D0028618

The
SURNAMES
of
IRELAND

Irish Families:
Their Names, Arms & Origins

Dr MacLysaght's major work on Irish family history is now in
its fourth edition. This volume, complete in itself, covers the
most widespread and prominent names with an article on
each. The book is handsomely illustrated by Myra Maguire
with 27 full-clour plates depicting 243 family arms.

More Irish Families

This second, companion, volume greatly expands the range of
Irish Families. It incorporates the author's earlier book of the
same title and his *Supplement to Irish Families*, and carries an
essay on Irish chieftainries.

'For anyone with an interest in genealogy this book is a must.
It is, and is likely to remain so, the standard reference work in
this field' *Cork Examiner.*

'Together with the original *Irish Families*, the book presents
the result of the labours of Dr Edward MacLysaght. . . .
Libraries and genealogists who wish to have an *encyclopaedia
of Irish name lore* at their elbow will invest in this *rara avis*, a
definitive work' *Nova Scotia Genealogist.*

'This compulsion to keep browsing on from name to name
can be ascribed to MacLysaght's captivating style, a unique
blend of the scholarly and the mundane. . . . This is the kind of
book it is — compendious, accurate, yet full of fascinating
anecdotes and witty asides' *Journal of the Cork Historical
and Archaeological Society.*

The
SURNAMES
of
IRELAND

SIXTH EDITION

EDWARD MacLYSAGHT
MA DLITT MRIA

IRISH ACADEMIC PRESS

This book was printed in Ireland
by Colour Books Limited, Dublin,
for Irish Academic Press Limited,
Kill Lane, Blackrock, Co. Dublin.

ISBN 0-7165-2364-7

First edition 1957
Second edition 1957
Third edition, revised 1972
Reprinted 1978
Fourth edition, revised and enlarged 1985
Reprinted 1991

Contents

Preface

This book is an epitome of the essential facts given in the three volumes of my *Irish Families* series, together with similar information on some 1,500 additional names not dealt with in them. To assist readers seeking a fuller account of a particular name, references to articles in the *Irish Families* series are given where this is available (such references will be found with about one-fifth of the names in this book), IF standing for *Irish Families, their names, arms and origins* and MIF for *More Irish Families* (incorporating *Supplement to Irish Families*). Variant forms account for a further four hundred additional entries. The method adopted in the presentation of variants is explained in the Introduction.

In my search for data relating to the more uncommon surnames still extant in Ireland I have received information from several people with specialized local knowledge. In addition to those whose help has already been acknowledged in the volumes of the *Irish Families* series I have pleasure in thanking also Sir Henry Blackall, Mr Hubert Butler, Dr Arthur Moore, Fr Patrick Egan, Mr Dermot Foley, Fr Peadar Livingstone, Mr Philip MacGuinness, Mr Seamus O Concobhair, Mr Muiris O Droighneain and Fr C.J. Travers whose suggestions have proved most helpful, and Mr Kenneth Nicholls, who was especially helpful in elucidating problems relating to the fourteenth to sixteenth centuries; and perhaps it would not be invidious to mention again the assistance I have derived from the extensive communications I received from Mr P.J. Kennedy and the late Mr C.J. MacDonagh, I would like also to thank Professor E. G. Quin, Mrs Mairin O'Daly, Professor Gerard MacNicholl and Mrs Nessa Doran who have with patience helped me in the difficult task of elucidating the derivation of Irish surnames. As I point out in the Introduction many of these are conjectural and I must make it clear that their help consisted of advice rather than final decisions.

EDWARD MacLYSAGHT

31 January 1985

Introduction

Ireland was one of the earliest countries to evolve a system of hereditary surnames: they came into being fairly generally in the eleventh century, and indeed a few were formed before the year 1000. The traditional belief that the system was introduced deliberately by Brian Boru is without foundation: it developed spontaneously in Ireland, as elsewhere, as the population increased and the former practice, first of single names and then of ephemeral patronymics or agnomina of the nickname type proved insufficiently definitive.

At first the surname was formed by prefixing Mac to the father's Christian name or O to that of a grandfather or earlier ancestor. Names with the prefixes Mac and even O, apparently surnames, will be found in the records relating to centuries before the tenth, but these were ephemeral not hereditary. After a time other types of surname were adopted, still with the prefixes Mac and sometimes O: for example those which introduced the words *giolla* and *maol* both usually meaning follower or servant, often in the sense of devotee of some saint e.g. *Mac Giolla Mhártain* (modern Gilmartin or Martin) or *Ó Maoilbhreanainn* (modern Mulrennan) from St. Martin and St. Brendan.* Perhaps the most numerous of the later names were those formed from the occupation of the father, as for example *Mac an Bháird*, son of the bard (modern MacWard and Ward) or *Ó hÍceadha—icidhe*, doctor or healer—(modern Hickey).

Similarly, but less often, the Mac and O were prefixed to some word denoting character or peculiarity of the father or grandfather, e.g. *Mac Dubhghaill*, black stranger (modern MacDowell). From this it was a short step to the incorporation of nicknames in permanent surnames, for instance *Mac an Mhadaidh—mada*, dog (now MacAvaddy etc., cognate with *Ó Madáin*, Madden).

The common practice of adding an epithet denoting some personal characteristic to the Christian name and surname eventually led in some cases to the loss of the surname proper and the substitution of the epithet for it. In that way arose Gaelic surnames without the distinctive Mac or O: thus *bán* (white) became Bane, *ruadh* (red) Roe, *láidir* (strong) Lawder, and so on. Similarly agnomina such as *Caomhánach* (Kavanagh) became hereditary surnames without a Gaelic prefix, though an O has sometimes been erroneously inserted in more modern times.

---

*For fuller consideration of the meaning of the words *maol* and *giolla* see footnotes pp. 3, 7 and 40.

I have used the word Gaelic, and this perhaps needs clarification. To many people unfamiliar with Ireland this word denotes a language once widely spoken in the Highlands of Scotland and still extant there. In Ireland when speaking English we call the Gaelic language 'Irish', though in Irish the word is, in the modern spelling, Gaeilge. As an adjective, however, 'Gaelic' is used to denote the race which has inhabited Ireland since prehistoric times. Scottish Gaelic is basically the same as the Irish language, of which it is an offshoot. The fact that the Gaels of Scotland are the descendants of Gaelic settlers from Ireland seems not be be generally known, though Scotland got its name from them, the word Scotus being the Latin for Irishman, as exemplified in the name of the famous ninth century Irish philosopher, Johannes Scotus Eriugena.

The majority of the surnames borne by Irish people of today are of Irish origin even in Ulster where, for reasons to be mentioned later, the proportion is smaller.

O names are somewhat more numerous in Ireland than Mac names. I need hardly again refute the once prevalent idea that the Mac is a sign of Scottish origin, since everyone must now be familiar with such essentially Irish names as MacMahon, MacGuire, MacNamara, MacCarthy etc. And here let me also refer to the fallacy that Mc is Irish and Mac Scottish (or was it vice versa?).

The practice of differentiating between Mac and Mc (not to mention the now almost obsolete M') is fortunately dying out. There is no difference: Mc is simply an abbreviation of Mac. This can be very irritating in indexes which separate them. An example of the absurdity of such differentiation is to be seen in the *Century Cyclopaedia of Names* (New York, 1954) where an individual McGillicuddy (so spelt) is dealt with on page 2684 while MacGillicuddy's Reeks, the striking Kerry mountain range called after that family, must be sought more than 100 pages away (page 2558) because the prefix in that case is arbitrarily given as Mac.

The prefixes Mac and O were very widely dropped during the period of the submergence of Catholic and Gaelic Ireland which began in the early seventeenth century, when English rule and influence in Ireland, little more than nominal prior to that outside the Pale, became really effective. The revival of national consciousness in the eighties resulting in the establishment of the Gaelic League in 1893 was reflected in the general resumption of the discarded Macs and Os. The statistics, taken from birth registrations and voters' lists, for a typical name—O'Sullivan —illustrate this.

Year	Percentage using the prefix O
1866	4
1890	13
1914	20
1944	60

I have no comparable figures for 1972 except those taken from current telephone directories: these show a further increase to 85 per cent; but these concern mainly urban communities, and for the country as a whole the percentage is probably nearer 70.

O'Connell is a comparable case, though the increase from 1866 to 1890 (9 per cent to 33 per cent) was more marked, due perhaps to the use of O by the 'Liberator' Daniel O'Connell. It is of interest to recall that his father was plain Morgan Connell, at least for legal purposes, though he was no doubt known as O'Connell by his neighbours in Kerry, most of whom, of course, normally spoke the Irish not the English language.

It is a curious fact that while widespread resumption occurred with some names, in others it scarcely took place at all. Murphy for example, the most numerous surname in Ireland, hardly ever appears with the prefix. Similarly Connolly, Donnelly, Doyle, Foley, Hogan, Kennedy, Nolan, Quinn and Sheridan, among the better known O names, seldom if ever use the O even today. O'Brien and O'Neill are two of the most important names in Ireland; in neither was the O discarded so widely: both had 50 per cent a century ago. The almost equally important O'Kelly on the other hand scored 0 per cent in 1866, 1 per cent in 1890 and can muster at most 8 per cent at the present time.

Mac has been more resistant to change. Apart from the existence of Scottish names in Ulster which retained the Mac, there are other reasons for this, particularly the fact that the omission of Mac often definitely alters the appearance of a name in a way not noticeable with O. Inerney and Namara for MacInerney and MacNamara, Guire and Grath for MacGuire and MacGrath illustrate this. When, however, Mac is shed its replacement is slow and often practically non-existent. Sweeney, it is true, has very often reverted to MacSweeney; but how few MacBradys, MacClancys, MacEgans and MacKeoghs one meets compared with Bradys, Clancys, Egans and Keoghs.

This resumption has led in some cases to the adoption of the wrong prefix. Chevalier O'Gorman, who should have known better, 'resumed' the O, whereas his family was formerly MacGorman. The former Premier of Ireland, John Costelloe, was officially described in documents in the Irish language as *Ó Coisdealbha* with the prefix O, instead of the correct Mac. Perhaps the most remarkable example of this tendency to substitute O for Mac is that of the Kerry author of *An tOileánach* ('The Islandman') Thomás Mac Criomhthain, whom Robin Flower, his mentor, called *Ó Criomthain* [*sic*] on the title page of the book. This essentially Kerry family is MacCrohan, never previously O'Crohan. The fact that Mac in the spoken language is in Connacht and Ulster often elided to 'ac is a contributory cause of this tendency: but that does not really apply to Kerry or to any part of Munster. Substitution of Mac for O is much less common. It can occur with names where the Mac form is numerous and the O rare, e.g. O'Gowan to MacGowan.

This name is one which leads me to another aspect of our subject. Many, perhaps the majority, of MacGowan families in Co. Cavan became Smith by translation—*Mac an Ghabhann, son of the smith.* No doubt legislation, mainly the Statute of Kilkenny (1367), had an effect in the Pale, but for the country as a whole the principal cause of the distortion of Irish surnames was the introduction of the English language and the fact that the documents relating to legal and official business were so often prepared by clerks who were unfamiliar with Ireland. A defeatist attitude on the part of an oppressed people has also something to do with it.

The changes which took place in Irish nomenclature after 1600 were much more drastic than the abandonment of the prefixes O and Mac. I have given an example of translation above. Mistranslation was more usual than correct translation: thus *Mac Giolla Eoin* could become Monday instead of MacAloon from the supposed similarity of the sound of the latter part of the name to *Luain* the Irish word for Monday. Similarly *Ó Dubháin* (Devane etc.) became Kidney. Examples of this could be cited *ad lib*.

Next we have abbreviation. To take my own name as an example: *Mac Giolla Iasachta* in Irish appears first in anglicized form *inter alia* as Macgillysaghta, a mouthful which soon became MacLysaght and eventually Lysaght.

Plain distortion gave us Mucklebreed for *Mac Giolla Bhrighde* (MacGilbride) and MacLice for *Mac Giolla Íosa* (MacAleese). The extent to which a name can mislead one is illustrated by Abraham. Of course that is Jewish elsewhere, but in Ireland it is the modern corrupt or distorted form of an ancient Gaelic surname, *Mac an Bhreitheamhan* (son of the judge). It was first anglicized MacEbrehowne, etc. which was shortened to MacEbrehan and MacAbrehan, later MacAbreham and so to Abraham. Other modern anglicized forms of this name are Breheny and Judge.

Another change which has been going on almost to the present day is the absorption of some rare names by better known ones of somewhat similar sound, e.g. Sullahan changed to Sullivan, Griffey to Griffin, Blowick to Blake and so on.

The name Cullen provides a good example of this. In the Registrar-General's report, published in 1909, he gives the following as synonyms of Cullen, reported by local registrars as appearing in recent registrations, with the union in which the birth occurred:

Colins	Banbridge
Collen	do., Armagh, Newry
Collins	do., Antrim
Colquhoun	New Ross
Culhoun	do.
Culleeny	Corofin
Cullinane	Callan
Cullion	Derry, Milford
Culloon	New Ross
Cully	Trim
Quillan	Cavan, Oldcastle, Granard
Quillen	do.

The most remarkable case of variant spellings I have met is that of the name MacEnaney. In the *Supplement to Irish Families* (p. 159) 38 variants are listed, of which of course many are merely occasional American mistranscriptions. More interesting is the case there cited of six members of one family on whose tombstones (to be seen in two cemeteries) the names of the six—father, mother and their four children —appear in six varying forms as McEneaney, McAneaney, McAneny, McEnaney, McEneany and Bird, the last being an example of pseudo-translation made in the mistaken belief that the derivation is from *éan* a bird. Many other cases are on record of the use of interesting synonyms by different members of the one family: a single example will suffice, Sruffaun and Bywater (the Irish word *sruthán* means a stream). Variant spellings are very numerous. I have already referred to MacEneany as a remarkable example of this. It was not, of course, necessary to specify all these variants separately in the text but it is obviously desirable to give one beginning with MacA and one MacE. Similarly with Gallagher, of which 23 variants have been noted, it is deemed sufficient to list only two, viz. Gallagher and Gollagher, the others being obvious variants.

There are many MacGil names with variant forms beginning MacIl and MacEl (see MacIlveen, p. 166, for example); and similarly MacG names, especially in Ulster, have been shortened to Mag (e.g. MacGee to Magee, MacGuinness to Maginnis etc.). By no means all such have been duplicated in the text, but the reader looking for a rare name may anticipate this possibility.

It is hardly necessary to mention, even for the benefit of readers unfamiliar with the subject, that the duplication of consonants and the alternative use of GH and H and of short internal vowels can be disregarded. To take an example which illustrates all these points, Hanahan, Hannaghan, Hanihan, Hanehan, Haneghan, Hanneghan etc. are all variant anglicized forms of the Irish *Ó hAnnacháin*.

Reverting to the question of the different types of surnames in Ireland, there are many of Norman origin which are now rightly regarded as essentially Irish such as Burke, Cruise, Cusack, Dillon, Nagle, Power, Roche, Taaffe, to mention just a few of these. Some became completely gaelicized like Costello (the first Norman name to assume the Mac prefix); others retained in Irish the prefix De. Parenthetically I may mention that this, though sanctioned by custom, is often an error for Le, as *De Buitléir* for *Le Buitléir*—neither De nor Le is used in the English forms. De is sometimes misleading, as when a Gaelic family of Devlin chose for reasons of snobbery to write their name as D'Evelyn and de Moleyns was adopted instead of Mullins.

A number of the Hiberno-Norman names begin with Fitz (French *fils*). Fitzgerald is the best known of these: it is called *Mac Gearailt* in Irish. The almost equally well known Fitzpatrick, however, is not of Norman origin but is the Gaelic *Mac Giolla Phádraig* normanized.

There are three other sources of surnames closely associated with Ireland. A few are pre-Norman Norse names—Harold and Trant for example. In the seventeenth century there was an influx of Huguenots who gave us such names as Lefroy, Lefanu, Trench, Guerin and Saurin. Incidentally I may mention that the two last names are also used as the anglicized forms of Gaelic-Irish surnames. Co. Limerick has still a number of Palatine names, the best known of which are Ruttle, Bovenizer and Switzer.

Lastly of course there are English names. A number of these came into Ireland in mediaeval times, but where they are still found here they are in almost every case the result of comparatively recent immigration. The earliest of the permanent English settlers were Elizabethans, like the Edgeworths and the Bagenals. They are not numerous and, though they had some influence on the fortunes of the country, as we are considering Irish surnames rather than Irish history I need not say anything further about them here. The main causes of the widespread introduction of British names were the Plantation of Ulster in the first decade of the seventeenth century and the Cromwellian Settlement of the 1650s. The Plantation of Ulster had a very considerable and permanent effect on that province, until then the most completely Irish part of Ireland. It is of interest, however, to note that in only two of the nine Ulster counties do English or Scottish names now predominate (Antrim and Down) and these were not among those 'planted': this condition is due rather to modern commercial infiltration. The Cromwellian Settlement was different because the immigrants it introduced were widely scattered over the country. In this case they were for the most part eventually assimilated and became an integral part of the Irish nation. Generations of intermarriage with native Catholic Irish have made them, apart from a few landlord families, otherwise indistinguishable from their neighbours who bear Gaelic or Hiberno-Norman names.

More recently, especially during the past 150 years, there has been a steady, though small, infiltration of English names, arising mainly from commercial activity, not confined to Ulster, but to some extent also in quite recent times to the attractions of Ireland as a pleasant country free from the hustle of its overcrowded neighbour.

When examining birth registers from time to time I noted many which struck me as curious. In some one can at least guess what the disguise conceals: for example Anguish is presumably Angus and Junk is probably for Junkum, a variant of Jenkins; but the majority, if not foreign names brought in by immigrants, have lost all resemblance to their original form.

It is practically impossible to determine now what proportion of English names to be seen in directories and voters' lists are really of English origin. Take Smith as an example: in and around Co. Cavan nearly all Smiths are MacGowans or O'Gowans in disguise, while Smith families unconnected with that Breffny country or south Down are probably of English descent. Similarly in Kerry, Cliffords are almost certainly O'Cluvanes, but elsewhere probably non-Gaelic.

In that connection it may not be out of place to say that in spite of modern conditions Gaelic surnames are still mainly to be found in the part of the country to which their sept belonged: thus practically all Conneelys and Keadys come from Co. Galway, Teahans and Sugrues from Kerry, Lehanes and Riordans from Co. Cork: examples could be multiplied from all parts of the country. This is the case even with names which have become very numerous and are inevitably found in Dublin and the larger towns: Moriartys and MacElligotts are still mainly in Kerry, O'Mahonys and O'Driscolls in Co. Cork and so on.

The most difficult aspect of our subject is the derivation of the old surnames of Gaelic origin. In many cases there is no doubt about them, as for example with those mentioned above on page ix or, to take another obvious one, Ahearn, *Ó hEachthighearna,* in which *each* means steed and *tighearna* lord. Such have been included in the text without comment. With many, however, which look obvious one can be led astray. An Old-Irish or Middle-Irish word incorporated in a surname often looks exactly like a modern Irish word of quite different meaning: thus, to take one example, *Ó Calgaigh* (Callagy) which one might expect to be from the adjective *calgach*, is, I am informed, more probably from the Gaelic personal name *Calggach* which derives from *colgg*, an old word for sword. *Sloinnte Gaedhael is Gall* is a most valuable work, based as it is largely on that of John O'Donovan eighty years earlier, but Father Woulfe makes the mistake of attempting to give derivations for almost every Gaelic name in the book: many of these are guesses and, as that great authority, the late Professor M. A. O'Brien, often mentioned to me, quite untenable. Today we have the advantage of being able to consult both scholars and printed sources not available to Woulfe fifty years ago, notably the Royal Irish Academy's *Dictionary of the Irish Language*.

In some cases where I had little doubt that Woulfe was right I found competent scholars in that field rejecting his interpretation: I would for example have accepted *inreachtach*, lawful, for Enright, but Dr. John Ryan, S.J. tells me that it comes from an adjectival form of *indreacht*, meaning attack, whence the old personal name *Indrechtech*.

The very word *inreachtach*, illustrates one of the difficulties inherent in these linguistic problems. The prefix *in* is used both intensively and negatively, so that unless one is acquainted with the word in question it may have either of two exactly opposite meanings. In this case we do know that *inreachtach* denotes lawful, the *in* being intensive; but were it not a familiar word it could equally well mean unlawful.

In this connection it would be relevant and explanatory to quote a letter from Dr. Ryan, late Professor of Early and Medieval Irish History, University College, Dublin, in reply to my enquiry as to the origin of the name Ryan.

'What the *Rian* in the surnames Ó Riain and Ó Maoilriain is has never been satisfactorily explained. Rian, like Niall, seems to be so ancient that its meaning was lost before records began. It is tempting to think of the Old Irish word *rian*, "water", which goes back to a form ren, found in Rhenos, the Rhine, and to connect the personal name with the cult of an ancient water deity. But *rian*, in this sense, has a genitive, *rein*, found in Ireland in the place-name Mag Rein, Co. Leitrim. A genitive riain seems to be etymologically impossible. For that reason the surname Ó Maoilriain must be excluded from the category of such names as Ó Maolanfaidh and Ó Maolgaoithe which preserve a memory of the cult of natural elements, the storm and the wind.

'My colleague, Rev. Professor Shaw, thinks that the word rian was originally disyllabic, like *trian*.

'He notes that the late Professor M. A. O'Brien, in his index to the "Corpus Genealogiarum Hiberniae", gives the nominative as Rian, with short *i* and a long â. O'Brien therefore did not associate the name with *rì*, "a king". Otherwise a form *Rian* (beside *Rîgân*) would naturally come to mind, in the fashion of Cûan, beside Conân. Another suggestion would be the Irish root *riin* cognate with the Latin *ritus*. In this case the personal name *Rian* would mean a person who sets in order or marshals.

'If the a of -an was long, as Dr. O'Brien indicated, the ending would be diminutive. If the a is short the form Rian has an ending found also in many personal names.'

In the text of the present work wherever, like Ryan, a surname is formed from an old personal name of obscure meaning it is left without comment; this applies also where a surname is formed simply from one of the well-known Christian names with the prefix Mac or O, e.g. *Mac Diarmada,* son of Dermot or *Ó Briain* descendant of Brian, though in some cases where the identity of the Christian name would not be easily apparent to a person unacquainted with the Irish language it is stated, thus with *Mac Aodha* or *Mac Aoidh* the equation of *Aodh* with Hugh is mentioned.

For English surnames the best published work is P. H. Reaney's *Dictionary of British Surnames* (London, 1958) and he is my authority for most of the derivations given in the text for names of English origin. It is, however, so misleading in regard to Irish surnames that it is necessary to criticize this otherwise very valuable work. Dr. Reaney pleads restriction of space as his excuse for the omission of many interesting English names (e.g. Cromwell, Gladstone, Shelley etc.) yet he fills up space with some Irish (though they are not British) and those which he does give are chosen quite without method. Thus the comparatively rare O'Looney is one of the mere 22 names with prefix O included, and those with Mac give rise to the same confusion. The book is particularly misleading in its treatment of those English names which have been widely used as the anglicized forms of Irish surnames: there is no indication in the entries for Collins, Farren, Moore or Traynor (to take four examples at random) that these are anything but exclusively English, and this deficiency is accentuated by the fact that in other names (e.g. Hughes) the alternative Irish origin is stated. Bardsley's *Dictionary of English and Welsh Surnames* (London, 1901) is much more comprehensive but less scholarly. Weekley's *Surnames* (London, 1916) is an entertaining and valuable essay, but of not special Irish interest. I have found *A History of Surnames of the British Isles* by C. L'E. Ewen useful too, but he knows little about Irish surnames. G. F. Black's *Surnames of Scotland* is an authoritative work so far as Scotland is concerned but when Irish names in Scotland are under consideration Woulfe's derivations are accepted without question.

The books mentioned above are the principal modern printed works dealing with surnames; others by Lower (1849) and Ferguson (1858 and 1883) have been largely superseded. Readers who contemplate making a close study of the subject are advised to consult the bibliographies printed in earlier editions of *Irish Families* and *More Irish Families*. The bibliography of family histories is now published in a slim volume of its own.

It is not thought necessary to include a general bibliography in this volume, as that is fairly fully covered in *Irish Families* (pp. 331–6) and in *More Irish Families* (pp. 289–90). The only works of importance in this category which have appeared since those books were published are the eleven-volume *Manuscript Sources of the History of Irish Civilization*, edited by Dr. R. J. Hayes, the late Dr. M. A. O'Brien's *Corpus Genealogiarum Hiberniae*, Rev. Paul Walsh's *Irish Chiefs and Leaders*, Rev. P. K. Egan's *The Parish of Ballinasloe* and the third and fourth volumes (Galway and Clare) of the *Books of Survey & Distribution* series and Dr. R. C. Simington's *Transplantation to Connacht and Clare*. A few books of which I have made frequent use were omitted from the bibliographies printed in my earlier volumes, notably the *Calendar of Documents, Ireland, 1171-1307*, edited by H. S. Sweetman, John O'Donovan's editions of *The Tribes and Customs of Hy Many* and *Hy Fiachrach* and the mediaeval registers of archbishops Alen and Swayne and of Gormanston. Two outstanding diocesan periodicals which I have frequently consulted were also not included, viz. *The Clogher Record* and *Seanchas Ardmacha*. I should add that the Tudor Fiants begin in the reign of Henry VIII not Edward VI and that a calendar of the earlier patent rolls (Henry II to Henry VII) commonly known as Tresham was published in 1828 by the Irish Record Commissioners, whose other publications are also very useful.

Attention should be drawn to the fact that in *More Irish Families* an appendix of 34 pages is devoted to additional information (including the correction of some errors) relating to names dealt with in *Irish Families*; and the final volume of the series again contains an appendix serving a similar purpose. Slips and misprints were for the most part corrected in the second edition of *Irish Families*: curiously enough, though my attention was drawn to a number of these by reviewers, no one noticed the one major error the book contained, viz. the arms ascribed to Mannix: this was pointed out by myself in a letter to the *Irish Times* dated November 1st, 1957 and corrected in the third edition published in 1972.

There are other interesting aspects of Irish nomenclature besides those briefly dealt with in this Introduction, such as the legal position regarding changes of name, the incorporation of surnames in place-names, changes in pronunciation of names etc. These and other cognate matters of interest are the subject of chapters or sections in the first two volumes of the *Irish Families* series.

Explanation of Technical Terms used in Text

Adventurer A person who subscribed ('adventured') a sum of money for the equipment of an army to suppress the Rising of 1641 on the security of lands to be confiscated from Irish proprietors.

Aspiration The addition of the letter H to a consonant, thereby modifying its sound, e.g. BH = V. (Cf. PH in English, which gives the sound of F.)

Barony A territorial division next in order of size to the county, each county comprising from 5 to 20 baronies according to its extent.

Brehon (Irish *breitheamh*, genitive *breitheamhan*, a judge). The terms Brehon Law and Brehon System refer to the Gaelic legal system in force before the Norman invasion: this system was not completely superseded until the seventeenth century.

Census The so-called census of 1659 was not a complete census of population in the modern connotation of the word. There is a difference of opinion as to its exact purpose.

Co-arb The following passage is quoted from J. F. Kenney's *Sources for the Early History of Ireland:* 'By the eleventh century . . . in the average church the abbot, generally known as the *comharba* (co-arb), "heir", of the saintly founder, or, if it were not the saint's principal establishment, the *airchinnech* (erenagh), "head", had become a lay lord, whose family held the office and the church property from generation to generation . . . In some cases, apparently, all trace of a church-establishment had disappeared, except that the incumbent claimed for his lands the *termonn* of the ancient monastery, those privileges and exemptions which had from of old been accorded to ecclesiastical property; but generally the *comharba* or *airchinnech* maintained a priest.'

Eclipsis. The suppression of a consonant at the beginning of a word by the insertion before it of another consonant of the same class, e.g. M before B (labials), D before T (dentals).

Eponymous ancestor The individual from whom the family name was taken.

Erenagh See Co-arb above.

Fiant This is short for 'Fiant litterae patentes'. Fiants were warrants to the Chancery authority for the issue of letters patent under the Great Seal. They dealt with matters ranging from commissions for appointments to high office and important government activities to grants of 'English liberty' and 'pardons' to the humblest of the native Irish.

Gaelic See Introduction, p. x.

Galloglass (Irish *gallóglach*). A heavily armed mercenary soldier, usually, but not always, of Scottish origin.

Kern (Irish *ceithearnach*). An Irish soldier, lightly armed.

Locative name One formed from a physical feature or location not an actual place-name.

Ollav A professor or learned man; a master in some art or branch of learning.

Palatines Families from the Palatinate of the Rhine who settled in Co. Limerick early in the eighteenth century.

Pale, The The district centred on Dublin under the full control of the government of the King of England. It varied greatly in extent as the power of the English waxed and waned. At the end of the fifteenth century it comprised only Co. Dublin and parts of Louth, Meath and Kildare.

Sodhan A pre-Gaelic race in the Uí Maine country.

Toponymic A surname formed from a place-name.

Townland The territorial sub-division of a parish, each townland greatly varying in size, commonly averaging from 250 to 400 acres. The term has no relation to a town or city, being derived from the Old-English word *tun* signifying enclosure.

Undertaker A person, usually English, who, as a condition of obtaining a grant of lands confiscated from Irish proprietors, undertook to plant thereon English or Scottish settlers in place of the dispossessed occupiers.

Wild Geese A term applied to Irish exiles to the Continent of Europe in the seventeenth and eighteenth centuries. Originally denoting those who became soldiers in continental armies it was later extended to refer to their descendants.

Location of Ancient Territories

The following ancient territories, in existence from prehistoric times to the break-up of the Gaelic order in the sixteenth century, are mentioned occasionally in the text: their locations are given below.

Breffny (Breifne) Cavan and west Leitrim.
Corca Laoidhe South-west Cork.
Dalriada North Antrim.
Decies (Déise) West Waterford.

Desmond (Deasmhumhan) Kerry and much of Co. Cork.

Iar Connacht West Connacht, mainly Connemara.

Muskerry (Muscraidhe) North-west and central Cork.

Oriel (Orghialla) Cos. Armagh and Monaghan and parts of south Down, Louth and Fermanagh.

Ormond (Urmhumhan) Much of Co. Kilkenny and north Tipperary.

Ossory The extent of the ancient kingdom of Osraighe was approximately the same as that of the diocese of Ossory, i.e. Co. Kilkenny and some adjacent areas.

Thomond (Tuathmhumhan) Most of Co. Clare with adjacent parts of Cos. Limerick and Tipperary.

Tirconnell (Tír Chonaill) Co. Donegal.

Tirowen (Tír Eoghain) Co. Tyrone with adjacent part of Co. Derry.

Population Groups

The following population groups are referred to:

Cenél Conaill The race name of the O'Gallaghers, O'Boyles and other families traditionally descended from Conall Gulban, son of Niall of the Nine Hostages, located in Tirconnell.

Cenél Eoghain The clan name of O'Neills etc. descended from Eoghan, son of Niall of the Nine Hostages, located in Tyrone and south Derry.

Dál gCais Otherwise called the Dalcassians; embraces the main septs of Thomond.

Eoghanacht The clan name of the descendants of Eoghan, son of Oilioll Olum, to which many of the main families of south Munster belonged.

Síol Anmchadha A branch of the Uí Maine.

Síol Muireadhaigh (Silmurray) The clan name of the O'Connors and other north Connacht septs.

Uí Fiachrach The northern and more important, i.e. Uí Fiachrach Muaidhe, were located in north Mayo and Sligo; the other branch (Aidhne) occupied that part of south Galway covered by the small diocese of Kilmacduagh.

Uí Maine (At one time anglicized Hy Many); mid-Galway and south Roscommon.

Abbreviations

IF: See *Irish Families*.   MIF: See *More Irish Families*.   Bibl.: See *Bibliography of Irish Family History*.   App.: See appendices to this book.

A

Abberton An English toponymic found in south-east Galway, locally classed as one of the 'Oultaghs', i.e. families which migrated from Ulster early in the eighteenth century.

Abbott *Abóid.* This old English name (usually of nickname type) is in Ireland since the fourteenth century and is now quite numerous in Dublin.

Abernethy This branch of the Scottish clan Leslie has been established in north Ulster since the first half of the seventeenth century. It is now well known in east Cork.

(Mac) Abraham In Ireland Abraham as a surname is seldom of Jewish origin but is a corruption of *Mac an Bhreitheamhan* (son of the judge), first anglicized MacAbrehan etc. MacAbraham and even FitzAbraham occur in Co Cork in the thirteenth century. The synonym Brohoon is still extant. MIF

Acheson Though this name (the Scots form of Atkinson) occurs occasionally in mediaeval records (e.g. a monk at Trim in 1436) it was not established permanently in Ireland till the seventeenth century—first in Co. Wicklow and Fermanagh. It has since become scattered.

Achmooty See Aughmuty.

Acton This English toponymic occurs occasionally in Irish records from the early fifteenth century onwards. The Co. Wicklow family settled there in mid-seventeenth century but otherwise it has always been a scattered name in Ireland. Bibl.

Adair A Scottish name prominent in Ulster. It is also occasionally an anglicized form of *Ó Dáire,** formerly in Offaly. MIF   (where Robin Adair is identified).

Mac Adam This name has several origins in Ireland. In Co. Cork it was an Irish patronymic, *Mac Adaim,* assumed by a branch of the Norman Barrys; in Co. Armagh it is a synonym of MacCadden; in Co. Cavan it can be for MacCaw; Ballymacadam in Clanmorris barony, Co. Mayo, locates a family there. This place-name occurs also in Kerry and south Tipperary. In Dublin and Belfast MacAdam is often Scottish. MIF

Adams This well-known English name has been used synonymously with Aidy and Eadie in Co. Down. Bibl.

Mac Adarra A variant form of (Mac) Darragh found in Co. Louth.

Addis This English name (a pet form of Adam) came to Ireland early in the seventeenth century, first to Westmeath, later to Co. Cork. It

---

*Dáire is an old Irish personal name. The derivation of the majority of pre-Christian personal names is uncertain. See Introduction, p. xv.

has since become more numerous in north-east Ulster, where the variant form Addy is also found. Neither has been closely identified with any particular area.

Addy See Aidy.

Adley See Audley.

Adlum See Odlum.

Mac Adoo See Cunniff.

Mac Adorey *Mac an Deoraidh* (son of the stranger). A rare Co. Antrim name.

Adorian A variant of Doran in Co. Down. As Dorian it is found in Co. Donegal.

Adrain *Ó Dreáin.* Woulfe's derivation from *dreán*, wren, is improbable. There is an older word *drenn*, which has several meanings including rough and firm. The name is sometimes shortened to Drain. This erenagh family was originally of Co. Roscommon but later under pressure from the MacDermots, settled in Ulster. MIF

Adrian When not used as a variant of Adrain this is a form of the Latin Adrianus. It is not a synonym of Adorian.

Mac Afee See Mahaffy.

Affleck See Flack.

Agar See under Eagar.

Agarty An occasional variant of Hegarty.

Aghoon *Ó hEachdhubháin* (*each*, steed—*dubh*, black). Now usually changed by mistranslation to Whitesteed. Both these names are now rare.

Mac Aghy See MacCaughey.

Aglish See Church.

Agnew *Ó Gnímh* (*gníomh*, action). A literary family under the O'Neills whose name was formerly anglicized O'Gneeve. Some Agnews, also of Ulster, are of Norman (d'Agneau) descent. There was a family of *O Gnimha*, anglicized O'Gnew, located near Doneraile, Co. Cork, early in the thirteenth century. Bibl; MIF

Aherne *Ó hEachthigheirn* or *Ó hEachthighearna* (*each*, steed—*tighearna*, lord). Originally Dalcassian, this sept migrated from east Clare to Co. Cork. In Co. Waterford the English name Hearn is a synonym of Ahearn. IF   Map Clare.

Ahessy A variant of Hahessy in Co. Waterford.

Aide See under Heade.

Aidy, Addy See Adams and Addis. Adie is a sept of the Scottish clan Gordon and MacAdie of the clan Ferguson.

Aiken An old Scottish diminutive of Adam, having many variant spellings including Aitken. Since mid-seventeenth century it has been numerous in north-east Ulster. The form Eakin is also used, especially in Co. Derry and adjacent areas. The earliest Irish reference to the name I have met outside Ulster is in a Dublin Funeral Entry of 1654: it is of interest to note that the arms given there bear no resemblance to those of the Scottish and Ulster Aikens. Woulfe's suggestion that Aiken may have been sometimes used for O'Hagan (*Ó hAogáin*) may be tenable, having regard to the location of the latter. Egan has also been used as a synonym of Aiken in Co. Down. MIF

Airey An English toponymic found in Ulster.

Mac Alarney See under Mullarney.

Alcock This English name is in Co. Waterford since late seventeenth century. No less than 47 Alcocks were students of Dublin University between 1605 and 1845; the earliest were not of Co. Waterford.

Alcorn An English name (from old corn) fairly prominent in Ulster since mid-seventeenth century and particularly associated with Co. Donegal.

(Mac) Aldin I have failed to find the origin of this name which has long been in Co. Monaghan and south Down, where both MacAldin and occasionally Haldan are variants. In his earlier work Woulfe gave the form in Irish as *Mac Ailín* but in his later larger book he evidently rejected that, as he gives none of the variants mentioned above as anglicized forms of *Mac Ailín*. Some Irish MacCaldins are certainly of planter stock.

Mac Aleary, -Alary A north Connacht sept, with a branch in Co. Antrim. Map Sligo. See MacCleary. IF

Mac Alee, -Alea *Mac an Leagha*. This name, as the Irish form indicates, is that of a medical family. It is located in Ulster, mainly in Co. Antrim, where it is also anglicized MacClay and MacLea and sometimes MacKinley. IF

Mac Aleenan A synonym of MacAlinion, not of MacAlinden. See Lyness.

Mac Aleer *Mac Giolla Uidhir* (*odhar*, gen. *uidhir*, dun-coloured or weather-beaten). A numerous Co. Tyrone sept. See MacClure.

Mac Aleery A variant of MacCleary.

Mac Aleese *Mac Giolla Íosa* (son of the devotee of Jesus*). The name of a prominent Derry sept. There are many variants of the name such as MacIleese, MacLeese, MacLice, MacLise etc. The best known of this spelling, the painter Daniel MacLise, was of a family of the Scottish Highlands, known as MacLeish, which settled in Cork.

Mac Aleevy See Dunlevy.

*As names beginning with *Mac Giolla* followed by a saint's name, especially those with anglicized forms beginning with Gil and Kil, will be found frequently in the text of this book the words 'Son of the devotee of' will not be repeated there. See note under MacAreavy.

3

Mac Alernon A variant of MacLarnon.

Mac Alesher See MacIllesher.

Alexander This English name is numerous in Down and Antrim. Less than a century ago fourteen synonyms of it were recorded in Ulster birth registrations, e.g. Elshinder, MacCalshender, all now rare. Woulfe gives *Mac Alsandair* as the form in Irish. MacAlister and MacEllistrum are of similar Scottish origin. Bibl.

Algeo, Algee Possibly a derivative of the English Elgar; found in Leitrim and north-west Ulster.

Mac Alilly See Lilly.

Mac Alindon *Mac Giolla Fhiondáin* (devotee of St. Fintan). A sept of Oriel. MIF 20; Map Armagh-Down.

Mac Alineeny A variant of MacIlhenny.

Mac Alinion, -Aleenen *Mac Giolla Fhinnéin* (devotee of St. Finian). Often changed in modern times to Leonard and distinct from MacAlindon which has seldom been so changed. MIF   Map Fermanagh.

Mac Alister *Mac Alastair.* An Irish-Gaelic family in Scotland, a branch of which returned to Ulster as galloglasses in the fourteenth century. MIF Map Antrim. See Alexander.

Mac Alivery See Winter.

Allen This is usually of Scottish or English origin; but sometimes *Ó hAillín* in Offaly and Tipperary has been anglicized Allen as well as Hallion. Occasionally also in Co. Tipperary Allen is found as a synonym of Hallinan. As Alleyn it occurs frequently in mediaeval Anglo-Irish records. The English name Allen is derived from that of a Welsh saint; for the Scottish see next entry. Bibl. MIF

Mac Allen *Mac Ailín (ail,* rock). Primarily the name of a war-like branch of the Scottish Campbells brought to Ulster by the O'Donnells. It is also a synonym of MacCallion in Cos. Donegal and Derry.

Alley This English name, of Scandinavian origin, is now rare in Ireland, but was numerous in the past in Cos. Kildare and Leix where it is frequently on record, e.g. in the Fiants for 1544.

Allingham An English toponymic associated with Ballyshannon, Co. Donegal, since 1613; later found also in Co. Leitrim.

Mac Allion See MacCallion.

Allison Synonymous with Ellison in Scotland. In Ireland it was found formerly in Co. Donegal, now mainly in Co. Antrim.

Allman Originally *de Allemagne* (probably from the German colony in Normandy), this name came to Ireland at the end of the twelfth century and first became established in Co. Louth, where the old place-name Almanston (later changed to Almondstown, Almond being a synonym of Allman) locates them. By the time of the

Cromwellian transplantation they had become fully hibernicized. A branch subsequently went to Kerry and from about 1800 became numerous in the area between Tralee and Killarney.

Mac Aloan See MacLoone.

Mac Alonan *Mac Giolla Adhamhnáin* (devotee of St. *Adhamhnán,* mod. Eunan). This was a famous Christian name in the diocese of Raphoe, taken from the saint so called. Cos. Antrim and Derry.

Mac Aloney Woulfe equates this Co. Derry name with MacElhinney. I think, however, that it is a variant of MacEldowney.

Mac Aloon A variant of MacGloin.

Mac Alpin *Mac Ailpín.* A Scottish name numerous in Ulster; the personal name *Ailpean* probably being derived from *alp,* lump. It is sometimes confused with Halpin elsewhere. The Mayo name Calpin is an abbreviation of MacAlpin.

Altimas The name of a Palatine family settled in Co. Wexford since the beginning of the eighteenth century for which Alton has sometimes been substituted.

Ambrose *Mac Ambróis.* This name has been mainly associated with west Munster since the fourteenth century and is still well known in Cos. Cork and Limerick. Earlier they were in Co. Wexford where Ambrosetown was named after them.

Amooty See Aughmuty.

Amory This and its variants Emery, Hembry etc. derive from the Old-German *Amalric,* work-rule. Bibl.

Mac Anabb A variant of MacNabb in Co. Cavan.

Mac Anally See Nally.

Mac Analty See MacNalty.

Mac Anaul An Ulster name, usually *Mac Con Uladh* (see MacCullagh). In Co. Dublin it has been recorded as a synonym of MacNally.

Mac Anawe See Kinnawe.

Anderson (son of Andrew). One of the most numerous English names in Ireland, it is found mainly in north-east Ulster. Bibl.

Mac Andrew *Mac Aindriu.* A Gaelic patronymic adopted by a branch of the Barretts. MIF   Map Mayo. See also Ross.

Andrews This English name is in Ireland in all the provinces since the early seventeenth century and is now numerous in Dublin and northeast Ulster. It has been sometimes used as a synonym of MacAndrew (see previous entry). Andrew(e), alias FitzAndrew, occurs frequently in mediaeval Irish records. In modern times it is found as a synonym of Andrews in Co. Dublin. Bibl.

Mac Aneany See MacEneaney.

Mac Aneave See Gilnagh.

Mac Anerney An Ulster variant of MacInerney.

Mac Anespie *Mac an Easpuig.* This rare name, mainly found in Tyrone, is sometimes abbreviated to Aspig or translated as Bishop. MIF

Angier See Aungier.

Angland See England.

(O) Anglim, Anglin *Ó hAngluinn* (probably from *anglonn*, champion). This name has always been associated with Co. Cork. MIF

Angus, Anguish See MacInnes.

Mac Aniff See Cunniff.

Mac Anilly See MacNeilly.

Mac Aninch, -Inch, -Ninch Ulster variants of the Scottish MacInnes.

Anketell An Anglo-Norman name still extant in Ulster. Authorities on British surnames disagree as to its derivation. The family settled in Co. Monaghan with a branch in Co. Cork. Bibl.

Mac Anlis A variant of MacCandless.

Annesley Coming to Munster from Nottinghamshire in 1606, this name has been very prominent in the Anglo-Irish aristocracy since in all the four provinces. It is now scattered and much less numerous than formerly.

Annett An English name derived from the woman's name Ann. It is fairly numerous in Co. Down, but of comparatively recent introduction.

Ansbery, Ansboro See Hanbury.

Anthony Though not very closely identified with any particular area this name has been associated with Waterford since the mid-seventeenth century. There are early references to Anthony and MacAnthony as an ephemeral surname.

Mac Anulla, -Nully These Ulster names, and sometimes also MacNaul, are synonymous; they are basically the same as MacCullagh, q.v. for derivation.

Mac Anulty A variant of MacNulty.

Aragan See Horgan.

Archbold *Áirseabóid.* (The variant Archibald indicates the derivation). Families of this name were very early settlers in east Leinster. Map Wicklow.

Archdale A family of English background which came to Ulster in the early seventeenth century and have since been established at Castle Archdale, Co. Fermanagh. Bibl.

Archdeacon See Cody. Map Kilkenny.

Archer *Áirséir.* This important Anglo-Norman family, one of the 'Tribes of Kilkenny', came to Ireland in the thirteenth century. The name is self-explanatory. Bibl; MIF   Map Kilkenny.

Ardagh *Árdacha.* This is one of the few Irish toponymics. It was formerly mainly found in Co. Louth but more recently in Co. Waterford. It has become rare. MIF

Ardiff A rare Co. Kildare name, the origin of which I have not yet ascertained.

Ardill Nowhere numerous, this name is mainly associated with Co. Tipperary. It is very rarely an abbreviation of MacArdle. MIF

Mac Ardle *Mac Árdghail* (*árdghal*, high valour). This sept is traditionally a branch of the MacMahons of Oriel. MIF Map Monaghan.

Mac Aready See under MacCready.

Mac Areavy *Mac Giolla Riabhaigh** (*riabhach*, grey or brindled). This is sometimes anglicized MacGilreevy and MacIlreavy in Antrim and Down. MacAreavy is also used as a synonym of MacGreevy.

Mac Aree *Mac Fhearadhaigh*. Woulfe gives the derivation as from *Fearadhach*, a personal name meaning manly, but it does not appear to have been in use as an adjective. This Co. Monaghan name is sometimes changed to King from its similarity in sound to *Mac an Rí* (*rí*, king). MIF See MacCarry.

Argue This Co. Cavan name is not of English origin, but, if Irish, the Gaelic form of it has not been determined with certainty. In Co. Leitrim, not far from Co. Cavan, there is a place called Killargue, which O'Donovan says is *Cill Fhearga* i.e. the church of St. Fearga. Killargue is also called Kilarga. It is probable therefore that the surname is *Mac Giolla Fhearga*. I think the family tradition that it is of Huguenot origin may be discounted. MIF

(O) Arkins *Ó hOrcáin*. (Woulfe's derivation from *orc*, pig, is conjectural). A Clare name distinct from the Donegal Harkin.

Arland This English name is now very rare; in the seventeenth century it was quite numerous in Co. Waterford.

Armitage Derived from the word hermitage, this English name first appears in Cos. Louth and Cork in mid-seventeenth century and has since been mainly established in north Tipperary and Offaly.

Armour See Larmour.

Armstrong An English name very numerous throughout Ulster as such; it is also often used as the anglicized form of Lavery and Traynor.

Arnold An English personal name used as a surname; in Ireland since the thirteenth century, now mainly found in Dublin and north-east Ulster.

Arnott This is a Scottish toponymic. It is perpetuated in Ireland by the townland of Ballyarnott in Co. Antrim.

Arragan See Horgan.

Arrell *Ó hEarghaill*. This name, also called Harrell, is etymologically the same as Farrell, q.v. for derivation. It belongs to Donegal and Tyrone.

Mac Art See MacCart.

*When *Mac Giolla* is followed by an epithet, *giolla* may be translated lad or fellow.

Mac Artan See MacCartan.

Arthur This pre-Norman family has been prominent in Limerick since the twelfth century. The name is of Norse origin. IF   Map Limerick.

Mac Arthur A Scottish name distinct from the foregoing. It is often called Arthur and sometimes MacCarter.

Mac Artney Bibl. See MacCartney.

Arundel An English (Sussex) toponymic associated with Co. Cork continuously since the end of the thirteenth century when Robert de Arundel was coroner of Ibawn. It is locally pronounced Aringale and gaelicized *Airinnéal*.

Mac Asey A corrupt form of MacCasey.

Ashe *Ághas*. This family was established in Meath and Kildare in the fourteenth century and is still there. The name denotes dweller by the ash tree. Bibl; IF

Mac Ashinagh *Mac an tSionnaigh* (*sionnach*, fox). Now usually called Fox, and sometimes anglicized phonetically as MacAtinney; an Armagh family, a branch of which migrated to Mayo, and Tinney, which is found in Donegal.

Mac Askie See Caskey.

Askin An English name sometimes used as a synonym of Heskin.

Mac Asparran See MacSparran.

Aspel A variant of Archbold in east Leinster.

Aspig See MacAnespie.

Mac Astocker See MacStocker.

Aston This and Ashton were formerly used synonymously: both are toponymics (but the former is also from the M.E. forename *Estan*). Aston, but seldom Ashton, occurs in mediaeval Irish records. Since the seventeenth century both names have become fairly numerous but widely scattered throughout Ireland. Bibl.

Mac Atamney See Timpany.

Mac Atasney *Mac an tSasanaigh* (*Sasanach*, Englishman—perhaps in a satirical sense). This name belongs almost exclusively to Cos. Armagh and Tyrone. MacAtarsney is a corrupt form.

Mac Atavy *Mac an tSámhaigh* (probably from *sámhach*, pleasant). A Co. Monaghan name sometimes abbreviated to Tavey. MIF

Mac Atee A form of MacEntee found in Oriel.

Mac Ateer *Mac an tSaoir* (*saor*, craftsman). An Ulster name for which the Scottish MacIntyre, of similar derivation, is widely substituted. Ballymacateer is a place-name in Co. Armagh, which is its homeland. *Mac an tSaoir* is sometimes anglicized Wright in Fermanagh. MIF 23.

Athy *Ataoi*. One of the 'Tribes of Galway' of Norman stock, but first settled in Co. Kildare about 1300. The name is derived from the place in that county. IF   MIF

Mac Atilla See Flood.

Mac Atinney See MacAshinagh.

Atkins An English name derived from Adkin, a pet form of Adam. It is well known in Co. Cork where it was established in the seventeenth century. MIF

Atkinson Of similar derivation (Adkin, diminutive of Adam), mainly found in Ulster, Atkinson is much more numerous than Atkins.

Mac Attegart See MacEntaggart.

Attridge, Now numerous in Co. Cork, though of comparatively late introduction. It is derived from the latinized (*Aethericus*) form of an old English personal name.

Aubin See Obins.

Audley This English name was well established in Co. Down before mid-sixteenth century; since the eighteenth it has been found in small numbers in Connemara. I may mention without corroboration that Woulfe suggests that there it is of Irish origin—Ó *hÁdhlaigh*—of which he gives no derivation.

Augher See Orchard.

Aughey An abbreviated form of MacCaughey.

Aughmuty A Scottish toponymic. This family coming at the time of the Plantation of Ulster first settled in Co. Cavan and later in Co. Longford. MIF

Mac Aughney, -Haughney *Mac Fhachtna*. A Co. Carlow name. Facthna is a saint's name once popular as a Christian name.

Auld. App.

Mac Auley, -Awley There are two distinct septs of this name, viz. *Mac Amhalghaidh* of Offaly and Westmeath, and the more numerous *Mac Amhlaoibh*, a branch of the MacGuires which as *Mag Amhlaoibh* gives the form Gawley in Connacht. Both are derived from personal names. The latter must not be confused with MacAuliffe. Bibl; IF Map Westmeath and Fermanagh.

Mac Auliffe *Mac Amhlaoibh*. An important branch of the MacCarthys whose chief was seated at Castle MacAuliffe. The name is almost peculiar to south-west Munster. IF   Map Cork. See MacAuley.

Aungier A Huguenot family in Dublin from mid-seventeenth century, when an important family of the same name settled in Co. Longford. In Offaly Danger is a synonym, though according to Reaney the two names are of different derivation, not from d'Aungiers.

Austin On record in Ireland since early fourteenth century this English name is now fairly numerous but not closely identified with any particular area. Woulfe gives *Oistín* as the form in use in Irish, adding that *Mac Aibhistín* is found in Connacht.

Mac Avaddy *Mac an Mhadaidh*. The derivation from *madadh,* dog, is not fully accepted, though it seems probable. This family is also called Madden in its homeland, Co. Mayo.

9

Mac Avera, -Avery *Mac Aimhréidh*. A Co. Down name.

Averell See Ebrill.

Mac Avey, -Aveigh A synonym of both MacEvoy and MacVeagh in north Connacht; occasionally of MacEvoy in Ulster.

Mac Avin See MacGiven.

Mac Avinchey *Mac Dhuibhinse*. Woulfe suggests 'of the black island', from *dubh* and *innis*, which is conjectural. A rather rare name found in Cos. Armagh, Tyrone and Derry. It has been sometimes changed to the English name Vincent there.

Mac Avinney See MacEvinney.

Mac Avinue See MacGivney.

Mac Avish A variant of MacCavish.

Mac Avoy See MacEvoy.

Mac Award See Ward.

Mac Aweeney A Cavan form of MacWeeney.

Mac Awley See MacAuley.

Aylmer *Aighlmear*. This Anglo-Saxon name came to Ireland after the Norman invasion and, settling in Leinster, families so called became hibernicized. Bibl; Map Kildare.

Aylward *Aighleart*. This Anglo-Norman family is closely associated with the city of Waterford since the fourteenth century, now numerous in Co. Kilkenny. In the Carrick-on-Suir area it is also called Elward. Map Waterford. Bibl.

Ayres, Eyres These are variants of Eyre (not used by the main family of Eyre). There are many other variants of Eyre, e.g. Heyer, but these are not in Ireland except very rarely as mistaken variants of (O)-Hehir.

B

Babe An Anglo-Norman name (*le Babbe*), gaelicized as *Báib*, formerly prominent in Co. Louth, now rare.

Backas Though very rare now this locative name (derived from bake-house) was well known in Waterford from late seventeenth century until comparatively recently. It is on record in Co. Derry as Backhouse.

Bacon Anglo-Norman *le Bacoun*, (i.e. the pig, implying pig-keeper); this one of the many such surnames which have been given the prefix *de* instead of *le* in their gaelicized form.

Badger See Brick.

Bagenal See Bagnall.

Bagge Bibl.

Bagley An English toponymic occasionally used as a synonym of Begley.

Bagnall Named from an English village this family came to Ireland in the sixteenth century, and were later prominent in the Catholic-Irish cause. The principal family was located in Co. Carlow and is remembered in the place-name Bagenalstown (now Muine Bheag). Bibl; MIF 24. See Beglin.

Bagot *Bagóid.* A family of importance in the Pale from the thirteenth century. They were also in Co. Limerick where Baggotstown locates them. Bibl; Map Dublin.

Bagwell In Co. Tipperary since late seventeenth century, when the well-known Clonmel family was established there.

Bailey, Bailie *Báille.* This English name which, often as *le Bailiff*, occurs frequently in mediaeval Irish records, is numerous in all the provinces except Connacht. It is an occasional synonym of Bellew. Bibl.

Bain See Bayne.

Baird The name of a Scottish clan, derived from Gaelic *bárd* (a bard), numerous in Antrim and Down.

Baker An English occupational name found in all the provinces. It was in Ireland, as *le Bakere,* as early as the thirteenth century.

Bakey See Beakey.

Baldrick This name, sometimes spelt Boldrick, came from England in mid-seventeenth century and is now quite numerous in north Donegal but rare elsewhere. The name is derived from an Old-English word meaning bold-rule.

Baldwin, Baldoon *Baldún.* This name (derived from an Old-German word meaning bold friend) came to Ireland from Germany via Flanders and was well established in Waterford and neighbouring counties before 1500. In Co. Donegal Baldwin is occasionally used as an anglicized form of *Ó Maolagáin,* normally Mulligan (*maol* is the word for bald in Irish). Bibl; MIF See Boden and Bodkin.

Balfe *Balbh.* A name of the epithet type—*balbh* means stammering—used by an immigrant family settled in Meath in the thirteenth century. IF MIF

Ball An English name of early introduction into Ireland and now scattered, mainly in Leinster and Ulster. Reaney gives four different derivations for Ball. Bibl.

Ballagh An epithetic surname formed from the Irish adjective *ballach* (speckled, marked). Frequent up to the seventeenth century as an ephemeral agnomen. MIF

Ballard See under Bollard.

Ballentine A Scottish toponymic fairly numerous in Ulster but of comparatively recent introduction.

Ballesty *Bailiste.* An old Co. Westmeath surname formed from the Old-French *ballestier* (cross-bowman).

Ballinger An English name of French origin found in Co. Clare.

(O) Ballivan *O Balbháin* (stammerer). An old Co. Tipperary name, now rare.

Balmer App.

Balton See Bolton.

Bambury A Northumbrian toponymic mainly found in Kerry. There were several mediaeval mayors of Limerick of this name.

Bambrick The origin of this name is uncertain; it is possibly derived from the Scottish place-name Bambreich. It has been closely associated with Co. Leix since 1600. MIF

Bamford App.

(O) Banane See Bannon and Bunyan.

Bane, Bawn An epithetic surname mainly found in Cos. Clare and Galway. It is formed from the Irish adjective *bán* (white) and often used synonymously with White. Irish surnames beginning with Ban, however, are seldom from *bán*, white, (unless the A is definitely long) but possibly derived from *ban*, indicating woman. MIF

Banfield, Banville Co. Wexford forms of Bonfield.

(O) Banigan *Ó Banagáin*. A name found in Cos. Donegal and Monaghan and quite distinct from Banaghan.

Banim A form of Bannon found in the Ormond country. MIF

Banks See Brohan.

(O) Ban(n)aghan *Ó Beannacháin* (*beannach*, beaked). Of Co. Sligo and east Connacht. MIF

Bannister A metonymic from Old-French *banastre*, basket, occasionally found in mediaeval Ireland; more numerous since seventeenth-century immigration when families of the name settled in Cos. Carlow and Cork.

(O) Bannon, Banane *Ó Banáin*. The name of several distinct septs, the most important in Lower Ormond and Fermanagh. Though White is sometimes used as a synonym of *Banáin* that is not derived from *bán*, white. See Bane. Leap Castle in Co. Offaly, near Roscrea, is *Léim Uí Bhanáin* in Irish; and the name is also incorporated in Ballybannon on the west side of Lough Mask in Co. Mayo, which locates a third sept not marked in the Map. MIF   Map Offaly, Fermanagh.

Barbour, Barber i.e. *le Barbier*. In Dublin since the thirteenth century; now mainly in Ulster. Bibl; MIF

Barclay An English toponymic from Berkeley in Gloucestershire, sometimes still so spelt. Barkley is the usual form in Ulster, where it was introduced at the time of the Plantation. Bibl.

(O) Bardon, Barden, Bardane *Ó Bárdáin* (*bárd*, a bard). A bardic family listed in Petty's 'census' of 1659 as a principal name in Cos. Longford and Westmeath, it is now found chiefly in Co. Wexford, where it has sometimes been changed to Barnes. Bardane is found in Co. Waterford.

Barker Though this occupational name (tree-stripper) is mainly of Cromwellian origin in Ireland (when not of recent immigration) it was in fact in Dublin as early as mid-sixteenth century and is on record occasionally before that. It is now fairly numerous in both Leinster and Ulster.

Barlow An English toponymic on record in Dublin from 1584 and since settled in other parts of the country, notably Co. Tipperary.

Barnacle A synonym of Coyne by translation.

(O) Barnane *Ó Bearnáin.* A west Cork name; sometimes changed to Bernard.

Barnard This is a variant of Bernard which is derived from Old-German word meaning bear-brave. Bibl.

Barnes This English locative name is used as a synonym of Barron. It is found in small numbers in all provinces. See Bardon.

Barnett App.

Barneville, Barnewall *de Bearnabhal.* An Anglo-Norman family of much importance in the Pale. Bibl; MIF

Barr An English name of three different origins. It is also a Scottish toponymic very numerous in north-east Ulster. Woulfe is misleading as he treats it solely as an anglicized variant of the rare west Cork name *Ó Báire,* which has been anglicized as Barry and so is now indistinguishable from the Norman Barry.

(Mac) Barragry, Berochry, Biracrea These are some of the variants of the name usually called Berkery.

Barrett *Baróid* in Munster, *Bairéid* in Connacht. These families, which were branches of the same stock, came with the Anglo-Norman invasion and became completely hibernicized. IF   Map Cork and Mayo.

Barrington This English toponymic occurs occasionally in mediaeval Irish records. The family first settled in Ireland temp. Elizabeth I (Leix); the main family is Cromwellian (Cork). The name is occasionally used as an anglicized form of *Ó Bearáin* (see Barron). Bibl; IF

Barron *Barún.* Though this name is derived from the English word baron, it is not English. It has two origins: one, MacBarron, a branch of the O'Neills; the other Barron, of the Fitzgeralds (Waterford-Kilkenny area). Barron is also used for *Ó Bearáin* (Berrane). Barron is also Scottish (of Angus); the Frazers were known as MacBarron. Bibl. MIF   Map Armagh and Kilkenny.

Barry *de Barra.* The majority of this name are of Norman origin, i.e. *de Barri* (a place in Wales); they became completely hibernicized. Though still more numerous in Munster than elsewhere the name is widespread throughout Ireland. Barry is also the anglicized form of *Ó Báire* (see under Barr) and of *Ó Beargha* (meaning spear-like, ac-

13

cording to Woulfe) a small sept of Co. Limerick. Bibl; IF   Map
Cork. See MacAdam.

Barter Since this occupational name came from England in the seventeenth century it has been associated exclusively with Co. Cork. Bibl.

Bartley See MacPartlan.

Barton *de Bartún*. This English toponymic is in Ireland since the thirteenth century, but the leading family, mainly identified with Straffan, Co. Kildare, came in 1599. Bibl; MIF

(O) Baskin *Ó Baiscinn*. Originally of the Corca Bhaiscinn in west Clare, now very rare.

Basnett Derived from *basynet*, a form of helmet, this name was prominent in Dublin throughout the sixteenth century, but has since become rare. Bibl.

Basquill A rare name found in Co. Mayo; it is probably a variant of Baskwell, which is from Baskerville.

Bassett From Old-French *basset* (of low stature). This name is in Ireland since the thirteenth century but is not closely associated with any particular area.

Bastable *de Bastábla*. A west country English toponymic well known in Cos. Cork and Kerry since the seventeenth century. MIF

Bastick See Bostock.

Bateman This English name (meaning servant of Bartholomew) has been fairly numerous in Co. Cork since the seventeenth century. It appears occasionally in Irish records as early as 1292. MIF

Bates Usually derived from the forename Bartholomew, this English name is quite numerous in Dublin and north Ulster. It is on record in Ireland since mid-seventeenth century.

Bathe This English toponymic, now rare, is the name of an Anglo-Norman family very prominent in Leinster in mediaeval times.

Battersby An English toponymic quite numerous in Cos. Monaghan and Fermanagh since mid-seventeenth century.

Battle *Mac Concatha* (*cú*, gen. *con*, hound—*cath*, battle). An indigenous Irish sept belonging to Co. Sligo, formerly anglicized MacEncaha. The form Concagh is extant in Co. Galway. It has no connection in Ireland with the mediaeval Anglo-Norman *de la Bataille*. MIF

Bawn See Bane.

Baxter Quite numerous in Ulster this name came from Scotland where *Mac an Bhacstair* is a branch of the Clan MacMillan. Baxter is an old word for baker. MIF

Mac Bay A variant of MacBeth and occasionally of MacVeigh.

Bayly Bibl.

Bayne An English name occasionally used as a synonym of Bane. As a Scottish name Bayne also derives from the adjective *bán*, white.

Beaghan See Behan.

Beakey, Bakey *Ó Béice*. A Clare name, also found in Co. Wicklow. *Béice* means weeping in Irish, but Woulfe's derivation of the name from this word is open to question.

Beamish An Anglo-Norman name of French toponymic origin, identified with Cos. Cork and Kerry since the sixteenth century. Bibl; MIF

Mac Bean See under MacVann.

Beard On record in Leix and Dublin and in Co. Waterford in the sixteenth century this name is now rare, except as an occasional variant of Baird, from which, however, it is basically quite distinct, being a translation of the French *barbe*.

(O) Beary *Ó Béara*. A small Offaly sept being an offshoot of the O'Dempseys.

Beasley *Béaslaoi*. A Lancashire toponymic, in Ireland since mid-seventeenth century.

(O) Beasty *Ó Biasta*. A small Mayo sept claiming descent from an early king of Connacht.

Beatty Usually the name of Scottish settlers in Ulster, but in other parts of the country it is the anglicized form of *Biadhtach* (public victualler) still extant as Beatagh and Betagh in the Athlone area; this is thus an occupational surname. MIF   Map Meath. See Betty.

Beaumont See Bowman.

Becher The name (derived from beech tree) of a landed family in Co. Cork since the end of the sixteenth century.

Beck An English name (of four distinct derivations) which occurs in mediaeval Irish records, now mainly found in Ulster. According to O'Donovan it is also an anglicized form of *Ó Béice* (see Beakey). Bibl.

Beckett This English name (usually of early French derivation) is now numerous in north-east Ulster and in Dublin but, though occasional references to it as early as the fourteenth century occur, it did not become established in Ireland till a century later, mainly in east Leinster; its close association with Ulster is later.

(O) Beegan A variant of Behan in the Ballinasloe area.

Beggane See Biggane.

Begg(e) In Leinster this is mainly the epithetic surname of a Norman family formed from the adjective *beag* (small), as is Bueg in Co. Cork; in Ulster, as Beggs, it is sometimes a variant of the English name Bigge. SIF 15.

(O) Begley *Ó Beaglaoich* (*beag*, little—*laoch*, hero). Originally of Co. Donegal. A branch of that sept migrated to Co. Kerry as galloglasses in the fifteenth century and the name is now mainly found in west Munster. MIF   Map Cork and Donegal.

(O) Beglin, Beglan *Ó Beigléighinn* (*beag*, little—*léighinn*, scholarship).

A rare name of Westmeath and Longford, sometimes anglicized Bagnall. MIF 25.

Begney An occasional synonym of Beglin, sometimes changed to Bagnall.

(O) Behan, Beaghan *Ó Beacháin* (perhaps from *beach,* bee). A Leinster sept, found also in Kerry in later times. For connection with Co. Clare see MIF   Map Kildare.

(O) Beirne *Ó Birn, Ó Beirn* (from the Norse forename *Bjorn*). This important north Connacht sept is quite distinct from O'Byrne. IF 54; MIF 186, 245. Map Mayo and Roscommon.

Bell This name, usually from Old-French *bel,* beautiful, mainly found in the four north-eastern counties of Ulster, is among the ten most numerous purely English names in Ireland. There are several different derivations of it. Bibl. App.

Bellew This Norman toponymic (*de Belleau*) is in Ireland since 1200. It is perpetuated in Bellewstowns in Cos. Louth and Meath; and Mount-bellew, Co. Galway. Bibl; MIF   Map Louth.

Bellingham This family is prominent in Co. Louth since the seventeenth century. There are three places in England so called. Castlebellingham in Co. Louth perpetuates this family. Bibl.

Belton This is a modern form of the Anglo-Norman de Weldon. More often, however, particularly in the case of immigrants of the seventeenth century and later. Belton is a simple English toponymic derived from one of several places so called. See Weldon.

(Ó) Benane This is a variant of Banane which is a north-Connacht anglicization of *Ó Banáin.* See Bannon.

Benbo See MacNaboola.

Benison A variant of Benson; in Ireland it is used as a curious synonym of Gildea.

Bennett A prominent Anglo-Irish family (of French origin, ultimately Latin *benedictus*) in Kilkenny and adjacent counties since the fourteenth century. The name appears as MacBennett in Oriel. MIF See also Bunyan.

Bennis An old English name of uncertain derivation (possibly son of Ben) mainly associated with Limerick since the seventeenth century.

Benson This English name is fairly numerous in Belfast and Dublin. See Benison.

Bentley An English toponymic which occurs occasionally in mediaeval Irish records. It was firmly established in Cos. Clare and Limerick in the seventeenth century—in some cases before Cromwell.

Berachry, Berocky See Barragry, Berkery.

Beresford An English toponymic. The family first came to Ireland at the time of the Plantation of Ulster; later they became prominent in Co. Waterford. Bibl; IF

(O) Bergin *Ó hAimheirgin (aimhirgin,* wondrous birth) lately contracted to *Ó Beirgin.* This family has spread from its original territory (Geashill) into Leix. MIF   Map Offaly. See Berrigan.

(Mac) Berkery *Mac Bearthagra.* Woulfe suggests the doubtful derivation *bear,* sharp—*tagradh,* pleading. This name of Co. Tipperary and east Limerick has many variant spellings.

Berkley See under Brickley and Barclay.

Bermingham One of the great Anglo-Norman families. The more hibernicized branches adopted the Irish patronymic *Mac Fheorais* (son of Piers) which became Corish. Bibl; MIF   Map Galway and Kildare.

Bernal This, like Burnell, is a variant of Berneval. See Barneville.

Bernard This English name is used in west Cork as a synonym of Barnane. Bibl. See Barnard.

(O) Berne A variant of Beirne.

Berney See MacBirney.

(Mac) Berochry See Barragry.

(O) Berrane A Mayo name. See Birrane and Barron.

(O) Berreen *Ó Birín (birín,* small spike). A Co. Sligo name.

Berrigan, Bergan Variants of Bergin.

Berrill, Birrell *Boiréil.* A Co. Louth name there since the Anglo-Norman invasion. Authorities of English surnames differ as to its derivation.

Berry This English name, usually a variant of Bury, is fairly numerous in Ireland since the seventeenth century, but widely scattered. It is also used as a synonym of Beary in Offaly.

Berth A Co. Clare variant of Brett.

Besnard Bibl.

Best The Irish Bests came from Kent, England, and settling in Leinster in the seventeenth century became prominent in Carlow and adjacent counties. The name is now mainly found in Cos. Antrim, Armagh and Tyrone due to more recent immigration from England. The derivation is from Old-English *best* (beast) denoting one in charge of cattle. MIF

Beston An English toponymic associated in small numbers with Co. Limerick and east Clare since the sixteenth century.

Betagh See Beatty.

Mac Beth, -Beath *Mac Beatha (beatha,* life). A Scottish name confused with MacVeagh and MacEvoy in Ulster.

Bethel In Co. Limerick this is a Palatine name. In Ulster, where it is on record since mid-seventeenth century, it is of Welsh origin, *Ap Ithel.*

Betty A variant of Beatty. Both occur in Co. Fermanagh as synonyms of MacCaffrey.

Bevan Bibl.

Bewley Bibl.

Bickerstaff See Biggar.

(O) Biggane, Biggins *Ó Beagáin* and *Ó Bigín*. This has been largely superseded in Munster by the English names Little and Littleton (*beag*, little). Beggan(e) is the Ulster spelling, mainly Co. Monaghan. Biggins is used in Co. Mayo.

Biggar This is normally of Lowland Scottish toponymic origin; but some Biggars and even Bickerstaffs of Co. Down are actually of the sept MacGivern. MIF

(O) Biggy *Ó Bigigh*. Presumably derived from *beag* (small). It is mainly a Co. Mayo name.

Bigley A variant of Begley.

Binane See Bunyan.

Binchy This family came from England in mid-seventeenth century and has since been closely associated with Charleville and adjacent areas of north Cork.

Bindon Though the Bindons first settled in Co. Tipperary in 1580 the family has since the following century been prominently associated with Co. Clare. MIF

Bingham An English toponymic now numerous in Ulster but formerly associated with Co. Mayo, where Binghamstown locates them. Bibl.

(Mac) Biracrea See Barragry.

Birch A locative name of mid-seventeenth century introduction. Families of the name settled in Offaly and adjoining areas. Bibl.

Bird This well-known name is used in Ireland as a synonym (by pseudo-translation) of Heany, Hegney, Henaghan and MacEneany. MIF

(Mac) Birney See Burney.

(O) Birrane *Ó Bioráin*. As modernized forms of this Byrne, Byron and even Burns have been recorded in various parts of Connacht and Munster. Woulfe suggests *bear*, a spear, as the derivation of this and the cognate Berrane.

Birrell See Berrill.

Birt, Burt, Byrth In Munster these are occasional synonyms of Brett. A family of English origin, using the variants Burt, Birt, Bert and Byrth has been established in Co. Derry since early eighteenth century. The name Birt occurs in the Pale in the mediaeval period as a variant of Britt.

Bishop This well-known English name is used in Ireland as a synonym of MacAnespie and Gillespie by translation.

Bissett A Scottish family in the Glens of Antrim, who adopted the Irish patronymic of *Mac Eoin,* Mac Keown. Bibl.

Blacagh A synonym of Blake found in bi-lingual areas of Connacht.

Black A Scottish name (connected with three clans—Lamont, MacGregor and MacLean of Duart) very numerous in Ulster. It is also used as a translation or synonym of Duff and Kilduff. Black again is a common English name. Bibl; App.

Blackall, Blackhall This name first appears in Ireland in mid-seventeenth century in Ulster and Limerick. It has since been mainly associated with Limerick, Co. Clare and Dublin where they were prominent in civic affairs. According to Reaney the name indicates dweller by the dark nook.

Blackburn(e) This English (Lancashire) toponymic, which is on record in Ireland since the fourteenth century, recurs in later centuries as that of landowners in the area from Co. Roscommon to Co. Donegal. There was also a branch in Co. Meath. There are several variant spellings including Blackbyrne.

Blacker A name of Norse origin, in Co. Armagh since mid-seventeenth century. Bibl.

Blackney An English toponymic in Co. Carlow since mid-seventeenth century and in Dublin before that. Bibl.

Blackwell This is an English toponymic much in evidence among the Cromwellian 'adventurers', but there were families of the name settled in Co. Clare earlier in the seventeenth century. MIF

Blackwood App.

Blair A Scottish territorial name very numerous in north Ulster.

Blake *de Bláca* (more correctly *le Bláca*). One of the 'Tribes of Galway'. An epithet name meaning black which superseded the original Caddell. They are descended from Richard Caddell, Sheriff of Connacht in 1303. They became and long remained very extensive landowners in Co. Galway. A branch settled in Co. Kildare where their name is perpetuated in three townlands called Blakestown. Bibl; IF   See also Blowick.

Blanchfield This is a modern form of the Norman *de Blancheville* which is associated with Co. Kilkenny since the thirteenth century. SIF 17.

Blaney The Blaneys or Blayneys came from Wales at the end of the sixteenth century and settled in Co. Monaghan where they gave their name to the town of Castleblayney. Bibl; MIF

(O) Bleahan, Bleheen *Ó Blichín*. An east Galway name synonymous with Melvin. MIF

Bleakley, Blakely An English toponymic first appearing (apart from an isolated instance in the fifteenth century) in Ireland in the seventeenth century, now numerous in Cos. Cavan, Monaghan and Antrim.

Blennerhassett An English family, originally of Cumberland, settled in Kerry, basically quite distinct from the Irish Hassetts. The other family, formerly prominent in Fermanagh, is no longer there. Bibl. MIF See Hassett.

Blessing See Mulvanaughty.

Blevins Of Welsh origin; found in Co. Tyrone.

Blewett See Bluett.

Bligh *Ó Blighe*. In Connacht this is derived from a Norse personal name, elsewhere a synonym of Blythe, which is of dual origin; from the adjective *blithe* and the place Blyth: as such the form used in Irish is *de Blaghd*.

Blood Though by a coincidence, settled in the Uí Bloid country in Co. Clare the Bloods are not of Irish origin; they came from Derbyshire, England, in 1595 being originally Welsh, *ap Lloyd*. MIF

Bloomer A synonym of Gormley.

Blosse-Lynch A branch of the Lynch family in Co. Galway.

Blowick *Ó Blathmhaic* (*blath,* fame, not flower,—*mac,* son). A Connacht name sometimes changed to Blake in Co. Mayo and Fermanagh. IF 55.

Bluett, Blewitt This name derived from the French *bleu,* is in Ireland since the Anglo-Norman invasion. It occurs continuously from the thirteenth century in records relating to Cos. Cork and Limerick.

Blunden A landed family of note in Co. Kilkenny since mid-seventeenth century.

Blunt Norman *le Blount,* i.e. the blond or fair-haired. Now very rare, this name was one of the most numerous of the Anglo-Norman names in Ireland in the Middle Ages. It was usually changed to White by semi-translation.

Blythe, Bly See Bligh.

Boag A variant of Bogue.

Boal Mainly found in Cos. Antrim and Down. Boal is a synonym of the Irish Boyle, also sometimes of the English name Boles or Bowles. MIF

Boar See Bower.

Boddy A derivative of Baldwin found in Co. Leitrim.

Bodell See Bothwell.

Boden The well-known name Boden is perpetuated in the place Bodenstown, Co. Kildare, where Boden is a variant of Baldwin; but there is also a rare Irish name *Ó Buadáin* so anglicized. MIF

Bodkin *Boidicín* (originally Bowdekyn, a diminutive of Baldwin). One of the 'Tribes of Galway'. Traditionally said, perhaps erroneously, to be an offshoot of the Fitzgeralds. IF

(O) Bogan, Boggan *Ó Bogáin* (*bog,* soft). Mainly associated with Cos. Donegal and Wexford. MIF

(O) Bogue *Ó Buadhaigh* (*buadhach,* victorious). Bogue is the usual anglicized form in Co. Cork, Bowe mainly in Cos. Kilkenny and Waterford, and Bowes and Bowie in the midland counties. In modern times Bogue (in Ulster of Scottish origin) is more numerous in Co. Fermanagh than elsewhere. See also Boyce. MIF   Map Cork.

(O) Bohan(e) *Ó Buadhacháin.* Derivation as previous entry. It takes the form Bohan in Connacht (mainly Leitrim and Galway) and Bohane, Boughan and Buhan in Cork, while in Clare it is usually Bohannon, which in Ulster is a synonym of the Scottish Buchanan. MIF   Map Cork. See Bowen.

Bohannon See previous entry.

(O) Bohelly, Bouhilly See Buckley.

Bohill See Boyle.

Boileau A Huguenot name.

(O) Bolan(d) *Ó Beolláin* (formed from a Norse personal name). The name of two distinct septs: one of the Uí Fiachrach, the other Dalcassian, as Map. Bibl; IF   Map Clare and Sligo.

Bolasty A variant of Ballesty in Co. Westmeath.

Boldrick See Baldrick.

Bole A variant of Boal found in Oriel.

(O) Bolger *Ó Bolguidhir*. I accept Woulfe's derivation (*bolg*, belly— *odhar*, yellow) though it has been disputed. Chiefly notable as a medical family. MIF 38; Map Wexford.

Bollard Of Dutch origin, this name came to Ireland in the early seventeenth century, and soon became prominent in the commercial life of Dublin. The quite distinct Norman name Ballard (Middle-English bald head) goes back to early mediaeval times.

Bolster An English name well known in Co. Cork since early eighteenth century. Like Bowler it denotes a maker of bowls.

Bolton This, derived from an English place-name, has been in Ireland since mediaeval times. It is scattered and is fairly numerous in all the provinces. In Co. Clare it has become Balton. Bibl. MIF

Bonar This name is very numerous in Ulster but not elsewhere in Ireland. In Co. Donegal, where it is mainly found, it is a synonym of Crampsey and Kneafsey. See Bonner.

Bonass An English toponymic distinct from Bones.

Bond Anglo-Norman *le Bonde* (unfree tenant). In Ireland since early fourteenth century and now found in small numbers in all the provinces, least in Connacht.

Bones This is *Mac Cnámhaigh* in Connacht sometimes English elsewhere. The rare Bone is for de Bohun. The Irish word for bone is *cnámh*.

Bonfield *de Buinnbhíol*. Anglo-Norman *de Bonneville*, mainly associated with Limerick and Clare.

Bonner A variant of Bonar in north Ulster; in Co. Limerick it is a Palatine name from French *bonnaire* (courteous).

Boohan A Co. Limerick form of *Ó Buadhacháinn*. See Bohan.

Booth An English occupational name (for a cowman) prominent since mid-seventeenth century in Dublin and Co. Sligo. Of the latter was Constance Countess Markievicz of 1916 fame.

Bor Bibl.

(O) Boran, Burrane *Ó Bodhráin* (probably from *bodhar,* deaf). East Limerick and west Tipperary.

Borris An occasional variant of Burris or Burrowes.

Borrowes, Borroughs See Burrowes.

Bostock The establishment of this English toponymic in Ireland dates from the sixteenth century. As Bastick, another toponymic with which it is confused, it was later found mainly in Co. Offaly.

Bothwell This is a Scottish name, derived from the lordship of Bothwell in Lanarkshire. It is in east Ulster since the first half of the seventeenth century and is still quite numerous there. In mediaeval times in Scotland it was spelt Boduel, whence the present variant Bodell in Ulster.

Boucher, Bossher *Buiséir.* Norman and Irish forms of the English Butcher, on record in Ireland since the thirteenth century especially in Co. Wexford; now mainly found in Cos. Cork and Waterford. Busher and Bouchier are variants.

Boughan See Bohan.

Boughla, Bouhilly See Buckley.

Bourchier Usually a synonym of Boucher. Bibl.

Bourke See Burke.

Bourne In Ireland since the sixteenth century, mainly Cos. Dublin and Kildare. Many families of the name in Mayo have now become Burns, while elsewhere it has been often changed to Byron thus concealing its origin and sometimes inevitably to Byrne. Bibl.

Bovaird A name of French origin formerly quite numerous in Co. Donegal, now rare.

Bovenizer A Palatinate name in Co. Limerick alias Boonizer, sometimes abbreviated to Neazer.

Bowden See Boden.

Bowdern, Bowdren *de Búdráin.* A Co. Waterford name, probably an Anglo-Norman toponymic, *de Boderan.* MIF

Bowe See Bogue.

Bowen It is usually of Welsh origin (*Ap Owen*), as is the well-known family of Bowenscourt, Co. Cork, which was Cromwellian. The name, however, was prominent in Queen's County in the sixteenth century. It is also used sometimes for Bohane and for Norman de Bohun. Bibl.

Bower An occasional synonym by mistranslation of MacCullagh in Co. Sligo. Boar, more obviously so, is also used.

Bowes, Bowie See Bogue.

Bowler *Bóighléir.* In the Pale this is an occupational name (maker of bowls). It has long been associated with Co. Kerry, where Ballybowler indicates its location. There Bowler is a later variant of the earlier *le Fougheller,* which was first anglicized as Fuller and Fowler. It is perhaps from the Norman-French *le oiseleur.* MIF

Bowles, Boles See under Boal.

Bowman In north Ulster this is said to be a corruption of Beaumont; it is found in Co. Limerick as a Palatine name.

Bowyer A well-known English name derived from Middle English *bowyere* (maker of bows) on record in Dublin from 1644, since when it has been continuously in Dublin and also in Cos. Longford and Westmeath.

Boyce An English name of Norman origin (from French *bois*) established in various counties. In Donegal and the west it is an anglicized form of *Ó Buadhaigh* (Bogue).

Boycott Capt. Boycott, whose connection with Irish land agitation less than a century ago gave a word to the English language, was the first of the family to settle in Ireland. There are two places in England called Boycott. MIF

Boyd This Scottish name is very numerous in Ulster. It appears erroneously as O'Boyd in some of the northern hearth money rolls. In Scotland and Ireland it is usually derived from Bute; there is also a Manx name basically the same as the Irish MacElwee but changed to Boyd. The Boyd branch of the Stuarts claim that it derives from the adjective *buidhe*, yellow. App. Bibl.

Boydell An old Cheshire and Lancashire name, probably a toponymic. The well-known Dublin family only came from England in 1862, but the name was found in Co. Meath as early as 1710.

Boyer A variant of Bowyer.

Boyes Usually a variant of Boyce, but it is also found as a synonym of Bohill in Co. Down.

(O) Boyhan A Westmeath name. Woulfe suggests *Ó Buadhacháin* (see Bohane) as the Irish form. This seems improbable. For the cognate MacBoyheen see under Boyne.

(O) Boylan *Ó Baoighealláin*. A sept of Dartry (Co. Monaghan). Before being subdued by the MacMahons they were influential from Fermanagh to Louth. See next entry. IF 56.

(O) Boyle *Ó Baoighill*. This sept shared with O'Donnells and O'Doghertys the leadership of the north-west. Boyle and Boylan are among the many names the derivation of which is uncertain. However, in this case there is general agreement that the root word (modern *geall*) means pledge. The name is occasionally made Bohill in Co. Down. Bibl; IF   Map Donegal. See p. 304.

Boyne Possibly a modern form of *Mac Baoithin* (*baoth*, foolish) formerly MacBoyheen which was one of the more numerous names in Co. Leitrim in the seventeenth century but is now almost extinct there. MIF

Boyton This name is of dual origin: it is de Boyton in Co. Tipperary and probably *Ó Baodáin* (*baotán*, simpleton) in Connacht.   MIF

Brabazon Nowhere numerous, this name is found in all provinces. It denotes inhabitant of Brabant. Bibl.

(O) Bracken *Ó Breacáin (breac,* speckled). In the Map this sept should have been placed slightly more to the north than it is, viz. on the Kildare-Offaly border. It has been closely identified with that area since mediaeval times. MIF

(O) Bradden See Salmon and Bredin.

Bradfield This English toponymic is not a name about which I have useful information before early nineteenth century. I include it because since then it has been numerous in west Cork.

Bradford An English toponymic of seventeenth-century introduction, since when it has been in Ulster, mainly Co. Down.

(O) Bradigan *Ó Bradagáin.* A Co. Roscommon name which has become Brodigan in Cos. Meath and Louth. The variant Bredican (*Ó Bradacháin*) occurs in Cos. Sligo and Mayo. See Brady for possible derivation.

Bradish The earliest reference to this name I have met is to a customs officer in Co. Wicklow in 1616. From that time till the present day the name has been found in the south-eastern counties and Kilkenny. I have yet to discover its origin.

Bradley Though this is an English name it is seldom of English origin in Ireland where it is a synonym of O'Brallaghan.

Bradshaw This English toponymic, which occasionally occurs in mediaeval Irish records, was well established in Ireland in the early seventeenth century and has since been mainly found in Co. Tipperary and Oriel as well as in Dublin and Belfast. Bibl.

(Mac) Brady *Mac Brádaigh* (possibly *bradach,* spirited, from *brad,* urging). A powerful Breffny sept. IF   Map Cavan. For Brady in Co. Clare see O'Grady.

(O) Bragan *Ó Bragáin.* Formerly Co. Louth, now very rare.

(O) Brahan *Ó Bracháin.* A rare name formerly found in Cos. Limerick and Wexford.

Brakey See Breakey. **Braly** Bibl. p. 368.

(O) Brallaghan *Ó Brollacháin* (from *Brollach,* an old Irish personal name presumably derived from *brollach,* breast). Mainly Derry, Tyrone and Donegal. There is a Cork branch which is called Bradley. IF   Map Donegal.

Mac Bran *Mac Brain.* West Clare. See Brann.

Brandon In Kerry this is *Mac Breandáin,* a branch of the Fitzmaurices; elsewhere, as *de Brandon,* of English origin. Brendon is an occasional synonym.

(O) Braniff *Ó Branduibh* (presumably derived from *bran,* raven—*dubh,* black). A rare Co. Down name.

(O) Branigan, Brangan *Ó Branagáin* (*bran,* raven). A sept of the Cenél

Eoghain, now found mainly as in Map. MIF   Map Armagh-Monaghan.

Brann This east Ulster name is distinct from the Clare MacBran, though both derive from the word *bran*, a raven.

Brannagh, Brennagh *Breat(h)nach*. Now widely superseded by the translation Walsh, but still extant in Connacht. IF

(Mac) Brannan *Mac Brandin* (*bran*, raven). An important name in north Connacht, to be distinguished from Brennan, though that form is often used. IF 60; Map Roscommon.

(O) Brannan *Ó Brandin*. An erenagh family of Fermanagh, now often called Brennan.

(O) Brannelly, Branley *Ó Branghaile* (*branghal*, raven valour). Peculiar to east Galway.

Brannock This, with its variant Brennock, is a Welsh toponymic from Brecknock quite distinct from Brannagh. It is indisputable, however, that both do frequently appear as synonyms of Walsh, as official birth registrations testify.

Bransfield An English toponymic associated with west Waterford and south-east Cork. Richard Foley considered it to be a corrupt form of Blanchfield.

Brassil See Brazil.

Mac Bratney See under Britton.

Brawley See Brolly.

Brawn A variant of Birrane.

Bray Of dual origin: Bray may be a toponymic, *de Bré* (in Cornwall; seldom Bray, Co. Wicklow) also modernized Bree; or the Irish *Ó Breaghdha* (indicating a native of Bregia, a territory in Meath), formerly well known in Munster. MIF

(O) Brazil, Brassill *Ó Breasail* (possibly from *bres*, strife). Mainly a Co. Waterford name.

Breadon See Bredin.

Bready A variant of Brady in Connacht and parts of Ulster.

Breakey This is quite numerous in Co. Monaghan and adjacent areas since the late seventeenth century. Brakey is a variant.

(Mac) Brearty, Mac Murty *Mac Muircheartaigh* (son of Murtagh). MacMurty has been confused with MacMurtrie which is a sept of the Scottish clan Stuart of Bute. MacBrearty is mainly found in Co. Donegal, MacMurtry and MacMurty in Antrim. MIF

(O) Bredican See Bradigan.

Bredin, Breadon These and other variants (Braden, etc.) are mainly found in Tyrone and Fermanagh. In Leitrim, as well as Bradden, they are anglicized forms of *Ó Bradáin*. In Leinster Breadon is an Anglo-Norman toponymic.

Bree Found in Cos. Sligo and Mayo. See Bray.

(Mac) Breen *Mac Braoin.* This sept so called of Co. Kilkenny is now extinct or indistinguishable from O'Breen. IF   Map Kilkenny. See MacBryan.

(O) Breen *Ó Braoin.* Of Brawney as Map. Also anglicized as Bruen in Co. Roscommon, where an important sept of *Ó Braoin* was located. IF 59; Map Offaly, Roscommon.

(Mac) Brehany, -Brehon *Mac an Bhreitheamhnaigh.* Now largely translated as Judge. MIF   Map Sligo.

Brendon See Brandon.

Brennagh See Brannagh.

(O) Brennan *Ó Braonáin.* (The word *braon* has several meanings, possibly sorrow in this case). The name of four unrelated septs, located in Ossory, east Galway, Kerry and Westmeath. The Co. Fermanagh sept of *Ó Branáin* was also anglicized Brennan as well as Brannan. Bibl; IF   Map Kerry and Kilkenny. See also Brannan.

(O) Brennigan This variant of Branigan is found in west Connacht.

Brennock See Brannock.

Brereton An English toponymic. The family, of Norman origin, came to Ireland in the sixteenth century and is now mainly found in Co. Tipperary where it is quite hibernicized. MIF   Bibl.

(O) Breslin, Breslane *Ó Breasláin.* (The derivation is perhaps the same as *Ó Breasail.* See Brazil). One of the principal brehon families. MIF   Map Donegal, Fermanagh and Sligo.

(O) Bresnahan, Bresnan See Brosnan.

Brett, Britt Formerly *le Bret* (Old-French *Bret*, i.e. Breton). In Ireland since the twelfth century. Now mainly found in Cos. Waterford, Tipperary and Sligo. MIF

Brew This is of varied origin: a Norman surname *de Berewa*; a Manx name MacVriew; or an anglicized form of *Ó Brugha,* Broe (*brughaidh,* farmer) a small Ossory sept. MIF

Mac Briar The form used in Co. Down for the Scottish name MacBrair (*bráthair,* brother or friar).

Brice See Bryce.

Briceson See Bryson.

(O) Brick *Ó Bruic.* Though originally a Thomond name it is now seldom found outside Kerry, except in the translated form Badger in Co. Galway. As *Ó Bric* it is the name of Decies sept of some mediaeval importance, now very rare. MIF   Map Waterford.

Brickley, Breckley Probably a corrupt form of Berkeley in Co. Cork from the thirteenth century and formerly numerous there.

Mac Bride *Mac Giolla Bhrighde* (devotee of St. Brigid). This name belongs mainly to Co. Donegal, where it is that of a prominent ecclesiastical family. In east Ulster it is sometimes of Scottish origin. IF

Bridgeman See Drought. See page 304.

Bridget This name is not derived from the Christian name Brigid but is an abbreviated form of Uprichard. It is in Ireland since the seventeenth century, mainly in Ulster.

Mac Brien See MacBryan.

O Brien *Ó Briain*. A Dalcassian sept, deriving its name and historical importance from the family of King Brian Boru. Now very numerous in other provinces as well as Munster, being the fifth most numerous name in Ireland. In some cases O'Brien has been made a synonym of O'Byrne and in others of the Norman Bryan. Bibl; IF MIF Map Clare, Limerick, Tipperary, Waterford.

Briggs App.

(O) Brinane This is on record as used synonymously with Brennan in Co. Cork.

Mac Brine See MacBryan.

Mac Brin(n) *Mac Broin*. A Co. Down name now usually made Byrne, one of the many names derived from *bran*, raven.

(O) Briody *Ó Bruaideadha*. (From the old Irish personal name *Bruaided*). North Longford and west Cavan.

Briscoe This English toponymic is in Ireland since the sixteenth century, but is not closely identified with any county. MIF

Brislan(e), Brislawn Variants of Breslin.

Britt See Brett.

Britton, Brittain This is derived from Brittany in France not from Great Britain—it was *le Breton* in mediaeval times in Ireland, not *de Bretagne* as in England. It is to be distinguished from the Co. Antrim Mac-Britany *(Mac Breatnaigh)* now usually MacBratney. MIF

Brocas The well-known artists of this name were all Dublin, where the family settled in the seventeenth century. It is apparently not a variant of the English Brookhouse, but according to Bardsley of French origin. Bibl; MIF

Brock This is usually of English origin. Like the Irish Brick it is derived from *broc* which is the word for badger in both Irish and Old-English.

Broder, Broderick, Browder *Ó Bruadair* (derived from a Norse forename). The name of several septs, two of which are extant, viz. of Barrymore (with a branch in Ossory) and of Co. Galway. IF Map Cork and Kilkenny.

Brodie The Scottish form of O'Brollaghan. MIF

(O) Brodigan See Bradigan.

Mac Brody *Mac Bruaideadha*. A literary family attached to the O'Briens of Thomond. Map Clare. See Briody.

Broe See Brew.

(O) Brogan *Ó Brógáin*. A sept of the Uí Fiachrach located in north Connacht. The origin of the name is uncertain. Woulfe's derivation from *brón,* sorrow is not accepted by Celtic scholars. MIF   Map Mayo.

Brohal See Broughall.

(O) Brohan *Ó Bruacháin.* An Offaly family often by pseudo-translation called Banks. The true meaning of the word is probably corpulent. MIF

(Mac) Brohoon A phonetic synonym of Brehony or Abraham *(Mac an Breitheamhan).*

(O) Brollaghan See Brallaghan.

(O) Brol(l)y, Brawley *Ó Brolaigh.* A sept of Co. Derry still represented there. For possible derivation see Brallaghan. Brolly is also an anglicized form of the French *de Broglie* but this rarely if ever applies to Ireland.

Brontë See Prunty.

Brooke This family came to Ulster in the sixteenth century; to be distinguished from Brooks, which is of later introduction. IF

(O) Brophy *Ó Bróithe.* A numerous and well-known sept of mid-Leinster. The origin of this name is obscure. I have never seen even a tentative suggestion. MIF   Map Leix.

(O) Brosnan, Brosnahan *Ó Brosnacháin.* This name, also anglicized as Bresnahan, etc., belongs almost exclusively to Co. Kerry. It probably derives from the place-name Brosna. MIF   Map Kerry.

Brothers A synonym of Broder.

Broughall There are references to this name in Irish records from the fourteenth century, mainly in east Leinster. The derivation is uncertain. MIF

Broughan See Brohan.

Browder See Broder.

Browne *De Brún,* more correctly *le Brún* (brown). One of the Tribes of Galway. Other important families of Browne were established in Ireland from the Anglo-Norman invasion onwards. The Brownes of Killarney, who came in the sixteenth century, intermarried with the leading Irish families and were notable for their survival as extensive Catholic landowners throughout the period of the Penal Laws. (The Kenmare associated with their name is in Co. Limerick.) The Browne family shown on the Map in Co. Limerick is of Camus and of earlier introduction. Yet another important family of the name was of the Neale, Co. Mayo. In that county Browne has also been used as a synonym of (O) Bruen. App. IF   MIF   Map Galway and Limerick.

Brownlee App.

Brownlow Bibl.

Brownrigg Bibl.

Broy This can be O'Broy *Ó Bróithe* (see Brophy), or de Broy. The former was of Co. Kilkenny. The name is rare now. MIF

Bruce This name, mainly associated with Scotland (though ultimately of French origin), is numerous in Ulster, where it has been found since early eighteenth century; it was in Co. Cork before that.

(O) Bruen This is a variant form of Breen usual in Co. Roscommon, the homeland of one of the *Ó Braoin* septs. The main family were erenaghs of St. Coman at Roscommon. MIF

Brugha See Burgess and Brew.

(O) Brunty See Prunty.

Bruodin, Broudin Synonyms of MacBrody.

(O) Brusnahan See Brosnahan.

Bruton An English toponymic in Ireland since the sixteenth century; rare formerly, now quite numerous in Dublin. It is occasionally used synonymously with Britton. It has been recorded also as a synonym of Brereton in Co. Offaly.

Bryan The name of a prominent Anglo-Norman family settled in Co. Kilkenny. Sometimes used for O'Brien and also occasionally for Byrne in Co. Kildare. MIF

Mac Bryan This form of *Mac Braoin* (Breen) as well as MacBrine is usual in Co. Fermanagh where it is the name of a branch of the Mac-Manus sept. It is frequently written MacBrien and has sometimes been changed to O'Brien there and in Co. Cavan.

Bryce This is an English name long found in Ireland. It, like Bryson, has been used in Donegal as a synonym of Breslin.

Bryson This English name, alias Briceson, is used in Cos. Donegal and Derry as the modern form of *Ó Muirgheasáin*, first anglicized as O'Mrisane and later sometimes O'Morison. *Muirgheas* (sea valour) equates with Maurice. MIF

Buchanan A well-known Scottish toponymic quite numerous in Tyrone and other Ulster counties. Bibl. See also Bohannon and Mawhannon.

Buckley The numerous English name Buckley is used as the normal anglicized form of *Ó Buachalla*, a sept located in Offaly in mediaeval times, where it is still extant as Buhilly and Boughla. Buckley is now found mainly in Cos. Cork and Tipperary. The root word *buachaill* means boy. IF

Budran A variant of Bowdern.

Bueg See Begg.

Buggle An English toponymic associated with Dublin since late sixteenth century and later with Co. Kildare.

(O) Buggy *Ó Bogaigh* (*bog*, soft). An old and well-known name in Cos. Wexford and Kilkenny.

Bugler This name, peculiar in Ireland to east Clare, is an English (Dorset) toponymic not an occupational name. MIF

29

(O) Buhan See Bohan.

Bulfin Probably a variant of Bullfinch, this name is associated with Co. Offaly but not of great antiquity in Ireland.

(O) Bulger See Bolger.

Bullen This name, formerly Boleyn (from the French place-name Bologne), first came to Ireland early in the sixteenth century through association with the Ormond Butlers. From the end of the seventeenth century it has been mainly found in Co. Cork.

Bullman This well-known English name has been in Co. Cork since before 1650, but is seldom found elsewhere in Ireland.

Bullock Bibl.

Bulmer A Huguenot name found in Ulster.

Bunbury Derived from an English place, this name is in Cos. Tipperary and Carlow since early seventeenth century.

Bunting This English name, of nickname type, has been in Cos. Tyrone and Armagh since the first half of the seventeenth century. It is famous on account of Edward Bunting's life work in the field of traditional Irish music. MIF

Bunton A variant of Bunting especially in Cos. Armagh and Down.

Bunworth An English family established in Co. Cork in the late seventeenth century.

Bunyan, Bunion An English family settled in Co. Kerry (of Ballybunion). The name is now generally changed to Bennett. Binnane and Banane have also been used as synonyms of it in Kerry. MIF

Burbage An English toponymic found in Cos. Leitrim and Longford, on record in Ireland since the sixteenth century.

Burchill See Burtchell.

Burdon This name is found in Co. Down where it is that of a branch of the Scottish clan Lamont; in Co. Cork, where it is on record as early as the fourteenth century, it is of English, ultimately French, origin.

Burgess See under Burrowes.

Burke, de Burgh *de Búrca*. This is one of the most important and most numerous Hiberno-Norman names. First identified with Connacht it is now numerous in all the provinces (least in Ulster). Many subsepts of it were formed called MacHugo, MacGibbon, *Mac Seoinín* (Jennings), MacRedmond, etc. IF   MIF   Map Galway, Mayo and Tipperary.

Burnell This, like Brunell, is derived from Old-French *brun,* brown: the name of an Anglo-Norman family in Meath and Dublin since the thirteenth century and in Clare from the sixteenth. It is occasionally a synonym of Bernal. Bibl.

Burnett Derivation as previous entry. The name is in Co. Monaghan and Dublin since mid-seventeenth century.

(Mac) Burney, Birney *Mac Biorna*. A Scottish name of Norse origin of comparatively recent introduction in Ireland, now numerous in north-east Ulster.

Burns This Scottish locative name, numerous in Ulster and to a lesser extent in Munster, is widely used for O'Beirne, Birrane and Byrne. It is also the modern form of *Mac Conboirne*, formerly anglicized Conborney, a north Connacht sept. Bibl; App.

Burnside An English locative name in Co. Derry since early seventeenth century. Bibl.

Burrane See Boran.

Burrell A variant form of Berrill in Co. Armagh.

Burrowes, Burris(s) An English name (dweller at the bower-house) now numerous, especially in Ulster, but little known in Ireland before the seventeenth century. It has been wrongly gaelicized *Brugha* which is for Burgess, a distinct name of obvious derivation. MIF

Burt See Birt.

Burtchaell Though since the seventeenth century associated with Cos. Wicklow and Kilkenny the name (spelt Burchill) is now more numerous in Co. Cork.

Burton This well-known English toponymic is, in Ireland, mainly associated with Co. Cork. Bibl.

Bury The name of an English family of Norman descent which came to Ireland in the late thirteenth century with the Prestons. MIF

Busher One of the earliest Anglo-Norman families which settled in Co. Wexford. See Bouchier.

Bustard This English name, of obvious derivation, is, in Ireland, peculiar to Co. Donegal; it is of comparatively modern introduction.

Busteed This name is almost peculiar to Co. Cork where it has been since the first half of the seventeenth century. I have not ascertained its origin. MIF

Butler Always called *de Buitléir* in Irish, though it is of course properly *le* Butler not *de*. It is one of the great Anglo-Norman families which, however, did not soon become hibernicized like the Burkes etc. Historically it is mainly identified with the Ormond country. It is now very numerous in all the provinces except Ulster. Bibl; IF   MIF Map Kilkenny-Tipperary.

Butt Apart from the political leader, Isaac Butt, born in Co. Donegal, this name has no close association with Ireland, though it does occur in a few isolated cases in the seventeenth century.

Butterly An English toponymic in Co. Louth since late seventeenth century.

Buttimer The earlier form in England was Botymer. A well-known name in Co. Cork since the sixteenth century. MIF

Bwee This is for *Ó Buadhaigh* (Bogue, Boyce) in Donegal and for *Mac Giolla Bhuidhe* (MacEvoy) in east Ulster.

Byers This name in England is derived from Old-French *byre*, cowman. In Scotland, whence Byers families in Ireland mainly came, it is from the old barony of Byers in East Lothian. It is fairly numerous in Ulster being mainly associated with Cos. Cavan and Armagh.

Bynane See Bunyan.

(O) Byrne *Ó Broin* (*bran*, raven). A foremost sept in east Leinster, prominent in Irish history, especially in the resistance to English conquest. Byrne is now one of the most numerous names in Ireland. Bibl; IF 68; Map Wicklow. See MacBrinn, Burns, Beirne and Byron.

Byron This English name is used occasionally as a synonym of O'Beirne, Birrane and Byrne. For derivation see Byers.

Bywater A synonym of Sruffaun in Co. Waterford (*sruth, sruthán*, a stream).

C

Mac Cabe *Mac Cába*. A galloglass family with the O'Reillys and the O'Rourkes which became a recognized Breffny sept. Woulfe suggests *cába*, cape, a surname of the nickname type as the derivation. Having regard to their origin it is more likely to be from a non-Gaelic personal name. Bibl; IF   Map Cavan.

Mac Cadam An occasional variant of MacAdam.

Caddell Welsh *Cadwal*. In Cos. Galway and Dublin since the thirteenth century; in Co. Galway this name became Blake.

Mac Cadden *Mac Cadáin*. An old erenagh family in Co. Armagh. See also MacAdam.

(Mac) Caddo, Caddow Two of the many anglicized forms of *Mac Conduibh*. See Cunniff.

(O) Cadogan, Cadigan *Ó Ceadagáin*. A Co. Cork sept, to be distinguished from the Welsh family of Cadogan who were prominent in Dublin and Meath in the seventeenth century and on record in Co. Limerick as early as the thirteenth century. Woulfe's derivation from *céadach*, (possessing hundreds) is untenable. The root word may be from *cet* (a blow or buffet). MIF

Mac Caffelly See MacCaughley.

(Mac) Cafferky, Cafferty *Mac Eachmharcaigh* (*each*, steed—*marcach*, rider). The former anglicized form is more usual in Co. Mayo, the latter in Cos. Donegal and Derry. It is sometimes shortened to Caffrey. IF

(Mac) Caffrey *Mac Gafraidh* (*Gafraidh* or *Gothraidh* equates with the English Godfrey). A branch of the Maguires of Fermanagh, located around Rosmacaffrey. MacCaghery and MacCahery are variants. IF   See Betty.

Mac Caghey See Caughey and Hackett.

(O) Cagney *Ó Caingne* (*caingean*, tribute or exaction). A sept of the Corca Laoidhe. Map Cork.

Mac Cague A Co. Monaghan variant of MacTeige.

(O) Cahalane *Ó Cathaláin* (*cathgal*, battle mighty). Formerly of Co. Limerick, now Cork and Kerry. As a Co. Roscommon name it is now rare if not extinct. MIF See Culhane and Callan.

Mac Cahan, -Cahane *Mac Catháin*. This west Clare surname, also anglicized Keane, is distinct from O'Cahan. The family were co-arbs of St. Senan of Iniscathy. IF

(O) Cahan *Ó Catháin*. See O'Kane, Keane.

(O) Cahany See Canny.

Caheerin See Keheerin.

(Mac) Cahern, -Caughran *Mac Eachráin*. Occasional synonyms of MacGahern.

O Caherny *Ó Catharnaigh* (*catharnach*, warlike). Map Offaly. See Fox and Kearney.

(Mac) Caherty, -Caugherty Co. Down forms of MacCafferty.

Mac Cahery See MacCaffrey.

Mac Cahey A variant of MacCaughey.

Mac Cahill *Mac Cathail*. (The personal name *Cathal*, now generally made Charles, means valour). Mainly Donegal and Cavan. See MacCall.

(O) Cahill *Ó Cathail*. This is the name of several distinct septs (as Map); that of Galway is now found in Clare. IF Map Galway, Kerry and Tipperary. See previous entry.

(O) Cahir *Ó Cathaoir*. (Cahir is an old forename in Ireland). A rare Co. Clare name. Though MacCahir appears very frequently in such sixteenth-century records as the Fiants, these are ephemeral patronymics occurring in the Kavanagh and other great Leinster families. The prefix is O, wherever a man bore this as a hereditary surname, and it rarely (if ever) occurs in Leinster. The statement that in Co. Limerick it is a toponymic, viz. *de Cathair*, can be discounted.

Mac Cahon Usually a variant of MacCaughan; sometimes of Mac-Gaghan in Ulster, but not of the Co. Clare name MacCahan (Mac-Keane).

Cahoon A variant form of Colhoon.

Mac Caig An anglicized form of *Mac Thaidhg* found in Co. Galway. See MacTeige.

Cain, Cane English names used in Mayo for Kane.

Mac Cainsh See MacCance.

Cairns A Scottish toponymic numerous in Ulster, occasionally substituted for Kieran. Bibl.

Mac Calden See MacAldin.

Calderwood See Catherwood.

Caldwell An English name now generally used as an anglicized form of *Ó hUarghuis* or *Ó hUairisce* (Horish, Houriskey) in Tyrone, and of Cullivan and Colavin (*Mac Conluain*) in Co. Cavan. MIF

Calfe Of Norman origin. See Veale.

Calfer See Colfer.

Calhoun See Colhoun.

Mac Call One of the many anglicized forms of *Mac Cathmhaoil* (see Campbell) of the Cenél Eoghain in use in Tyrone and Armagh. Also sometimes a synonym of MacCahill. MIF   See Caulfield.

Mac Calla In Donegal this is a variant of MacCauly: in Armagh of MacCall.

(O) Callaghan *Ó Ceallacháin*. The derivation from *ceallach*, strife, which is usually given, is questioned but no acceptable alternative has been suggested. The eponymous ancestor in this case was *Ceallacháin*, King of Munster (d. 952). The sept was important in the present Co. Cork until the seventeenth century and the name is still very numerous there. The chief family was transplanted under the Cromwellian regime to east Clare, where the village of O'Callaghan's Mills is called after them. Bibl. IF Map Cork. See Kealaghan.

(O) Callagy *Ó Calgaigh*. An old Co. Sligo name, now also in Co. Galway. Woulfe's derivation from *calgach*, peevish, is questioned; *colgg*, sword, is perhaps more probable.

Mac Callan This form of the name MacCallion is long established in Co. Fermanagh where it has sometimes been changed to Collins.

(O) Callan *Ó Cathaláin*. A mainly Oriel sept ethnologically distinct from, though etymologically the same as, Cahalane. Callan is very rarely a toponymic. MIF   Map Armagh-Monaghan.

(Mac) Callery This is not the same as Colleary. It is probably a north Connacht variant of the Clare name anglicized as Gallery.

(O) Callighan (Sometimes corruptly without the H) a form of Callaghan.

(Mac) Callilly, Callely A variant of MacAlilly.

(O) Callinan *Ó Callanáin*. The main sept was a medical family to the MacCarthys; another of the name was an erenagh family in Co. Galway. MIF

Mac Callion *Mac Cailín*. A galloglass family with the O'Donnells. Still almost exclusively found in Cos. Donegal and Derry. Ballymacallion is in Co. Derry. See Campbell and MacCallan.

Mac Callister See Alexander.

Callow Usually cognate with the Irish Calvey. The English name Callow is derived from Old-English *calu* (bald). Callow is rare and found only in Leinster. Cf. Irish *calbhach,* the modern meaning of which is bald (see Calvey).

Mac Callum A variant of MacColum.

Mac Calmont A sept of the Scottish clan Buchanan; the name is fairly numerous in Co. Antrim since the seventeenth century. MIF See MacColman.

Calnan A variant of Callinan.

Calpin See MacAlpin.

(Mac) Calshender See Alexander.

Calter A variant of Colter in Co. Armagh.

Calvert App.

(Mac) Calvey, Calway MacCalvey is recorded as a synonym of MacKelvey but Woulfe treats it as a different name, viz. *Mac an Chalbhaigh* (so it could be *calbhach,* bigheaded). Modern statistics show that Calvey is mainly found in Cos. Mayo and Sligo.

Camac Bibl.

(Mac) Cambridge With the prefix Mac this is *Mac Ambróis* of Scottish origin and found mainly in north-east Ulster; without the prefix it is usually an English toponymic. It is occasionally changed to Chambers.

Cameron One of the great Scottish clans, numerous in north-east Ulster. The Gaelic form *Camshrón* signifies crooked nose. Woulfe says it has been made *Ó Cumaráin* in Irish in Co. Mayo.

Mac Camley, -Comley Synonyms of MacAuley in Antrim and Armagh.

Mac Cammon See Hammond.

Campbell *Mac Cathmhaoil (cathmhaoil,* battle chief). An Irish sept in Tyrone; in Donegal it is usually of Scottish galloglass origin, viz. Mac Ailín a branch of the clan Campbell (whose name is from *cam béal,* crooked mouth). Many Campbells are more recent Scottish immigrants. See MacCawell. The name has been abbreviated to Camp and even Kemp in Co. Cavan. Bibl. App. MIF

Campion This name, derived from a Norman-French word denoting a combatant in an arena (akin to champion) was well established in the midlands by the seventeenth century, and by 1850 it was very numerous in Cos. Leix and Kilkenny. MIF

Canally A variant of MacAnally.

(O) Canavan *Ó Ceanndubháin.* This family provided hereditary physicians to the O'Flahertys of Connemara. Whitehead and Whitelock are occasionally synonyms by mistranslation, taking the termination as *bán* white and ignoring *dubh,* black. MIF   Map Galway.

Canaway An occasional variant of Conway in east Ulster.

Mac Cance A variant of MacNish and MacInnes in north-east Ulster.

Mac Candless *Mac Cuindlis.* This name appears in six variant forms

(MacAndles, MacCanliss etc.). It is fairly numerous in Ulster.

Cane See Cain.

Mac Cann *Mac Cana* (*cano*, wolf cub; the form *Mac Anna* is incorrect). A leading sept in Clanbrassil. IF MIF Map Armagh.

Canniff See under Cunniff.

Canning The two best-known families of this name came to Co. Derry from England in the seventeenth century; but some Cannings may possibly be *Ó Cainín* of Westmeath and Offaly, which Woulfe equates with *Ó Coinín* (Cunneen). Canning is also an occasional synonym of Cannon. MIF

(Mac) Cannon See MacConnon.

(O) Cannon *Ó Canáin* (*cano*, wolf cub). When met in south Connacht this name is that of a sept of Uí Maine. *Ó Canáin* is also the modern form of *Ó Cananáin*, a sept of Tirconnell. IF Map Donegal.

(Mac) Canny *Mac Annaidh* of Thomond. This name is well known in Tyrone as well as in Clare. MIF Map Clare.

(O) Canny *Ó Caithniadh* (*caithniadh*, battle champion) of Erris. MIF 48; Map Mayo.

Cantillon, Cantlin Norman *de Cantelupe*. In Kerry from early thirteenth century. Bibl. MIF 49; Map Kerry.

Cantrell An English toponymic well known in Ireland as the name of a Quaker family in Co. Leix since the seventeenth century. It was evidently in Co. Dublin earlier as the place-name Cantrellstown, near Castleknock, occurs in a Fiant of 1574.

Cantwell *de Cantual*, i.e. of Kentwell. An English family completely hibernicized from the twelfth century. Bibl. MIF Map Kilkenny.

(O) Canty *Ó an Cháintighe* (*cáinteach*, satirical). A bardic family of west Cork also called County. MIF 50; Map Cork.

Capel When this name appears in the same part of the country as Caples or Caplice it is a synonym thereof; elsewhere it is a variant of Keppel, an English name found in Co. Carlow.

Caplice, Capplis Variant forms of an English name almost peculiar to Co. Tipperary and north Cork. It is also found as Capples in that part of Munster. See Capel.

Mac Cappin A Scottish variant of MacAlpin found in north-east Ulster.

Cappock *de Ceapóg*. A Co. Louth toponymic; there since the thirteenth century, now rare. Keppock is a variant form.

Carabine A variant of Corribeen almost peculiar to Co. Mayo.

Caraher See Carragher. Bibl.

Carbery The more important sept of this name was that of Clonlonan, as Map; a branch of it were erenaghs of Galloon in Co. Fermanagh. They were usually *Ó Cairbre* in Irish, but *Mac Cairbre* was also used. The Carberys of Co. Waterford are distinct: they are *Mac Cairbre*;

Ballymacarbry in that county locates them. The personal name *Cairbre* is said to have denoted charioteer, but this derivation is uncertain. MIF 51; Map Westmeath.

Cardell, Cardwell An English name which has been used in Co. Down as a synonym of Caldwell and even of Carroll. Cardell is a variant of Cardwell and is seldom found as a substitute for MacArdle.

Carden An English toponymic mainly associated with Co. Mayo as well as Dublin. One prominent family settled in Co. Tipperary in the mid-seventeenth century.

Cardiff A Cambro-Norman toponymic in east Leinster since the thirteenth century. The variant Kerdiff is now extremely rare.

(Mac) Cardle See MacArdle.

Carduff See Corduff.

Carew *de Carrún*. Of Norman origin, formerly de Carron, this family is long associated mainly with Co. Tipperary, but formerly prominent also in Cos. Cork, Carlow and Mayo. Bibl. MIF

Carey This is used as the anglicized form of seven Gaelic Irish surnames, *Ó Ciardha, Mac Fhiachra* etc. (see MacCary, Crean, Currane, Keary, Kerin, Kerrane, Keighry); also as a synonym of the Norman Carew. IF 73.

(Mac) Cargill, Carrigle A Scottish toponymic. See MacGirl.

Cark(h)ill The Clare form of *Mac Fheargail*, see under MacGirl; also an occasional variant of MacCorkill.

Carland See Carlin

Carleton A variant form of O'Carolan. It is seldom now of English origin in Ireland, though it occurs as such in mediaeval records. IF 74.

Carley This name is of two entirely distinct origins. It is an English name long established in Co. Wexford, hence the place-name Carleysbridge in that county. In Connacht it is that of the sept *Mac Fhearghaile*, formerly anglicized as MacCarrelly, which in variant spellings occurs frequently in sixteenth-century Fiants relating to Co. Roscommon.

(O) Carlin, Carlan(d) These are forms of Carolan often used in Tyrone and neighbouring counties.

Carlisle This English toponymic is in Co. Antrim since 1588.

Carlos See Corless.

Carlton See Carleton.

Carmichael This is a sept of the Scottish clan Stewart, now numerous in north-east Ulster.

(O) Carmody *Ó Cearmada*. An old Thomond name still found in east Clare and south-west Munster. MIF Map Clare.

Mac Carn An abbreviated form of MacCarron found in Co. Monaghan.

(O) Carnahan A variant of Kernaghan.

Mac Carney *Mac Cearnaigh (cearnach,* victorious). Originally of Ballymacarney, Co. Meath, this name has long been located in Ulster, but the prefix Mac having been widely discarded, it is usually indistinguishable from (O) Carney. MIF

(O) Carney See Kearney.

(O) Carolan *Ó Cairealláin.* Of Clondermot, Co. Derry; also *Ó Cearbhalláin* in south Ulster and Meath. Both these surnames are derived from obsolete personal names. IF   Map Cavan-Meath and Derry-Tyrone.

Carpenter Usually for *Mac an tSaoir* (MacAteer), though sometimes of English origin.

(O) Carr The English name Carr has been used as the anglicized form of several different Irish surnames. See Carry, MacElhar, Kerrane, Mulcair. It is also a variant of the Scottish Kerr. MIF

(Mac) Carra(g)her *Mac Fhearchair* (man dear). An Oriel name, numerous on the Monaghan-Armagh border. Some of the Scottish (Caraher) branch re-settled in Ireland in the 17th century. Bibl. MIF

Carrick See Carrig.   **Carreen** See Curreen.

(Mac) Carrig, Carrigy *Mac Concharraigh (con,* hound—*carraig,* rock). Carrig and Carrick may also be *de Carraig,* referring to some notable rock, or, in the case of the Anglo-Norman family, to Carrick in Ayrshire, Scotland. Carrig is confined to Cos. Clare and Limerick, but MacCarrick is mainly found in Ulster and in Co. Roscommon.

(O) Carrigan, Carrogan See Corrigan.

Mac Carrison A variant of Carson, not of Harrison.

(Mac) Carroll *Mac Cearbhaill.* Two distinct septs: one in south Leinster; for the other see MacCarvill. These are quite distinct from O'Carroll. Bibl. IF MIF

(O) Carroll *Ó Cearbhaill.* Several different septs were so called: those of Ely O'Carroll and Oriel are important; minor septs were in Kerry and Leitrim. IF   Map Kilkenny, Louth, Offaly.

(Mac) Carrolly A synonym of Carley found in Westmeath.

Mac Carron, -Carroon *Mac Carrghamhna (gamhan,* calf, *carr* has many meanings). Of the southern Uí Néill, anglicized Carroon as well as MacCarron. Carron is also *Mac Cearáin,* a Tirconnell sept. This is found in Co. Monaghan. MIF   Map Westmeath. See O'Growney.

Carruthers See Caruth.

(Mac) Carry *Mac Fhearadhaigh* of Oriel. Woulfe also gives *Mac an Charraigh,* but this name, first anglicized as MacIncarrie, appears in the sixteenth century in Connacht and is probably extinct now. MIF   See MacAree.

(O) Carry *Ó Carraigh.* Often confused with Carr. Carry both as a Mac and an O name belongs mainly to Oriel. MIF

Carson A very numerous Scottish name in north Ulster. Bibl.

(Mac) Cart *Mac Airt.* MacArt is an example of a very common ephemeral patronymic becoming in some places a hereditary surname. As such it took the form MacCart, which is now mainly associated with Ulster. Cases of MacCarthy being abbreviated to MacCart are very rare.

Mac Cartan *Mac Artáin* (ultimately from the personal name Art). Of Kinelearty. IF   Map Down.

Carter This numerous English name, in Ireland as le Carter since the fourteenth century, is sometimes used for MacArthur.

Mac Carthy *Mac Cárthaigh (cárthach,* loving). The chief family of the Eoghanacht and one of the leading septs of Munster, prominent in the history of Ireland from the earliest times to the present. MacCarthy is the most numerous Mac name in Ireland. Bibl. IF Map Cork, Kerry.

Cartmill An English toponymic found in Cos. Louth and Armagh since the early fourteenth century. MIF

Mac Cartney *Mac Cartaine.* This Scottish name, cognate with the Irish MacCartan, is that of a branch of the clan Mackintosh which has been prominent in north-east Ulster since the mid-seventeenth century. It has been used as a synonym of Mulhartagh *(Ó Maolfhathartaigh* of Co. Tyrone) and of MacCaugherty (which is a synonym of MacCafferty). MIF

Carton An English toponymic mainly found in Ulster. It is occasionally used as a synonym of MacCartan.

(O) Carty *Ó Cárthaigh* (derivation as MacCarthy). This name often spelt Carthy, but to be distinguished from MacCarthy, is found mainly in Co. Wexford and in Connacht.

Caruth, Carruthers Scottish names in Ulster since the seventeenth century. MIF

(Mac) Carvey, Carway *Mac Cearbhaigh (cearbhach,* ragged). A Co. Sligo name.

Mac Carvill *Mac Cearbhaill.* Formerly anglicized MacCarroll. An Ulster sept noted for its musicians.

(O) Carvin, Carvan See Kerevan.

Mac Cary *Mac Fhiachra* for the east Galway-Westmeath sept, more usually anglicized Keaghry; *Mac Fhearadhaigh* in Ulster. See MacAree and MacKeary.

(Mac) Casement *Mac Asmuint.* An Antrim family of Manx origin. MIF

(Mac) Casey *Mac Cathasaigh.* An Oriel sept formerly numerous in

Co. Monaghan. Owing to dropping the prefixes Mac and O. Casey families properly MacCasey are now thought to be O'Casey. See next entry.

(O) Casey *Ó Cathasaigh* (*cathasach,* watchful). The name of six unrelated septs. Those of Fermanagh, Mayo and Roscommon were erenagh families. The name is now widely distributed in all the provinces except Ulster (especially south-west Munster). See Map. IF   Map Cork, Dublin, Fermanagh, Mayo, Limerick and Roscommon.

Cash This name, which appears frequently in mediaeval Dublin records as Cass and Casse, is still found in small numbers in the country between Tipperary and Wexford. With the prefix O, Casse is a corruption of O'Casey.

Cashell Of dual origin: Anglo-Norman *de Cashel* or native Irish *Ó Maolchaisil* (*maol Caisil,* chief of Cashel).* The de Cashel family was from the fourteenth to early seventeenth century prominent in Co. Louth and pro-Irish; the latter, occasionally anglicized as Mulcashel and even Mountcashel, belongs to Thomond and adjacent areas. See Cushlane.

(Mac) Cashin *Mac Caisín.* Often *O* for *Mac* in Munster. (Its derivation may be from *cas,* bent, or *cas,* pleasant). A medical family of Upper Ossory. The following variants are on record: Cashen, Casheon, Cashion, Cashon, Cassin, Cassion. MIF   Map Leix.

Cashlan(e) See Caslin.

Cashman See Kissane.

Caskey *Mac Ascaidh* (from a personal name of Norse origin). A well-known name in Tyrone and Derry. The form MacAskie is an occasional variant.

Casley See Cassily.

(O) Caslin, Cashlane *Ó Caiseáláin.* Almost exclusively a Roscommon and Leitrim name.

Cass See Cash.

Cassell(s) See Cushlane.

(Mac) Casserley *Mac Casarlaigh.* On record in Co. Roscommon from very early times.   MIF

(O) Cassidy *Ó Caiside.* A Fermanagh family of ollavs and physicians to the Maguires. Now numerous in all the provinces except Connacht. Bibl. IF

---

*Woulfe translates *maol* as chief in cases where its primary meaning of tonsured, hence devotee, is inapplicable. In fact *maol* does not mean chief, but MacFirbis says that the pagan Irish used the prefix *mal* in this sense, and this was continued later as *maol.*

(O) Cassily, Casley *Ó Caisile.* A sept of Co. Armagh. In 1609 it is described as Munter Cassely in that county. See Cushley.

Cassin The origin of this name is uncertain. It is now a variant of Cashin in Cos. Offaly and Tipperary; and it can also be *Ó Casáin,* a Sodhan sept in south Galway. MIF

Cathcart App.

Cather A Wesleyan family prominent in Co. Tyrone.

Catherwood A variant of the Scottish Calderwood, now the more numerous form.

Mac Catigan *Mac Aitigin* (son of Atkin). A Mayo name. It has no connection with Cadigan.

Mac Caughan *Mac Eacháin.* An Antrim and north Derry name. Some families have changed it to MacCaughey.

Mac Caugherty See MacCaherty.

Mac Caughey, -Cahey *Mac Eachaidh. Eachaidh* is a personal name anglicized Aghy, cognate with *Eochaigh,* Oghy, once a popular Christian name. Co. Tyrone. MIF   See Mulcahy.

Mac Caughley, -Caffelly *Mac Eachmhilidh* (*each,* horse—*mileadh,* soldier). Woulfe counts this Co. Down family a branch of the MacGuinness sept. MacCaughley has inevitably often become MacCawley.

Mac Caul See MacCall.

Mac Cauley See MacAuley.

Caulfield The name of a very prominent English settler family in Ulster. It is used as a synonym of MacCall, Caffrey and Gaffney, and occasionally of MacKeown and also in Ireland for the English Calfhill. Bibl. MIF

(O) Caulin See Cawlin.

Mac Causland This Scottish name, stated by Reaney to be derived from MacAbsolom, has been prominent and fairly numerous in Cos. Derry and Tyrone since the mid-seventeenth century.

Cavan A synonym of Keevan and occasionally of Kavanagh. It is not a toponymic.

Mac Cavana *Mac an Mhanaigh* (*manach,* monk). The Antrim form of MacEvanny. Quite distinct from Cavanagh, though the form *Mac Caomhánaigh* is sometimes erroneously used in Irish.

Cavanagh See Kavanagh.

Cavendish This aristocratic English name has been used as a rather pretentious synonym of both O'Kevane and Kavanagh.

(Mac) Cavey *Mac Dháibhidh.* Akin to MacDavitt.

(Mac) Cavish *Mac Thámhais.* A rare name found in Co. Cavan, akin to the Scottish MacTavish. Both MacCavish and MacTavish have sometimes been changed to Thomson or Thompson in Co. Cavan. See Holmes.

(Mac) Cavitt A variant of MacKevitt.

Mac Cavock See Davock.

Mac Caw *Mac Ádhaimh* (son of Adam). A Co. Cavan name now mainly found in Antrim.

Mac Cawell *Mac Cathmhaoil* (*cathmhaol*, battle chief). MacCawell is used colloquially for Campbell in Tyrone; also as a synonym of MacCall. MIF

(Mac) Cawley This variant of MacAwley is mainly found in north Connacht and Fermanagh.

(O) Cawlin, Caulin These are recorded as synonyms of Callan in Oriel. The name Coughlan is locally pronounced *Coho*lan (almost Cawlan) in Cork and is sometimes so written. Confusion with Cohalan may therefore arise.

Mac Cay An Ulster variant of Mackay.

(O) Cevlehan A variant of Kivlehan.

Chadwick Bibl.

Chaff An anglicized form of *Ó Lócháin* or *Ó Leochain* (Lohan) by supposed translation (*lóchán* means chaff). It is mainly found in Co. Galway.

Chamberlain Frequent in mediaeval Irish records, especially in Co. Cork; now rare. Bibl.

Chambers A numerous but scattered name of Anglo-Norman origin *(de la chambre)*. It is mainly found in Ulster and Mayo.   MIF See also MacCambridge.

Chamney This name, first spelt Champney, is the anglicized form of the French *le Champagnois* (i.e. native of Champagne). It was fairly well known in the Cos. Wicklow and Wexford in the seventeenth and eighteenth centuries but is now rare.

Chaney A variant form of Cheyney.

Chapman This English occupational name is fairly numerous in all the provinces in Ireland except Connacht, and there too it appears in Co. Roscommon in 1629. Other seventeenth-century references are to Westmeath, Wexford, Clare and Dublin. There are occasional references to *le Chapman* in Irish records as far back as the thirteenth century.

Charles Used as a synonym of Corless.

Charleton Though it has a Cromwellian connection with Co. Sligo the name Charlton or Charleton has been in Ireland since the fourteenth century. It became established in Cos. Tyrone and Fermanagh early in the seventeenth century. The name is now numerous in Ulster. Bibl.

Charters A French toponymic (*Chartres*) mainly of Huguenot origin in Ireland. It was first established in Co. Cork in the seventeenth century but in modern times has been found chiefly in Ulster.

Cheasty Woulfe makes this a Gaelic-Irish name, viz. *Ó Siosta* or *Ó Seasta*. I have found no evidence of this beyond a Co. Kerry place-name Kylmacollok O'Cestie which occurs in a sixteenth-century Fiant: it has been suggested that this is a corruption of *Tuath Ó Síosta* (Tuosist) in which parish Kilmacolloge is. Families called Cheasty have certainly been in Co. Waterford since mediaeval times.

Cheevers, Chivers (from Old-French *chièvre*, goat). In south-east Leinster since the Anglo-Norman invasion. In the old rhyme about the families of Forth in Co. Wexford the epithet used with Cheevers is 'laughing'. They were one of the Old-English families classed as Irish and Catholic at the time of the Cromwellian transplantation and suffered much hardship as such.

Chenevix Bibl.

Cherry An English occupational name, fairly numerous in Ulster since the seventeenth century. MIF

Chesney, Cheyney Apart from a few isolated mediaeval references, this name came to Ireland at the time of the Plantation of Ulster. It is derived from Old-French *chesnai*, oakgrove. MIF

Chesnutt App.

Chetwood Bibl.

(Mac) Cheyne A corrupt form of MacShane, found in Co. Down. Cheyne (with its variants Chesney, Chesnay etc.) is an Anglo-Norman name, from Old-French *chesnai*, oakgrove.

Chichester A prominent toponymic name in Ulster since the beginning of the seventeenth century. Bibl.

Chifley A rare name of uncertain origin; of interest in Ireland because the Australian prime minister of that name came of a Thurles family.

Childers From Old-English *cildra-hus* (orphanage).

Chinnery A family of Essex origin prominent in Co. Cork since mid-seventeenth century. Bibl. MIF

Chisholm The name of a Scottish clan now fairly numerous in Ulster. It is sometimes spelt phonetically as Chism.

Chivers See Cheevers

Chooke See Tuke

Christian Established in north-east Ireland since the sixteenth century, when it sometimes had the prefix Mac. Christianston is in Co. Louth.

Christopher *Críostóir.* This name has been continuously in Co. Waterford since the thirteenth century; it is recorded in the 1659 'census' as one of the principal Irish names in the Co. Waterford barony of Decies. MIF

Christy A Scottish name fairly numerous in Ulster. Woulfe gives *Mac Críosta* as the Irish form, but it is not a Mac name in Scotland.

Chrystal See Crystal.

Church Old-English *atte churche*; the name of a family settled in Ulster since the seventeenth century. Matheson says it has been made Aglish (*eaglais*, church) in Munster. MIF

Chute This name of English toponymic origin is quite distinct from Tuite. The Chutes have been prominent in Co. Kerry since early seventeenth century.

(O) Clabby *Ó Clabaigh* (Woulfe derives this from *clabach*, wide-mouthed). An erenagh family of St. Patrick's, Oran. Map Roscommon.

(Mac) Clafferty A variant of MacLafferty.

(Mac) Claffey Claffey is the midland form of *Mac Laithimh* anglicized MacClave in Ulster. *Laitheamh* is a variant form of *flaitheamh*, lord or ruler. See Hand.

(O) Clahane, Clehane *Ó Cathaláin*. A west Limerick name. See Cahalane of which it is a variant.

(Mac) Clamon See MacClement

(Mac) Clancy *Mac Fhlannchaidh*. (Woulfe says this means ruddy warrior, but I am informed by Celtic scholars that the termination *caidh* denoting warrior is unknown.) There are two prominent septs of this name: that of Thomond provided hereditary brehons to the O'Briens; the other was of Rosclogher. IF   Map Clare and Leitrim.

Clandillon The origin of this rare name, which does not appear in Ireland as such before the nineteenth century, is obscure. The tradition that it is simply Dillon with the addition of Clan, arising from some notion on the part of one of the Wild Geese, would appear to supply its most probable origin, though I have not found definite evidence of this. Less likely are the other conjectural suggestions which have been made in this connection, viz. that it is: (1) an Irish toponymic, but no such place-name exists, the nearest being Clondullane in Co. Cork (sometimes spelt Clandullan in the seventeenth century); (2) A corrupt variant of Cantillon; (3) a variant of Clandinnen which is itself a variant in Ireland of the Scottish Glendinning.

Clare See Clear.

Clarke An English name which usually stands for O'Clery in Ireland. Bibl; App.

Clarkin A variant of Clerkin. See under Clerihan.

Mac Clarnon See MacLarnon.

Mac Clary See MacLary.

Clashby, Clasby See Gillespie.

Mac Clatchey An Ulster name of Scottish origin, mainly associated with Co. Armagh. Black gives the Gaelic form as *Mac Giolla Eidich*.

Mac Clatton See MacIlhatton.

Clausson, Classon See MacNicholas.

(O) Clavan *Ó Clamháin*. A variant form of Clavin.

Mac Clave *Mac Laithimh* (formerly *Mac Fhlaithimh* from *flaitheamh*, lord). This is also anglicized as Claffey, now Hand, in Co. Monaghan by pseudo-translation (*lámh*, hand).

Mac Claverty See MacLaverty.

(O) Clavin, Claveen *Ó Claimhín*. A sept of Leix and Offaly. The name is sometimes anglicized as Swords, from *claidheamh*, sword; though probably it is actually from *clamh* indicating a sick person. MIF

Clay A well-known English name of obvious derivation. For MacClay see MacAlee.

Clayton An English toponymic associated with Co. Cork since seventeenth century and now found in all the provinces of Ireland. Bibl.

Mac Clean, -Lean *Mac Giolla Eáin* (*Eán*, an old form of *Eoin* or *Seán*, John). A galloglass family of Scottish origin, numerous in Antrim and Derry. MIF

Clear, Clare *de Cléir*. These names, mainly associated with Cos. Wexford and Kilkenny, are usually synonymous toponymics (not derived from County Clare); occasionally used for O'Clery. MIF

Mac Cleary This was MacAleary in Sligo and became MacCleary on migration to Ulster. *Mac Giolla Arraith* is the accepted Irish form of this name there, but Woulfe's suggested derivation from *rath*, prosperity, is improbable. *Mac an Chléirigh* (*cléireach*, clerk) is another origin of MacCleary (in Co. Cavan).

(O) Cleary See Clery.

Cleeve Derived from an Old-English word denoting dweller by the cliff. This name has been in Co. Tipperary since mid-seventeenth century.

Clegg Ewen derives this name from the Cornish *clegg*, a rock; but it is more probably a Lancashire toponymic. It has been fairly numerous in Ulster since early eighteenth century, whence it has spread to Dublin.

(O) Clehane See Clahane.

Mac Clelland See MacLellan.

Mac Clement *Mac Laghmainn* formerly called MacLamond. It is a branch of the Scottish clan Lamont. It is represented in Ireland by the Co. Derry family whose name has been widely changed to Clements.

Clements An English name long associated with Cos. Leitrim and Donegal. See foregoing.

Mac Clenaghan, -Lenahan *Mac Leanacháin* (*leanach*, possessing mantles) in Tyrone in the sixteenth century, now almost exclusively Co. Derry and Antrim. MIF

Clendinning A variant of Glendinning.

45

(O) Clerian Clerian of Co. Monaghan has no connection with Clerihan of Co. Limerick, though possibly the Irish form is the same (*Ó Cléireacháin*).

O Clerihan, Clerkin *Ó Cléireacháin* (*cléireach,* clerk). A sept belonging to the barony of Cosmha now rare there. Map Limerick.

(O) Clery, Cleary *Ó Cléirigh* (*cléireach,* clerk). One of the earliest hereditary surnames. Originally of Kilmacduagh (Co. Galway) the sept was dispersed and after the thirteenth century settled in several parts of the country; the most important branch were in Donegal where they became notable as poets and antiquaries. In modern times the name is found mainly in Munster and Dublin. Bibl. IF See Clarke. Map.

Clibborn There are several variants of this name extant in Ireland, e.g. Clayburn, Clebburn. The main family is Cromwellian and settled at Moate, Co. Westmeath; but the name was in Ireland before that, e.g. William Clyburn, dean of Kildare 1642; and it also occasionally occurs in mediaeval records.

(Mac) Clifferty I am informed by Fr. P. Ó Gallachair that this Tyrone name is *Mac Raibheartaigh* in Irish and that it has been much corrupted to Clifford.

Clifford This English toponymic is, in Ireland, mainly the anglicized form of *Ó Clumháin*. See under Cluvane and Colman. For Co. Fermanagh see Crifferty and Clifferty.

Cligott See MacElligott.

Mac Climmond, -Climent, -Clammon Variants of MacClement.

Clinch A name of English origin (meaning dweller by the hill) very frequent in Leinster records since the early fourteenth century. It is called *Clinse* in Irish. MIF

Mac Clinchy See MacGlinchy.

Cline An abbreviated form of Kilcline.

Mac Clinion See MacAlinion.

Mac Clintock *Mac Giolla Fhionntóg.* A Scottish name numerous in Antrim and Derry. Black says this, like MacClinton, refers to St. Fintan.

Clinton *de Cliontún.* Rare now, this name was prominent in mediaeval Irish records. The famous American Clintons were of Clintonstown, Co. Louth. Bibl. MIF See next entry

Mac Clinton *Mac Giolla Fhionntáin* (devotee of St. Fintan). A west Ulster name distinct from the English Clinton. Confusion is inevitable when the prefix Mac is dropped.

Clisham This name belongs exclusively to Co. Galway. As Klisham it is found in Clare. Woulfe suggests *Mac Cliseam* as the Gaelic form; the initial C presumably comes from the prefix Mac. Crisham is a variant.

Clogher This name is found in Co. Roscommon. It is not derived from any of the numerous places called Clogher but is probably an abbreviation of MacCloughry.

(O) Clo(g)herty *Ó Clochartaigh*. A Connemara name. Though also called Stone by 'translation', the word *cloch,* stone, is apparently not a component part of this name.

(O) Clohessy *Ó Clochasaigh*. Of Ballycloghessy, Co. Clare. The name is still found there but is now more numerous in Co. Limerick.

Clone An abbreviated form of Cloney.

(O) Cloney *Ó Cluanaigh* (*cluana* has three meanings—deceitful, flattering and rogue). A Co. Wexford name. Clooney and Clowney are usual variants. Clooney is also a synonym of MacLoonie in Co. Down. MIF

Mac Cloon Occasionally spelt MacClune this is an Ulster variant of MacAloon but not of MacClune of Co. Clare.

(O) Cloonan *Ó Cluanáin* (for derivation see Cloney). Essentially a Co. Galway name.

(O) Clooney See Cloney.

Mac Cloran *Mac Labhráin* (*labhraidh,* spokesman). The name is cognate with the Scottish MacLaren. Woulfe says Cavan, but I find it in Co. Galway. However, this Cloran is probably distinct as it appears as O'Cloran there in the seventeenth century.

Mac Clory *Mac Labhradha* (derivation as Mac Cloran). This name belongs almost exclusively to Co. Down and adjacent parts of Co. Armagh. It was formerly *Mag Labhradha* anglicized MacGlory. As such it is on record in Co. Down at least as early as 1447.

Close Some families of this name are of Yorkshire origin and some are of Irish—(*Ó Clusaigh*); both are found in Antrim and adjacent counties. MIF

Mac Closkey, -Cluskey *Mac Bhloscaidh*. A branch of the O'Cahans with whom *Bloscaidh* was a favourite forename. Map Derry.

Clossick Originally of Swinford, Co. Mayo, Clossick is now found also in other parts of Connacht. *Mac Lusaigh* has been suggested as its Irish form from *lusach,* dealing in herbs, but this is conjectural.

Clossy An abbreviated form of Cloghessy.

Mac Cloughry *Mac Clochaire* (*clochaire,* stone-mason). A Scottish family in Cos. Donegal and Longford. See Kingston.

(Mac) Cloven A Co. Carlow variant of Cluvane.

Mac Clowry A variant of MacClory found in mid-Leinster.

Mac Cloy A fairly numerous name in Co. Antrim, being that of a branch of the Scottish clan Stuart of Bute. Black makes MacCloy son of Lewie. Woulfe equates it with *Mac Dhuinnshléibhe* (Mac-Aleevy) but I have no evidence of this. See Fullerton.

Mac Cluggage Dr. Ó Raifeartaigh tells me that his suggested derivation of this name (from *clogad*, helmet) must not be taken as authentic. It now seems probable that it is from *Mac Lúcáis*, usually anglicized MacLucas in Scotland where the variant form MacLugash was formerly found.

(Mac) Clune *Mac Clúin*, formerly *Mac Glúin* (*glún*, knee). A Dalcassian family of Ballymaclune, to be distinguished from MacCloon and Cluvane. MIF   Map Clare.

(Mac) Clung MacClung and MacClurg are two Scottish names found in Ireland for which Woulfe gives *Mac Luinne* and *Mac Luirg*. Black, however, an authority on Scottish names, gives *Mac Luinge* (*long*, ship) and *Mac an Chléirigh* (*cléireach*, clerk).

(Mac) Clure MacClure in Ulster is mainly a Scottish name, numerous in Galloway to which location it probably originally came from Ireland, the Gaelic form being basically the same as that for Mac-Aleer. MIF

Mac Clurg See under MacClung.

Clusby See Gillespie.

Mac Clusker *Mac Bhloscaire*. A Co. Armagh name. Woulfe suggests that it is a local corruption of MacCluskey.

Mac Cluskey See Closkey.

(O) Cluvane *Ó Clúmháin*. This name, rare now as Cluvane, has been widely changed to Clifford. As such it is mainly, if not exclusively, of Co. Kerry. O'Cluvane was also the name of a notable ecclesiastical family in Co. Sligo. MIF   Map Kerry.

Clyde App.

Clyne(s), Cloyen See Kilcline.

Coady A spelling variant of Cody.

Coakley See MacKehilly and Colclough.

Mac Coan *Mac Comhdhain*. Co. Armagh. This is now widely superseded by Cowan.

Coates A locative name (denoting residence at the cottage or sheep-cote) established in Tyrone after the Plantation of Ulster (*c*. 1609), later Antrim, now quite numerous in Dublin as well as in Ulster. Cott, of similar derivation, is on record in Ireland since the fourteenth century, mainly in Co. Cork.

Cobbe Cob is a derivative of the Christian name Jacob. Since the introduction of the surname Cobb or Cobbe in Dublin early in the seventeenth century its location has been almost entirely in Leinster, particularly the midland counties of Leix, Offaly and Kildare. However, one 'titulado' is recorded in the 'census' of 1659 as of Co. Limerick, where the name is still found.

Coburn This is a well-known and quite numerous name in Co. Louth and other parts of Oriel. There is a tradition that this is not the Scottish Cockburn nor the English Colborne but a modern form of

Mac Conboirne (see under Burns). No documentary evidence to support this tradition has yet been discovered.

Cochrane A Scottish toponymic numerous in Ulster. It is occasionally used as a variant of Cuggeran and Corcoran.

Codd *Coda.* Usually this is Old-English, as such peculiar to Co. Wexford from the thirteenth century. It is sometimes a variant of Cody. Bibl. MIF   Map Wexford.

Cody *Mac Óda.* A Gaelic patronymic assumed by the Archdeacon family who are in Co. Kilkenny since the thirteenth century. MIF 61; Map Kilkenny.

Codyre See Eyre.

Coe A variant of Coey.

Coen A synonym of Coyne in Connacht and occasionally of Cowan in Co. Down. The name Cohen is also so used and has usually no Jewish connotation in Ireland.

(O) Coey This is the anglicized form of *Ó Cobhthaigh* used by the north Ulster sept, distinct from those usually called Coffey; it has not any connection with MacCooey.

(O) Coffey *Ó Cobhthaigh* (*cobhthach,* victorious). There were three main septs of this name, viz. of the Corca Laoidhe (west Cork); Uí Maine (Cos. Galway and south Roscommon); and a bardic family of Westmeath. Bibl. IF   Map Cork, Galway and Meath–Westmeath.

Cogan, Coggan *de Cogán.* A Welsh toponymic. The first of this family came to Ireland with Strongbow and settled in Co. Cork. Later the name became Gogan and Goggin. It is also a synonym of Coogan. Bibl. MIF   Map Cork. See also Cogavin.

(Mac) Cogan *Mac Cogadháin* (from the personal name Cuchogaidh *cú,* hound— *cogadh,* war). Of Co. Leitrim and quite distinct from the foregoing. MIF

(Mac) Cogavin *Mac Cogaidhín.* A rare variant of *Mac Cogadháin.* See previous entry.

(Mac) Coggeran See Cuggeran.

Coggins A variant of Cogan in Co. Sligo.

Coghill The name of a Yorkshire family which came to Ireland in the second half of the seventeenth century and has since been identified mainly with Co. Kilkenny. Bibl.

Coghlan See Coughlan.

(O) Cogley See Quigley.

Cohalan See under Culhane.

(O) Cohane This is a synonym of Keohane and occasionally of Cahan.

(O) Cohee, Cohey Variant spellings of Cowhey.

Cohen See Coen.

(O) Coholan This is an occasional misspelling of Cohalan. See also under Cawlin.

Cohoon A variant of the Scottish Colhoun in Cos. Donegal and Derry.

Cokeley See Coakley.

(O) Colahan See Colohan.

(Mac) Colavin, Cullivan *Mac Conluain*. (Woulfe makes this a corrupt form of *Mac Anluain*). A sept of the Uí Fiachra in north Connacht and later in Co. Cavan. O'Donovan says *Mac Conluain* is anglicized MacColwan.

Colbert *Cólbárd*. This name, of Anglo-Saxon origin (formerly Accolobert) is in Munster since early fifteenth century.

Colclough This English toponymic is the name of a family established in Co. Wexford in the sixteenth century. See Coakley. Bibl. MIF

Coldrick A variant form of Goldrick in Meath and Cavan.

Col(d)well See Caldwell.

(Mac) Cole See MacCool. Cole is also a numerous English name, prominent as such in Fermanagh since the Plantation of Ulster. Bibl.

Coleman See Colman.

Colfer An old Co. Wexford name. As 'cross' Calfer (the earlier form) it is among the names of Forth families in the old rhyme about that barony. MIF

(Mac) Colgan *Mac Colgan*. There were two main septs of this name, viz. one of Tirkeeran and Donaghmore, the other of Kilcolgan (as Map). The former were also called O'Colgan. IF   Map Derry and Offaly.

Colhoun Woulfe gives *Ó Cathluain* for this, which he says is a Breffny name now dispersed throughout Ulster. He overlooks the more usual origin of Ulster families of the name, viz. the Scottish clan Colquhoun.

Coll *Col*. Usually of Norse origin; in some cases locative from Old-English *coll*, hill. Best known as the name of a Co. Limerick family, in Ireland since the fourteenth century. Coll as a numerous Donegal name is for *Mac Colla*, a galloglass family, sometimes changed to MacColley. See MacCullagh. MIF

(Mac) Colleary *Mac Giolla Laoire*. Of north Connacht. Distinct from MacAleary. MIF

(O) Collen An Oriel variant of Cullen.

(O) Colleran *Ó Callaráin* (not *Mac Allmhuráin*). Almost exclusively a Mayo and north Galway name. MIF

Colles Bibl. See Collis.

Colleton See Culliton.

Colley As an indigenous Irish surname (MacColley) it belongs to Cos. Roscommon and Galway. This may be *Mac Colla*, but it has been suggested that Colley is here a variant of Cooley. The main

English family came to Ireland *temp.* Henry VIII; later they acquired the Wellesley property and name. MIF

Collier, Colyer *Coiléir.* This English occupational name, on record in Ireland since 1305, was well enough established in Co. Meath to be reckoned in Petty's 'census' of 1659 as a principal Irish name there. It is now mainly found in Cos. Carlow, Kilkenny and Wexford. MIF

(O) Colligan A variant of Colgan.

Mac Collin *Mac Cuilinn (cuileann,* holly). This belongs to Oriel. Also anglicized as MacQuillan and (Mac)Cullen.

Colliney See Culliney.

Collins Though this is a well-known English name, in Ireland it is nearly always the anglicized form of *Ó Coileáin (coileán,* whelp) which is also Cullane. This sept is of Co. Limerick. Another sometimes spelt *Ó Cuileáin* is of the Corca Laoidhe. In west Ulster Collins is *Mac Coileáin.* IF   MIF   Map Cork and Limerick.

Collis On record in Ireland since 1638, this name has since that time been continuously associated with Co. Kerry. It denotes son of Col, a diminutive of Nicholas. MIF

Colliton See Culleton.

(O) Collopy *Ó Colpa.* Almost exclusively a Co. Limerick name. My own suggestion that it comes from *colpa,* collop, a farming term still in use, is not improbable. Woulfe says that it is from *Colptha,* a personal name denoting the calf of the leg.

Mac Colman A variant of MacCalmont, quite distinct from O'Colman.

(O) Colman *Ó Colmáin.* (The personal name Colman is derived from *colm,* dove). A sept of the Uí Fiachrach. Also *Ó Clumháin,* which as Coleman and Clifford belongs to Co. Cork. Coleman is an English name, but few Irish Colemans are of that origin. The name is now numerous in all the provinces except Ulster. The spelling Coleman is now more numerous than Colman. IF   Map Sligo. See Cluvane.

(O) Cologhty, Coonlaghty *O Conlachta.* An east Clare name, now rare.

(Mac) Colohan See Cuolahan.

Coloo, Coloe Woulfe treats these as anglicized forms of *Mac Conuladh* (see MacCullagh), a predominantly Ulster name—Ballycullo is in Co. Antrim. As Culloe and Culloo it has long been established in Co. Clare: while Coloe is fairly numerous in Griffith's *Valuation for Westmeath (c.* 1850).

Colpoys Coming from Hampshire in the first half of the seventeenth century, this name was prominent among the Anglo-Irish gentry in Co. Clare for two centuries. Bibl.

(Mac) Colreevy See Culreavy.

(O) Colter, Coulter *Ó Coltair.* (Woulfe says this is an abbreviated form of the obsolete name *Ó Coltaráin).* Of Ballycolter. Map Down.

Colton, Coulton An English toponymic found in Oriel. The use of prefix O with this name is incorrect, except perhaps in south Galway where, according to Woulfe, it is *Ó Comhaltáin*. Fr. Livingstone says this also applies to Tyrone. The Four Masters use the form *Mac Comhaltain* for Derry.

(Mac) Colum *Mac Coluim* (*colm*, dove). With the prefix Mac this is an Ulster name; without the prefix, Colum is mainly found in Co. Longford, where it is probably another and distinct *Mac Coluim* sept. SIF 38.

Columby This name is almost peculiar to Westmeath. Its origin is uncertain. It is probably from the French Columbat, but possibly from the English Columbine.

Colvan A variant of Colavin and sometimes of Colville.

Colvill(e) A Scottish name of French origin which came to Ireland, mainly to Ulster, in the seventeenth century. It is sometimes confused with Colvin. Woulfe equates it with Coldwell, due perhaps to an occasional mistaken use of these as synonyms. Bibl.

Colvin In Ulster this is usually of Anglo-Saxon origin; occasionally a synonym of Colavin.

Colwan See Colavin.

Colyer See Collier.

(O) Coman A variant of Commane.

Mac Comb(e), -Come *Mac Thom*. The name of a Scottish family now fairly numerous in north-east Ulster. MacComish and Mac-Combs (*Mac Thómais*) are variants in Co. Down; MacCome is an old name in Co. Armagh. MIF See Holmes.

Comber, Comer *Ó Ciaragáin* (the basic word in this is *ciar*, black or dark). A synonym of Kerrigan in Galway and Mayo, occasionally also of *Ó Ciaráin* (Kerin), both by mistranslation (*cíor* means comb).

Comberton A variant of Comerford.

Mac Combie A sept of the Scottish clan Mackintosh.

Comerford *Comartún*. A hibernicized English family, prominent in Ireland since 1210. The name is occasionally used for Cumiskey in the Cavan-Longford area. MIF Map Kilkenny.

Comey, Coomey, Cowmey These are normally synonyms but Woulfe differentiates, making Comey *Mac Giolla Chóimdheadh* and Coomey *Ó Camtha*. Both are mainly found in Breffny and occasionally in Co. Cork.

Comish See MacComb and Holmes.

(Mac) Comiskey, Cumesky *Mac Cumascaigh* (*cumascach*, confuser). Originally of Co. Monaghan but now mainly found in Cos. Longford, Cavan and Westmeath. MIF See Comerford.

(O) Commane, Commons *Ó Comáin* (in Munster) and *Ó Cuimín* (in

Connacht). Usually called Commons in Co. Wexford and Cummins in Co. Cork. *Ó Comáin* has become Hurley in some parts of Cos. Clare and Cork, due to the mistaken belief that it derives from *camán*, a hurley. Woulfe says it is from *cam*, crooked, which is equally unacceptable. IF   Map Mayo.

Comyn The name of a Norman-Irish family which is also used in Co. Clare as the anglicized form of *Ó Cuimín*, see previous entry. Bibl. IF

(O) Conaghan *Ó Connacháin*. A Donegal-Derry name now usually changed to Cunningham.

Mac Conaghy, -Conkey *Mac Dhonnchaidh* (son of Donagh). The name of a branch of the Scottish clan Robertson numerous in east Ulster. Ballymaconaghy is near Newry.

(O) Conalty *Ó Conallta* (*cú*, wolf—*allta*, wild). A rare name of Ulster origin.

(Mac) Conamy, Conomy *Mac Conmidhe* (hound of Meath). A Co. Derry and Tyrone name, where it has been often changed to Conway. Though etymologically the same as MacNamee they are seldom used synonymously.

(O) Conan In Connacht this is a variant of Queenan and Cunnane; in Offaly and other midland counties usually of Coonan. In England Conan is a name of Breton origin.

(O) Conaty An abbreviated form of Connaghty found in Co. Cavan.

(Mac) Conborney See Burns.

(O) Conboy, Conaboy *Ó Conbhuidhe* (*con*, hound—*buidhe*, yellow). A sept of the Uí Fiachrach found in all Connacht counties, often also called Conway. Map Sligo. See Cunnaboy.

Concagh See Battle.

(O) Concannon *Ó Concheanainn*. (Woulfe's derivation—fairheaded hound—is possible). A sept of the Uí Briúin prominent in the territory of Uí Maine in Co. Galway. IF   Map Galway.

Mac Conchy See MacConaghy.

Condell This name, which first appears in Ireland in mid-seventeenth century, became quite numerous in Co. Carlow and is also found in Co. Wicklow. It is probably from the English place-name Caundel or Cundell.

Condon *Condún*. The toponymic name of a hibernicized Cambro-Norman family, formerly de Caunteton. The barony of Condons, Co. Cork, is named from them. Bibl. IF Map Cork.

Condrick See Kendrick.

(O) Condron *Ó Conaráin*. Also called Conran. This sept, which originated in Offaly, is now numerous in mid-Leinster. Muintir Coneran were a co-arb family in Co. Fermanagh but this has now died out, unless it survives under a different name. MIF

Condy Though of comparatively recent introduction this name (from the French *Condé*) has become quite numerous in Co. Tyrone.

Mac Cone See MacCoan.

(Mac) Conefry *Mac Confraoich* is the Irish form. *Fraoch* is probably a place-name derived from the word for heather. *Con* is the genitive of *cú*, hound. The name belongs almost exclusively to Co. Leitrim.

Coney A rare variant of Cooney. Also an English name.

Coneys This name, found in Co. Galway, is said to be of Cromwellian origin there. Cunniss is a variant.

Conheady A Co. Clare name possibly *Mac Conéidigh* in Irish (*éidigh*, ugly). For *con* see Conefry.

(Mac) Conheeny *Mac Conanaonaigh* (*con*, hound—*aonach*, fair, market). A rare south Connacht name sometimes made Rabbitt by pseudo-translation. It is distinct from MacEneaney.

Coniam See Cunniam.

MacConigly *Mac Congaile*. Almost peculiar to Co. Donegal.

Mac Conkey See MacConaghy.

(Mac) Conley *Mac Connla*. A sept of Co. Offaly. Conly is also an occasional variant of Connolly. MIF

(Mac) Conlogue See MacConnellogue.

(O) Conlon See Connellan.

Mac Conmee A synonym of MacNamee, according to O'Donovan. See MacConamy.

Mac Conn *Mac Mhíolchon*. A rare Co. Down name. MacIlchon is an earlier anglicized form.

(Mac) Con(n)agher *Mac Conchobhair*. A rare name found in Co. Galway. *Conchobhair* is anglicized Conor as a forename.

Connaghty, *Ó Connachtaigh* (*Connachtach,* man from Connacht). A Breffny name confused with, but properly distinct from, Mac-Connaghty which is an occasional synonym of MacConaghy.

(O) Connahan See Conaghan.

(Mac) Connalty The Clare form of MacNulty.

Connarty A corrupt form of Connaghty.

(O) Connaughton *Ó Connachtáin*. An important Connacht sept which migrated from Co. Sligo to Co. Roscommon. Often confused with O'Naughton and sometimes corrupted to Connorton or Connington. MIF   Map Sligo.

(Mac) Conneely *Mac Conghaile* (*con*, hound—*gal*, valour) MIF Map Galway. See Neely and Corneely.

Conneff See Cunniff.

Mac Connell Usually *Mac Dhomhnaill* not *Mac Conaill* (i.e. son of Daniel not Connell). Very numerous in Cos. Antrim, Down and Tyrone. MIF

O Connell *Ó Conaill*. One of the most important Kerry septs. Daniel

O'Connell was of the leading family of Derrynane. Bibl. IF Map Kerry.

(O) Connellan *Ó Conalláin* and *Ó Coinghiolláin* in Connacht; *Ó Caoindealbháin* in Munster and Leinster. The anglicized form is now usually abbreviated to Conlan or Conlon, both of which are numerous in all the provinces, especially in Connacht. IF 86. See also Kindellan, Quinlan and Quinlivan.

Mac Connellogue, -Conlogue *Mac Dhomhnaill Óig* (*óg,* young or junior). A Donegal name, mainly of Inishowen.

(O) Connelly See Connolly.

Conner A variant of O'Connor. Bibl.

Connerney A Co. Galway name formerly Connerneen, sometimes used as a variant of MacInerney.

Connerton See Connaughton.

(O) Connery *Ó Conaire.* A Munster name, mainly found in Cos. Cork and Limerick. It is confused with the Connacht name Conry, e.g. in the case of the author Pádraic Ó Conaire.

(O) Conney See Cunnea.

(Mac) Connick *Mac Conmhaic* (*con* gen. of *cú,* hound—*mac,* son). Woulfe calls this family a branch of the O'Farrells of Co. Longford; the name is now associated with Co. Wexford, where it appears among the proprietors in the barony of Forth in 1659.

Connigan See Cunnigan.

Connington See Connaughton.

(O) Connolly *Ó Conghaile* (Connacht and Monaghan), *Ó Coingheallaigh* (Munster). Spelt Connelly in Co. Galway where the family is of the Uí Maine. The name is widely distributed over all the provinces. James Connolly was of a Co. Monaghan family. Bibl. IF   Map Galway, Fermanagh, Meath and Monaghan.

Mac Connon *Mac Canann* (*cano,* wolf cub). An Oriel name still mainly found in Co. Monaghan. It is also anglicized MacCannan which has been changed to MacCann, as MacConnon has become MacConnell. MIF

Mac Connor *Mac Conchobhair* (son of Connor). MacConnor was formerly much used erroneously by officials, e.g. Petty's census enumerators, for O'Connor; the true MacConnors of Ulster are now usually called MacNaugher, No(c)her etc.

O Connor *Ó Conchobhair.* The name of six distinct and important septs. (See Map.) In Connacht there were O'Connor or O'Conor Don (of which was the last High King of Ireland) with its branches O'Conor Roe and O'Conor Sligo; also O'Conor Faly (i.e. of Offaly), O'Connor Kerry and O'Connor of Corcomroe (north Clare). The prefix O, formerly widely discarded, has been generally resumed. Similarly the variant form Connors has become O'Connor again.

It is one of the most numerous names in Ireland particularly in Co. Kerry. Bibl. IF   Map Clare, Derry, Galway, Kerry, Offaly, Roscommon and Sligo.

Connorton See Connaughton.

Connoty See Conaty.

(Mac) Connulty The Clare form of MacNulty.

(O) Conole *Ó Coineoil.* This is now mainly found in west Clare, but was originally an erenagh family of Co. Sligo. MIF

Mac Conomy See Conamy.

Conoo, Cunnoe *Mac Conmhaigh* (*condmach,* head smashing). Now widely changed to Conway. Though originally Dalcassian this was returned as a principal name in west Cork in 1659 and has since spread to Offaly. The Annals of the Four Masters use the Irish form *Ó Connmhaigh.* (See derivation given above which I got from the late Professor M. A. O'Brien). MIF 93.

(O) Conrahy *Ó Conratha.* (Woulfe derives this from *rath,* prosperity, which is doubtful). A Leix-Offaly name, where it has often been erroneously changed to Conroy.

(O) Conran See Condron.

Mac Conready See under MacCready.

(O) Conroy, Conree, Conary, Conry These mainly Connacht names, owing to the similarity of the anglicized forms, have become virtually indistinguishable. They represent four Gaelic originals, viz. *Mac Conraoi* (Galway and Clare), *Ó Conraoi* (Galway), *Ó Conaire* (Munster) and *Ó Maolchonaire* (an important literary family of Co. Roscommon). IF   Map Galway (Mac Conry). See also Conrahy, Connery and King.

Mac Conry *Mac Conraoi.* See previous entry. Ballymaconry is in west Galway. Map Galway.

(Mac) Considine *Mac Consaidín.* A Dalcassian sept, a branch of the O'Briens, IF   Map Clare.

Mac Consnave See Kinnawe. Map Leitrim.

(Mac) Convery *Mac Ainmhire.* This belongs to the Magherafelt district in south Derry. For derivation see cognate Hanbery.   MIF

(Mac) Convey See Conway, of which it is a synonym.

Mac Conville *Mac Conmhaoil.* The name of an Oriel sept mainly found in Cos. Armagh, Louth and Down. MIF See Conwell. Conwell.

Conway This is used as the anglicized form of several Gaelic-Irish surnames, the more important being *Mac Connmhaigh* (Thomond), *Mac Conmidhe* (Tyrone), *Ó Conbhuidhe* (Easky, Co. Sligo) and *Ó Connmhacháin* (Co. Mayo). See Conamy, Conboy, Conoo, Kanavaghan and MacNama. Bibl. IF

(Mac) Conwell Formerly this was the more usual form of the name now called Conville in Oriel. Conwell is still found in Donegal.

Conyers The well-known family of Cos. Kerry and Limerick was originally *de Coignières.* Elsewhere the name was adopted by a few families of O'Connor anxious to conceal their Irish origin. MIF

Conyngham See Cunningham.

Mac Cooey *Mac Cumhaighe.* This is the Irish form given by Fr. Paul Walsh. It is an Oriel name quite distinct from MacCoy.

Mac Coog See Cooke.

(O) Coogan *Ó Cuagáin.* A sept of the Uí Maine; now scattered to Cos. Kilkenny, Monaghan etc. Map Galway. See Cogan.

(Mac) Coo(g)han *Mac Cuacháin* (probably from *cuach,* cuckoo). Map Leitrim. See MacGoohan.

Cooke There are three distinct origins for the name in Ireland. In Leinster it is mainly an English occupational name, in many cases long established there: nine place-names in the province (Cookstown, Cooksland etc.) attest this. In Ulster it is usually Scottish— MacCook or MacCuagh, a branch of the clan MacDonald of Kintyre. Cookstown, Co. Tyrone, was founded by Alan Cook in 1609. In Connacht Cooke is the modern anglicized form of *Mac Dhabhoc* (also called *Mac Uag*) the name of a branch of the Burkes: it is anglicized MacCooge in some places. The MacCoogs of south Co. Galway were first named MacHugo from Hugo Burke.

(Mac) Cool *Mac Giolla Comhghaill* (devotee of St. Comhghal) or *Mac Comhghaill.* This name has been made Cole in the Glenties area. In Scotland MacCool is a variant of MacDougall. MIF Map Donegal.

Cooley In Ulster this is a variant of Cowley and occasionally also of Colley. For the name in Clare and Galway see Kilcooley. Mac-Cooley is found in Oriel where it is possibly a variant of MacCawley.

(O) Coolican and **Coolahan** See Cuolahan.

Cooling The correct pronunciation of this name stresses the second syllable. Richard Foley gives *Ó Cúilfhinn* as the Irish form. It is mainly found in Co. Wicklow. MIF

Coomey See Comey.

Coon See Cunningham.

(O) Coonaghan See Counihan.

(O) Coonan *Ó Cuanáin* (probably from *cuan,* elegant). Originally of Co. Sligo, this name is now found in Offaly and north Tipperary. Conan is usually a variant. MIF See Conan.

(O) Connerty *Ó Cuanartaigh.* A Co. Clare name seldom found elsewhere.

(O) Cooney *Ó Cuana* (for probable derivation see Coonan). Originally of Tyrone this family later migrated to north Connacht. The Cooneys of east Clare and south-east Galway may be of different origin.

Ballycooney there indicates their homeland. It is now fairly numerous in all the provinces except Ulster. IF   Map Roscommon.

(O) Coonlaghty See Coloughty.

Cooper This English occupational name has been prominent among the Anglo-Irish gentry since mid-seventeenth century in four counties, particularly Co. Sligo. Bibl.

Coote An influential Anglo-Irish family since 1600, principally associated with Cos. Cavan and Leix. The name is a nickname from the bird. Bibl. MIF

Copeland App.

Copley An English toponymic in Co. Cork since the seventeenth century.

Coppinger The name is of Norse origin. This family settled in Cork city and county in the early fourteenth century. Bibl; Map Cork.

Corbally One of the few surnames formed from an Irish place-name. It is found, with its synonym Corballis, in Co. Louth.

(O) Corban(e), Corbett Corbett is an old English name. In Ireland it is usually like Corbane for *Ó Corbáin* (Munster) or *Ó Coirbín* (Connacht). MIF   See Corribeen.

(Mac) Corboy, Corby *Mac Corrbuidhe* (possibly from *corr*, crane— *buidhe*, yellow). Leix, Offaly and north Tipperary. See p. 304.

(Mac) Corcoran *Mac Corcráin* (*corcair*, purple). A sept of the Ely O'Carroll country. IF   Map Offaly. See Cochrane.

(O) Corcoran *Ó Corcráin* (derivation as previous entry). An ecclesiastical family located near Lough Erne. IF   Map Fermanagh. See Cochrane.

Mac Cord An Ulster name, possibly a variant of MacCourt.

(O) Cordan A rare variant of Corridon.

Cordue An east Clare name believed to be of Spanish origin. It might also be for the English toponymic Cardew. MIF

Corduff Though Woulfe gives *Ó Corrdhuibh* for this name, which is rarely found outside Donegal and Mayo, I think it is more correctly *Mac Corrdhuibh*. The only instance I have found in authentic records of Corduff or Carduff appearing with the prefix is in the Donegal hearth money rolls of 1665 where it is Mac. Modern usage, however, makes the use of O allowable. In any case it can be accepted as a Gaelic-Irish name, not a toponymic taken from any of the numerous places called Corduff.

Corey Often used in Tyrone for Corry.

Corish *Mac Fheorais* (son of Piers). A Gaelic patronymic adopted by the Berminghams of Connacht. The Leinster branch were located in Co. Wexford where the name Corish is now mainly found. MIF

Mac Corkell, -Corkhill *Mac Thorcaill* (from a Norse personal name).

A branch of the Scottish clan Gunn, mainly found in Cos. Donegal and Derry. In the Isle of Man it is Corkhill.

Corkeran A variant of Corcoran.

(O) Corkery *Ó Corcra* (*corcair*, purple). All families of this name originated in south-west Munster. It is still almost exclusively found in west Cork and adjacent areas.

(O) Corkin, Corken *Ó Corcáin*. An Ulster name, Woulfe says it is *Mac Corcáin* in Co. Wicklow.

(Mac) Corless This appears early as *Mac Coirleasa*, later *Mac Cathail* and (mod.) *Mac Carluis*. The forename *Cathal* is equated with Charles. The family is of the Uí Maine and the name is now found mainly in Co. Galway.

(Mac) Corley A variant of Curley, mainly found in Cos. Mayo and Sligo.

Mac Cormack, -Cormick *Mac Cormaic*. This like MacCormican is formed from the forename Cormac. This name is numerous throughout all the provinces, the spelling MacCormick being more usual in Ulster. For the most part it originated as a simple patronymic; the only recognized sept of the name was of the Fermanagh-Longford area. Many of the MacCormac(k) families of Ulster are of Scottish origin, being a branch of the clan Buchanan–MacCormick of MacLaine. Bibl. IF

(O) Cormican *Ó Cormacáin*. It is in fact now often changed to MacCormack. Septs of the name were in Thomond, Roscommon, Galway and Down. It is now chiefly found in Co. Galway. Woulfe lists MacCormican as distinct from O'Cormican, but I think the use of the prefix Mac in this case is due to a not uncommon sixteenth-century clerical error.

Mac Cormilla A synonym of Gormley in Co. Monaghan.

Corneely A corrupt variant of Conneely formerly common in Co. Galway, now rare.

(O) Corneen See Curneen.

Corneille A Palatine name in Co. Limerick.

Corner Found in Co. Armagh since late seventeenth century. Corner is of dual derivation: locative or Anglo-French *cornier* (hornblower).

(O) Corr This is the usual anglicized form of *Ó Corra* of northern Ulster. There are so many words from which this may be derived that it is impossible to make a definite statement. Woulfe says it is from *corra*, spear. MIF   Map Derry. See Corry.

Corra See Weir.

(O) Corrain, Corren Variants of Curran in Donegal and Tyrone.

(O) Corree, Corr(e)y Variants of O'Curry found in Co. Clare.

(O) Corribeen *Ó Coirbín* (possibly from *corb*, chariot). Found in Cos. Mayo and Galway. See Corbett.

(O) Corridon *Ó Corradáin*. Now of Kerry, this was originally of south Clare on the opposite side of the Shannon. It is not a variant of Corrigan. MIF

(O) Corrigan *Ó Corragáin*. Akin to the Maguires, originally of Fermanagh, now scattered. Ballycorrigan, for example, is in Co. Tipperary, though possibly this place-name may not be derived from the surname. As Currigan and Courigan it is now found in east Connacht, and as Carrocan in Co. Clare. IF 95.

(Mac) Corry, Corrie *Mac Gothraidh* (*Gothraidh* or Godfrey). A branch of the Maguires, sometimes contracted to Corr. MIF Map Fermanagh.

(O) Corry A synonym of both Curry and Corr. Bibl. MIF Map Cork and Tyrone.

Corscadden An Irish variant of the English Garscadden. The root word in this name is *gart*, field (cf. Irish *gort*). Found in Co. Leitrim.

Cosby An important Anglo-Irish family in Co. Leix since the sixteenth century.

(Mac) Cosgrave *Mac Coscraigh* (*coscrach*, victorious). An erenagh family of Clones. MIF Map Monaghan. See Cushley and Coskerry.

(O) Cosgrave *Ó Coscraigh*. Distinct from MacCosgrave, though of the same county and derivation. Another sept of the same name, often anglicized Cosker, is of south-east Leinster. The spelling Cosgrove is nearly as usual as Cosgrave. In Connacht, where it is fairly numerous, it is the name of a distinct sept originating there. MIF Map Monaghan and Wicklow.

Cosgriff A variant of Cosgrave in Co. Cork.

(Mac) Cosh, Cush *Mac Coise*. Woulfe suggests the derivation from *cos*, foot, leg. Foote and Legge are used as synonyms of it whether by translation or pseudo-translation. MacCosh is mainly found in Co. Antrim; Cush in Tyrone and Oriel. See Cushnahan.

(Mac) Cosker See Cusker.

(O) Coskeran See Cuskeran.

Coskerry A variant of Cosgrave both in Down and Kerry.

(Mac) Costello(e) *Mac Oisdealbhaigh*. *Oisdealb* was the name of the father of Gilbert de Nangle, and this is the first example of a Norman family assuming a Mac name. The use of the prefix O is erroneous, though it does occasionally occur in seventeenth-century records. The barony of Costello in east Mayo is named from them. IF Map Mayo.

Costen *Mac Oistin*. According to Woulfe *Oistin* is a form of Augustine. Costen is found in Waterford and east Cork.

(Mac) Costigan *Mac Oistigín* and corruptly *Mac Costagáin*. Woulfe says *Oistigín* comes from the English name Roger, pet form Hodgkin. A branch of the Fitzpatricks of Ossory. MIF   Map Leix.

Costley An occasional variant of Costello; but in Antrim an English name.

Cott See under Coates.

(Mac) Cotter *Mac Coitir* formerly *Mac Oitir*. This is an old Gaelic-Irish family though their name is formed from a Norse personal name. Ballymacotter locates their homeland. Bibl. IF   Map Cork.

(O) Cottle *Ó Coitil* (from a Norse personal name). A small sept of the Uí Fiachra in Co. Sligo, perpetuated in the place-name Cottlestown. It is distinct from Kettle.

Cotton An English toponymic associated with Dublin and south-east Leinster since the seventeenth century. Ballycotton in Co. Cork is not derived from this surname.

Mac Coubrey *Mac Cúithbreith* (son of Cuthbert). This Scottish name is closely associated with Downpatrick and adjacent areas.

(Mac) Coughlan *Mac Cochláin*. For many centuries a leading family in Co. Offaly. Their territory in the Banagher-Clonmacnois area was formerly known as Delvin MacCoughlan. For derivation Woulfe gives *cochal,* cape or hood. IF   Map Offaly. Bibl.

(O) Coughlan *Ó Cochláin*. The well-known Munster sept of Barrymore. The prefix O in this case and Mac in the foregoing have been almost entirely dropped. Coughlan and Coghlan are more numerous in Co. Cork than elsewhere. IF   Map Cork. See Cawlin.

(O) Coulahan See Cuolahan.

Coulter See Colter.

Coumey See Comey.

(O) Counihan *Ó Cuanacháin* (derivation as Coonan). A Kerry name. Counihan is occasionally a synonym of Cunningham.

County See Canty.

de Courcy This Anglo-Norman name came to Ireland in 1177 in the person of Sir John de Courcy who, until he was displaced by de Lacy, was a leading figure in Ulster. As Barons of Kinsale, they were prominent in west Cork, where branches of the family have since been established. A century ago, when they were mainly located around Clonakilty, the prefix de had been dropped, but today most bearers of the name are called de Courcy. The form used in Irish is *de Cúrsa,* from the Norman place-name Courci. Map Cork.

(O) Courigan See Corrigan.

(O) Cournane, Courneen See Curnane, Curneen.

Coursey See de Courcy.

Mac Court *Mac Cuarta* or *Mac Cuairt*. An Oriel sept. I have found no evidence to support the statement that it is a variant of MacCurdy. MIF   Map Armagh-Louth. See Courtney.

(O) Courtayne See Curtayne.

Courtney A Norman name (*de Courtenai*). Usually, however, an anglicized form of Cournane (see Curnane) and occasionally of MacCourt. MIF

Cousins See Cussen.

(Mac) Coveney *Mac Coibheanaigh* (*coibhdheanach,* tropper). A small Ossory sept of Cranagh (as Map). In quite modern times mainly found in Co. Cork. The prefix O is sometimes used with this name. Map Kilkenny.

MacCovera A variant of MacCoubrey.

MacCovey *Mac Cobhthaigh.* A rare Louth–Down name. For derivation see Coffey.

Cowan *Ó Comhdhain.* The name of a Kilkenny–Waterford sept now, I think, extinct. Cowan, however, is numerous in Ulster where it is used frequently as a synonym of MacCoan, Coyne and MacKeown and sometimes as an abbreviated form of MacIlhone. MIF

(O) Cowhig, Cow(h)ey Munster forms of Coffey. Map Cork.

(Mac) Cowhill, -Cowell An occasional anglicized form of *Mac Cathmhaoil.* See MacCawell.

Cowley One of the ten 'Tribes of Kilkenny'. The name is usually an English toponymic. Bibl. See next entry and Cooley.

(Mac) Cowley A variant of MacAuley in north Connacht and Donegal and also in the Isle of Man where, however, the Mac is not retained.

Cowman Used synonymously with Commons and Cummins in Co. Wexford. MacCowman is listed as one of the principal Irish names in east Wexford in the 'census' of 1659. That would be *Mac Comáin* rather than the usual *Ó Comáin.* Cowman of English origin, appears as a Quaker name in Dublin in 1741.

Cowmey See Comey.

Cowper See Cooper.

Cox See under MacQuilly.

Mac Coy One of the several anglicized forms of *Mac Aodha* (son of Hugh). Woulfe says it is almost peculiar to Co. Limerick, but in fact it is mainly found in north Ulster, where it is a galloglass family. IF

Coyd See Quoid.

(Mac) Coyle *Mac Giolla Chomhgaill* (devotee of St. Comgal); formerly anglicized Mac Ilhoyle, which is still extant. Coyle is also confused with MacCool. MIF   Map Donegal and Monaghan.

(O) Coyne *Ó Cadhain* (*cadhan,* wild goose). A sept of the Uí Fiachrach. This and its synonym Kyne are essentially Connacht names. IF Map Mayo. See Barnacle and Kilcoyne.

Craan, Cran See Crahan.

Mac Cracken *Mac Reachtain*. An Ulster form of MacNaughton. This substitution of R for N is not unusual. Map Antrim–Derry.

Craddock *Creadóc,* (Welsh *Caradoc*). This name is prominent in the midlands since the thirteenth century. Places called Craddockstown are located in Cos. Meath, Kildare and Kilkenny.

(O) Craffy A variant of Croffy.

Crahan This rare name has several different origins: a form of MacCrohan (Kerry); of O'Creaghan (Mayo); in Leinster Crahan has been changed to Craan and even Curran.

Craig This Scottish name (from crag) is very numerous in Cos. Antrim, Derry and Tyrone. App.

Mac Crainor See Traynor.

Cramer See Creamer.

Cram(p)sey See Kneafsey.

Crampton Prominent in the commercial life of Dublin since early eighteenth century. There are occasional references to this name in earlier Irish records.

Crane This well-known English name (a nickname from the bird) has been used as a variant of Crean; in Kerry it is occasionally a synonym of Curran.

Craney See Cranny.

Crangle Woulfe equates this with Cronelly, but that is an Offaly–Galway name; in fact Crangle, which is a Manx form of MacRannall, is mainly found in Co. Down.

Cranley An English toponymic, which is sometimes used as a synonym of Cronelly.

Mac Cran(n) See Rinn.

(Mac) Cranny Cranny is not closely associated with any particular area, but its synonyms Crany and Creaney are definitely of Cos. Armagh and Down. Woulfe suggests *Mac Bhranaigh* as a possible Gaelic form.

Craughwell This surname belongs exclusively to east Galway. The village of Craughwell is in that area so the presumption is that it is a toponymic. The fact that it is called *Ó Creachmhaoil* in the spoken language does not preclude this.

Cravane, Craven, Creavan *Ó Crabháin* in Co. Galway; *Mac Crabháin* in Louth–Monaghan. As an English toponymic Craven is very rare in Ireland.

Crawford Bibl; App.

Mac Crawley An Oriel name, where *Mac Raghallaigh* is the Irish form. Elsewhere Crawley is occasionally a variant of Crowley.

Mac Crea, -Crae, -Cray *Mac Raith, Mac Craith*. A Scottish name, numerous in Ulster, akin etymologically to MacGrath.

Mac Cready *Mac Riada.* An erenagh family in the barony of Raphoe, Co. Donegal. In Co. Derry MacCready has been used as an abbreviated form of MacConready, alias MacAready, i.e. *Mac Conriada.* MIF

Creagh *Craobhach.* An adjectival surname, formed from *craobh,* branch, assumed by the O'Neills of Co. Clare. IF 98; Map Limerick.

Creamer, Cramer There are several origins for this name. The well-known Co. Cork family were Von Kramer; there is an English name derived from creamer, a pedler; and in Leitrim it can be a corruption of MacCreanor, a variant form of Traynor. Bibl.; MIF

(O) Crean, Creaghan, Crehan *Ó Croidheáin (croidhe,* heart). A Cenél Eoghain sept of Donegal, with a branch in Co. Sligo. Crehan is the usual form in Cos. Clare and Galway. These names are also anglicized forms of *Ó Criocháin,* alias *Mac Criocháin* of Ardstraw. IF   Map Mayo and Tyrone. See Curreen for Creen or Crean of Kerry.

Creaney See Cranny.

(Mac) Creanor See Traynor.

Mac Creary See MacCreery.

Creaton See Creighton.

(O) Creavan See Cravane.

Creed, Creedon Properly *Mac Críodáin,* but changed to *Ó Críodáin* in modern times. Creed is an abbreviation of Creedon. Both are Co. Cork names. MIF

Mac Creedy A variant spelling of MacCready.

(O) Creegan See Cregan.

Creely See Crilly.

Creen Used as a variant of both Crean and Curreen.

Mac Creery *Mac Ruidhri.* A variant of *Mac Ruaidhri* (MacRory) in Co. Tyrone where the Irish sept of the name originated.

Mac Creesh *Mac Raois.* A branch of the sept of MacGuinness in Oriel. The name is probably a corruption of *Mac Aonghuis* (Mac Guinness).

Mac Creevy An occasional variant of MacGreevy.

Cregan While it is definite that Creegan of Connacht is *Ó Croidheagáin (croidhe,* heart) it would appear probable that Cregan of Munster and Leinster is *Mac Riagáin:* this view, however, must be accepted with reserve until further evidence is forthcoming. In north Connacht Creegan is much confused with Crehan. See Crean.

Cregg The Co. Roscommon form of Craig.

(O) Creghan See Crean.

Mac Creight *Mac Creacht.* One of the non-Highland Scottish names; it came to Ireland from Galloway, possibly Irish originally.

Creighton A Scottish territorial name, prominent in Ulster, also sometimes used as a synonym of Creaghan and Crehan.

Crelly, Creilly Variants of Crilly.

(O) Cremin, Cremeen *Ó Cruimin* (*crom*, bent). Traditionally a branch of the MacCarthys. Seldom found outside west Munster. MIF

(O) Crennan *Ó Críonáin* (*críon*, old, worn out). Mainly found in Cos. Kilkenny and Leix between Castlecomer and Abbeyleix. See Crinion.

(O) Crennigan *Ó Críonagáin* (from *críon* as foregoing). Cos. Westmeath and Roscommon.

Cribben For MacCribben see under Gribben. *Ó Croibín* is a Mayo variant of *Ó Coirbín*. See Coribeen.

Crickard A Co. Down form of MacRicard.

Crighton Bibl. See Creighton.

(Mac) Crifferty *Mac Raibheartaigh*. A Fermanagh name now often disguised as Clifford.

(Mac) Crilly Woulfe gives *Mac Raghallaigh*, thus equating the name with Crawley, which is conjectural. Historically this family is mainly of Oriel. The better-known erenagh family of Tamlaght was also called O'Crilly. MIF 72 Map Derry.

(O) Crimmeen, Crimmins Variants of Cremin.

(O) Crinigan See Crennigan.

(Mac) Crinion *Mac Críonáin*. Of Meath and adjacent areas. This is probably a variant of *Ó Críonáin*; see Crennan.

Mac Crink A Scottish name found in south Down.

Crisham A synonym of Clisham also found in Co. Galway.

Cristopher See Christopher.

Croan See Crowne.

Crockett App.

(O) Croffy *Ó Crábhthaigh* (*cráibhtheach*, religious) is the traditional Irish form in east Galway where this name belongs. MIF

Crofton An English toponymic. Families of the name settled permanently in Connacht in the sixteenth century, where they became connected with that of O'Connor Don and a century later were staunch supporters of the Catholic cause, though some of the name were found on the other side. Bibl; MIF

Crofts The name (derived from the English word croft) of a well-known landed family which settled in Co. Cork late in the sixteenth century.

Mac Crohan *Mac Criomhthainn* (a word for a fox). The name of a branch of the O'Sullivans associated with the Dingle peninsula and the Blasket islands. The use of the O prefix with this name is erroneous. MIF Map Kerry. For Croghan and Croughan see Crowne.

Croke *Cróc*. In Co. Tipperary since the thirteenth century. IF MIF

Croker The main family is in Co. Limerick since the early seventeenth century. It was earlier in Co. Kilkenny. The Anglo-Norman *le Crocker* (maker of pots) was in Ireland in the thirteenth century. Bibl. IF

Croly, Crolly These are used both for Crilly in Oriel and Crowley in Munster.

Cromie, Crombie This name is peculiar to Co. Armagh, south Down and adjacent areas. Cromie is a Scottish toponymic but families called O'Cromy were in Co. Armagh in the seventeenth century, so the Irish form *Ó Cromtha* (*crom*, bent or crooked) can also be accepted. SIF 44.

Cromley See Crumley.

Cromwell, Grummell This English toponymic in either variant is now very rare in Ireland; it was prominent in the city of Limerick for two centuries before the time of Oliver Cromwell. MIF

(O) Cronan *Ó Crónáin* (*crón*, brown or swarthy). A variant of Cronin. It is mainly found in Co. Tipperary.

Crone An adjectival name; *crón* means swarthy. It is not closely associated with any particular area. Bibl.

(O) Cronekan Woulfe gives *Ó Crónagáin* (from *crón*, see Crone). Richard Foley, who had special knowledge of the area around Youghal to which this name belongs, considered that the correct Irish form is *Ó Crónmhacháin*.

(O) Cronelly, Cronley *Ó Crónghaile* (probably from *crón*, brown or swarthy, and *gal*, valour). Originally of the Uí Maine, later also Offaly.

(O) Cronin, *Ó Cróinín* (from *crón*, as previous entry). A sept of the Corca Laoidhe. The leading family were erenaghs of Gougane Barra. The name is now very numerous in Cos. Cork and Kerry. MIF Map Cork. See Cronan.

Cronogue *Cronóg*. A Co. Leitrim name, sometimes there strangely changed to Crowley.

Crooke (derived from *crook*, a bend). An Anglo-Irish family which gave its name to Crookstown, Co. Cork, formerly Moviddy. Crooks, an English toponymic numerous in Ulster, is of different origin. These names are often confused. Both have been in Ireland since early seventeenth century.

Mac Crory See MacRory.

Crosbie This English toponymic was adopted by a family of Mac-Crossan of Leix who espoused the English cause and migrated to Kerry in the seventeenth century. MIF

Croskery A corrupt form of Coskery numerous in Co. Down.

Cross This English locative name is sometimes used as a synonym of MacCrossan.

(Mac) Crossan *Mac an Chrosáin* (*cros*, cross). The name of two distinct septs; the more numerous is of north Ulster now mainly Tyrone, the other of mid-Leinster. Ballymacrossan lies on the border of Leix and Offaly. MIF   Map Donegal and Leix. See Crosbie.

Crossley Bibl.

Crothers A form of the Scottish Carruthers numerous in Cos. Antrim and Down.

(O) Crotty *Ó Crotaigh*. Originally of Thomond. The majority of the sept migrated to east Munster. MIF 76; Map Waterford.

Crough This form has been used in the Cashel area as a synonym of both Croke and Crowe.

(Mac) Croughan A variant of Crohan. See Crowne.

Croughwell See Craughwell.

Crowe See MacEnchroe.

(O) Crowley *Ó Cruadhlaoich* (*cruadh*, hard—*laoch*, hero). A branch of this sept is said to have migrated from their homeland, Moylurg, Co. Roscommon; it became a leading west Cork sept. Bibl. IF Map Cork.

(Mac) Crowne, Croan *Mac Conchruacháin* (hound of Croghan). A Co. Roscommon name formerly anglicized MacCroghan. MIF See Crohan.

Crowton Bibl.

Crozier This occupational name is listed in the 'census' of 1659 as one of the principal English names in Fermanagh; it is now more numerous in Co. Armagh.

Mac Crudden See Rodden.

Cruise *de Crúis*. Always de Cruys not le Cruys in mediaeval Irish records. One of the oldest of the Hiberno–Norman families, mainly identified with Cos. Meath and Dublin. Map Dublin.

Mac Crum *Mac Cruim* (*crom*, bent). This name came to Co. Down from Islay, Scotland.

(O) Crumley, Cromley This name belongs to Cos. Donegal and Derry. Woulfe suggests *Ó Cromlaoich* (bent hero) as the Irish form but in some cases at least it is a variant of Crumlish.

Crumlish Modern usage gives this Donegal name the Mac prefix. Woulfe suggests *Ó Cromruisc* (meaning the descendant of the squint-eyed man), as the form in Irish which is doubtful.

Crummell See Cromwell.

Crummy A variant of Cromie.

(O) Cryan, Crynes Co. Roscommon forms of Crean.

(Mac) Crystal Chrystal is a diminutive of Christopher. It is a Scottish name in Cos. Armagh and Tyrone since the seventeenth century. MIF

Cubbard Probably for Cutbird, a corrupt form of Cuthbert. One of the non-Gaelic names associated with the Claddagh of Galway.

Mac Cudden A variant of MacCadden.

(O) Cuddigan A Co. Cork variant of Cadogan.

(O) Cuddihy, Cuddy, Quiddihy *Ó Cuidighthigh* (*cuidightheach*, helper). Definitely a Co. Kilkenny name though the form *Mac Cuidithe* appears in Co. Cork in 1214. MIF

Cudmore A west of England name established in Co. Cork since the seventeenth century. MIF

Mac Cue Formerly MacCoo, a form of MacHugh (*Mac Aodha*) found in Fermanagh and adjacent Ulster counties.

Cuffe This has three origins; (a) *Maċ Dhuibh*, see MacDuff (b) *Ó Duirnin* see Durnin (c) An English name associated with Co. Kilkenny. MIF

(Mac) Cuggeran *Mac Cogaráin* (possibly from *cogar*, whisper). The prefix O is now often substituted for Mac in this east Clare name. It has no real connection with the Scottish Cochrane. MIF

Culbert This Ulster name is of Huguenot origin. Culbrath is an eighteenth-century variant of it in Co. Monaghan.

(O) Culhane This is the anglicized form of *Ó Cathaláin* (Cahalan) in Co. Limerick, its original homeland. It is called Cohalan in Co. Cork. MIF Map Limerick.

(O) Culhoun, Culloon *Ó Cuileamhain*. Of south Leinster, now almost entirely absorbed by Cullen. According to O'Curry the famous Cardinal Cullen was of this minor sept. For Ulster see Colhoun.

Culkin, Culkeen See Quilkin.

Cull A variant of Coll in Co. Limerick.

Mac Cullagh, -Collough *Mac Cú Uladh* or *Mac Con Uladh* (hound of Ulster). A numerous name in Ulster. Also, as MacCulloch, Scottish. MIF 76. See MacColla and MacCullow.

(O) Cullane See Collins.

Culleeny See Culliney.

(Mac) Cullen *Mac Cuilinn* (*cuileann*, holly). Mainly found in Co. Monaghan. A variant of MacCollin; also confused with MacQuillan. SIF 90.

(O) Cullen *Ó Cuilinn* (derivation as MacCullen). Primarily a numerous sept of south-east Leinster. Also the synonym of several other somewhat similar names. See Introduction p. xiii. Bibl. IF
Map Kildare. See Cullinane and Culhoon.

(Mac) Culleton, Colleton *Mac Codlatáin* (sleeper). The prefix O is sometimes substituted for Mac in this predominantly Co. Wexford name; it is also found in Co. Carlow and Kilkenny. MIF

(O) Culligan See Quilligan.

Mac Cullin See Holly, MacCollin and MacCullen.

(O) Cullinan(e) *Ó Cuileannáin* (probably from *cuileann*, holly). A branch of the Corca Laoidhe. In Clare and Tipperary the spelling is

Cullinane and sometimes Quillinane. Another sept so called, of Donegal, have become Cullen. IF   Map Cork.

(Mac) Culliney, Culleeny A Clare name also found in Mayo. Probably *Mac an Laighnigh*, son ot the Leinsterman.

Cullington A Connacht form of Culliton.

Mac Cullion This is *Mac Coileáin (coileán*, whelp) in Co. Fermanagh where it is sometimes changed to MacCullen.

Cullivan See Colivan.

Culloo See Cullow.

(O) Culloty, Cullity *Ó Codlata (codladh*, sleep). Kerry and west Cork.

Mac Cullow, Cully Forms of MacCullagh found respectively in north-east Ulster and Co. Tyrone. Culloo is found in Co. Clare. MIF   See Coloe.

(O) Cully *Ó Colla*. This name, found in Cos. Armagh and Antrim, is distinct from *Mac Colla*. See Coll and Colley.

(O) Culnane See Cullinane.

(Mac) Culreavy *Mac Cathail Riabhaigh (Cathal*, Charles—*riabhach*, grey or brindled). A Co. Longford and Leitrim name, a branch of the O'Rourkes. Some families of the name have become Gray.

Cummane See Commane.

Cumming(s), Cummins See Commons.

(Mac) Cumiskey, Cumisk See Comiskey.

Cummerford See Comerford.

(O) Cundlish A variant of Quinlish.

Cuniam See Cunniam.

Mac Cune A variant of MacKeown in north Ulster.

(O) Cunlaghty See Cologhty.

Cunlisk A variant of Quinlisk.

Cunnaboy A variant of Conboy found in Co. Galway where it is usually of Uí Maine not Uí Fiachrach origin.

(O) Cunnaghan A variant of Conaghan.

Cunnagher A curious synonym of Joyce in Mayo, possibly a patronymic—*Mac Conchobhair*. See Connagher.

(O) Cunnane See Kinnane and Queenan.

(O) Cunnea, Conney *Ó Coinne*. Cunnea is a west Ulster name, now sometimes changed to Quin in the Glenties district of Co. Donegal. Mr. J. C. MacDonagh treats it as a Mac name. Conney is scattered. See Quinney.

(Mac) Cunneen *Mac Coinín*. A literary family of Erris, often by mistranslation or possibly translation called Rabbitt. See next entry. Cunnane is an occasional variant in Connacht. IF MIF Map Mayo.

(O) Cunneen *Ó Coinín*. Two septs were so named—of Thomond and Offaly—both were sometimes changed to Rabbitt (*coinín*, rabbit).

The name is also said to be from *cano,* wolf cub. IF Map Offaly. Map Offaly.

Mac Cunnegan *Mac Cuinneagáin.* A Sligo sept of the Uí Fiachra whose name was often anglicized Cunningham. IF Map Galway.

(O) Cunnegan *Ó Cuinneagáin* or *Ó Connagáin.* A sept of the Uí Maine, anglicized Cunningham as the foregoing. Woulfe says, probably correctly, that both are derived from the personal name Conn. IF 104; Map Galway.

Cunniam Cunniamstown in Co. Wicklow is called *Baile an Choinniamaigh* in 'Leabhar Branach' which shows that Cunniam is an old name in Ireland. It is sometimes a synonym of Cunningham.

(Mac) Cunniff *Mac Conduibh (cú,* gen. *con,* hound—*dubh,* black). In addition to variant spellings such as Coneffe, this name is also anglicized Kinniff, MacNiff, Caddo, MacAdoo, MacEndoo etc. The latter show that the D in the Gaelic form need not be aspirated. These are found in many parts of Connacht and west Ulster. Canniff may be a synonym of MacAniff or MacNiff; but in Co. Cork it is *Ó Ceannduibh* (black head). MIF

(O) Cunning An Ulster variant of Gunning.

Cunningham The name of Scottish settlers, widely adopted as the modern form of Irish surnames. Matheson in his report on synonyms in birth registrations gives no less than 20 for Cunningham, e.g. Cunnegan, Kinnegan and even Coon. See also under Dongan. Bibl; IF 104.

Cunnion An occasional variant of Cunneen.

Cunniss See Coneys.

Cunnoo See Conoo.

(O) Cunny See Quinney.

Cunree A synonym of Conry.

(Mac) Cunreen *Mac Conriain* (Ryan's hound). A rare Co. Roscommon name, made King by pseudo-translation.

(Mac) Cuolahan *Mac Uallacháin (uallach,* proud). A branch of the Síol Anmchadha. Formerly an important family in the barony of Garrycastle. MIF Map Offaly.

(O) Cuolahan *Ó Cúlacháin.* A sept of the Uí Fiachrach in Mayo. Coolican is a modern variant. MIF

Cupples App.

Mac Curdy *Mac Mhuircheartaigh.* An Antrim variant of MacMurty and Mac Brearty.

(Mac) Curley *Mac Thoirdealbhaigh.* A variant of the Ulster Turley, mainly found in Galway and Roscommon; the place-names Ballymacurley and Curley's Island are in the latter. IF

Curlin, Curland See Kerlin.

(O) Curnane *Ó Curnáin.* An earlier form of the modern Courtney in Kerry. The derivation from *corn,* a drinking horn, is doubtful.

(O) Curneen *Ó Cuirnín.* A family of ollavs to the O'Rourkes of Breffny. The name is etymologically the same as the foregoing. Bibl; Map Leitrim.

Curphy *Mac Mhurchada.* The Manx form of Murphy found in Ulster.

Curragh In Oriel since the fifteenth century. This can be either an Irish toponymic or an Irish form of the Scottish MacCurrach, a branch of the clan MacPherson. MIF

(O) Curran This name is now numerous in all the provinces. The usual Irish form is *Ó Corráin.* In the sixteenth and seventeenth centuries it was mainly found (a) in Cos. Waterford and Tipperary; (b) in Cos. Galway and Leitrim—there they are of the same stock as the O'Maddens, the older Irish form being *Ó Curráin*; (c) in Co. Donegal, but there they may be Curreen changed to Curren and Curran; (d) in Co. Kerry where, however, the variant Currane is now almost invariably used. Bibl. IF   Map Galway.

(O) Currane See previous entry.

(Mac) Curreen, Curren *Mac Corraidhín (corradh,* spear). A sept of the Uí Fiachrach mainly in Leitrim, now more often called Mac-Gurrin, i.e. *Mag Corraidhín.* Curreen has not only become Curran in some places but has also been abbreviated to Crean, which is sometimes quite erroneously made Creen.

(O) Curreen, Currin Woulfe gives *Ó Cuirín* and states that it is a variant of Curran: Curreen and Currin have certainly been widely absorbed by Curran, but etymologically they are cognate with MacCurreen, see previous entry. Curreen is mainly found in Co. Waterford. This name is further complicated by the fact that the numerous Creens of Kerry are *Ó Cuirín.* Carreen is a variant in U.S.A.

(O) Currid *Ó Corthaid.* Closely identified with Co. Sligo.

(O) Currigan See Corrigan.

(O) Currivan Probably a form of Corbane, found in Co. Tipperary.

Mac Curry A variant of MacCorry.

(O) Curry *Ó Comhraidhe.* This is the name of two septs, unconnected, of Thomond and Moygoish. In some cases it is a variant of Corry. Currie is Scottish, a branch of the clan MacDonald. IF   Map Clare and Westmeath.

Curtayne *Mac Curtáin.* A variant form of Curtin. The statement that it is the Munster form of MacCartan can be disregarded.

(Mac) Curtin Formerly *Mac Cruitin* now *Mac Cuirtín (cruitin,* hunchback). An old Thomond sept later found chiefly in Co. Cork. Up to the end of the sixteenth century MacCruttin was the anglicized form. In the 'census' of 1659 MacCurtaine and O'Curtaine in Cos. Cork, Kerry and Limerick are treated as synonymous, thus accounting for the use now of the prefix O as well as the more correct Mac. IF   MIF   Map Clare.

(O) Curtin See previous entry.

Curtis Though gaelicized *de Cuirtéis* this name, in Ireland since the thirteenth century, is the Norman *le Curteis,* i.e. the well-educated man. Mainly found in east Leinster.

Cusack In Ireland this name dates back to the Anglo-Norman invasion of 1171. The family became fully hibernicized. First called de Cussac it became *Ciomhsóg* in Irish. Cusack in Clare is of different origin, viz. *Mac Iosóg,* first anglicized MacIsock and later MacCusack. MacIsaac is the corresponding Scottish name. IF Map Meath. Bibl.

Cush See Quish.

(Mac) Cushely, Cuskley *Mac Giolla Choiscle.* This Co. Tyrone name is easily confused with Cassily, especially as it belongs to almost the same part of the country. It has also been mistakenly changed to Costello, while in Co. Monaghan it has been wrongly anglicized as Cosgrave. Woulfe's derivation from *cos,* leg—*clé,* left, seems far-fetched.

Cushing, Cushion These are forms of Cussen found in Co. Wexford and Tipperary.

Cushlane A variant of Caslin. This and Cashlane have been corrupted to Cassell(s).

Cushnahane, Cushanan *Ó Cosnacháin (cosnach,* defender). A north Ulster name.

Cuskelly See Cushely.

Mac Cusker, -Cusker Principally a branch of the MacGuires in Fermanagh, centred at Ballymacosker; also synonyms of Cosgrave in Oriel. Without the prefix Mac, Cusker and Cosker are so used in Co. Wexford.

(Mac) Cuskeran *Mac Coscracháin* (derivation as Cosgrave). A Co. Down name cognate with and often changed to Cosgrave. The prefix O is sometimes used in Irish.

(O) Cussane *Ó Casáin.* Located in the Uí Maine country in Co. Galway but of a different race. Woulfe derives this name from *cas,* curly. In Connacht this is often called Paterson by pseudo-translation *(casán,* path). It is distinct from Cussen and Kissane.

Cussen *Cúisín.* Hibernicized Norman families of this name settled in Munster and Leinster, chiefly Cos. Limerick, Cork and Wexford. It was occasionally changed to the English name Cousins. Reaney says Cussen is from Cutison, i.e. Cuthbertson, but in Ireland the more obvious derivation denoting relationship is more probable. MIF

(Mac) Custy See Hosty.

(Mac) Cutcheon A branch of the Scottish clan MacDonald *Mac Uisdin* in Scottish Gaelic and *Mac Úistin* in Irish. The name is cognate with Hutchinson, Hutchin being a diminutive of Hugh. There are nine variant anglicized forms, e.g. MacQuestion, MacWhiston, Houston. Kitchen is a synonym in Co. Down and Hutchinson in Scotland. MIF

D

Dacey A variant spelling of Deasy.

Mac Dacker See Harden.

Mac Dade See MacDaid.

Dady See Deady.

(O) Daffy *Ó Deabhthaigh*. Woulfe suggests the modern word *deabhthach*, quarrelsome, for its derivation. Essentially a Co. Clare name.

Dagg Derived from Old-French *dague*, a dagger, this name came to Co. Wicklow and Wexford from England in the seventeenth century. MIF

Mac Dagney *Mac an Deagánaigh (deagán,* dean). An Ulster name now usually changed to Deane.

(O) Dahill *Ó Dathail*. Though believed to be originally of the Silmurray (Co. Roscommon) this name is on record in central Munster from very early times. It is now almost exclusively a Co. Tipperary name. MIF

(O) Dahony A rare variant of Doheny.

Mac Daid *Mac Daibhéid*. This is also anglicized (Mac)Davitt and (Mac)Devitt and sometimes Davison, but in its homeland (Donegal and Derry) MacDaid is more numerous. The meaning of these names, or course, is son of David. MIF   Map of Donegal.

Dale This can be a name of the agnomen type, *dall* (blind), occasionally found with the prefix Mac; or English, derived from dale, valley.

(O) Dallaghan *Ó Dalacháin*. A Connacht name, originally a clerical family in the diocese of Clonmacnois, it was reduced at the time of the Cromwellian transplantation. The derivation from *dálach*, as Daly, is unacceptable; *dall*, blind, is more probable.

(O) Dallagher *Ó Dalachair*. Formerly Dologher, this name belongs to Co. Limerick.

Dallas A Scottish name established in Co. Derry. Dalhouse was an earlier form. Derivation [dweller at] the dalehouse.

Dallon An occasional variant of Delane.

(O) Dally A variant of Daly.

Dalton *de Dalatún*. This toponymic was formerly written D'Alton. An Anglo-Norman family which became completely hibernicized. A branch settled in Co. Clare. IF   Map Westmeath. See Daton.

(O) Daly, Dawley *Ó Dálaigh* (*dálach*, from *dáil*, assembly). One of the greatest names in Irish literature. Originally Westmeath, but subsepts in several different localities as Map. As that in Desmond appears in the records as early as 1165 it is probable that this was a distinct sept. Bibl. IF   Map Clare, Cork, Galway, Westmeath.

Dalzell A Scottish toponymic in Louth and Down since the seventeenth century; pronounced Dee-ell.

(O) Dana(g)her *Ó Danachair* earlier *Ó Duineachair*. This sept which originated in Lower Ormond has long been located mainly in Co. Limerick. MIF   Map Tipperary.

(O) Danahy A variant of Dennehy.

Dancey A form of the English Dauntsey in use in Co. Cavan. Seldom on record before the eighteenth century.

(O) Dane *Ó Déaghain* (*déaghan*, dean). A sept of Co. Roscommon. Dane is also an English name derived from Old-English *denn*, a valley. MIF See Deane.

Danger See Aungier.

Mac Daniell As a synonym of MacDonnell this was formerly very widespread, but is not numerous now. In Co. Kerry, according to Nicholls, MacDaniel was the Irish patonymic assumed by a family of Welsh origin settled there in the thirteenth century. MacDaniell is also the name of a Scottish family.

O Daniel A variant of O'Donnell found in Co. Tipperary. Bibl.

Mac Dara See Darragh.

Darby Darby is the name of an English family which came to Co. Leix in the sixteenth century. For Darby as a native Irish name see under Darmody.

Darcy *Ó Dorchaidhe* (*dorcha*, dark). One of the 'Tribes of Galway' (see note under Kirwan) also anglicized Dorcey, it is the name of two septs, one in Mayo and Galway, the other in Co. Wexford. Most Darcy families in Leinster are usually of Norman origin, viz. D'Arci. Bibl. IF   Map Mayo (O'Dorcy) Meath (D'Arcy). See Mac-Gourkey.

Dardis The importance of this Hiberno-Norman family is evidenced by the fact that there are four places called Dardistown and one Dardisrath in north Leinster. The name, formerly D'Ardis, is said to be derived from the Ards, Co. Down, but d'Artois is a possible alternative. MIF

(O) Dargan The Leinster form of *Ó Deargáin* (*dearg*, red). In Co. Cork it takes the form Dorgan and is perpetuated in the place-name Ballydorgan. IF

Darley Though this name is an English toponymic it is better known in Ireland than in England. It has been associated with Dublin and adjacent counties since the seventeenth century. MIF

Darling In Dublin since mid-seventeenth century this name, of obvious epithetal derivation, is now equally numerous in the Belfast area.

(O) Darmody, Dermody *Ó Diarmada*. Mainly found in Co. Tipperary and adjacent Leinster counties, where it has sometimes been changed to MacDermott, though the names are basically quite distinct. This has also happened in the case of Darby (formerly MacDarby) both in that same area and further north in Leinster. The forename *Diarmaid* is anglicized Darby as well as Dermot, hence *Mac Diarmada* for Mac-Darby. MIF See Dermond.

(Mac) Darragh *Mac Dubhdara* mod. *Mac Dara*. This name, chiefly associated with Co. Antrim, is sometimes anglicized as Oakes by translation of *dair*, oak. Darren is a corrupt variant. The cognate Darroch is a branch of the Scottish clan MacDonald. MIF

Daton, Daughton Of Norman origin *(d'Auton)*. Prominent in Co. Kilkenny from the thirteenth century. It is now usually made Dalton by assimilation.

Daugherty A variant of Doherty.

Daunt This family settled in Co. Cork in the sixteenth century. Bardsley suggests that the name is a shorter form of Davenant. Bibl; IF

Davane This is usually a Connacht variant of Devane *(Ó Dubháin)*; Woulfe, however, treats it as a distinct name—*Ó Damháin*—and locates it in Ulster, but I do not find it there except as a very occasional variant of Devine. For derivation see Davin.

Davenport Though this English toponymic was mainly introduced in the Cromwellian period it is on record occasionally in Dublin as early as 1477. For Davenport in Munster see Donarty.

Davern See Davoren.

Davey, Davy An English name occasionally used synonymously with MacDavitt and even Davin.

Mac David Distinct from MacDavitt. A family of MacDavid was a branch of the MacDermots of Moylurg. See under Davis.

Davidson The name of a Scottish clan numerous in north-east Ulster. Davison and Davie are branches of that clan.

Mac Davie, -Davy The name of a branch of the Burkes of Connacht. In the sixteenth century a large area of Co. Galway (barony of Ballymoe) was known as MacDavie's country. Map Galway.

Davies Bibl.

(O) Davin *Ó Daimhín* (*damh*, ox or stag; not from *dámh*, poet). A Co. Tipperary name often confused with Devine.

Davis This well-known Welsh name is associated with Mallow through Thomas Davis. O'Donovan's statement that it is also a synonym of MacDavid or MacDavymore, a branch of the MacMurroughs in Co. Wexford, is disputed. IF App.

Davitt This, with the prefix Mac, is usually a Mayo variant of Mac-

Devitt. It is also the name of a branch of the Connacht Burkes. MIF 80.

(Mac) Davock *Mac Dabhóc*. Like the cognate MacCavock and Mac-Cooke this is a branch of the Burkes of Connacht. SIF 51. See Cooke.

(O) Davoren *Ó Dábhoireann*. The name of a Dalcassian brehon sept, which in its original form *Dubhdábhoireann* denotes black, two and Burren, the north Clare barony. IF   Map Clare.

Davy See Davey and MacDavie.

Mac Davymore See under Davis.

Davys Bibl. See Davis.

Daw An occasional synonym of O'Dea.

Dawley See Daly.

Dawney See Doheny.

Dawson An English family prominent in Cos. Monaghan and Tipperary since mid-seventeenth century. Bibl; MIF

Dawton See Daton.

Day See O'Dea.

O Dea *Ó Deághaidh* mod. *Ó Deá*. One of the principal Dalcassian septs. Away from its homeland it is usually mispronounced as O'Dee which, though cognate, is a distinct name, viz. *Ó Diaghaidh*. This, no doubt accounts for the use of Godwin in Mayo as its synonym. The prefix O is now almost always used, but a century ago Dea was quite usual and the English Day was regarded as synonymous. IF   Map Clare. See Daw.

(O) Deady *Ó Déadaigh*. Its variant *Ó Daoda* is anglicized Dady which is the local pronunciation of Deady also. Both these forms belong to Cos. Kerry and Limerick.

Deakin, Deacon Woulfe regards these names as anglicized forms of the very rare *Ó Deocáin*. His earlier opinion that Deakin is a synonym of Deegan was altered. As far as I know there is no evidence of it being used as an anglicized form of *Ó Deagánaigh*—see Deane. In any case as a rule Deacon, if not Deakin, is an English name which came to Ireland in the seventeenth century.

Deale, Daile Though occasionally variants of Dahill, these are normally English names derived from the word dale (a valley). The quite distinct MacDeale appears in Co. Armagh hearth money rolls, 1664.

(O) Dealy Woulfe states that this is a variant spelling of Deeley which is probable, but the fact that in Co. Cork it has been recorded as a synonym of Daly should be remembered. In Irish names EA is normally sounded AY rather than EE. See O'Dea.

Deane One of the 'Tribes of Galway', originally *le Den*. For north Connacht see Dane. Another family of Ormond was *de Denne*. Some Tipperary families, however, are *Ó Déaghain*; while those of Donegal are *Mac an Deagánaigh* (from Irish *déaghan* also *deagáin* and Latin *decanus,* dean). MIF

Deany, Deanie Ulster variants of Denny; seldom for Deeney. See observation under Dealy.

Dease *Déise.* Named not from Decies but from Deece, Co. Meath, in which county the family has been continuously since the thirteenth century. MIF   Map Meath.

Deasy *Déiseach* (i.e. of the Decies, Co. Waterford). Now mainly found in Co. Cork. Woulfe says it is found in Co. Sligo as *Mac an Déisigh*: I have no evidence of that. MIF

(O) Dee *Ó Diaghaidh.* An attenuated form of *Ó Deághaidh* found in south Munster. See O'Dea.

(O) Deegan *Ó Duibhginn** (*dubh,* black—*ceann,* head). Also anglicized Duigan, especially in Co. Leix. The O'Deegans of Cloncouse, Co. Leix, were keepers of the bell of St. Molua. MIF   Map Leix.

(O) Deehan *Ó Díochon.* Woulfe gives the derivation as great hound, but this is not generally accepted. A scattered name mainly found in Co. Derry. Sometimes changed to the English name Dickson. See Deighan.

(O) Deeley *Ó Duibhghiolla** (*dubh,* black—*giolla,* lad). Families of this name all originated in Co. Galway. See Devilly which is synonymous with it.

(O) Deenihan, Dinaghan *Ó Duibhneacháin* (for derivation see Deeny). The name of a small Co. Limerick sept now found mainly in Co. Kerry. MIF

(O) Deenihy A variant of Dennehy.

(O) Deeny *Ó Duibhne* (*duibhne,* disagreeable). This east Donegal and west Derry name is now usually mistranslated as Peoples from the similarity of the word *daoine* in sound to Deeny.

(O) Deerane See Dirrane.

(O) Deere See Diver.

Deering A branch of the very old Kent family of Dering settled in Leix in the sixteenth century which soon acquired much property in adjoining counties. They held many important official positions. The name is now mainly found in south-east Leinster. MIF

(O) Deery *Ó Daighre.* A notable ecclesiastical family in Ulster. To be distinguished from, though often confused with, O'Derry. MIF Map Derry.

(O) Deevy *Ó Dubhuidhe** or *Ó Duibhidhe.* These are also anglicized Devoy. One of the 'Seven Septs of Leix' now mainly found in Cos.

---

*The majority of names beginning with *Dubh* or *Duibh* in Irish are derived from the adjective *dubh,* black; the second part of such names is usually speculative being often obsolete forenames. Similarly those beginning with *Donn* and *Duinn* are mainly from *donn,* brown.

Kilkenny and Leix. The form Devoy is rather more numerous but less confined to its original homeland. MIF

Deey This name is now very rare but in the eighteenth century it was well known in Dublin and also in Mayo. I have yet to ascertain its origin. Bibl.

(O) Deffely See Devilly.

(O) Degidan *Ó Duibhgeadáin.** A rare east Clare name. I do not think that Woulfe's statement that it has been changed to Dixon is correct, though of course a single instance of this may have occurred.

Deheny A variant of Doheny.

Deighan Used as a synonym of both Deegan and Diggin. In Oriel it is *Ó Díochon*, see Deehan. In Antrim it has been changed to Dickson.

Deignan See Duigenan.

Delacour See Deloughery.

(O) Delahunt(y) *Ó Dulchaointigh* (*dulchaointeach*, plaintive, satirist). This has several variants, e.g. Dulanty. It is the name of an important sept in Ely O'Carroll. MIF   Map Offaly.

Delahyde An Anglo-Norman family which came to Ireland in the thirteenth century. Map Dublin. See Hyde and Skinnion.

Delamer (from La Mare in France). The name of a distinguished Westmeath family of Norman origin; now rare. The chiefs of the family assumed the patronymic MacHerbert. Bibl.

Delane *Ó Dalláin* (the basic word is *dall*, blind). Sometimes used as an abbreviated form of Delaney. See Dallon.

(O) Delaney *Ó Dubhshláine** (*dubh*, black—*Sláine*, perhaps the river Slaney). The prefix O has been almost completely discarded in the anglicized form of the name. It appears as Delane in Mayo. Both now and in the past it is of Leix and Kilkenny. IF   Map Leix. See Doolady.

Delap See Lappin.

(O) Delargy *Ó Duibhlearga** (*learga* is more likely to be from *learg*, plain or slope, than a place-name). This sept migrated from Mayo to Antrim where they had become well established before mid-seventeenth century. MIF

Delea, Delay See Dunlea.

Delmege A Palatine name, formerly Dolmage, prominent in Co. Limerick.

Deloughery *Ó Dubhluachra* (another case of *dubh*, black, with a place-name). This is fairly numerous in Co. Cork where it is found under nine different spellings such as Deloorey and Dilloughery, as well as its synonym Dilworth. The use of the form de Loughry is an attempt to make a native Irish name appear to be Norman.

*See footnote on p. 77.

(O) Dempsey *Ó Diomasaigh* (*diomasach*, proud). A powerful sept in Clanmalier. O'Dempsey was one of the very few chiefs who defeated Strongbow in a military engagement. Many of his successors distinguished themselves as Irish patriots and they were ruined as a result of their loyalty to James II. The name is now numerous in all the provinces. IF   Map Leix-Offaly.

Dempster Derived from the Manx word for a judge this name, numerous in Co. Down, is occasionally used as a synonym of Dempsey.

Denham Bibl.

Denieffe On record in Co. Kilkenny since the eighteenth century, fairly numerous in the nineteenth, now rare; sometimes abbreviated there to Neef. Reaney says it is derived from an Old-English personal name.

(O) Denihan A variant of Deenihan.

Denivan See Dingevan.

Denn This name is found in Cos. Waterford and Kilkenny. See de Denne under Deane.

(O) Dennan(y), Denneny *Ó Doineannaigh* (*doineannach*, tempestuous). This name, now rare, has always been associated with Cavan and adjoining counties.

(O) Dennehy *Ó Duineacha*. Woulfe's derivation from *duineachaidh*, pure, is not accepted by Irish scholars. Numerous in Cos. Cork and Kerry, rare elsewhere. Bibl. MIF   See Denny.

Dennery A rare name belonging to Cos. Mayo and Roscommon.

Dennigan, Denegan Connacht variants of Donegan.

Denning An occasional variant of Dinneen.

Dennis A scattered name of various origins, viz. Old-French *le Danei* (the Dane); from the French Christian name derived from Dionysius; or a semi-translation of MacDonagh (as the latter it is more often Dennison); and, finally the rare *Ó Donnghusa* is also anglicized similarly. Neither is numerous. Dennis is mainly found in Dublin and Cork, Dennison in Ulster.

Dennison See previous entry.

Denny A leading family of this name (which is cognate with Dennis) came from England in the sixteenth century and became prominent in Co. Derry. It has been used in Kerry for Dennehy. Bibl. MIF

(O) Denroche *Ó Duibhinnreachtaigh** (*innreachtach*, lawful). A rare Connacht name, also called Dunroche.

Denvir Traditionally descended from the Norman D'Anver of Norfolk. Irish Denvirs mainly belong to Co. Down. MIF

Derenzy Formerly de Renzi. Associated with Cos. Wexford and Dublin since early seventeenth century.

Dergan An occasional variant of Dargan.

*See footnote on p. 77.

Derham See Durham.

(O) Derivan See Dervan.

(O) Dermody, Darmody *Ó Diarmada.* A fairly numerous but scattered name mainly in Cos. Cavan, Westmeath, Kilkenny and Galway; in the latter though spelt Dermody it is pronounced Darmody.

(O) Dermond *Ó Duibhdhiorma (dubhdhiorma,* black troop). Often changed to MacDermot and occasionally to Darby in its homeland, Donegal and Derry. MIF Map Donegal.

Mac Dermot *Mac Diarmada.* There are three branches of this very important sept, all in Connacht. The Chief of the principal branch of Moylurg (Co. Roscommon) is styled Prince of Coolavin. The head of the other branch is MacDermot Roe (*ruadh,* red). IF Map Roscommon.

(O) Derrane See Dirrane.

Derrick An English name of Dutch origin, seldom a variant of Derrig.

(O) Derrig *Ó Deirg (dearg,* red). A family of the Uí Fiachrach. Map Mayo.

(O) Derry *Ó Doirighe.* An erenagh family in the diocese of Raphoe, distinct from Deery though the two are often confused. MIF Map Donegal.

(O) Dervan, Derwin Usually called *Ó Doirbheáin* or *Ó Doirbhín* in Irish: the form *Ó Dearbháin* (from *dearbh,* certain) is preferable. This name is now rare but is still found in Co. Roscommon and adjacent areas. MIF

(O) Desmond *Ó Deasmhumhnaigh* (descendant of the Desmond man—*deas,* south—*Mumhan,* Munster). This sept migrated from west to east Cork. It is now very numerous throughout the county and the great majority of families so named are of that origin. It is possible that some may be descended from a junior branch of the Fitzgeralds of Desmond. MIF

(O) Devally A variant of Devilly in south Galway. This is now pronounced De-valley but the emphasis should properly be on the first syllable as in Devilly. MIF

Devane See Dwane.

(O) Devanny *Ó Duibheannaigh.* Mainly found in Donegal and adjacent areas of Connacht. Also *Ó Duibheamhna* in Oriel, derived from *dubh,* black—*Eamhain,* the place in Co. Armagh. Much confusion arises between Devany, Diviney and Devane. MIF

(O) Deveen A variant of Davin in Co. Tipperary; also used for Devine.

(O) Deven, Devon Variants in Co. Louth of Devin.

Devenish An Old-English surname denoting Devonshire origin, on record in Ireland since the fourteenth century. It is confused with Devereux in Co. Wexford. Bibl.

(O) Devenny A variant of Devanny.

(Mac) Dever See Diver.

Devereux *Dearbhrús*. Originally this name was *d'Evreux*: it is that of one of the most powerful of the Anglo-Norman families in Co. Wexford. Bibl. MIF   Map Wexford. See next entry.

Deverill, Devery Used as synonyms of Devereux in Cos. Leix and Offaly.

(O) Devilly *Ó Duibhghiolla* (*dubh*, black—*giolla*, lad). The name of two Co. Galway septs. That of the southern Uí Fiachra is usually placed in the south-west of the county at Kinvarra; and the other, Síol Anmchadha, in the south-east. Local authorities, however, place the latter nearer to the Co. Mayo border. MIF

(O) Devine The Irish form, according to O'Donovan, is *Ó Daimhín* (see Davin). In Co. Louth it became Devin, which in Co. Tipperary is a synonym of Davin. IF   See Divine and Devin; and p. 304.

(O) Devinney A variant of Devany.

(Mac) Devitt See MacDaid.

(O) Devlin *Ó Doibhilin*. Of Munterdevlin: a leading Ulster sept. There was also a distinct sept in Co. Sligo, but there the name has strangely often become Dolan. Bibl. IF   Map Tyrone.

Devon One of the many variants of Devine.

Devonport See Davenport.

(O) Devoy See Deevey. Map Leix.

Dexter Bibl.

(O) Deyermott See Dermond.

(O) Diamond, Dimon(d) *Ó Diamáin*. An erenagh family in east Derry. The name is now found also in Donegal and north Connacht. Map Derry.

Diarmod See Dermond.

Dick This is simply the pet form of Richard used as a surname; it was introduced from Scotland in the seventeenth century and is now fairly numerous in Antrim and Down. Dix is a synonym.

Dickey App.

Dickson, Dixon One of the more numerous English names in Ireland. See Deehan and Deighan. Bibl.

(O) Diffin A variant of Duffin in Tyrone and Armagh.

(O) Diffley, Duffley Variants of Devilly.

(O) Diffney A variant of Diviney.

(O) Digan A variant of Deegan.

(Mac) Digany, Digney *Mac an Deagánaigh*. See Deane.

(O) Diggin *Ó Duibhginn* (*dubh*, black—*ceann*, head). The Kerry form of the name elsewhere called Duigan and Deegan, but it is not used synonymously with them.

(O) Dignam, Dignan See Duigenan.

(O) Dilgan A rare west Clare name. Woulfe suggests *Ó Duibhleacháin*, cognate with Dullahan.

Dill This English name was in Donegal in the first half of the seventeenth century and is still found there. Bibl.

(O) Dillahan A variant of Dullahan.

(O) Dillane *Ó Duilleáin*. A Co. Limerick and north Kerry name, sometimes disguised as Dillon. It is a variant of Delane.

(O) Dilleen *Ó Duillín*. A variant of the foregoing in Clare and south Galway.

Dillon *Diolún*. A Hiberno-Norman family which has three branches (as Map). It has always been prominent in Irish history. Bibl. IF Map Meath, Westmeath and Roscommon. See Dillane.

Dilworth, Dilloghery See Deloughery.

Dimond See Diamond.

(O) Dinahan Map Limerick. See Deenihan.

(O) Dinan, Dynan *Ó Daghnáin*. Now chiefly Cos. Clare and Cork. Quite distinct from Dinneen though in Cork Dynan has sometimes been changed to Dinneen. MIF Map Tipperary.

(O) Dingevan, Dinnevan *Ó Dinneabháin*. A south Munster name sometimes changed by attraction to Donovan with which it is etymologically cognate. See also Ginnevan.

(O) Dinkin *Ó Duinnchinn* (brown head). A north Connacht name which has now been much changed to Duncan.

(O) Dinneen *Ó Duinnín*. The personal name Donn from which this is formed is from *donn*, brown. A family famous as poets and historians. IF   MIF   Map Cork.

(O) Dinnegan *Ó Duinnegáin*. A variant of Donegan found in Co. Longford.

Dinsmore This is a variant of the old Scottish (Fifeshire) toponymic Dunsmore used in Ireland. It is mainly located in Cos. Derry and Donegal.

(O) Dirrane, Derrane *Ó Dearáin*. Almost exclusively of Co. Galway. Map Galway.

(O) Dirreen *Ó Dirín*. A rare Co. Kilkenny name, possibly a variant of the foregoing.

(O) Diskin *Ó Díscin*. Originally of Ballydiscin, Co. Sligo, now mainly south Connacht. Woulfe suggests that the name is derived from *díosc*, barren.

Disney Derived from a French place-name and originally written D'Isigny etc., the name Disney occurs quite frequently in the records of several Irish counties in the south and midlands since the first half of the seventeenth century. MIF

Divane See Dwane.

Diver *Ó Duibhidhir** (sometimes with *Mac* prefix). The name of a well-

---

*See footnote on p. 77.

known Tirconnell sept, sometimes elided as Deere. Diver is peculiar to Donegal, it has become (Mac) Dever in Mayo. Map Donegal. See MacDyer.

(O) Divilly See Devilly.

(O) Divine, Diveen This name is sometimes *Ó Duibhín* of Tyrone-Derry. Elsewhere it is indistinguishable from Devine.

(O) Diviney, Divenny *Ó Duibheanaigh*. A Mayo name. Like most names beginning with Div this is derived from *dubh,* black. Woulfe suggests that its second part is a place-name, *Eanach*. It is cognate if not identical with Devanny. MIF

Dix This name has been well known in Dublin since mid-seventeenth century. It is a variant of Dick. It is of interest to note that some Irishmen of the name in France were called d'Aix.

Dixon Bibl. See Dickson.

Doag, Doak Ulster forms of Davock.

Doane A variant of Duane.

Dobbin *Doibín*. (Dob is an old English diminutive of Robert). Families of the name were associated with Co. Kilkenny and the city of Waterford from the fourteenth century. The name has also been continuously in Co. Antrim, the families in question being unrelated. It is now much more numerous in Ulster than in the south. Bibl. MIF

Dobbs This is one of the few English families which settled in Ulster as early as the sixteenth century. They have since been associated with Co. Antrim where their home is called Castledobbs. Dobb is an old pet form of Robert.

Dobson This English name is fairly numerous in Co. Leitrim.

(Mac) Dockery The original form, *Mac Dháil Ré Dochair,* of this east Connacht name was corrupted to *Mac Giolla Deachair,* thus giving rise to the use of Harden as a synonym (*deacair,* hard). In modern times the Gaelic form is *Ó Dochraigh* which is very far from the original. The MacDockerys were one of the septs attached to the O'Connors in a military capacity. In Ireland Dockery has no connection with the English toponymic Dockray. MIF   Map Roscommon.

Dockrell The origin of this Dublin name has not been determined. It is improbable that it is the modern form of the historic Dockwra because it first appears as Dogerell. It came to Ireland from Wiltshire in the second half of the seventeenth century.

Dodd This is the name of an ancient English (Shropshire) family settled in Co. Sligo in the late sixteenth century. It is now scattered, though mainly found in Cos. Armagh and Down. Occasionally Dodd is a corrupt synonym of Dowd in Ulster.

Dodwell Bibl.

Doey, Dooey Variants of Duffy in north-east Ulster.

Doggett Established in Leinster since 13th century.

(O) Doheny *Ó Dubhchonna.** A sept of the Corca Laoidhe. It spread to east Munster where the name has been sometimes made to look English by changing it to Dawney. MIF   Map Cork.

(O) Doherty *Ó Dochartaigh* (*dochartach*, hurtful). The leading sept of Inishowen. Doherty is now one of the most numerous names in Ireland, it is still mainly found in Ulster. Bibl. IF   Map Donegal. See Doorty and Dorrity.

Doig Seldom a variant of Doak. See under Doog.

(O) Dolan The generally accepted form in Irish today is *Ó Dúbhláin* (mod. *Ó Dúláin*) as given by Woulfe and others. I have little doubt that in the first edition of this work I was wrong to accept that and its supposed derivation. In fact O'Doelan, later Dolan, derives from *Ó Dobhailen*, the name of a family on record since the twelfth century in the baronies of Clonmacnowen, Co. Galway, and Athlone, Co. Roscommon, in the heart of the Uí Maine country and quite distinct from *Ó Doibhilin* (Devlin). There has been a movement north-eastwards so that now the name Dolan is numerous in Cos. Leitrim, Fermanagh and Cavan as well as in Cos. Galway and Roscommon.

Dolier Formerly D'Olier. This Huguenot name was formerly well known in Dublin but has now become very rare.

(O) Dollaghan See Dolohan.

(O) Dollagher See Dallagher.

Dollard, Dullard A descriptive name in Co. Dublin since the thirteenth century.

(O) Dolly *Ó Dathlaoich* (*laoch*, hero or champion—*dath*, swift). This name is still around Galway city. The sept was once of some importance in Connemara.

(O) Dolohan A variant of Dullaghan and of Dallaghan.

Dolohunty A variant of Delahunty.

Dolphin *Doilfin*. Of Norse origin this family came to Connacht from England at the time of the Anglo-Norman invasion settling in Co. Galway where they became completely hibernicized, with a chief of the name as in the leading Irish septs. MIF

(O) Domegan *Ó Domagáin* (*doma*, poor). A rare east Leinster name. The form Dumigan occurs in Co. Down.

Domville An old Cheshire family very prominent in Dublin in the 17th and 18th centuries. The name is now rare.

Mac Donagh *Mac Donnchadha* (son of Donagh). A branch of the MacDermots of Connacht where the name is very numerous. In Connemara the name is usually that of a branch of the O'Flahertys. The MacDonagh sept in Co. Cork were a branch of the MacCarthys: the name is now rare there and apparently many of these resumed the name MacCarthy. Bibl. IF   Map Sligo.

*See footnote on p. 77.

(O) Donagher A Co. Roscommon variant of Danagher.

(Mac) Donaghy *Mac Donnchaidh.* A variant in Tyrone and Derry of MacDonagh.

Mac Donald The name of a Scottish clan. Sometimes a synonym of the Irish MacDonnell. Bibl.

Donaldson See Donnellson.

(O) Donarty *Ó Donndubhartaigh** (*dubhartach,* aggressive). A south Tipperary family who have widely adopted Dunworth and even Davenport as synonyms. Map Tipperary.

Dondon, Dundon *Dondún.* Anglo-Norman *de Auno,* to be equated with Dawnay in England. The family settled in Co. Limerick in the thirteenth century.

(O) Donegan, Dunnigan *Ó Donnagáin.** The name of several unrelated septs. In addition to the Co. Cork sept shown in the Map, which was important until subdued by the Barrys, there was another, an erenagh family, in the south-west; the north Tipperary sept is scattered, while that of Co. Monaghan is now indistinguishable from MacDonegan. In the seventeenth century the name was also numerous in Cos. Roscommon and Westmeath. Dunnigan is sometimes used as a synonym of the Offaly name Dunican *(Ó Duinacháin).* MIF   Map Cork and Tipperary. See Dongan.

Doney As occasional variant of Downey.

Dongan Of dual origin: an English family long settled in Co. Kildare and Dublin; also for MacDonegan, i.e. *Mac Donnagáin* of Co. Down which also became Cunningham. Map Down. See Donegan.

(O) Donlan See Donnellan.

(Mac) Donlevy See Dunlevy.

(O) Donly A variant of Donnelly.

(O) Donnan *Ó Donnáin.* This name belongs to Co. Down, but is often confused with Doonan. The Donnans of Donnanstown, Co. Cork, were of Norman origin.

Mac Donnell *Mac Domhnaill.* Of three distinct origins: (a) a galloglass family of the Glens of Antrim; (b) a native sept of Thomond; and (c) a west Ulster sept. Bibl. IF   MIF   Map Antrim, Clare and Fermanagh. See MacConnell.

O'Donnell *Ó Domhnaill.* The main sept, one of the most famous in Irish history, especially in the seventeenth century, is of Tirconnell; another is of Thomond and a third of the Uí Maine. Bibl. IF
Map Clare, Donegal and Galway.

(O) Donnellan *Ó Domhnalláin* (diminutive of *Domhnall,* Donnell). K. Nicholls in his Survey of Uí Maine shows that the O'Donnellans, though later settled in that territory, were from the eleventh century a

*See footnote on p. 77.

notable bardic family seated at Ross-O'Donelan, near Elphin. Minor septs were in Tyrone and Offaly. IF   Map Galway.

Donnellson App.

(O) Donnelly *Ó Donnghaile* (*donn*, brown—*gal*, valour). A Cenél Eoghain sept of Ballydonnelly, akin to the O'Neills. IF 122; Map Tyrone.

(O) Donoghue, Donohoe *Ó Donnchadha*. An important sept in Desmond: they were driven from their original habitat in Co. Cork to Co. Kerry where their name was perpetuated in the territory called Onaght O'Donoghue. There are also two others in Co. Galway and Co. Cavan where the spelling Donohoe is usual. According to Dr. John Ryan there was another O'Donoghue sept in Co. Tipperary of Eoghanacht descent. For derivation see MacDonagh. IF   Map Kerry and Cavan.

Mac Donough See MacDonagh.

(O) Donovan *Ó Donnabháin*.* Originally of Co. Limerick, they became a leading sept in south-west Cork. A branch settled in Co. Kilkenny, of which was Dr. John O'Donovan, to whom we owe so much on the subject of Irish names and families. IF   Map Cork.

Donworth See Donarty.

(O) Doocey See Ducey.

(O) Doody A synonym, in Kerry, of O'Dowd.

(O) Dooey, Doey Variants of Duffy in north-east Ulster.

(O) Doogan See Duggan.

Doog(ue) In Munster this is synonymous with Doohig; in Leinster with Doig, which Reaney states is derived from St. Cadoc.

(O) Doohan *Ó Duacháin*. Mainly found in Donegal; also in Co. Clare where it is probably a variant of Doughan. MIF

(O) Dooher, Dougher *Ó Dubhchair* (black dear). This rare name is mainly found in north Connacht and Donegal.

(O) Doohey A synonym in Donegal of Duffy.

(O) Doohig See Duhig.

(Mac) Dool A variant of MacDowell, in the north midlands.

(O) Doolady *Ó Dubhladaigh*.* A family of Co. Leitrim, where the name has been sometimes changed to Delany.

(O) Doolaghan A variant of Dullaghan.

(O) Doolaghty *Ó Dubhlachta*.* A Clare name.

(O) Doolan In Connacht this is *Ó Dubhlaing*: see Dowling. Doolan and Doolin are the anglicized forms of *Ó Dubhlainn* (*dubhshláin*, challenge) in Munster, which in Leinster is made Dowling. Doolan is also an occasional synonym of Dolan in Connacht. IF

(O) Doole A variant of Doyle used in north-east Ulster.

*See footnote on p. 77.

86

(O) Dooley *Ó Dubhlaoich* (*dubh,* black—*laoch,* hero or champion). Originally of Westmeath this sept later became important in the Ely O'Carroll country. IF   Map Offaly.

Dooling A Munster variant of Dowling.

Doona The agnomen of a branch of the O'Sullivans—*Ó Súileabháin an Dúna* (of the fort). It has usually become Downey in modern times.

(O) Doonan *Ó Dúnáin.* An erenagh family in Fermanagh; also found in Leitrim and Roscommon. Woulfe's equation of this name with Donnan is improbable, though they are sometimes used synonymously. SIF 56.

(O) Dooner *Ó Dúnabhra, Ó Donnabhair* (*donn,* brown—*abhra,* eyebrow), A rare name found in Roscommon and Leitrim, The Annals record several notable men of the name in the early mediaeval period.

(O) Dooney See Downey.

(O) Doonigan, Dunican *Ó Donnagáin,* sometimes written *Ó Dúnagáin.* Formerly one of the erenagh families of Galloon, Co. Fermanagh, now fairly numerous in the area between Athlone and Longford.

Doordan See Dordan.

(O) Doorey A variant of Durey. See Durr.

(O) Doorish *Ó Dubhruis,* earlier *Ó Dubhrosa* (*dubh,* black—*ros,* wood). The sept originated on the Fermanagh-Monaghan border, whence it spread to Co. Tyrone and in the other direction to north Longford. The supposed connection with Co. Limerick arose from O'Dures, the plural of O'Dure, an early anglicized form of *Ó Doghair,* now Dore.

(O) Doorley *Ó Dubhurthuille.** (Woulfe is my only authority for this Irish form). Nicholls says that *Ó Dubhurla* occurs in fifteenth-century Papal Registers). A sept of the Uí Maine. Another of Corca Laoidhe is almost extinct. MIF   Map Galway and Offaly.

(O) Doorty *Ó Dubhartaigh.** A co-arb family in Co. Tipperary, correctly anglicized as Doorty in Clare; often made Doherty in Co. Cork.

(O) Doran, Dorran *Ó Deoráin.* One of the 'Seven Septs of Leix', and the great brehon family of Leinster. The earlier form was *Ó Deoradháin,* the word denoting exiled person. IF   Map Leix and Westmeath.

(O) Dorcey See Darcy. Map Mayo.

(Mac) Dordan, Doordan *Mac Dubhradáin* (*dubhradán,* pigmy). Essentially a Mayo name.

(O) Dore Dore is *Ó Doghair* and also *de Hóir* (of Norman origin) in Co. Limerick, but elsewhere may be from the French Doré. MIF   See Durr and Doorish.

(O) Dorgan See under Dargan.

Dorian See Adorian.

(O) Doris A variant of Doorish.

*See footnote on p. 77.

Dorman An English name (meaning dear man, friend) established in Co. Cork in the seventeenth century, but now mainly Co. Down; sometimes used as a variant of Dornan.

Dormer An English name of French origin associated with Co. Wexford since the sixteenth century. Dormer has also been used as an anglicized form of *Ó Duibhdhiorma*—See Dermond. Bibl. MIF

(O) Dornan *Ó Dornáin*. The east Ulster form of Durnin. MIF

(O) Dorney Woulfe makes this Cork and Tipperary name *Ó Doirinne* deriving it from the non-existent word *doireann*, sullen. It takes the form Durney in east Munster. MIF See Torney.

(O) Dorohy *Ó Dorchadha* (*dorcha*, dark). This name is almost peculiar to the Kenmare area of Co. Kerry. Dorothy is said to be a variant but this is not found in Co. Kerry. MIF

Dorragh A west Ulster variant of Darragh.

Dorran See Doran.

Dorr See Durr.

(O) Dorrian, Durrian, Durran Co. Down variants of Doran. MIF

(O) Dorrigan An occasional variant of Dorgan in Co. Cork.

Dorrity A corrupt form of Doherty found in Oriel.

(O) Dougan See Duggan.

(O) Doughan *Ó Dubhchon** (*dubh*, black—*con*, hound). Originally a Corca Laoidhe sept, it settled later in north Tipperary and Offaly. MIF

(O) Dougher See Dooher.

(O) Dougherty See Doherty.

Doughty An English adjectival name associated with Dublin since mid-seventeenth century.

Douglas *Dubhghlas*. The name of a well-known Scottish clan very numerous in Ulster.

Doupe A rare Palatine name in Cos. Limerick and Clare.

Dovany See Devany.

Dove See Dow.

Dow This Scottish name, found in Ulster, is that of a branch of the Scottish clan Buchanan and is used synonymously with MacCalman, whence obliquely Dove (*colm*, dove). In Scotland Dow and Dove are also from the adjective *dubh*, black.

O Dowd(a) *Ó Dubhda.** A leading sept of the northern Uí Fiachrach. A branch settled in Kerry where they are called Doody. Another small sept of *Ó Dubhda* was in Co. Derry and they are usually Duddy now. Bibl. IF   MIF   Map Sligo. See Dodd.

Dowdall *Dubhdal*. This family has been prominent in the Pale since the Anglo-Norman invasion. The name is from Dovedale, an English

*See footnote on p. 77.

place-name. In this case the *dubh* is not from the adjective meaning black, but see Dudley.

(O) Dowdican, Dudican *Ó Dubhdacáin.** This name belongs almost exclusively to Cos. Sligo and Donegal. It is cognate with O'Dowd.

Dowdie, Dowds Often used in Ulster for O'Dowd.

Mac Dowell *Mac Dubhghaill* (*dubh*, black—*gall*, foreigner). This is the Irish form of the name of the Scottish family of MacDugall which came from the Hebrides as galloglasses, and settled in Co. Roscommon where Lismacdowell locates them. It is now mainly found in north Ulster, largely due to more recent immigration. MIF   Map Roscommon.

Dower A variant of Dore in east Cork and Co. Waterford.

(O) Dowey A synonym of Duffy in Ulster.

Dowland A Palatine name distinct from Dowlane.

(O) Dowlane Though this was a distinct name in Co. Down in the sixteenth century, it now stands for Dowling in Co. Carlow and for Doolan in Co. Longford.

(O) Dowler A north Connacht variant of Dollagher.

(O) Dowley A variant of Dooley.

(O) Dowling *Ó Dúnlaing.* One of the 'Seven Septs of Leix'. Their territory beside the river Barrow was known as *Fearrann ua nDúnlaing*, i.e. O'Dowlings country. A leading branch was transplanted to Co. Kerry. They are now numerous throughout south Leinster. Bibl. IF Map Leix. See Doolan.

Dowman Bibl.

Downer Probably a variant of Dooner.

Downes One of the several forms of *Ó Dubháin*, found in Clare and Limerick. MIF   See Dwane.

Downey This abbreviated form is sometimes used for Muldowney and for MacEldowney as well as O'Downey. See Doona.

(O) Downey *Ó Dúnadhaigh* (the basic word is *dún*, fort). The larger of the two septs so called is of west Munster where it is often made Downing; the other of the Síol Anmchadha. Bibl. IF   Map Galway and Kerry.

(O) Downing *Ó Dúinín*. Though Downing is a well-known English name, in Ireland it is usually a Kerry variant of *Ó Duinnín*—Dinneen. Bibl. See Downey.

Dowse Derived from French *douce*, sweet, this name is in Dublin and adjacent counties since the early fourteenth century. Bibl. MIF

(O) Doyle *Ó Dubhghaill* (for derivation see MacDowell). This is one of the most numerous names in Leinster. The main sept is of Norse origin, well established before the Anglo-Norman invasion. IF Map Wexford. In Co. Roscommon Doyle is found as a synonym of MacDowell.

*See footnote on p. 77.

(O) Doyne   The old form of Dunne.

(O) Draddy   *Ó Dreada*. Almost exclusively a Co. Cork name, but occasionally a synonym of Drudy (*Ó Draoda*) in Connacht. MIF

(O) Draffin   *Ó Druifin*. A rare name mainly found in Cos. Monaghan and Cavan.

Drain   See Adrain.

Drake   This name is derived from an Old-English word meaning dragon. The Drakes of Drakestown, Co. Wexford, are Cromwellian, but those of Drakerath and Drakestown, Co. Meath are there since the thirteenth century. Bibl. MIF

Draper   One of the few Anglo-Irish names dating from the seventeenth century which is not numerous now in Ulster, though its early connection with that province is perpetuated in the Co. Derry place-name Draperstown. It has since been associated with west Cork.

Draycott   Bibl.

(O) Drea   See Drew.

(O) Drean   See Adrain.

Dreelan   A south Leinster name, possibly a variant of the English Dreeland. Nicholls, however, suggests that the use of *An Drithleánach* for the Norman name *de Druhull,* prominent in Co. Kilkenny, in the fifteenth and sixteenth centuries, points to that as its origin. Dreiling is listed as a principal name in Co. Kilkenny in the 'census' of 1659.

(O) Drennan   *Ó Draighneán* (*draighneán*—blackthorn). In Connacht, where the sept originated, it has been frequently changed to Thornton by semi-translation. MIF   Map Galway.

Drew   Usually of English origin, even in Clare where *Ó Draoi,* anglicized Drew, is also a native family of Thomond. For derivation see Drury. Drea is another anglicized form of it. Bibl. MIF   See Drury and Drough.

Drewry   See Drury.

(O) Drinan   A Co. Cork variant of Drennan.

Dring   A well-known landed family in Co. Cork since mid-seventeenth century. The name is derived from *dreng,* an Old-English word denoting free tenant.

(O) Driscoll   *Ó hEidersceoil* (*eidirsceol,* intermediary); the later form is *Ó Drisceoil*. One of the principal Corca Laoidhe septs. The name is very numerous in Co. Cork but not elsewhere. Bibl. IF   MIF Map Cork.

(O) Drislane   *Ó Drisleáin*. A rare Co. Cork name derived from *dris,* briar.

(O) Dro(g)han   *Ó Druacháin*. This name is originally of Co. Cork; it is now well known in Cos. Waterford, south Kilkenny and to some extent in Co. Wexford. MIF

Dromey   A variant of Drummy.

Dromgoole, Dromgould See Drumgoole.

(O) Droney, Drooney *Ó Dróna.* This name, well known in east Clare, is rarely found elsewhere.

(O) Droody, Drudy *Ó Draoda.* A Connacht name which in Mayo and Roscommon has often been changed to Drury. See also Draddy.

(O) Droogan, Drugan *Ó Druagáin.* An ancient Co. Armagh family quite distinct from Droohan and Druhan. It is found as far west as Co. Leitrim but is nowhere numerous.

Drough, Drugh These forms are found in Westmeath and Roscommon as synonyms both of Drought and Drew.

(O) Drought This name has several origins. Apart from supposed immigrants from Holland etc. and confusion with Drew, it is definitely an anglicization of two Irish names, *Ó Drochtaigh* of Leinster, and *Ó Droichid* (from *droichead,* bridge) of Limerick and Clare, now usually made Bridgeman. MIF 92. See p. 304 for Bridgeman in Co. Clare.

(O) Drudy See Droody.

(O) Druhan, Droohan Variants of Drohan.

(O) Drum(m) *Ó Droma* (*drom,* ridge). An erenagh family of Kinawley on the Cavan-Fermanagh border, where the name has to some extent been corrupted to the Scottish Drummond. A branch migrated to Co. Cork, where they are called Drummy. MIF Map Cavan.

Drumgoole, Drumgold There are several other variant spellings. This is one of the few Irish toponymics, being taken from *Dromgabhail* in Co. Louth whence the modern name Drumgoolestown. The family were prominent as Jacobites. MIF

Drummy, Drummond See Drum.

Drury *Mac an Druaidh.* This Irish form is erroneously anglicized Drew(e)ry in Cavan, Drury in Roscommon and more correctly Drew in Louth and Monaghan. Drewry or Drury is also an English name derived from an old French word meaning sweetheart. *Druadh* and *draoi* both mean druid. See Droody.

(O) Drynan See Drinan.

Duan(e) See Dwane.

(O) Duany A variant of Devany.

(O) Duarty See Doorty.

(O) Ducey, Doocey *Ó Dubhghusa* (*dubh,* black—*gus,* action). An east Munster name. See footnote on page 77.

Duck A far-fetched synonym of Lohan supposedly from Irish *lacha,* duck.

(O) Duddy See O'Dowd.

Dudgeon A diminutive of Dodge, in west Ulster since 1689; later mainly associated with Co. Monaghan.

(O) Dudican See Dowdican.

Dudley Usually of English toponymic origin; according to Woulfe it is sometimes *Ó Dubhdáleithe* (*dá*, two—*léithe*, sides) in Co. Cork, which has also been anglicized Dowdall.

Duff As well as being a surname of the epithet type (*dubh*, black) Duff occurs as an abbreviated form of Duffin in Co. Wexford, of Mac-Elduff in Co. Tyrone, and of Duffy in several counties. MIF See Black.

Mac Duff The name of a Scottish clan found in Ulster.

(O) Dufferley A Roscommon variant of Doorley.

(O) Dufficey The Connacht form of *Ó Dubhghusa*, see Ducey.

(O) Duffin *Ó Duibhinn*, earlier *Ó Duibhghinn** (perhaps *dubh* and *ceann*, head). Though found in Munster in mediaeval times and still in Co. Waterford, Duffin has been mainly found in east Ulster and Louth. MIF

(O) Duffley See Diffley.

(O) Duffy *Ó Dubhthaigh.** A numerous name in all the provinces except Munster. Modern statistics show that it is now the most numerous name in Co. Monaghan. Bibl. IF   Map Donegal, Monaghan and Roscommon. See Duhig.

(O) Dug(g)an *Ó Dubhagáin.** The principal septs of this name are two in Munster and two in Connacht as Map. In the west it is pronounced Doogan. This spelling is used in Donegal, Dougan in east Ulster. I cannot say whether these represent a distinct sept or a branch of one of those referred to above. IF   Map Cork, Galway and Mayo.

(O) Dugidan A variant of Degidan.

(O) Duhig, Doohig The south Munster form of *Ó Dubhthaigh* elsewhere called Duffy.

(O) Duigan See Deegan.

(O) Duig(e)nan *Ó Duibhgeannáin* (for possible derivation see Duffin). Located in east Connacht this was one of the principal learned families of Gaelic Ireland. The branch which moved eastward into Westmeath, Longford and Cavan use the variant forms Deignan, Dignam, etc. Bibl. MIF   Map Roscommon.

Duke Usually from the French *duc* (leader); occasionally an abbreviation of Marmaduke. Some are in Ireland since the sixteenth century, others are Cromwellian immigrants; the name is now scattered, being mainly found in north-east Ulster and also to some extent in north Connacht.

Dulanty, Dulhunty Bibl. See Delahunty.

(O) Dullaghan *Ó Dubhlacháin.** An Oriel name mainly found in Co. Louth.

Dullea See Dunlea.

*See footnote on p. 77.

Dullard See Dollard.

(O) Dumigan See Domigan.

Dunbar The name of a Scottish clan which came to Ireland early in the seventeenth century and has since been mainly associated with Cos. Fermanagh and Donegal. At least one branch was identified with the Catholic and Irish cause from the time of James II. Dunbar is a toponymic.

Duncan A Scottish name sometimes used in Ireland as a synonym of Donegan. See Dinkin.

Dundas The name of a Scottish clan found in Cos. Leitrim and Fermanagh.

Dundon See Dondon.

Dunford, Dunfort Co. Waterford synonyms of Donarty.

Dungan See Dongan.

Dunican, Dunigan See Donegan.

Dunkin See Dinkin.

(O) Dunlea Woulfe gives *Ó Duinnshléibhe** for this and treats the family as a branch of the famous MacDunlevys of Ulster. This statement cannot be accepted without definite evidence, as Dunlea and its variants Dullea and Delea are essentially and almost exclusively west Cork names. MIF See Dunlevy.

(Mac) Dunlevy *Mac Duinnshléibhe** (*sliabh*, mountain). A royal family of Ulidia till the twelfth century. Thence they migrated to Tirconnell under the O'Donnells and followed those who went to north Connacht in 1602. A branch went to Scotland, where they became Dunlop and Dunlief. The prefix O is sometimes used instead of the more correct Mac. Bibl. IF   Map Donegal and Down.

Dunlop, Dunlief See Lappin and Dunlevy.

(O) Dunn(e) *Ó Duinn* or *Ó Doinn*.* Usually spelt with the final E. One of the most numerous names in the midland counties. Formerly called O'Doyne (lords of Iregan). Bibl. IF   Map Leix.

(O) Dunnigan See Donegan.

Dunning This English name, found around Athlone, is sometimes used as a synonym of Downing. It is also a Scottish toponymic.

Dunnion A Donegal variant of Downing.

Dunny A variant of Downey in the midland counties.

(Mac) Dunphy *Mac Donnchaidh*. Cognate with MacDonagh. This is quite distinct from (O) Dunphy.

(O) Dunphy, Dunfy *Ó Donnchaidh*. A small Ossory sept: though of the same name in Irish, unrelated to the O'Donoghues elsewhere. IF   Map Kilkenny.

Dunroche See Denroche.

*See footnote on p. 77.

Dunshea(th) In Cos. Tyrone and Antrim since the seventeenth century. MIF

Dunwoody A Scottish toponymic found in Ulster. In Scotland Dinwoodie is the usual form.

Dunworth See Donarty.

(O) Durack *Ó Dubhraic*.* Woulfe's derivation from *rath,* prosperity, is improbable. An east Clare family, notable in Australia. Bibl; Map Clare.

Durham An English toponymic: the alternative form Derham is now the more usual. It is on record in Ireland since the fourteenth century, associated mainly with Dublin, Drogheda and Cork.

Duris, Duross Variants of Doorish in Tyrone.

(Mac) Durkan, Dorcan *Ó Duarcáin*, also *Mac Duarcáin* (pessimist). Sometimes anglicized as Gurkin. Numerous in north Connacht only. MIF 94; Map Sligo.

(O) Durley A variant of Doorley.

(O) Durnane A variant of Durnin in Co. Louth.

(O) Durney See Dorney.

(O) Durnin, Durnian *Ó Duirnín* (possibly from *dorn,* fist). Of Louth and east Ulster. Ballydurnian is in Co. Antrim, but Durnian is the more usual form in west Ulster. Durnan(e) and Durneen are variants. The English Durning is an occasional synonym. MIF

(O) Durr, Durry *Ó Doraidh*. A Leitrim and Roscommon name. Dore and Dorran occasionally used as variants. MIF See Dore.

(O) Durrian See Dorrian.

Duvick A rare synonym in Westmeath of Devereux.

(O) Dwane *Ó Dubháin*.* This is usually anglicized Dwane in west Munster (also Divane in Kerry), Downes in Thomond, Duane in Connacht and occasionally Devane. There were several septs of *Ó Dubháin*, the two of importance being of Corca Laoidhe and south Connacht. MIF 95.

(O) Dwyer *Ó Duibhir** (*dubh* and *odhar,* gen. *uidhir,* duncoloured). Of Kilnamanagh, a leading sept in mid-Tipperary. A great name in resistance to English domination. Bibl. IF Map Tipperary.

Dyer An English occupational name, but in Ireland mainly for MacDyer. See next entry.

Mac Dyer, -Dwyer *Mac Duibhir*. Though often written MacDwyer this Donegal name has no connection with O'Dwyer. Without the prefix Mac, Dyer is mainly found in Cos. Sligo and Roscommon. It is cognate with Diver. MIF

Dyermott A synonym of Dermond.

*See footnote on p. 77.

Dymond A variant of Diamond.

(O) Dynan See Dinan.

Dynes An English name of Old-French origin found in Co. Armagh and adjacent Ulster counties. Dyne, without the final S, is an occasional synonym of Doyne.

Dyra A Mayo name. I have not discovered its origin.

E

Eadie See Adams.

Eagar This is the spelling used by families in Kerry where they have been prominent since the mid-seventeenth century: Eager is found in north Louth and Down. Another English name, Agar, has been recorded as a synonym, but this family, which settled in Co. Kilkenny, is of different origin. Reaney states that both are derived from the name Edgar. Bibl. MIF

Eakin See Aiken.

Eames Derived from Middle-English *eme* (uncle), this name is fairly well known since mid-seventeenth century and is now in small numbers in all the provinces.

Earle, Earls These two names are quite distinct. The Earls family has been settled in Co. Galway since the thirteenth century; Earle, of much later introduction, is not closely associated with any particular area. It, like most names denoting titles, presumably began as a nickname. MIF

Early *Ó Maolmhoichéirghe* (*mochéirghe,* early rising) now shortened to *Ó Mochóirghe*. The name of an ecclesiastical family of Breffny. Occasionally a synonym of Loughran. The earlier alternative anglicized forms Mohery and Mulmoher are now rare. MIF Map Cavan, Leitrim. See Loughry. See p. 304.

Earner See Seery.

Eason Of dual origin in Ireland: one of the many anglicized forms of *Mac Aoidh* or the Scottish variant of Adamson.

Eastwood Though this English locative name is now almost exclusively found in Ulster earlier references to it in Irish records nearly all relate to Dublin and Louth. There are a number of them in the seventeenth century but it was not established in Ireland before that.

Eaton An English toponymic in Ireland since late sixteenth century; now fairly numerous in Ulster and Leinster but scattered.

Ebrill Probably, like Averill, this name is a variant of the French *Abrill*. It is associated with Cos. Limerick and Tipperary since mid-seventeenth century. It also came to Ulster at the time of the Plantation. MIF

Eccles App.

Mac Echern A variant of MacGahern.

Echlin A well-known Scottish family, a branch of which came to Co. Down early in the seventeenth century: twenty-six of the name are recorded as students of Dublin University, many of whom had distinguished careers. The name is taken from that of a territory in west Lothian. Bibl.

Eddery *Mac an Ridire* (*ridire,* knight). An Irish patronymic assumed by the Fitzsimons family of Co. Mayo.

Edgar App.

Edgeworth This famous family is in Co. Longford since 1583. Their name, which is an English toponymic, is perpetuated in Edgeworthstown (Meathus Truim). Bibl. IF

Edwards Bibl.

(Mac) Egan *Mac Aodhagáin* (son of Egan). An important brehon family originally of Uí Maine, settled in Ormond. The prefix Mac is now seldom retained with this name. Bibl. Map Galway and Tipperary. See Keegan.

Eivers See Ivers.

Elder This English name (denoting senior) though not of antiquity in Ireland is now fairly numerous in Ulster, being mainly associated with Cos. Derry and Donegal.

Mac Elderry* Woulfe gives *Mac Giolla Dorcha* (*dorcha,* dark) as the Irish form, which is probably correct. It is a well-known Tyrone name now numerous in Co. Antrim. MIF

Mac Eldowney *Mac Giolla Domhnaigh* (son of the devotee of the church). A Co. Derry name. (Mac) Gildowney is a variant in Co. Down where Muldowney is also used, but erroneously.

Mac Elduff See Kilduff.

Mac Eleavy A Co. Down variant of MacDunleavy.

Mac Elfatrick A variant of Gilpatrick.

Elgee Bibl.

Mac Elgunn See Gunn.

Mac Elhair *Mac Giolla Chathair* (devotee of St. Cathair). Variant forms are MacIlhair, MacIlcar and Kilcarr all found in Co. Donegal, where Carr is also often used synonymously with them.

Mac Elhargy See MacIlhagga.

Mac Elheron *Mac Giolla Chiaráin* (devotee of St. Kieran). Also spelt MacIlheron and MacLeheron. A small sept of east Ulster. MacElheron is also a branch of the Scottish clan MacDonald. The occasional use of Heron as an abbreviated form, as well as the variants MacIlheron and MacLeheron, indicate the correct pro-

---

*Almost all names beginning with MacEl- have also the alternative spelling MacIl-.

nunciation of MacElheron, in which the El is now wrongly stressed. MIF

Mac Elhill A form of *Mac Giolla Choille* found in Co. Tyrone. See MacIlhoyle and Woodman.

Mac Elhinney A synonym of Kilkenny peculiar to Cos. Derry and Donegal.

Mac Elholm See MacIlholm.

Mac Elhone *Mac Giolla Comhgháin*. Another rare name found mainly in Co. Tyrone.

Mac Elhoyle See MacIlhoyle.

Ellard This name, cognate with Aylward, is mainly found in Cos. Cork and Wexford.

Elliffe, Liffe Forms of the English name Ayliff (of Scandinavian origin) found in Westmeath.

Mac Elligott *Mac Uileagóid* is the current form in Irish. Four different theories as to the origin of this name have been put forward in the past (see MIF).   Another, perhaps the most probable, is that of the late Prof. E. Curtis for which Mr. K. W. Nicholls has recently found further evidence. It is that they were a Cambro-Norman family first called FitzElias. As such they were in Kerry from the middle of the thirteenth century. There are a number of indications suggesting this identification. The surname FitzElyoth, which appears in Kerry in 1455, would represent a transitional form and, of course, the tendency was for Fitz to be changed to Mac. The FitzElias family was associated with the same area as were the MacElligotts at a later date. MIF   Map Kerry.

Mac Ellin *Mac Ailín*. A small Co. Roscommon sept, distinct from the galloglass MacAllens.

Elliott Though occasionally occurring in mediaeval records, for the most part this name came to Ireland at the time of the Plantation of Ulster. It has since been mainly, though by no means exclusively, associated with Co. Cavan and Fermanagh, but in the nineteenth century it was numerous in Co. Leitrim also. As an English name it is cognate with Ellis.

Ellis This name, derived from the Old-English Christian name Ellis, or Elias, appears in Dublin as Elys in 1282 and occurs frequently in Irish records in every subsequent century; it has never been closely identified with any particular area and is now found mainly in Dublin and many parts of Ulster. Bibl.

Ellison English families of this name have settled in Ireland from time to time since the early seventeenth century up to recent times. I can find no evidence of the existence of the Irish form given by Woulfe except one isolated and very early instance in the 'Four Masters'. MIF

Mac Ellistrum *Mac Alastrum*. A Gaelic patronymic assumed by a Norman family in Co. Kerry, perhaps of Geraldine origin. MIF

Mac Elmeel *Mac Giolla Mhichil* (devotee of St. Michael). An Oriel name mainly found in Co. Monaghan. Distinct from MacElmoyle, which is *Mac Giolla Mhaoil* of Antrim and Derry. In surnames *maol* usually denotes tonsured but here may be simply bald. MIF

Elmore This is an English toponymic, but in Co. Louth, where it is on record since the seventeenth century, it is also found as a synonym of Gilmore. Elmer is a variant in the Dundalk area.

Mac Elmoyle See under MacElmeel.

Mac Elmurray *Mac Giolla Mhuire* (*Muire*, B.V. Mary). This name is mainly in Fermanagh and Tyrone where it is synonymous with Gilmore and sometimes abbreviated to Murray. Kilmary is a variant in Co. Derry.

Mac Elnay The Monaghan form of *Mac Giolla na Naomh* (*na naomh*, of the saints). This is corrupted to *Macgiollarnath* in Connacht and so mistranslated Ford. See also Gilnagh.

Mac Elreavy See MacIlravy.

Elrington Bibl.

Mac Elroy See Gilroy.

(Mac) Elshinder See Alexander.

Mac Elveen See MacIlveen.

Mac Elvenna, -Elvaney *Mac Giolla Mheana*. This name is mainly found in north Ulster.

Elvery This name, well known in Dublin but rare elsewhere, is probably synonymous with Alfrey (Old-English *Aelfrith*). For other possible origins see MIF

Mac Elvogue *Mac Giolla Mhaodhog* (devotee of St. Mogue). A Tyrone name.

Mac Elwain See MacIlwain.

Elward See under Elwood.

Mac Elwee *Mac Giolla Bhuidhe* (*buidhe*, yellow, *giolla* here means fellow or youth). MacGilloway is a variant of this Donegal–Derry name which is sometimes wrongly equated with MacEvoy. See also MacKelvey.

Elwood I can find no evidence to support Woulfe's statement that this is a synonym of Aylward, though Elward is. Reaney derives it from Old-English *Aelfweald*. Elwood has been a distinguished Anglo–Irish name in Co. Mayo for the past two centuries; it was previously established in east Leinster.

Ely Bibl.

Emerson App.

Emery See Amory.

Emison Bibl.

Emmet This family was established in Co. Tipperary in the seventeenth century. The name of Robert Emmet associates it with Dublin. It is derived from the woman's name Emma. Bibl. IF   MIF

Emo This name is quite numerous in Cos. Fermanagh and Cavan, where it is on record as a synonym of Seymour. Emor is an intermediate form. It has no connection with the place-name Emo in Co. Leix.

Mac Enally A variant of MacNally.

Mac Enchroe *Mac Conchradha*. Now generally Crowe (which is also an English name). All Crowes in their homeland, Thomond, are of native Irish stock. In Ulster they are mainly of English origin. IF Map of Clare.

Mac Endoo See Cunniff.

Mac Enealis See MacNelis.

Mac Eneany The name of two septs. That of Co. Roscommon is now almost extinct; that of Oriel is numerous under many variants (for a very remarkable example of this see p. xiii *supra*). A study of this name which appeared in the Clogher Record (1960) presents evidence (which I have verified elsewhere) to prove that its Irish form is not the generally accepted *Mac Conaonaigh* (*cú*, hound—*aonach*, fair) but *Mac an Dhéaghanaigh*, earlier *Mac an Déaganaigh*, (*déaganach*, dean). MIF   Map Monaghan and Roscommon.

Mac Enery See MacEniry.

England A synonym of English; occasionally also of Anglin. Angland is a variant in north Cork.

English First called *l'Angleis* etc. It is in Co. Limerick since the thirteenth century and completely hibernicized: *Aingléis* is the form used in Irish. MIF   See Gallogly.

Englishby, Ingoldsby See Gallogly.

Mac Enhill *Mac Conchoille* (*cú*, gen. *con*, hound—*coill*, wood). Now usually changed to Woods by semi-translation. Living near Omagh this family were hereditary keepers of the Bell of Drumragh, which is now kept at the Sacred Heart church there. The family are still resident in that parish.

Mac Eniff See Cunniff.

Mac Eniry, -Enery *Mac Innéirghe* (the basic word here denotes easily roused early). One of the Uí Cairbre group. Sometimes modernized as MacHenry or even Henry. IF   Map Limerick.

Ennis *Ó hAonghuis* (descendant of Angus). This is a variant of *Ó hAonghusa* (O'Hennessy) of Moyfenrath, on the border of Meath and Westmeath. It was well known in that and adjacent areas in its earlier forms Ennos, Enos etc. It has no connection with the town of Ennis. Occasionally Ennis is a synonym of the Scottish Innes which is cognate with MacGennis. MIF

Mac Enny An occasional variant of MacKenna.

(Mac) Enright, Enraghty *Mac Ionnrachtaigh*. For a consideration of the derivation of this name see Introduction p. xvi. It belongs to Cos. Limerick and Clare. MIF   Map Clare.

Mac Enroe *Mac Conruabha* (*Ruabha* is here probably a place-name). Sometimes abbreviated to Roe. Mainly of Cos. Cavan and Leitrim.

Ensor An English toponymic (d'Ednesor) occasionally on record in mediaeval Ireland. The family became established in Co. Armagh in mid-eighteenth century.

Mac Entaggart *Mac an tSagairt* (*sagart*, priest). An Ulster name with many variants, e.g. (Mac) Taggart, Attegart etc. Even Tiger has been recorded. It is perpetuated in the place-name Ballymacataggart. MIF   Map Fermanagh.

Mac Entee *Mac an tSaoi* (*saoi*, scholar). A sept of Oriel, where both MacAtee and MacGinty are used as synonyms. MIF   Map Armagh–Monaghan.

Mac Entyre A form of MacIntyre.

Ercke *Ó hEirc*. A Co. Tyrone name. This sept claims descent from Erc of the Ulster Collas. For Saint Erc see Mullarkey. MIF

Mac Erlean *Mac Fhirléighinn* (*fearléighinn*, learned man). A Sligo family whose principal branch settled in Co. Derry. MIF   Map Sligo.

Erley An English toponymic to be distinguished from Early. Bibl.

Erraught The Kerry form of Enright.

Mac Errigle A variant of MacGarrigle.

Errington A variant of Harrington.

Errity A rare variant of MacGerety.

Erskine App.

Mac Ervell A variant of MacCarville.

Ervine, Erwin See Irvine, Irwin.

Esbal(d), Esble These are two of six spelling variants of Archbold all found in Co. Derry.

Eskildson Bibl.

Esler App.

Esmond *Easmonn*. Reaney states that this name is derived from Old-English *eastmund*, favour protection. This family is influential in Co. Wexford since the Anglo–Norman invasion. IF   MIF   Map Wexford.

d'Esterre Bibl.

Etchingham An English toponymic associated with Co. Wexford since the sixteenth century. Also spelt Itchingham.

Mac Ettigan See MacGettigan.

Eurell See Yourell.

Eustace *Iústás* (the Latin form *Eustachius* derives from a Greek word meaning fruitful). An Anglo–Norman family of the Pale, prominent in Irish history. Bibl. MIF   Map Kildare.

Mac Evaddy A form of MacAvaddy.

Mac Evanny *Mac an Mhanaigh* (*manach*, monk). Now usually called Monks except in Mayo. See also MacCavana.

Evans Usually a Welsh name; occasionally an anglicized form of the rare *Ó hÉimhin* of Ormond: this is derived from a word meaning swift.

(Mac) Evatt This name, often with the prefix Mac, is a variant of the Oriel name MacKevitt. Evatt and Evett are English too.

Mac Eveagh, -Eveigh Rare forms of MacVeagh found in Mayo.

Everard An important Anglo-Norman family settled in Meath and Tipperary. The name is derived from Old-German *everhard*, boar hard. Map Tipperary.

Everett A variant of Everard.

Evers Originally Norman *d'Evere* or *d'Evers* this name has been prominent in Co. Meath since the fourteenth century. It occurs frequently among those attainted for participation on the Irish side in the wars against Cromwell and William III. In Munster Evers is sometimes used synonymously with Ievers.

Mac Evey, -Evay See under Vahey.

Mac Evilly *Mac an Mhílidh* (*míleadh*, warrior or knight). An Irish patronymic assumed by the Stauntons of Mayo. MIF   Map Mayo.

Mac Evin A variant of MacGiven.

Mac Evinney, -Avinney *Mac Aibhne*. A branch of the O'Cahans of Derry with whom the forename *Aibhne* was frequent. Also an anglicized form of *Mac Dhuibhne* (MacGiveney) of Breffny. I am informed by Fr. Livingstone that in Fermanagh it is *Mac Giolla Coimhne*, erenaghs of Callow Hill.

Mac Evoy *Mac Fhiodhbhuidhe* (probably from *fiodhbhadhach*, woodman). One of the 'Seven Septs of Leix'. Sometimes MacEvoy is for *Mac Giolla Bhuidhe*, see MacElwee. Without the prefix Mac, Evoy is found in Co. Wexford. See also MacVeagh. IF   Map Leix.

Ewart App.

Mac Ewen See Ewing.

Ewing According to several Celtic scholars this name is ultimately derived from the Greek *eugenes* (well-born), cognate with the Irish *eoghan* (but Bergin disputes this). It is sometimes a synonym of MacEwen which is the Scottish form of the Irish *Mac Eoghain*. It is quite numerous throughout Ulster and appears frequently in the seventeenth-century hearth money rolls of that province. MIF

Eyre An influential Cromwellian family in Co. Galway, where the place-names Eyrecourt and Eyreville perpetuate it. Codyre, found near the city of Galway is said to be a derivative of Eyre, viz. *cuid* Eyre. Apart from the family just mentioned there were English officials named Eyre in Ireland in the sixteenth century. The name is of great antiquity in England. It is derived from an early form of the word heir. Bibl, MIF See Ayres.

F

Mac Fadden, -Fadyen *Mac Pháidín* (*Páidín*, a diminutive of *Pádraig*, Patrick). An Ulster name, of both Irish and Scottish origin. Without the prefix Mac it is found in Mayo. MIF   Map Donegal.

Fagan Usually of Norman origin in Dublin and Meath. Sometimes *Ó Faodhagáin* in Co. Louth which, however, is there usually anglicized Fegan. Dr. John Ryan and other scholars regard this as an Oriel sept distinct from O'Hagan, with which Woulfe equates it. Bibl. IF   Map Meath. See p. 304.

Faggy A synonym of MacFadyen in Co. Fermanagh.

(O) Fagheny See Feighney.

(O) Faherty *Ó Fathartaigh*. This Co. Galway sept was located on the east side of Lough Corrib. Their name has often been changed to the better-known O'Flaherty. Map Galway. See Faverty.

(O) Fahy, Faghy *Ó Fathaigh*. A sept of the Uí Maine centred near Loughrea where their territory was known as Pobal Mhuintir Uí Fhathaigh, wherein we now find the modern place-name Fahysvillage. The use of Green as a synonym arises from the similar sound of the word *faithche*, which means a lawn or green. The name is said to be derived from *fothadh*, foundation, which is conjectural. IF MIF   Map Galway. See Fay.

Fair See Phair.

(O) Fairy *Ó Fearadhaigh* (for question of derivation see MacAree). A Donegal sept of the Cenél Conaill; as Ferry it is now quite numerous in Co. Sligo and frequent also in other parts of Connacht in sixteenth-century records.

(O) Falahee See Falsey.

Falkiner, Falconer This English name, numerous in Ulster, is occasionally recorded as a synonym of Fealy or Falvey in Kerry and of Faulkney in Mayo. The usual spelling in Co. Derry is Faulkner. Bibl. See Faughnan.

Mac Fall When not a synonym of Mulfaal, it is, in Ulster, a Scottish name, a branch of the clan Mackintosh. See Falls.

(O) Fallaher *Ó Faolchair* (wolf-dear). A Clare name; occasionally used as a synonym of Falvey. Flaher, a rare name found in Co. Tipperary, is presumably a syncopated form of Fallaher.

(O) Fallon, Falloon *Ó Fallamhain*. The main sept is that of the Uí

Maine located near Athlone. The form Falloon is peculiar to Cos. Armagh and Down. IF 138; Map Offaly and Roscommon. See Fullan and Folan.

Falls The Irish *Mac Pháil* has been used for this, though Falls is an English locative name settled in Ulster, mainly Tyrone, since mid-seventeenth century. For Fall see Lavelle.

(O) Falsey, Falahee *Ó Faolchaidh* (*faol*, wolf). Both forms are found in Co. Clare.

(O) Falvey *Ó Fáilbhe* (possibly from *fáilbheach*, lively). Mainly found in Co. Kerry where it has been continuously since surnames began. It is also well known in Cos. Clare and Cork. MIF   Map Kerry.

(O) Fanagan A rare variant of Finegan.

Fane An English name, meaning well-disposed, also used as a synonym of Feehin.

Fanning, Fannin *Fainín*. A name of Norman origin prominent in Co. Limerick where Fanningstown, formerly Ballyfanning, indicates the location. They were formerly of Ballingarry, Co. Tipperary, where in the fifteenth century the head of the family was, like Irish chiefs, officially described as 'captain of his nation'. Fannin is a variant. MIF   See Finan.

Fannon Mainly found in Cos. Roscommon and Galway. There it is an anglicized form of *Ó Fionnáin*. See Finan. Like Fannin it is also a variant of Fanning.

Fant Best known as one of the 'Tribes of Galway'. Also in Co. Limerick from the fourteenth century. Fantstown is in Co. Limerick. Of dual derivation, *l'enfaunt* and *de la faunte*.

Fanton A variant of Fenton.

Faraugher See Fraher.

Fardy An old Wexford name formerly numerous in the barony of Bargy. Probably a variant of the English Faraday.

Farker See Farquhar.

Mac Farland *Mac Pharthaláin*. A frequent variant of MacPartlan in Tyrone and Armagh.

Farley A common English name used as synonym of Farrelly especially in Co. Cavan.

Farlow This name, an English toponymic, was prominent on the Irish side at the Siege of Limerick, as well as on the English in the wars of the seventeenth century, but does not appear in Ireland before that. It is now rare.

Farmer Translation of *Mac an Scolóige*. The form MacScollog is still extant in Co. Monaghan. The erenagh family of Co. Fermanagh are now all called Farmer. As an English name Farmer is very rare in Ireland.

(O) Farnon, Farnan *Ó Farannáin*. An erenagh family of Ardstraw, Co. Tyrone.

Farquhar, Farker *Mac Fearchair* (man dear). A Scottish name in Co. Down, sometimes written Forker.

(O) Farraher See Fraher.

(O) Farrell, Ferrall *Ó Fearghail* (man of valour). A numerous and important sept of Annaly whose chief's seat was Longford, formerly called *Longphort Uí Fhearghail* (i.e. O'Farrell's fortress). The name is now widespread throughout the four provinces. IF   Map Longford.

(O) Farrelly Woulfe gives *Ó Faircheallaigh* but *Ó Fearghaile*, a variant of *Ó Fearghail*—see previous entry—is acceptable as an alternative. An important co-arb family. People of this sept are still numerous in its homeland as Map, not elsewhere. IF   Map Cavan.

(O) Farren The main sept, *Ó Faracháin* is of Donegal. There Farren is also substituted for Fearon and is then *Ó Fearáin*. MIF Map Donegal.

Farrington An English toponymic found in Ireland as early as the fourteenth century. Several families of the name came to Ireland in quite recent times. MIF

Farris This has been used in Connacht and adjacent areas for Fergus. It is mainly found in Leitrim and Cavan. Fr. Livingstone informs me that in Co. Donegal Farris is an anglicized form of *Ó Fearaigh*. See Fairy, Ferris and Paris.

(O) Farrissy *Ó Fearghusa* (*fear*, man—*gus*, action). Formerly an important sept in Mayo and Leitrim but now rare. Though seldom found now, it was also a Munster variant of Fergus; Ferris is much more often so used. MIF

(O) Farry Woulfe gives *Ó Farraigh* for this north Connacht name, saying that it is distinct from Fairy, of which, however, it is normally a synonym. See Fairy.

Farshin *Fairsing*. An adjectival agnomen from *fairsing*, generous, used by some MacCarthy families in Co. Cork.

Farty An American abbreviation of Faherty.

Mac Fatridge See MacFettridge.

(O) Faughnan *Ó Fachtnáin*. *Fachtna* is a very ancient forename much in favour with the O'Kellys with whom it was modernized as Festus. Faughnan belongs to Cos. Leitrim and Longford. The obsolete Faughney *Ó Fachtna*—now Faulkney or Faulkner—probably the same, was a sept of some importance in Co. Longford in mediaeval times. MIF

Faughton See Wharton.

(Mac) Faul See MacFall and Fawl.

Faulkner, Faulkney See Falkiner and Faughnan.

(O) Faverty An occasional variant of Faherty.

Fawcett, Fossitt There are many variant spellings of this English toponymic, which is found in all the provinces of Ireland. The first reference to it I have met in this country is to the gate-keeper of Maryborough fortress in 1587. It does not appear to have any connection with the mediaeval Fossard.

Fawl, Faul Found in Clare; an abbreviation of Mulfaul and MacFaul.

Fay *de Fae*. An Anglo-Norman family settled in Westmeath at the end of the twelfth century. Also sometimes a synonym of Fahy and of Fee. The Westmeath family spread to Cos. Cavan and Monaghan. IF MIF See Fee.

Fealty This name is found in Co. Donegal. I have not yet ascertained its origin.

Fealy A synonym of Falvey in Kerry; also sometimes for Fehilly. Fealy is distinct from, but often confused with, Feeley. See Feley.

Feane A corrupt form of Feighan.

(O) Fearon *Ó Fearáin* (possibly from *fear*, man). A sept of Oriel. Feran and Feron are variants. See Farren.

Feary This is used synonymously with Fairy as well as with Feighry.

Feddis Also written Fiddes, which is probably the modern form of the Norman *de Sancto Fide*: that may also be the original of the south Leinster name Sanfey or Sanphy. Feddis belongs to Co. Fermanagh.

(O) Fedegan *Ó Feadagáin*. Originally located in Co. Monaghan, where two place-names near Clones incorporate the surname, this Oriel sept has been continuously in the barony of Ardee in the adjacent county of Louth since the fifteenth century. MIF

Mac Fee See Mahaffy.

(O) Fee, Fey, Foy, Fye All these are variant anglicized forms of *Ó Fiaich*. They are occasionally changed to Fay by absorption or made Hunt by pseudo-translation; in modern contracted spelling *fiach* (raven) and *fiadhach* (hunt) are identical. The most numerous of the forms given above are Fee (in Fermanagh, Armagh and Cavan) and Foy (Cavan and north Connacht). MIF

(O) Feehan *Ó Fiacháin* (derivation as foregoing). This is a sept long located in the Tipperary–Kilkenny area probably originally the same as Feehin. The name has been confused with Fegan (*Ó Faodhagain*) of Co. Louth. MIF See p. 304.

Feeharry A rare synonym of Fitzharris quite distinct from Feehery.

(O) Feeheny See Feighney.

(O) Feehery, Feery See Feighry.

(O) Feehin, Feen *Ó Féichín*. A west Cork name cognate with Feehan and often so spelt. MIF

(Mac) Feely, Fehilly *Mac Fithcheallaigh* (*fithcheallach*, chess player).

105

A Donegal–Derry name quite distinct from O'Feely or O'Fehilly, though of similar derivation.

(O) Feely See Fehilly.

(O) Feenaghty See Finaghty.

(O) Feeney *Ó Fiannaidhe* (soldier) earlier form *Ó Feinneadha*. A sept of the Uí Fiachrach in north Connacht. The name Feeney is also in Co. Galway where *Ó Fidhne* is used as the Gaelic form. This, however, may be a branch of the Co. Sligo sept. O'Feeny, of Ballyfeeny, Co. Roscommon, is called *Ó Fighne* in the 'Annals of Connacht.' MIF

(Mac) Feerick *Mac Phiaraic* (a derivative of Peter). This name is very closely identified with Ballinrobe, Co. Mayo. It originated as a branch of the Berminghams of Dunmore, Co. Galway. MIF

Feery See Feighry.

Mac Feeters *Mac Pheadair* (son of Peter). A Tyrone–Derry name often translated Peterson.

(O) Fegan See Fagan and Feehan. Feighan is another variant.

(O) Fehill *Ó Fithchill*. An abbreviated form of Fehilly found in Co. Limerick.

(O) Fehilly *Ó Fithcheallaigh* (chess player). A sept of the Corca Laoidhe, often abbreviated to Feeley and sometimes anglicized Field. In modern times the form Feeley is mainly found in north Connacht, where it is a Silmurray sept. MIF   Map Cork.

(O) Feighney, Feheny *Ó Fiachna*. Often changed to Hunt. *Fiachna* is an old personal name: see Fee for note on the word *fiach*. Originally of Co. Roscommon, now rare. MIF 104.

(O) Feighry, Feery *Ó Fiachra*. This is also anglicized Feehery, Feary etc. and is often mistranslated Hunt (see Fee). Originally of Co. Tyrone, now rare. MIF   **Feighan** See page 304.

Felan See Phelan.

Feley A synonym of MacSharry in Co. Leitrim, presumably through confusion with Foley (*searrach*, foal, possibly extended to mean filly.)

Feltus A corruption of the English Felthouse of comparatively recent introduction, found in Cos. Carlow and Wexford.

(O) Fenaghty See Finaghty.

(O) Fen(e)lon *Ó Fionnalláin* (*fionn*, fair). Of Delvin, Westmeath. Fenelon in Ireland is occasionally of Huguenot origin. MIF

(O) Fennell *Ó Fionnghail* (fair valour). Apart from Dublin this is a Clare name; elsewhere it is confused with Fennelly. Fennell is also an English name found in Ormond since the fourteenth century. MIF

(O) Fennelly *Ó Fionnghalaigh* (for derivation see Fennell). This

Ormond name is now mainly found in Co. Kilkenny, Leix and Offaly. MIF

Fenner A toponymic: Fenner and its variant Finure are place-names found in many parts of Ireland, mainly Leinster. As a surname Fenner is on record since the fourteenth century in Cos. Dublin and Kilkenny; in the latter Fennerscourt indicates the location and there was also a place called Fennerstown there in the sixteenth century. Fennors is a variant form of the surname. It is called *Fionúir* in Irish, i.e. a modern spelling of *Fionnabhair*, the place.

(O) Fennerty A variant of Fenaghty or Finaghty.

(O) Fennessy, Finnessy *Ó Fionnghusa* (*fionn*, fair—*gus*, vigour or action). Mainly of Co. Waterford.

Fenning An English name mainly found in Belfast; also a modern variant of Fanning.

Fenton An English name, used in Kerry and Limerick as a synonym of Finaghty and occasionally of Feighney. MIF

Feore The Munster form of Furey. See under Fewer.

Feran, Feron Variants of Fearon.

(O) Fergus *Ó Fearghuis* (*fear*, man—*gus*, vigour). The name of two Connacht septs: (a) a medical family with the O'Malleys and (b) an ecclesiastical family in Leitrim. The name has become Ferris in Kerry. MIF   Map Mayo.

Ferguson A Scottish name (*Mac Feargusa*) numerous in Ulster. It is also used as a synonym of Fergus in Co. Leitrim. App; MIF

(O) Ferley A variant of Farrelly.

(O) Fernan Woulfe treats this as a distinct name, viz. *Ó Fearnáin*, a variant of *Ó hIfearnáin* (Heffernan) but it is usually a variant of Farnon (*Ó Farannáin*).

Ferns See Renehan.

Feron, Feran, Fern Variants of Fearon.

(O) Ferrall See Farrell.

Mac Ferran Woulfe gives *Mac Mheardáin* which he derives from *mear*, swift. This is conjectural, but I have no alternative suggestion to offer. In the sixteenth century this was a Co. Roscommon name, but it is now fairly numerous in Antrim and Down.

Ferrar Bibl.

Ferrick A variant of Feerick.

(O) Ferrigan *Ó Fearagáin* (possibly from *fearg*, anger or *fearagáin*, manikin). This is now mainly found in south Down and north Louth. In the sixteenth century it belonged to Breffny O'Reilly. MIF

Ferris In Kerry a variant of O'Fergus. It is also traditionally a cognomen of a branch of the Moriartys. In Ulster it is the name of a branch of the Scottish clan Ferguson formerly MacFergus. MIF
See Farrissy.

Ferriter *Feirtéir*. Of Ballyferriter since 1295. The name, of English origin, is derived from the verb to ferret, i.e. to hunt with ferrets, hence to search closely. IF   Map Kerry.

Ferrons A variant of Ferns. See Renehan.

(O) Ferry See Fairy.

Fetherston An English toponymic well known in Cos. Roscommon and Westmeath since the Cromwellian period. This name is also sometimes an abbreviated form of Fetherstonhaugh, another north of England toponymic.

Mac Fetrick *Mac Phádraic*. See next entry.

Mac Fettridge *Mac Pheadruis* (son of Petrus, not Patricius). The anglicized form is much confused with MacFetrick, both being located mainly in Antrim. MIF

(O) Fewer A variant of Feore found in Cos. Kilkenny and Waterford. Woulfe gives *Ó Fiodhabhair* as the Gaelic form with the probably correct derivation meaning bushy eyebrow; but he also equates Feore with Furey which the Four Masters call *Ó Foirreidh*, obviously a different name.

Fey See Fee.

Fiddes See Feddis.

Fidgeon See Pidgeon.

Mac Fie See Mahaffy.

Field(s), Fielding Mainly English in origin, but see Fehilly and Maghery. As *de la Felde* it occurs in mediaeval Irish records.

Figgis *Le Fykeis,* the original form of this name, derived from the Old-French *ficheis* (faithful), is found in mediaeval English records, but Figgis is of comparatively recent introduction in Ireland. MIF

(O) Fihelly See Fehilly.

(O) Filan A variant of Fyland.

(O) Filbin A variant of Philbin in Mayo.

Filgate The main family in Co. Louth is of Cromwellian origin in Ireland. The name, however, is on record in Dublin earlier in the seventeenth century. It is derived from the words field gate.

(O) Finaghty *Ó Fionnachta* (the second part of the name is from *sneachta,* snow). Now often corrupted to Finnerty. A Silmurray sept. MIF   Map Roscommon. See Fenton.

(O) Finan *Ó Fionnáin* (*fionn,* fair). A sept of north Connacht. Sometimes anglicized as Fanning elsewhere. MIF   Map Mayo.

Finch After its introduction from England in the early seventeenth century this name became established in Munster, but is now mainly found in Ulster. It is of nickname origin, from the bird.

Finglas *de Fionnghlas*. This is one of the few Irish toponymics. It appears frequently in records relating to Co. Dublin from the thirteenth century. MIF

Finlan A variant form of Fenlon found in the midland counties.

Finlay, Findley A branch of the Scottish clan Farquharson. Finlay is used as a synonym of Fennelly in Leix and Offaly.

(O) Finn *Ó Finn (fionn,* fair). There are three distinct septs of this name. Two, viz. of Coolavin, Co. Sligo, and of Kilcolgan, Co. Galway, survive. The name is now found also in Munster. IF   Map Monaghan and Sligo.

Finnamore A name of the nickname type, from Old-French *fin amour* (dear love), found in Leinster as early as the thirteenth century.

(O) Finnan See Finan.

(O) Finnegan *Ó Fionnagáin.* One sept of O'Finnegan belongs to the Galway–Roscommon border: there are two places called Bally-finnegan in those counties; the other to Oriel. It is now, both as Finnegan and Finegan, widespread and numerous. IF

Finnell, Finnelly See Fennell, Fennelly.

(O) Finneran *Ó Finnthigheirn (fionn tighearna,* fair lord). Cos. Galway and Roscommon. MIF

Finnerell Woulfe suggests *Ó Fiongardail* as the Irish form of this rare Co. Clare name but does not offer any derivation, nor have I traced it yet.

Finnerty See Finaghty.

(O) Finnessy See Fennessy.

Finney An Ulster variant of Feeney.

Finning A variant of Fenning.

(Mac) Finucane *Mac Fionnmhacáin* (the basic words are *fionn,* fair— —*mac,* son). A Co. Clare name. With the initial F aspirated it becomes **Kinucane,** also found in Clare.

Mac Firbis *Mac Firbhisigh.* (Woulfe's derivation—man of property— is possible). A famous Connacht family of historians and antiquaries. The name is now almost entirely replaced by the Scottish Forbes. Bibl. IF

Fisher Usually of English origin. It is also a synonym of Salmon; and occasionally an anglicized form of the Scottish MacInesker.

Fitch An abbreviated form of Fitzpatrick and Fitzsimons in Co. Down.

Fitton On record in Ireland since the thirteenth century. The main family came from England in the sixteenth century; later they were prominent Jacobites. The name is now rare.

Fitzelle Originally Norman. Frequent in Antrim in the seventeenth century. Now used for Fizzell in Kerry.

Fitzeustace Bibl.

Fitzgerald *Mac Gearailt.* One of the two greatest families which came to Ireland as a result of the Anglo-Norman invasion. It had two main divisions, Desmond (of whom are the holders of the ancient titles

Knight of Kerry and Knight of Glin); and Kildare, whose leaders held almost regal sway up to the time of the Rebellion of Silken Thomas and the execution by Henry VIII of Thomas and his near relatives in 1537. The name is now very numerous. Bibl. IF Map Cork, Kerry, Kildare and Limerick.

Fitzgibbon *Mac Giobúin*. The name of two unconnected Norman-Irish families; one of the same stock as the Burkes of Mayo, the other of west Munster whose head was the White Knight. IF Map Limerick.

Fitzharris The name of a distinguished Co. Wexford family, sometimes called Fitzhenry.

Fitzhenry A Norman family which in Connacht became *Mac Éinrí* (MacHenry). See Fitzharris and Henry.

Fitzmaurice *Mac Muiris*. A famous branch of the Norman Geraldines, lords of Lixnaw in Kerry, notable for their resistance to English invaders in the sixteenth century. The name Fitzmaurice is also connected with Mayo because some Connacht Prendergasts adopted it. Bibl. IF Map Kerry.

Fitzpatrick *Mac Giolla Phádraig* (devotee of St. Patrick). The only Fitz name of Gaelic-Irish origin, the main sept being located in Ossory. The name is numerous also in Fermanagh where families so called are said to be of MacGuire stock. Bibl. IF MIF Map Leix.

Fitzrery Bibl.

Fitzsimon(s), Fitzsimmons The main family of this name came from England to Leinster in 1323. Earlier than that it was in Mayo, for which see Eddery. It is now mainly found in Cos. Cavan and Down. IF 291; MIF 257; Map Westmeath. See under Kimmons.

Fitzwilliam Bibl. See under MacWilliam.

Fivey See Quigg.

Fizzell A Palatine name in Kerry.

Flack, Fleck This is a Scottish name fairly numerous in Ulster. It was formerly Affleck, a contraction of Auchinleck.

(O) Flahavan, Flavahan *Ó Flaitheamháin* (*flaitheamh*, ruler). This name belongs almost exclusively to west Waterford and east Cork. A third anglicized form, Flavin, is also found in the former. MIF

(O) Flaher See Fallaher.

(O) Flaherty, Flaverty *Ó Flaithbheartaigh* (bright ruler). The leading sept of Iar-Connacht. Another sept so called of Thomond is now found in Co. Kerry. For Ulster see Laverty. Bibl. IF MIF Map Galway.

(O) Flahive, Flahy See Lahiff.

(O) Flanagan *Ó Flannagáin* (*flann*, red or ruddy). Of the several septs of the name (see Map) that of Connacht is the most important:

their chief ranked as one of the 'royal lords' under O'Connor, King of Connacht. IF Map Fermanagh, Offaly and Roscommon.

(O) Flanahy *Ó Flannchaidh*. A rare Thomond name.

(O) Flannelly *Ó Flannghaile* (ruddy valour). A Co. Sligo sept quite distinct from, but often confused with, O'Flannery. MIF

(O) Flannery *Ó Flannabhra* (*flann*, red or ruddy—*abhar*, eyebrow). There are two septs of this name located as in Map. IF Map Limerick and Mayo.

Flatesbury An English name prominent in Cos. Kildare and Dublin from early fourteenth century; now rare. Bibl.

(O) Flatley *Ó Flaitile*; earlier form *Ó Flaithfhileadh* (prince poet). A sept of Uí Fiachrach in Co. Sligo, much confused with Flattery. MIF

(O) Flattery *Ó Flaitre*. Mainly Offaly. This is genealogically distinct from Flatley, but often found as a corruption of it. According to Woulfe the name itself is of similar derivation, which is conjectural. MIF Map Offaly.

(O) Flavahan, Flavin See Flahavan.

Flavelle An Anglo-Norman name meaning yellow-haired and found in north Armagh and adjacent areas. In Mayo it also occurs as the anglicized form of *Ó Flannghail*, an abbreviated form of *Ó Flann-ghaile*. See Flannelly.

(O) Flaverty See Flaherty.

Fleck See Flack.

Fleetwood The first of the name in Ireland was a 'Munster adventurer' who was granted 12,000 acres in Cos. Waterford and Cork in 1587. In the next century several were leading Cromwellians. These received grants in Cos. Meath and Kildare. Some branches in due course became Catholic and nationalist. Bibl.

Fleming (a man from Flanders). Usually gaelicized *Pléamonn*. Established at Slane in the twelfth century; now numerous in all the four provinces. Bibl. IF Map Meath.

Fletcher See under Lister.

Fleury An occasional synonym in Co. Galway of Furey. See p. 304.

Flinn A frequent variant of Flynn.

Flint An English name in Dublin since the thirteenth century.

Flinter Though one of the name appears as an official at Carlingford in 1499, Flinters did not settle permanently in Ireland till the seventeenth century; they have since been continuously in Cos. Kildare and Wicklow.

Flood Some Floods are of English extraction, but in Ireland they are mainly *Ó Maoltuile* or *Mac Maoltuile*, abbreviated to *Mac an Tuile* and *Mac Tuile*, anglicized MacAtilla or MacTully as well as Flood. *Tuile* means flood but probably it is here for *toile*, gen. of *toil*, will, i.e. the will of God. In parts of Ulster Flood is used for the Welsh Floyd (Welsh *llwyd*, grey). IF

Floody A variant of Flood found in Louth and Cavan.

Floyd Normally a variant of Lloyd but sometimes synonymous with Flood. It is mainly found in Munster.

(O) Flynn, Flyng *Ó Floinn* (*flann*, ruddy). This numerous and widespread name originated in a number of different places, including Kerry and Clare. Of the two in Co. Cork one was a branch of the Corca Laoidhe, the other, lords of Muskerylinn (*Muiscre Uí Fhloinn*); in north Connacht the O'Flynns were leading men under the royal O'Connors, and there was also an erenagh family there; while further west on the shores of Lough Conn another distinct erenagh family was located. For the name in Ulster as an indigenous sept see Lynn. IF MIF Map Cork and Roscommon.

(O) Fodaghan *Ó Fuadacháin*. This, like the cognate Foody, has been made Swift by pseudo-translation, mainly in the Cavan–Monaghan area.

Fodha A phonetic anglicization of the adjective *fada*, long, and thus synonymous with the surname Long.

(O) Fogarty *Ó Fógartaigh* (*fógartach*, expelling). A Dalcassian sept settled in the barony of Eliogarty which was named from them. IF Map Tippeary.

Folan(e) There was a brehon family of *Mac Fualáin* in Co. Galway, but Folan was formerly often used as a synonym of Fallon in Connacht, e.g. 'O'Folan's Country' for O'Fallon's Country. In seventeenth-century documents Folan sometimes appears as the anglicized form of *Ó Faoláin* (Phelan). Folan, however, belongs almost exclusively to Co. Galway and the adjacent part of Mayo. MIF

(O) Foley *Ó Foghladha* (*foghlaidhe*, plunderer). A very numerous name in south Munster. The distinguished English family of Foley is said to be of Irish origin. For Foley as a synonym of *Mac Searraigh* see Sharry. IF MIF

Follin Bibl.

Folliott Though the best-known families of this name acquired their property in Co. Donegal under the Plantation of Ulster, it is, however, on record in Dublin and Clonmel as early as 1409. The name is derived from French *follet*, gay. Bibl.

Folsey A variant of Falsey.

Font See Fant.

(O) Foody, Foudy Woulfe gives *Ó Fuada* for this. If it be *Ó Fuadaigh* it could derive from *fuadach*, plundering. A Mayo name, sometimes made Swift and Speed by pseudo-translation.

(O) Foohy See Fuohy.

Foote See Legge.

(O) Forahan. See Forhane.

(O) Foran *Ó Fuaráin.* Mainly found in Cos. Limerick and Waterford; also often changed to Ford. MIF   See Forhane.

Forbes A Scottish family settled in Co. Longford. Also a synonym of MacFirbis (e.g. in Co. Clare where it is pronounced Forbis). IF MIF

Ford(e) A well-known English name, widely used as a synonym of several Irish surnames, viz. MacKinnawe, MacElnay, Foran, Forhane. IF   Map Galway and Leitrim.

Forfee A variant of Furphy.

(O) Forhane, Forahan *Ó Fuarthháin.* Older forms of Foran used in Kerry and west Cork. (Woulfe's derivation of this from *fuar,* cold is very doubtful). MIF

Forke See Gooley.

Forker A variant of the Scottish Farquhar. See Carraher.

Forkin, Forkan *Ó Gabhláin* (*gabhal,* fork). *Ó Gabhláin* has also been anglicized Goulding. Forkin is found in Cos. Galway and Mayo.

For(r)estal From a dialect word meaning paddock, not a variant of Forester. A notable Anglo-Norman family. MIF   Map Kilkenny.

(O) Forrey A variant of Farry.

Forsythe This Scottish name, which is fairly common in Antrim and Down, has been there sometimes corrupted to Foursides. As well as its territorial derivation it also derives from *fearsithe,* man of peace.

(O) Fortune, Fortin, Forty *Ó Foirtcheirn.* Woulfe says this word, meaning overlord, is cognate with Old–English *vortigern.* It is almost peculiar to Co. Wexford. Occasionally it is a synonym of Farshing in Co. Cork. MIF   Map Carlow and Wexford.

Fossitt See Fawcett.

Foster App.

Fottrell An English toponymic in Co. Dublin since the fifteenth century.

(O) Fouhy See Fuohy.

Foursides See Forsythe.

Foudy See Foody.

Fourhan See Forhane.

Fowley A Co. Leitrim form of Foley.

Fowloo A phonetic form of *Ó Foghladha* (see Foley). This is sometimes corrupted to the English Fowler which, as such, is fairly numerous in Ulster since the time of the Plantation of Ulster, *c.* 1609.

Fox Though some English Foxes settled in Co. Limerick, Fox in Ireland is mainly a synonym of Kearney, MacAshinah, Shanahy or Shinnock. Bibl. IF   Map Offaly.

Foy See Fee.

Foylan *Ó Faoileáin (faol,* wolf). Of some note at Foylanstown in Co. Westmeath in the sixteenth century; now rare.

Foyle This name is not of Irish origin, but is derived from the French *fouille,* excavation. Found in Dublin since the thirteenth century, it later became established in Co. Leix. MIF

Foynes See Fyan.

(O) Fraher, Farraher *Ó Fearchair (fearchar,* man dear). Fraher is the south Munster form especially in Co. Waterford where **Raher** is a synonym. The earlier forms Farraher or Faraugher are almost exclusively of Cos. Mayo and Galway. MIF

(O) Frahill *Ó Freathail.* This metathesized form of Farrell, found in west Munster, is sometimes pronounced and written Fraul.

(O) Frahy See Frehy.

Frain, Frayne These are alternative forms of Freeney also found in Roscommon and north Mayo; occasionally for de Freyne.

Frame This name, which Bardsley says is from Old-English *frem,* stranger, first appears as a lessee on the Ormond estate in 1577, but was subsequently mainly found in Ulster: it is not numerous. MIF

Francis This name, which has no Gaelic background, being Norman *le Franceis,* the Frenchman, was nevertheless quite numerous as *Proinséis* in the Irish-speaking area near Galway city.

Franklin (Middle-English *frankeleyn,* freeholder). This name has been established in Cos. Limerick and Tipperary since late seventeenth century.

Franks By derivation this name means the Frenchman. A few isolated references to it occur in mediaeval Irish records. Families of Franks or Frank (formerly used synonymously) became established in Ireland in the seventeenth century and have since been prominent as Anglo-Irish gentry in Cos. Leix and Offaly. Frankford (now Kilcormac again) was named from them.

(O) Fraul See Frahill.

(O) Frawley *O Freaghaile.* A metathesized form of Farrelly in Cos. Clare and Limerick. MIF

Frayne Bibl. See Frain and de Freyne.

Frazer, Fraser The name of a Scottish clan numerous in Ulster, derived from, and sometimes a synonym of, Frizell there. Bibl.

Free An abbreviated form of Freeman found in and near Co. Kildare.

Freeborne Though the first record of this name in Ireland is in Co. Wexford in mid-seventeenth century it has subsequently been found mainly in Co. Donegal. The old English name Frebern inevitably later was treated as if free-born.

(O) Freely *Ó Frighile* A well-known name in Co. Mayo but rare elsewhere. It is cognate with O'Friel.

Freeman This English name, which is found in all the provinces, is sometimes used as the anglicized form of *Mac an tSaoir*. See Mac-Ateer.

Freeney *de Fréine*. Well known in Waterford and adjacent counties. The place called Freeneystown is in Co. Kilkenny. MIF   See de Freyne.

Freer See Prior.

(O) Frehill *Ó Frighil*. A form of Friel, found in Cos. Mayo and Roscommon.

(O) Frehy, Frahy *Ó Fearchaidhe*. A Co. Clare name.

French One of the more prominent 'Tribes of Galway', though first settled in Co. Wexford. Several places in Connacht incorporate the name notably Frenchpark in Co. Roscommon. Woulfe says the derivation is the same as de Freyne but Reaney and other authorities give the obvious, i.e. Frenchman. Bibl. IF   Map Galway.

Frew, Frewen Both these otherwise quite distinct names derive from the Anglo-Saxon personal name Freowine. Frew is fairly numerous in north-east Ulster, while Frewen is found in Dublin and Cork.

de Freyne An Anglo-Norman family in Co. Kilkenny. Freeney is a late popular variant. The name is derived from the Latin *fraxinus*. French *frêne*, ash tree.

Friar, Friary See Prior.

(O) Friel *Ó Firghil* later *Ó Frighil*. The name is etymologically the same as Farrell. The leading family were descended from a brother of St. Columcille and had the hereditary right of inaugurating O'Donnell as lord of Tirconnell. IF   Map Donegal.

Frisby An English toponymic continuously associated with Co. Kilkenny since mid-seventeenth century.

Frith Bibl.

Frizell (Norman-French the Friesian). Families of this name were established in Munster in the thirteenth century and gave their name to Frieselstown in Co. Limerick. They subsequently became scattered. MIF   See Frazer.

Frost The name of a family prominent in east Clare since 1700. It occurs occasionally elsewhere in mediaeval records.

Fry This English name is an occasional synonym of Ferris in west Ulster. Bibl.

Fuge An Anglo-Saxon name, a variant of Fulger, found in Co. Waterford and east Cork. Fudge is a variant which is on record in Co. Tipperary in 1664.

Fullam, Fulham This English toponymic has been continuously in Co. Dublin since the thirteenth century. MIF

Fullan, Fullen In Tyrone these are variants of Falloon (see Fallon) but Fullen is also a variant of the English Fulloon, derived from Old-English *fulun*, a fuller.

Fuller Well known in Co. Kerry since the sixteenth century. According to Woulfe this English name is also used as the modern anglicized form of the obsolete MacEnookery *Mac an Úcaire* (son of the fuller) of Co. Down. Bibl.

Fullerton A branch of the Scottish clan Stewart of Bute. MacCloy is a branch of Fullerton. Both are numerous in north-east Ulster. SIF 73.

Fulton A Scottish toponymic numerous in Ulster since the seventeenth century. Bibl.

(O) Fuohy *Ó Fuathaigh.* An east Cork name.

(O) Furey The Annals spell this name *Ó Foirreith* and *Ó Furreidh.* Woulfe gives *Ó Fiodhabhra* which is conjectural—its contraction *Ó Fiura* is, however, in current use. A branch of the O'Melaghlins who later migrated to Co. Galway. MIF   Map Westmeath. See Fewer.

Furlong This family settled in Co. Wexford at the end of the thirteenth century and the name occurs as one of the most numerous in five baronies of that county in the 'census' of 1659. MIF   Map Wexford.

Furnell An English name of French origin; it was prominent in Co. Cork and Co. Limerick in the eighteenth century.

(O) Furphy *Ó Foirbhithe (foirbhithe,* perfect). This name belongs to Cos. Tyrone and Armagh. SIF 73.

Fyan(s) This name, gaelicized as *Faghan,* is on record in Dublin since the fifteenth century, several of the family being mayors of the city. They became landowners in Co. Meath and gave their name to Fyanstown. Foynes, a rare name, is apparently a variant of Fyan. SIF 73.

Fye An anglicized form of *Ó Fiaich.* See Fee.

Fyfe A Scottish toponymic. It and Fyfee are used as anglicized forms of *Ó Fiacha* in Fermanagh and adjacent areas. See Fee.

(O) Fyland See Phylan.

Fynan See Finan.

G

Gabbett This family (Gabot in England) came to Co. Limerick in mid-seventeenth century.

Gaff See MacGagh.

Mac Gaffey *Mac Gaibhidh (gaibhidh,* a word usually denoting acquisition). A south Connacht name well known near Athlone. MIF   See MacGahey.

(O) Gaffigan See O'Gavigan.

Gaffney One of the most confusing of all Irish surnames as anglicized.

It may be *Ó Gamhna, Ó Caibheanaigh, Mac Conghamhna, Mac Carrghamhna* or *Mag Fhachtna*. See Caulfield, Keaveney, MacCarron and Gaughney. IF

Mac Gaffrey *Mac Gafraidh*. A variant of MacCaffrey found in Co. Leitrim.

Mac Gagh *Mag Eathach*.* A Galway-Mayo name. It takes the form Gaff in Co. Offaly. See MacGahey.

Gahagan A variant of Geoghegan.

Mac Gahan, Gahon *Mag Eacháin*. An Oriel name.

(O) Gahan Though this is an occasional variant of O'Gaughan, Gahan is mainly found in Cos. Wexford and Wicklow, where Woulfe says it is the anglicized form of *Ó Gaoithín* (derived from *gaoth*, wind). MIF 113. Map Wicklow.

Mac Gahern, -Gaughran *Mac Eachráin*. A Co. Cavan name distinct from, but sometimes confused with, MacGauran. MIF

Mac Gahey *Mac Eachaidh*. The personal name *Eachaidh*, anglicized Aghey, is a variant of the older *Eochaidh*, Oghy. MacGahey is an Ulster name akin to MacCaughey, not synonymous with MacGaffey. MIF   Map Monaghan. See Hackett.

Gaine See Geane.

Gainor, Geanor Variants of Gaynor.

Gaitens, Gattins Donegal synonyms of MacGettigan.

Galbally *de Gallbhaile*. One of the few Irish toponymics, on record in Co. Kildare as early as 1359.

Galbraith This well-known Scottish name came to Ireland (Cos. Tyrone and Fermanagh) at the time of the Plantation of Ulster (*c*. 1609) and is now numerous in that province. The Scots Gaelic form according to Black is *Mac an Breathnaigh*. (*Breathnach*, Welshman). One branch settled in Co. Leix (then Queen's County) and another in Co. Galway. The name is still in Leix. Bibl.

Gale For Gale when found in Leinster without the prefix Mac see Gaule.

Mac Gale, -Gall Variants of MacCall in Ulster especially Tyrone.

Gall See Gaule.

(O) Gallagher *Ó Gallchobhair*. This name (*gallchobhar*, foreign help) has at least 23 variant spellings in anglicized forms, several of them beginning with Gol instead of Gal. It is that of one of the principal septs of Donegal. Bibl. IF   Map Donegal.

(O) Gallahue *Ó Gallchú*. A variant of Gallagher. In east Cork it has been confused with Donohue.

(O) Gallen *Ó Gaillín*. Usually a Cenél Eoghain sept in Donegal. Alternatively a variant of Gallon.

(Mac) Gallery *Mac Giolla Riabhaigh* (*riabhach*, brindled). Formerly

---

* *Mag* is a form of *Mac* used before a vowel and some aspirated consonants.

117

MacGillereagh. MIF   Map Clare. See MacAreavy, Kilrea for other anglicized forms of this name.

Gallespy See Gillespie.

(O) Galligan *Ó Gealagáin.* A sept of the Uí Fiachrach in Co. Sligo, now often called Gilligan. It is numerous as Galligan in Co. Cavan where it is also called White (from *geal*, white). MIF

(O) Gallina(gh) *Ó Gailínigh* (possibly from *gailíneach*, flattering). A Donegal name.

(O) Gallivan See Galvin.

(Mac) Gallogly *Mac an Ghallóglaigh* (*gallóglach*, galloglass). Originally of Co. Donegal. Now changed to English and Englishby in Antrim. And sometimes even to Ingoldsby! As Gologly it is found in Co. Monaghan. MIF

(O) Gallon *Ó Galláin* (possibly from *gallán*, stone). A Breffny sept. Map Leitrim.

Galloway See Galwey.

(O) Galvin, Galvan *Ó Gealbháin* (*geal*, bright—*bán*, white). Originally a Clare sept, but now spread into neighbouring counties; very numerous in Kerry where it is more often spelt Gallivan. IF

Galt See Gault.

Galway The Tribes of: Athy, Blake, Bodkin, Browne, Darcy, Deane, Fant, French, Joyce, Kirwan, Lynch, Martin, Morris, Skerret.

Galwey, Gallwey *de Gallaidhe.* This name is found in Ireland since the thirteenth century, mainly in Ulster and in Cork, where the Galweys were for long a leading family. Those in Ulster doubtless derived their name from Galloway in nearby southern Scotland; but it is uncertain whether the southern Galweys derived theirs from Galloway or from the Irish city, more probably the latter. Bibl. IF

Gamble Families of this name, of Swedish derivation (*gamal*, old), were established both in Ulster and Co. Cork in the seventeenth century. Since then the latter have dwindled and the former have multiplied. MIF   **Gambon** See Gammon.

Gammell A variant form of Gamble.

(Mac) Gammon With prefix Mac a rare west Clare name (I have not found the form in Irish); elsewhere from French *gambon*, leg: in Co. Waterford it is so spelt.

(Mac) Ganly, Gantley *Mag Sheanlaoich* (*sean*, old—*laoch*, hero or warrior). A variant form of Shanly. MIF   Map Leitrim.

Mac Gann *Mag Annaidh.* A Connacht form of MacCann.

Gannessy A form of MacGuinness found in Co. Clare.

(Mac) Gannon *Mag Fhionnáin* (*fionn*, fair). An old Erris family. The Irish form is *Mag Canann* in Co. Clare. IF   Map Mayo. See MacConnon.

Ganter Anglo-Norman *le gaunter* (maker of gloves). This name occurs

118

in mediaeval Dublin records where it is still extant though never numerous.

O Gara *Ó Gadhra* (*gadhar*, dog). Akin to the O'Haras in Leyney. Lords of Coolavin up to 1650. The prefix O, formerly widely dropped, is now usual. IF   Map Mayo-Sligo. See Geary.

Garragan A variant of Garraghan found in Meath.

(Mac) Garahy Usually a variant of Garrihy; occasionally, in Offaly, of Geraghty.

Garavan A variant of Garvin in Co. Mayo.

Garde An east Cork family which came from Kent in the seventeenth century. Bibl, MIF). See Uniacke.

Gardiner App.

Gargan See Garrigan.

Garland *Gearnún*. The earlier form of this name, Gernon, has been almost entirely superseded by Garland. It has been very prominent in Cos. Monaghan and Louth since Roger de Gernon accompanied Strongbow in 1170. MIF   See MacGartlan.

Garner A variant of Gardiner.

Mac Garr See MacGirr.

(Mac) Garrahan, Garaghan *Mag Aracháin*. Originally of Fermanagh this family moved southwards to Cos. Cavan and Leitrim. MIF

(Mac) Garraher *Mag Fhearchair* (*fearchar*, man dear). A Donegal family which migrated to Co. Roscommon. MIF

(Mac) Garrell See MacGirl.

Garrett This is mainly of English origin in Ireland, but has also been used as a synonym of Fitzgerald. It is now numerous in north-east Ulster.

(Mac) Garrigan, Gargan *Mac Geargáin*, sometimes *Ó Geargáin* (*gearg*, the old word for grouse figuratively used for a warrior). A Breffny name found in Co. Cavan and also in Meath and Louth. MIF

Mac Garrigle See MacGirl.

Garrigy A Clare variant of MacGarry.

(Mac) Garrihy See Garry.

(Mac) Garrity A variant of Geraghty in Oriel.

(Mac) Garry *Mag Fhearadhaigh* (for *fearadhach*, see MacAree). Akin to the MacHughs of east Connacht in Cos. Leitrim and Roscommon. In Oriel it has been corrupted to O'Garriga and so mistranslated Hare *(girriadh)*. Garrihy is the form used in west Clare.

(Mac) Gartlan(d) *Mac Gartnáin*, a Cenél Eoghain sept; also *Mac Gartlan*. A gaelicized form of Garland.

(Mac) Garty A variant of Geraghty.

(O) Garvan *Ó Garbháin* (*garbh*, rough). A Munster family akin to the Moriartys in Kerry, now generally called Garvey. IF   See Garvin.

Mac Garvey *Mac Gairbhith* (*garbh*, rough). A Donegal family.

(O) Garvey *Ó Gairbhith*. A sept of the same stock as the O'Hanlons. IF   Map Armagh-Down. See Garvan and Garvin.

(O) Garvin *Ó Gairbhín*. Frequently anglicized Garvan. The name of a sept of the southern Uí Néill which migrated to Mayo. Sometimes changed to Garvey. See Garvan.

Gason See Gaussen.

Gaskin This is a modern form of Gascoigne (i.e. of Gascony). It is in Ireland since the thirteenth century, mainly in Leinster. Gaskinstown is in Co. Meath.

Gaston App.

Gatchell A Quaker family formerly prominent in the industrial life of Waterford.

(Mac) Gately *Mag* or *Mac Athlaoich*. I accept Dr. Arthur Moore's statement that this is the correct Irish form of this Co. Roscommon name rather than *Ó Gatlaoich* as given by Woulfe. See Keightley.

Gattins See Gaitens.

(O) Gaughan *Ó Gáibhtheacháin* (*gáibhtheach*, anxious). Lately abbreviated to *Ó Gacháin*. A sept of the Uí Fiachrach in north Connacht. MIF   Map Mayo. See Gahan and Gavaghan.

Mac Gaughey See MacGahey.

Mac Gaughney *Mag Fhachtna*. A rare name embodying an old Irish personal name. It has been changed to Gaffney in Co. Longford.

Mac Gaughran See MacGahern.

Gaule *Mac an Ghaill* (*gall*, foreigner). An Irish patronymic adopted by Stapletons. The Gaules of Gauletown, Co. Kilkenny, claimed to be a branch of the Burkes.

Gault An adjectival surname formed from *gallda* (foreign) mainly found in Antrim.

Mac Gauran See MacGovern.

(O) Gaussen *Ó Gusáin* (*gus*, action or vigour; a frequent component of Irish surnames). A rare Connacht name also anglicized as Gason.

(O) Gavaghan This is an alternative more phonetic form of *Ó Gáibhtheacháin* (Gaughan) almost peculiar to Mayo and Roscommon.

(O) Gavan, Gavin *Ó Gábháin, Ó Gáibhín*. (Woulfe derives these from *gábhadh*, want, which is conjectural). The latter form is the more numerous. Both are used in two areas to which these septs belong, viz. north Connacht, and south Munster. Mayo is their main location now. MIF   Map Cork.

(Mac) Gavigan This is recorded as a synonym both of Geoghegan and MacGuigan in Co. Dublin; and occasionally, also for Gaffigan.

(O) Gavigan A variant of Gavaghan.

Mac Gaw *Mag Ádhaimh* (a local form of Adam). A variant of MacCaw in Ulster; also the name of a branch of the Scots clan MacFarlane.

(Mac) Gawley See MacAuley. **Gawne** See under Gonne, page 304.

Gay This English name is an occasionally synonym of Gildea.

Gayer An occasional synonym of McGirr or of the English toponymic Gare. Bibl.

Gaynard An old Anglo-Norman family in Co. Galway from the thirteenth century, now mainly found in Mayo.

(Mac) Gaynor *Mag Fhionnbhairr* (*fionnbharr,* fair head). Gaynor has now superseded the older MacGinver except where the latter has become MacGinty, as in Co. Monaghan. With *Mac* for *Mag* it became Kinure in east Munster. MIF   Map Longford.

Mac Geady (This form in Irish uncertain, ?*Mag Géadaigh* or *Mag Éidigh*). This name is found in north-west Donegal.

Mac Geaghan, -Gegan Corrupt forms of Geoghegan.

Mac Geagh This Donegal-Derry name may be either *Mac Eathach* or *Mag Eachadha.* See MacGagh and MacGahey.

(O) Geane *Ó Géibhinn.* An abbreviated form of O'Geaney.

(Mac) Geaney *Mac Géibheannaigh* (*géibheannach,* fettered). A rare name in south Ulster and formerly in Co. Roscommon. MIF   See next entry.

(O) Geaney *O Géibheannaigh* (see previous entry). A Co. Cork name. I cannot accept Woulfe's equation of (O) Geaney with Guiney though that is occasionally true of (Mac) Geaney in Ulster.

Mac Gearn A Glenties (Co. Donegal) form of *Ó Géaráin.* See Sharpe.

Mac Gearty See Gerty.

Mac Geary, -Gerry Tyrone and Armagh forms of MacGarry. See next entry for Connacht.

(O) Geary In Co. Cork where Geary is mainly found, it is *Ó Gadhra,* the Munster branch of the O'Garas. It may also be for *Mac Gadhra* (MacGeary) of Co. Roscommon.

(O) Geaveney See Keaveney.

Geddes App.

Mac Gee *Mag Aoidh* (*Aodh* equates with Hugh). Usually spelt Magee in east Ulster where Island Magee on the Antrim coast locates that prominent sept. In addition some MacGee families are of north-west Ulster origin, some are of Scottish stock. Bibl. IF   Map Antrim and Westmeath. See Wynne.

Mac Geehan *Mac Gaoithín* (the basic word here is *gaoth,* wind). A Donegal name, often written Mageean. MIF   See Guihen.

(O) Geehan A variant form of the Wicklow name Gahan.

(O) Geelan *Ó Gialláin.* A Leitrim name. It may be derived from *giall,* hostage.

Mac Geeney See MacGeany.

Mac Geer See MacGirr.

Mac Geever A Donegal form of MacIvor.

(Mac) Geheran A north Connacht form of MacGahern.

(Mac) Gegan, Geogan Occasional variants of Geoghegan.

Mac Genis See MacGuinness.

(Mac) Geoffrey See Shaffrey.

(Mac) Geoghegan, Gehegan *Mag Eochagáin.* One of the main septs of the southern Uí Néill. The name is a derivative of *Eochaidh* (see Mac-Gahey). Wóulfe says this means rich in cattle, but I am informed by scholars in that field that this is not so. Bibl. IF   Map Westmeath.

(O) Geoghery See Goghery.

George Though there are some mediaeval Irish references to this name, including Georgestown in Co. Waterford, it was rare before the seventeenth century and has since been found mainly in Ulster, where it is of Scottish origin, as also is its synonym Georgeson, which is occasionally made McGeorge (though Black says this is a late form of McJarrow.) Gorges, now almost obsolete, is probably a variant. George is derived from a Greek word meaning farm-worker.

Mac Geough *Mag Eochadha* (for derivation see Geoghegan). This name belongs to the Oriel country where it is also called MacGoff and Mac-Gough. It is to be distinguished, however, from Gough. MIF

Mac Geown, -Geon Oriel synonyms of MacKeown.

(Mac) Geraghty, -Geretty *Mag Oireachtaigh* (*oireachtach,* member of assembly). There are many variants of the anglicized form of this name, e.g. Garrity, Gerty, Geroughty, Jerety, etc. It is that of an important Connacht sept which is akin to the royal O'Conors. Bibl. IF   Map Roscommon.

(O) Geran, Gerin See Guerin.

Gernon See Garland. Map Monaghan.

Mac Gerr See MacGirr.

Gerrard An English forename used as a surname; sometimes a synonym of Garrett. Bibl.

Mac Gerry A Co. Cavan variant of MacGarry.

(Mac) Gerty See Geraghty.

Gervais See Jervois.

Gethin See under Gettins.

Mac Getrick *Mac Shitric.* (*Sitric* was a Norse personal name). A variant of MacKetrick almost peculiar to Co. Sligo.

Mac Gettigan, -Ettigan *Mag Eiteagáin.* This Tyrone name had the O prefix *(Ó hEitigen)* in mediaeval times as well as the Mac. It is found now mainly in Co. Donegal. MIF

Gettins A synonym of MacGettigan. Gethin, however, a Welsh name, is seldom so used.

Getty Exclusively a Derry and Antrim name and is a known abbreviation of the Scottish Dalgetty, so this may be accepted as its usual origin. *Mag Eitigh* is used as the form in Irish.

(Mac) Ghee A Scottish form of MacGee.

Gibb A diminutive of Gilbert. See Gibson.

Mac Gibbon See Gibbons and MacKibben.

Gibbon(s) Disregarding English settlers so called, we have *Mac Giobúin* a branch of the Connacht Burkes, and also those Fitzgibbons who have dropped the Fitz. Bibl. IF   Map (MacGibbon) Mayo. See Fitzgibbon.

(O) Giblin *Ó Gibealáin.* The O'Gibellans, as they were formerly called, were noted as ecclesiastics in the diocese of Elphin. MIF   Map Roscommon.

(O) Gibney *Ó Gibne.* Woulfe may possibly be right in deriving this from a rare word meaning hound, but *gibne* usually means a lock of hair which seems preferable here. MIF   Map Cavan-Meath.

Gibson In Ireland usually a name of Scottish origin which, like Gibb, is a branch of the clan Buchanan. Gibson is very numerous in the Belfast area. Gibson and Gipsey have been occasionally assumed instead of Giblin.

Mac Giff See MacGuff.

(Mac) Giffen *Mag Dhuibhfinn* (perhaps *dubh,* black—*Finn,* gen. of *Fionn,* a personal name meaning fair). Fairly numerous today in Cos. Antrim, Derry and Tyrone, as it was in the seventeenth century.

(Mac) Gifford This Scottish name is fairly numerous in Co. Down.

Gihen See Guihen.

Gil- Names compounded with Gil usually begin with Kil in Connacht.

Gilbert This name has long been prominent in Leinster. Gilbertstown is now found as a place-name in five counties—two (Louth and Westmeath) in the sixteenth century.

Gilbey, (O) Gilboy Of dual origin; an English toponymic, or an anglicized form of *Ó Giolla Bhuidhe* (*buidhe,* yellow) which is usually anglicized Gilboy, but sometimes Ogilvy. The name of the Scottish clan Ogilvie is actually taken from a place so called. MIF

(Mac) Gilbride See Kilbride.

(Mac) Gilchrist *Mac Giolla Chríost* (devotee of Christ). An indigenous sept of north Connacht and Co. Longford. Gilchrist is also a Scottish surname quite numerous in north-east Ulster. MIF

(Mac) Gildea, Kildea *Mac Giolla Dhé* (*Dé* gen. of *Dia,* God). From Tirconnell, where this sept originated, many of the name moved southwards, and it is now found in Connacht and Clare. In Leitrim it has been made Benison by semi-translation. MIF

(Mac) Gildowney See MacEldowney and Muldowney.

Gilduff See Kilduff.

Giles Long associated with Youghal, Co. Cork. When this name occurs in or near Co. Louth it is often for *Ó Glaisne.* Elsewhere it is probably of English origin. Woulfe says it may also be *Mac Goill* in Co. Galway.

123

(Mac) Gilfillan See MacLellan.

(Mac) Gilfoyle *Mac Giolla Phóil* (devotee of St. Paul). A family of note in Ely O'Carroll. The form in Irish shows how the occasional synonym of Powell arose. IF   Map Offaly.

(O) Gilgan *Ó Giollagáin.* Of north Leitrim and Co. Sligo, this sept has no connection with the better known MacGilligan.

(Mac) Gilgar, Kilgar *Mac Giolla Gheáirr** (*geárr*, short). A north Connacht name.

(Mac) Gilgunn See Gunn.

Mac Gilheany A Breffny variant of MacIhenny.

(Mac) Gilhooly *Mac Giolla Ghuala* (*guala*, shoulder). An offshoot of O'Mulvey, prominent in Leitrim and Roscommon from the earliest times on record. It has been abbreviated to Gilhool in Co. Sligo. A branch settled in Co. Limerick. MIF   Map Leitrim.

Gilkinson According to Woulfe this name, mainly associated in Ireland with Tyrone, is an anglicized form of *Mac Uilicín* (see Quilkin); but Reaney says it is derived from the Christian name Gilchrist.

Gill There is an English name Gill, but in Ireland it is usually for MacGill. See next entry.

Mac Gill *Mac an Ghaill* (*gall*, foreigner). Spelt Magill in east Ulster. This name is also often an abbreviation of one of the many names beginning with *Mac Giolla*. MIF

(O) Gillan, Gillen *Ó Giolláin* (*giolla*, lad). A family of the Cenél Eoghain mainly found in Cos. Sligo, Donegal and Tyrone. See Gilligan and Gilliland.

(Mac) Gillanders *Mac Giolla Aindréis* (devotee of St. Andrew). Almost exclusively of Co. Monaghan. It takes the form MacLandrish on Rathlin Island. Glanders is an occasional synonym of both Gillanders and Landers.

(Mac) Gilleece, Gillice Fermanagh variants of MacAleese.

(O) Gilleen *Ó Gillín.* Cognate with Gillen and Gillan. Map Mayo. Gilleen is also an occasional synonym of Killeen.

(O) Gillen See Gillan.

(O) Gilleran Now *Ó Giollaráin.* (Woulfe says it was formerly *Mac Giolla Éanáin*). A Co. Roscommon name quite distinct from Gilloran.

Mac Gillereagh See Gallery.

(Mac) Gillespie *Mac Giolla Easpuig* (*easpog*, bishop). This family belongs by origin to Down but was early established in Donegal. Synonyms of the name are Clusby and Glashby in Co. Louth, Clasby in Co. Galway and also, by translation, Bishop. MIF   Map Donegal.

(Mac) Gillian *Mac Gileáin.* This name, of doubtful origin, is found in Cos. Tyrone and Derry.

*See footnotes on pp. 3 and 7.

Gilliard See under Killiard (which is not synonymous).

(Mac) Gillick *Mac Uilic* (*Uilic*, diminutive of William). A branch of the Burkes of Connacht, numerous in Co. Cavan.

(Mac) Gilligan *Mac Giollagáin*. (Another surname probably derived from *giolla*, lad). A leading sept of Co. Derry sometimes abbreviated to Gillan. The district in north Derry adjacent to Lough Foyle is called Magilligan's Strand. This name exemplifies the common practice in the north of eliding names beginning with MacG to Mag. MIF Map Derry. See Giligan.

(Mac) Gilliland An east Ulster variant of MacLellan. It is sometimes shortened to Gillan. **(Mac) Gillinan See p. 304.**

Gillis The Scottish *Giolla Íosa*, sometimes used for MacAleese in Ireland.

Gillman Cognate with *Guillaume*, the French form of William. Coming to Ireland with Essex in 1599 the family multiplied and became numerous in west Cork. Bibl. MIF

(Mac) Gillooly, Gillowly See Gilhooly.

(Mac) Gilloon A rare variant of MacAloon.

(Mac) Gilloran See Killoran.

Mac Gilloway This is another form of MacElwee.

Mac Gilly See Quilly.

Mac Gillycuddy *Mac Giolla Chuda* (?devotee of St. Mochuda). An important branch of the sept of O'Sullivan Mór. Bibl. IF   Map Kerry.

(Mac) Gilmartin *Mac Giolla Mhártain* (devotee of St. Martin). This sept is a branch of the O'Neills in Fermanagh and Tyrone. Those who moved into Connacht became Kilmartin. IF   Map Tyrone.

(Mac) Gilmer See under Gilmore.

(Mac) Gilmore *Mac Giolla Mhuire* (devotee of B.V. Mary) in Ulster, but *Mac Giolla Mhir* (*mear*, lively) in Sligo. The Ulster sept descends from an O'Morna (possibly the origin of the present Murney). MIF Map Down.

(Mac) Gilna(gh) *Mac Giolla na Naomh* (*na naomh*, of the saints). Gilnagh is found in Co. Longford. This Irish name has many variants, e.g. MacAneave in Co. Roscommon. See MacElnay and Ford.

(Mac) Gilpatrick An anglicized form of *Mac Giolla Phádraig* now rare. See Fitzpatrick. Map Kilkenny-Leix.

Gilpin An English name now concentrated in Cos. Armagh and Cavan. When found in Connacht families called Gilpin are probably of the Co. Sligo sept of *Mac Giolla Finn*, MacGilpin. MIF

Gilrain A Leitrim variant of Gilleran.

(Mac) Gilrea A variant of Kilrea.

(Mac) Gilreevy See MacAreavy.

(Mac) Gilroy *Mac Giolla Rua* (*rua*, red). Also anglicized MacElroy and

MacIlroy in Ulster (Ballymacilroy is in Co. Fermanagh) and Kilroy in Connacht. IF   MIF   Map Fermanagh.

(Mac) Gils(h)enan *Mac Giolla Seanáin* (devotee of St. Senan). This sept originated in Tyrone, but the name is now equally well known in north Leinster. Both Leonard and Nugent have been adopted as synonyms of Gilshenan, which is sometimes made Shannon in Co. Fermanagh.

Gilson In Offaly this English name is a synonym of Gilsenan.

(Mac) Giltenan *Mac Giolla tSeanáin*. A variant of Gilsenan used in Co. Clare, where it is also anglicized Shannon.

Mac Gilton An Ulster variant of MacGiltenan.

Giltrap A variant of the English toponymic Gilthorpe, mainly found in the Dublin-Wexford area and of comparatively recent introduction. MIF

(Mac) Gilvane A variant of Kilbane.

(Mac) Gilvany A variant of MacElvenna.

Mac Gilvarry *Mac Giolla Bhearaigh* (devotee of St. Barry). This name, a variant of the Scots MacGillivray, is peculiar in Ireland to north Connacht and Donegal.

Mac Gilvie This variant of MacKelvey has no connection with Ogilvie.

Mac Gilway, -Gilwee Variants of MacElwee in Donegal.

Mac Gimpsey *Mac Dhíomasaigh* (for derivation see Dempsey). This name is remarkable on account of its close concentration in one small area, viz. around Newtownards, Co. Down, where it is quite numerous. MIF

Gina, Ginnaw, Gna These are variants of MacKenna in use in Co. Kerry with prefix Mag for Mac in the Gaelic form.

(Mac) Ging, MacGinn, Maginn *Mag Fhinn (fionn,* fair). MacGing is the form almost invariably used in Mayo and Leitrim. MacGinn is usual in Tyrone and Maginn in Antrim and Down.   MIF

Mac Ginley *Mag Fhionnghaile (fionnghaile,* fair valour). A Donegal name to be distinguished from MacKinley. MIF

(O) Ginnane A west Clare name which is also quite numerous in north Tipperary and Offaly where it is spelt Guinane. Woulfe gives *Ó Cuinneáin* and *Ó Cuineáin* as the usual forms in Irish (deriving them from the forenames Conn and Conan, respectively). He also mentions *Ó Gaibhneáin,* without comment: this is presumably a modern synonym.

Mac Ginnelly The Mayo form of MacGinley.

(Mac) Ginnell *Mag Fhionnghail* (for derivation see MacGinley). The name of a branch of the MacGinleys of Donegal who settled in Co. Westmeath. MIF

(O) Ginnevan See Guinevan.

Mac Ginnis See MacGuinness.

(Mac) Ginty, Ginity, Maginnity *Mag Fhinneachta* (derivation as Finaghty). A Donegal sept, now more numerous both as Ginty or Genty in north Connacht. It is quite distinct from MacEntee, though MacGinty and MacGenty occur in Co. Monaghan as synonyms of the latter. MIF   See Gaynor.

Mac Ginver See Gaynor.

Gipsey See Gibson.

Girey A variant spelling of Guirey.

Mac Girl, -Gerl *Mag Fhearghail* (for derivation see Farrell). Also anglicized MacGarrell, MacGorl; now mainly Leitrim and Cavan. When *Mac* not *Mag* is used (*Mac Fheargail*) as in Donegal, the name becomes MacCarrigle whence Cargill and Carkill. MIF

Mac Girr *Mac an Ghirr*. An old Co. Armagh name, also found in adjacent Tyrone where it is sometimes made Short by translation of the word *geárr*, earlier *giorr*. The variant MacGeer is found in north Leinster. MIF

Girvan A Scottish toponymic found in Ulster, mainly Co. Antrim. MIF

(O) Gissane See Kissane.

(Mac) Given, Giveen *Mag Dhuibhin* or *Mag Dhuibhfhinn** (see Giffen) of Donegal. The variant *Mac Dhuibhin,* anglicized MacKevin and MacAvin, is also found in Donegal and adjacent Co. Sligo. MIF

Mac Givern *Mag Uidhrin* (*odhar*, of which this is a diminutive, means dun-coloured). Map Armagh-Down. Both Biggar and Montgomery are strangely used as synonyms of MacGivern in Co. Down.

Mac Givney *Mac Dhuibhne* (for derivation see Deeney). This sept was located in the eastern part of the diocese of Kilmore, especially Co. Cavan, where the variants MacAvinna, MacAvinue and MacEvinney are also found. MIF

(O) Glacken *Ó Glacáin.* Fairly numerous in Co. Donegal and adjacent areas.

(Mac) Gladdery *Mac Gleadra.* This name originated in the Uí Maine country (south Connacht), but by the mid-seventeenth century it was mainly located in or near Tyrone. The prefix O instead of Mac is also recorded. MIF

Mac Glade *Mag Léid.* It is probably as Woulfe suggests a variant of the Scottish MacLeod. MacGlade is also found as an abbreviation of MacGladdery.

(Mac) Glaffy A variant form of Glavy.

Mac Glanc(h)y A variant of Clancy in Breffny.

Glanders See Gillanders.

Glanny, Glenny One of our few locative surnames, i.e. *an Ghleanna* (of the glen).

**The use of *Mag* rather than *Mac* before *Dh* is not imperative.

Glanville, Glanfield An Anglo-Norman name on record in Ireland since the fourteenth century, mainly in the southern counties of Munster.

Glascoe See Glasscock.

(Mac) Glasgow In Tyrone and other parts of Ulster this is a variant of MacCloskey. Glasgow in Ireland may also be a Scottish toponymic. See Glasscock.

(Mac) Glashan Usually *Mac Glasáin*, sometimes *Mac Glaisín*. This Derry name is often changed to Green (the adjective *glas* means green or grey-green). See Glasheen.

Glashby, Glaspey See Gillespie.

(O) Glasheen *Ó Glaisín*. Originally south-east Cork, now chiefly Co. Tipperary. Distinct from (Mac)Glashan and Gleeson, but of similar derivation.

Glass An adjectival surname from *glas* (green) mainly found in Cos. Antrim and Derry.

Glasscock An English toponymic formerly numerous in Co. Kildare. Glascoe is a synonym of Glasscock not of Glasgow. MIF

Mac Glaughlin An Ulster spelling of Mac Gloughlin.

(Mac) Glavin *Mag Laimhín*, formerly *Mag Fhlaithimhín (flaitheamh,* ruler). This rare Ulster name, sometimes Hand by pseudo-translation, is quite distinct from O'Glavin. MIF   See Glavy.

(O) Glavin *Ó Gláimhín*. (The derivation from *gláimhín,* glutton is not accepted; it is a diminutive of *glám,* satirist). The name of a small Uí Fiachrach sept now rarely found outside Cos. Cork and Kerry. Hand is not used as a synonym.

(Mac) Glavy, Glave *Mag Laithimh,* formerly *Mag Fhlaithimh* (for derivation see MacGlavin). A Connacht name often changed to Hand in the mistaken belief that it is derived from *lámh,* hand.

Gleasure This (with its variant Glazier which indicates its derivation) is an English name of comparatively late introduction but now well known in Co. Kerry.

Mac Gleen A variant of MacGlynn in east Connacht.

Mac Gleenan *Mac Giolla Fhinéin*. This form is found in Co. Armagh. See MacAleenan.

Gleese This name appears in east Galway as *de Glys* in the fifteenth century and is still there.

(O) Gleeson *Ó Glasáin* or *Ó Gliasáin*. The anglicized form of this name in Kerry is Glissane. The main sept was located in Lower Ormond. IF   Map Tipperary.

Glenaghan Probably *Mag Leannacháin,* a variant of MacClenaghan.

Glenane A variant of Glennon, nearer to the Irish form, found in Co. Tipperary.

Glendenning A Scottish toponymic in Antrim and Tyrone since early seventeenth century.

Glendon, Glindon These and the intermediate form MacLindon, as well as Lindon, are abbreviated forms of MacAlinden. Linton is also on record as a synonym in Cos. Down and Armagh. Glendon and Glindon, however, were quite numerous in Cos. Tipperary and Kilkenny in the seventeenth century and these are thought to be of English origin. I have not yet sufficient evidence to make a definite statement as to that.

Glenn, Glenny See Glanny.

(Mac) Glennon *Mag Leannáin* (the basic word in this name is *leann*, cloak). This name belongs to the midland counties (Westmeath, Leix and Offaly) where it is quite numerous. In Co. Roscommon it is probably the Uí Fiachrach name *Ó Gloinín*. See p. 304.

Mac Glew An Oriel name, possibly one of the many synonyms of MacAleavy. In Dublin it has been changed to MacLeod.

Mac Glinchy *Mag Loingsigh* (*loingseach*, mariner). Families of this name are from Donegal, Derry and Tyrone. With prefix *Mac* for *Mag* the anglicized form becomes MacClinchy. Map Donegal.

Glinn See Glynn.

Glissane See Gleeson.

Mac Gloin, -Glone, -Gloon *Mac Giolla Eoin* (devotee of St. John). This name belongs to Tyrone and Donegal and is found also in Co. Leitrim; it is quite distinct from MacGlynn. In Fermanagh and Derry this, like MacAloon, has been absurdly changed to Monday, due to the similarity in sound of the word *Luain*, Monday. MIF

(O) Glorney *Ó Gloiairn* is the Irish form used in O'Heerin's 'Topographical Poem'; the modern form is *Ó Glóthairne*. A Kilkenny name much confused with Glory. MIF

(Mac) Glory, Glowry *Mag Labhradha* (spokesman). Properly this belongs to Cos. Armagh and Down but in Kilkenny it is used for Glorney. SIF 80. See Glorney.

Gloster An English toponymic, viz. Gloucester, established in Cos. Limerick and Kerry since early eighteenth century.

Mac Gloughlin *Mag Lochlainn*. A variant of MacLoughlin.

Glover An English occupational name found in Ireland in mediaeval times and now fairly numerous in Ulster.

(Mac) Glynn *Mag Fhloinn* (*flann*, ruddy). This sept originated in the Athlone area and the name has now spread throughout Connacht and Clare. Glynn is also of Welsh origin, *de Glin*, but this is seldom the case in Ireland. MIF

Gna See Gina.

Goaley Found in Co. Galway. See Gooley.

Goan An Ulster form of Gowan often changed to Smith.

(O) Gobban See Gubbins.

Godfrey This well-known English name does duty in Ireland for *Mac*

Gothraidh, the name of a branch of the Maguires of Fermanagh, which is also anglicized MacCorry. MacCurry, MacGorry (with and without the prefix Mac). See also Gohery and MacGoffrey.

Godsell An English toponymic. The name of a family settled in Cos. Cork and Limerick since the end of the seventeenth century.

Godwin, Goodwin Both these have the same derivation, viz. Old-English *god*, good—*wine*, friend. In Ireland, when not of immigrant origin, they are synonyms of different native names: Godwin for O'Dea in Connacht (but not in Clare, the homeland of the O'Deas), Goodwin for MacGoldrick in Tyrone and for MacGuigan in Cos. Derry and Tyrone. Goodwin is also well known in Mayo where it is anglicized form of *Ó Goidín*.

Mac Goey A Leitrim-Longford variant of MacGaughey.

Goff An English name, used as a synonym of Gough as MacGoff is of MacGeough.

Mac Goffrey A variant of Caffrey.

Gogan, Goggin A later form in Co. Cork of Cogan. As Gogan it is perpetuated in Co. Cork place-names Goganrath and Gogganshill, which was earlier called Knockgogan.

(Mac) Gogarty *Mag Fhógartaigh*. The prefix O with this name is a modern corruption. Gogarty, which is on record in Co. Meath since the eleventh century, is quite distinct from Fogarty though etymolically cognate. MIF   Map Meath.

(O) Gohery *Ó Gothraidh*. This is derived from the Norse name *Gothfrith*. It is often changed to Godfrey and sometimes confused with MacGoffrey. Gohery and its variant Geoghery belong to the north Tipperary-Offaly area. MIF

Going Of dual origin, viz., a synonym of (Mac)Gowan, and an anglicized form of the French *Gouin*. It has been well known in Co. Tipperary since the end of the seventeenth century. MIF

Golden, Goulding As English names these are of different origin; but in Ireland, when not the name of an immigrant family which was prominent in Cork, are anglicized forms of *Ó Góilín, Ó Goilín* also of Co. Cork. Woulfe says *Mag Ualghairg* (MacGoldrick), often anglicized Golden and Goulding, is a branch of the O'Rourkes of Leitrim. MIF

Goldie A synonym of Goulding mainly found in Co. Offaly.

Mac Gol(d)rick See Golden. MIF   Map Fermanagh-Leitrim.

Goldsmith Prominent in Ireland from the mid-sixteenth century, when several of the name occupied official positions in Dublin and other cities, till the end of the eighteenth. It is now rare outside the Belfast area.

Goligher See Gallagher.

Golightly, Gologly Synonyms of Gallogly.

Mac Gomory *Mag Iomaire.* A modern gaelicization of Montgomery.

Mac Gonigal, Magonagle *Mag Congail.* This sept is notable for the number of distinguished ecclesiastics it has produced. MIF Map Donegal.

Gonne No convincing evidence of the origin of this name has been found. Woulfe makes it a synonym of the English or Scottish Gunn. It may possibly derive from the epithetic name Gawne (*gann*, short or stunted) which occurs in sixteenth-century Fiants for Cos. Cork and Kerry. The suggestion that Gonne derives from O'Gone, an early variant of O'Gowan, is not borne out by the distribution of the name Gonne in the eighteenth century. See p. 304.

Mac Gonnell Used for MacConnell in Oriel.

Gonoude *Mag Nuadhat, Mag Nuad.* A synonym of MacNowd or Mac-Nutt; also of Conway in Co. Offaly, where Gonoude stands also for Conoo.

Good An English name fairly numerous in Ireland especially Co. Cork, first settled in Co. Leix in the sixteenth century.

Goodall In Dublin since the sixteenth century, subsequently mainly in Co. Wexford. It is of dual derivation denoting brewer of good ale, or from a Yorkshire place-name. Bibl.

Goodbody This Quaker family, well known in the industrial life of Ireland, came to Co. Offaly from Yorkshire in mid-seventeenth century.

Goodfellow I am informed by Fr. P. Ó Gallachair that in Tyrone and adjacent parts of Ulster this English name is used as an anglicized form of *Mac Uiginn* (see MacGuigan).

Goodman This English name was prominent on the Irish side in Cos. Dublin and Wicklow in 1641 and following years. Balegodman is an obsolete place-name in Co. Dublin. Goodman occurs also as a synonym of MacGuigan in Co. Monaghan, as do Goodwin and even Goodfellow in Co. Tyrone.

Goodwin See Godwin and Goodman.

Mac Googan, Gookin See MacGuigan.

Mac Goohan *Mac Cuacháin* or *Mag Cuacháin.* A Leitrim name. Possibly from *cuach*, cuckoo. See MacCoohan.

Goold See Gould.

Gooley This name usually as Goly is found in records of Cos. Cork and Limerick from 1307. There are three non-Gaelic origins for it and Gulley, but the fact that it often occurs in the sixteenth and early seventeenth centuries with the prefix O suggests that in Ireland it is *Ó Gabhlaigh*, which is the name of an early bishop of Clonfert. It is derived from *gabhlach* (forked) and Forke has been used as a synonym of it.

(O) Goonan(e) *Ó Gamhnáin* (for derivation see next entry). This Clare name has sometimes been changed to Gooney and Gunning.

(O) Goonery *Ó Gamhnaire* (calf keeper from *gamhain,* calf). This name is found in Co. Meath where it has been changed to Montgomery.

Gooney See Goonan.

Gooravan See Gorevan.

Mac Goorty See MacGourkey.

Gordon This Scottish surname, very numerous as such in Ulster, has been used as a synonym of Magournahan, i.e. *Mag Mhuirneacháin* which also takes the form MacGourneson in Co. Down. Bibl.

Gore Several families of this English locative name (*gor,* a strip of land) were prominent among the Anglo-Irish landed gentry from the seventeenth century, especially in Cos. Mayo, Sligo and Clare.

Gorevan According to Woulfe this is a variant of MacGovern. I disagree and accept Richard Foley's opinion that it is a variant of Garvin. Gorevan with its variants Goravan and Gooravan belongs mainly to Cos. Sligo and Mayo.

Gorey See Gorry.

Gorges Bibl. See George.

Gorham The evidence available suggests that this name may be of dual origin in Ireland. It is mainly associated with Connemara and there it seems possible that it is of native Irish origin and that the Irish form *Ó Guarim,* now in use there, was anglicized Gorham. In Kerry, however, it is definitely of English, ultimately Norman, origin.

Mac Gorish *Mag Fheorais.* Cognate with Corish, found in Co. Monaghan.

Mac Gorl, Gorrell See MacGirl.

Mac Gorlick A variant of MacGoldrick.

(Mac) Gorman, O Gorman *Mac Gormáin.* The prefix O has been widely substituted for Mac, especially in the case of the Clare sept who followed the mistaken example of the famous 'chevalier'. That of Co. Monaghan has to some extent retained the Mac. IF   MIF Map Clare. See Gormley.

(O) Gormican, Gormagan Variants of Cormacan.

(O) Gormley, Gormally *Ó Gormghaile* in Connacht and *Ó Goirmleadhaigh* in Ulster according to O'Donovan, who regarded these septs as quite distinct. A study of this interesting and important name is complicated by the fact that in some cases in Ulster it has been changed to Gorman and to Grimes. IF   Map Donegal, Mayo, Roscommon and Tyrone.

Mac Gorry *Mac Gothraidh.* The name of a branch of the O'Reillys in Co. Cavan. For derivation see Gohery.

(O) Gorry, Gorey, Gurry *Ó Guaire* (noble). This is fairly numerous in north Leinster. It has no relation to the town of Gorey. SIF 81.

Mac Gorty See MacGourkey.

Goslin See Gosnell. Gosling, however, is normally a different name of English origin, located in east Leinster.

Gosnell A family settled as tenants in west Cork in the eighteenth century, some of whom became Gosling. Ewen says Gosnell is derived from the Irish word *góiséir*, hosier, which is very doubtful.

Gossan See Gaussen.

Gough *Goch*. A Welsh family called Coch (*coch*, red) came to Ireland in the thirteenth century and settled in Co. Waterford and Dublin. This family has been closely identified with the Irish national cause, especially in the seventeenth century. The name Gough is occasionally a synonym of MacGeough. Bibl. MIF

Gould, Goold *Gúl*. This old English name, derived from the word gold, is intimately associated with Cork since mediaeval times. MIF Map Cork.

Goulding See Golden and Forkin.

Mac Gourkey, -Gourtey According to Fr. Travers the Irish form of this, *Mac Dhorchaidh* (*dorcha*, dark), has occasionally resulted in it being anglicized Darcy in Co. Fermanagh. Map Leitrim.

(Mac) Gourley *Mag Thoirdealbhaigh*. A variant of MacTurley in Cos. Tyrone and Antrim.

Mac Gourneson See Gordon.

Mac Gover(a)n, -Gowran, Magauran *Mag Shamhráin* (*samhra*, summer). A Breffny sept of note. The centre of their territory is indicated by the village called Ballymagauran. Bibl. IF Map Cavan.

Governey Now associated with Carlow, formerly Co. Leix. Its origin is uncertain. Its equation with Coveney cannot be accepted. It may be from the Huguenot *Gouvernet*.

Gow *Gabha*. This is the Irish form for blacksmith and Smith is actually used as a synonym of Gow in Co. Cavan and north Meath. See MacGowan.

Mac Gowan *Mac an Ghabhann, Mac Gabhann*. In Co. Cavan, the homeland of this sept, the name has been widely changed by translation to Smith (though Smithson would be a truer translation); but in outlying areas of Breffny MacGowan is retained. IF Map Cavan.

O Gowan *Ó Gabhann*. Though this has also become Smith it is distinct from MacGowan. O'Gowan has an early connection with Breffny, where it was a clerical family of note, but it is primarily of north Oriel. Bibl. IF Map Armagh-Down.

Gowen, Gowing See Going.

Mac Gowran See MacGovern.

Grace *Grás*. The Norman family of Grace has been prominent in Irish history since the first *le Gras* came to Ireland about 1200. Bibl. MIF Map Kilkenny.

Gracey App.

MacGrade See MacGread.

(O) Graddy *Ó Greada* (perhaps from *greit*, gen. *greada*, champion). Mainly found in Co. Cork where it is probably a synonym of Draddy.

Mac Grady *Mag Brádaigh*. A Co. Down variant of MacBrady as also are MacGraddy and MacGrade.

(O) Grady *Ó Grádaigh* (*gráda*, illustrious). A Dalcassian sept. The leading family went to Co. Limerick but the majority are still in Clare where the prefix O is retained more than elsewhere. An important branch changed their name to Brady in the late sixteenth century. The well-known name Grady has to a large extent absorbed the rarer Gready which is properly a Mayo name. This resulted in the name Grady being numerous in north Connacht and adjacent areas of Ulster. Bibl. IF   MIF   Map Clare and Limerick.

Graecen See Greacen.

Graham This Scottish name, very numerous in Ulster, is used as an anglicized form of two Irish surnames, viz. Gormely and Grehan. App.

Grahan A variant of both Grehan and Graham.

Mac Grail See MacGreal.

Grailis A Connemara form of Grealish.

Grainger This name (from French *grangier*, farm steward) is quite numerous in Antrim since mid-seventeenth century, but is not confined to Ulster. References to Le Graunger occur in mediaeval Irish records, mostly in central Leinster.

Gralton The prevalence of this name in Cos. Leitrim and Roscommon, but nowhere else, indicates that its origin is some indigenous Irish surname beginning with *Mag-R-*, but if that is so, I have yet to trace this. I do not find Gralton as an English toponymic.

Mac Granahan, -Grenaghan *Mag Reannacháin* (possibly from *reannach*, sharp-pointed), later form *Mac Grennacháin*. This sept is of Donegal and is still well known in their homeland, Mevagh.

Mac Grane Woulfe gives *Mag Raighne* for this mainly Leinster name, which is spelt Magrane in Dublin and Louth. This would equate it with Granny (see next entry) which is questionable. It is also in Tyrone and Armagh where it is pronounced and often spelt Mac-Grann. MIF

(Mac) Graney, Granny *Mag Raighne*. A north Ulster name sometimes changed to Grant. *Raigne* is a pet form of *Raghnall* which equates with Reginald. MIF

Granfield, Granville Granfield, sometimes spelt Grandfield, is a modern form of the Norman *de Granville*. Granfield is fairly numerous in Kerry, where it has been since late sixteenth century. It is very rare elsewhere in Ireland.

Mac Grann This is a variant of MacGrane not of MacCran.

(Mac) Grannell *Mag Raghnaill*. This form of MacRannall is found in Co. Wexford. See Graney.

Mac Grannon *Mag Raghnainn*. A Mayo name cognate with MacRannall or Reynolds.

Grant This Scottish name is numerous in all the provinces except Connacht. It is an occasional synonym of Granny. It was well established in Munster before the end of the sixteenth century and as *le Graunte* the name frequently occurs in mediaeval records in other parts of the country also, especially in Co. Kilkenny. Bibl.

Mac Grath, Magrath *Mac Graith, Mag Raith*. The personal name in this case is *Craith* not *Raith*. The name of two distinct septs; viz. (i) that of Thomond who supplied hereditary ollamhs in poetry to the O'Briens, a branch of whom migrated to Co. Waterford; and (ii) of Termon MacGrath in north-west Ulster, a co-arb family. MacGrath is often called MacGraw in Co. Down and MacGragh in Donegal. IF Map Clare, Donegal-Fermanagh, Waterford.

(Mac) Grattan *Mag Reachtain* has been accepted, without much authority, as the Gaelic form of Grattan. MacGrattan is a not uncommon name in Ulster today. There is an English name Gratton which may be the origin of some Irish Grattans. Grattans were well established in Co. Tipperary and also in Dublin in the seventeenth century. Bibl. IF

Graves An Old-English name derived by some authorities from a word denoting grove (from residence there) and by others from one denoting steward: it is in Ireland since the sixteenth century (then often spelt Greaves) and has long associations with Cos. Cork, Offaly and Tyrone but is best known for its connection with Dublin University. Bibl. IF   See Greeves.

Mac Graw See MacGrath.

Gray This name is usually of English or Scottish origin; but for Connacht and Co. Longford see Culreavy. IF   MIF

Grayhan See Grehan.

Greacen, Grayson A Co. Monaghan name, derived from grieve, a steward.

Mac Gread, -Grade Abbreviated forms of MacGrady found in west Ulster; occasionally synonyms of MacGrath.

Mac Gready, -Greedy *Mag Riada*. This family, whose name has been corrupted to *Ó Griada,* belongs to Mayo and Roscommon. For Gready without the prefix see Grady.

Mac Greal *Mag Réill* formerly *Mac Néill*. A galloglass family established in Mayo and Leitrim. The Uí Fiachrach sept of MacNéill of Carra, Co. Mayo, was extinct a century ago in O'Donovan's time, he said.

(Mac) Grealish *Mag Riallghuis.* A Connacht form of MacNelis. In Ulster it sometimes takes the form MacGrellis or MacGrillis.

(Mac) Greally *Mag Raoghallaigh, Raoghallach* is a variant of *Raghallaigh,* i.e. Reilly. Greally, usually without the prefix Mac, is almost exclusively a Galway-Mayo name.

Greaney *Ó Gráinne (Gráinne* is a woman's name). This is fairly numerous in Kerry. When found in Connacht the prefix Mac is used. MIF See Graney.

Greaves See Greeves.

(O) Greefa An older and more phonetic form of Griffey.

(O) Greehy *Ó Gríocha.* A variant of *Ó Gríobhtha* (see Griffey) peculiar to east Cork and west Waterford.

Mac Green Woulfe equates this name with MacGrane and MacGrean. MacGreen, however, is quite distinct, being a well-known west Clare name. It is not *Mac Grianna* which is a Donegal name. I have yet to determine its origin in Clare, where Green without the prefix Mac, i.e. *Ó hUaithín* (Honeen), is numerous. Possibly it is an example of the not infrequent substitution of O for Mac, though this is unusual combined with translation. See Greene.

(O) Greenan *Ó Grianáin* (for derivation see Grennan). A rare name found in Cavan and Sligo, also anglicized as Greene.

Greenaway This English locative name (dweller by the green way) has been in Ireland since mid-seventeenth century when Henry Greenaway, one of the Cromwellian commissioners, became a prominent settler in Co. Galway. It is now quite numerous in Ulster where Greenhay is a variant.

Green(e) This well-known English name does duty in Ireland for a number of Irish names, see Houneen, MacGreen, Fahy, MacAlesher, MacGlashan, Greenan and Guerin. It is also an O'Sullivan agnomen, *glas.* Bibl. IF MIF

Greer This is a variant of the Scottish MacGregor, *Mac Grioghar,* numerous in north Ulster since the time of the Plantation of Ulster. MIF

Greeves, Greaves Though Reaney distinguishes between Greaves and Graves, deriving the former from an Old-English word meaning thicket or grove but Graves (and also Grieve) from one denoting steward or farm bailiff, it is impossible to differentiate them in Ireland unless relevant evidence is available in particular cases; and the uncertainty is increased if we accept Woulfe's statement that the Irish *Ó Gríobhtháin* has been anglicized Grieve as well as O Griffen, etc. There is an occasional reference to Greves in records relating to Cork as early as the fourteenth century but seldom occurs until the seventeenth century when it came from England as Grieve and has since been found mainly in Ulster, where it is now numerous as Greeves. See Graves.

Mac Greevy *Mag Riabhaigh* (*riabhach,* grey or brindled). A north Connacht sept of importance in mediaeval times. Their chiefs were lords of Moylurg. MIF   Map Roscommon. See MacAreevy.

(Mac) Gregan *Mag Riagáin.* This is a Mac name distinct from Grehan. It appears occasionally in mediaeval and early modern records in east Leinster. It is rare now and seldom found outside Leinster. See Cregan.

Gregg App.

Gregory An Anglo-Irish family first settled in Kerry in the seventeenth century; later well known as of Coole in Co. Galway. Bibl. IF

(O) Grehan, Greaghan *Ó Gréacháin.* (Woulfe's derivation from *créach,* blind, is not accepted for the personal name *Gréachán*). This name is mainly found in Connacht and the adjacent part of Westmeath. It has a number of variant forms, e.g. Graham, Grayhan, and has even been corrupted to Grimes, which, however, when it occurs in Tyrone, is for Gormley, not Grehan. Grimes has been fancifully gaelicized *Ó Greidhm.*

(Mac) Grellis(h) See Grealish.

(Mac) Grenaghan See Granahan.

(O) Grennan *Ó Grianáin* (probably from *grian,* sun, *grianach,* sunny). A Connacht family originating and still found in Mayo; in Offaly and midland counties the name is of Norman origin (from Old-French *gernon,* moustache) and sometimes spelt Grennon. It is numerous in Co. Monaghan where it is probably of Irish origin. Both are quite distinct from Grannon. MIF

Grenville See Granfield.

Grew See under Mulgrew.

Grey See Gray.

Gribben This name is now widespread in the north-eastern counties of Ulster and has long been on record in Cos. Down and Armagh as O'Gribben (*Ó Gribín* in Irish). Where it is found as MacGribben it is a variant of MacCribbin, i.e. *Mac Roibín,* a Connacht name (*Mag Roibín* in Ulster). Its synonym MacRobin is now very rare. MIF

Grier See Greer.

Grierson A branch of the Scottish clan MacGregor. Bibl.

Grieve See Greeves.

Grifferty A variant of Crifferty with prefix *Mag* for *Mac.*

(O) Griffin, Griffey *Ó Gríobhtha* (*gríobhtha,* griffin-like). Griffin has almost entirely superseded the earlier Griffey. The main sept is of Thomond. Another was located near Kenmare. Some Irish Griffins are of Welsh origin, i.e. Griffith. IF   Map Clare.

137

Griffith A Welsh name, used synonymously with Griffin in Co. Kilkenny. IF

Mac Grillan, Magrillan *Mag Rialláin*. An Ulster name formed from *Niall* with the not uncommon substitution of R for N.

(Mac) Grillis See Grealish.

Grimes See Grehan and Gormley.

Grimley A Co. Armagh variant of Gormley.

Mac Griskin A Co. Leitrim name for which rather dubiously Woulfe suggests *Mac Cristín* (son of Christian) as the form in Irish which is conjectural.

(Mac) Groarke, Grourke *Mag Ruairc*. A small sept of the southern Uí Néill, but now mainly found in Mayo.

Mac Groarty *Mag Robhartaigh*. A Co. Donegal name. The family of Ballymagroarty were keepers of the psalter of St. Colmcille. See MacRoarty.

Groden An anglicized form of *Mag Rodáin* found in Connacht. Magrudden is another. See Rodden.

Mac Grod(d)y *Mag Rodaigh* (*rod*, strong). An erenagh family of Desertegney, Inishowen, Co. Donegal. The spelling MacGruddy is also usual in that county.

(O) Grogan, Groogan *Ó Gruagáin*. (Woulfe suggests alternatively *gruag*, hair and *grúg*, fierceness). Few septs have been so widely dispersed as this from their original homeland, in this case Co. Roscommon. The prefix O has not been resumed. In Ulster the variants Grugan and even Groggan are found. MIF

(Mac) Gronan A synonym of Reynolds in Co. Armagh, giving *Mag Raghainn* as a variant in Irish.

Mac Grory A variant of MacRory, with *Mag* for *Mac*.

Mac Grotty A rare name found in Cos. Derry and Tyrone. Woulfe tentatively suggests *Mag Ratha* as the form in Irish.

Grove(s) An English locative name associated mainly with Co. Cork since seventeenth century. See Graves.

Mac Growder, -Grudder *Mág Bhruadair*. (Broder was a Norse personal name). An Oriel name.

(O) Growney *Ó Gramhna*. A corrupt form of *Mac Carrghamhna*, MacCarron. Map Westmeath.

Grubb An English family settled in Cos. Waterford and Tipperary since the mid-seventeenth century. The name is occasionally, but seldom, a synonym of MacRobb. Bibl. IF

Mac Gruddy See Groddy.

(O) Grugan A variant of Grogan.

Grumley A Leinster variant of Gormley, but not of Crumley.

Grummell See Cromwell.

Mac Guane *Mac Dhubháin* (*dubh*, black). In Donegal this has been absorbed by MacGowan but in Clare the form MacGuane is retained.

Gubbins In Donegal and Derry this is *Ó Goibín* and *Ó Gobáin* (*gob*, mouth), also anglicized Gobban; but in Limerick, where it is well known, it came from England in the seventeenth century, its origin being probably the Old-French *Giboin* or Old-German *Gebawin*. MIF

Mac Guckin, Guckian See MacGuigan and Hackett. Guckian is found in Co. Leitrim. Also distinct as *Mag Eochaidhín* in Ulster.

Guerin This name is fairly numerous in Co. Limerick. In Kerry it has taken the form Geran and Gerin. It has been changed to Green in the Athlone area, and in Ulster it is an occasional synonym of Mac-Givern. Guerin is also a Huguenot surname. Its connection, if any, with the now almost extinct Mayo sept of *Ó Gearáin* is tenuous.

MacGuff, -Giff(ie) *Mac Dhuibh* (*dubh*, black). A north Connacht name.

(Mac) Guffin A variant of MacGiffen.

Guidera, Guider I have not ascertained the origin of this name. It has been found in north Tipperary at least since the mid-seventeenth century; there it was formerly called Gidery. *Mac Giodaire* is the modern Irish form in use in Co. Derry, where the name is also found. MIF

Mac Guigan *Mag Uiginn*. The following are the more usual of the many variant forms of this Co. Tyrone name: MacGoogan, MacGookin, MacGuckian, MacQuiggan, MacWiggin; some of these without the Mac, as Wigan, or with the Mac combined, as Maguigan. Fidgeon and Pidgeon are also used as synonym of MacGuigan (sometimes *Mac Guagáin*) in Co. Monaghan. MIF   See MacQuiggan, Godwin and Goodfellow.

(O) Guihan, Guihe(e)n *Ó Gaoithín* (*gaoth*, wind). The name of this Roscommon sept is also anglicized Geehan. Either a branch of this, or a distinct sept, is established in Co. Kerry: there were a number of families of the name on Blasket Island. MIF   See also Gahan.

(Mac) Guilfoyle See Gilfoyle.

Mac Guill *Mag Cuill*. A variant of MacQuill not of MacGill, long associated with Co. Armagh.

Guina A variant of Gina. See MacKenna.

(O) Guinan(e) See Ginnane.

Guinee A variant of Guiney, indicating the correct pronunciation of that name.

Guinevan Woulfe gives the Irish form as *Mac Dhuinneabháin* treating it as an attenuated form of O'Donovan. It may also be a synonym of Canavan in Co. Waterford.

(O) Guiney *Ó Guinidhe*. This name is mainly found in Kerry and Cork. Map Kerry. See Guinee and Geaney.

Mac Guiney A variant of MacGeaney mainly found in Co. Cavan.

Mac Guinn *Mac Guinn*. A form of MacQuinn in north Connacht.

(Mac) Guinness, Mac Genis, Magennis *Mag Aonghusa* or *Mag Aonghuis* (son of Angus) of Iveagh. One of the leading septs of Ulster. The world-famous brewers descend from a junior branch. Bibl. IF Map Down.

Mac Guire, Maguire *Mag Uidhir* (*odhar,* gen. *uidhir,* dun-coloured). The leading sept of Fermanagh. Many members of this sept have been distinguished in the history of Ireland. Bibl. IF Map Fermanagh.

Mac Guirk, -Gurk *Mag Oirc* (not *Mag Cuirc*). A Tyrone sept descended from Niall Naoighiallach numerous in that county and also in Antrim. Ballygurk, in Co. Derry near Co. Tyrone, is *Baile Mhic Oirc* in Irish. MIF

(O) Guiry The Co. Limerick and Waterford form of *Ó Gadhra*. See Geary.

(O) Guissane A west Clare form of Kissane.

Gullen A variant of Gillan in Co. Donegal.

Mac Gullian, Magullion *Mac Gilleáin*. This is mainly found in Cos. Leitrim and Longford, where Gillen is often a synonym.

Gunn In Ireland this English name is usually an abbreviation of Gilgunn and MacElgunn—*Mac Giolla Dhuinn* (*donn,* brown)—which are still found in Co. Fermanagh, the homeland of the sept. Gunn is also the name of a Scottish clan. MIF

Gunnell As an English name Gunnell has two distinct derivations, but in Ireland, especially in Co. Louth, it usually occurs as a synonym of MacGonigal.

(O) Gunning *Ó Conaing*. A Dalcassian sept originally of Castleconnell (more correctly Castlegunning) now numerous in Offaly. Gunning is also an English name fairly numerous in Ulster. MIF Map Limerick.

Gunshenan A corrupt form of Gilsenan found in Co. Longford. See Magunshennan.

Mac Gurk See MacGuirk.

Gurkin A variant of Durkin.

Mac Gurl See MacGirl.

Mac Gurnahan *Mag Mhuirneacháin* (*muirneach* has several meanings, here probably loving or lovable). A rare name. This family were early followers of the Savages of the Ards and have always been associated with Co. Down. See Gordon.

Mac Gurrin See Curreen and Kiverkin.

Gurry See Gorry.

Mac Gushen *Mag Oisín*. A rare name found in Leitrim and Meath.

MacGusty *Mag Oiste*. A name of Welsh origin, derived from a gaelicized form of Hodge.

Guthrie A Scottish name used as a synonym of Lahiff in Co. Clare.

Guy Of Old-French derivation from a personal name, in Ulster since early seventeenth century.

Gweehin A variant of Guihen. See also Wynne.

Gwynn This family of Welsh origin (*gwyn*, white) is in Ireland since the sixteenth century. The most distinguished members of it have been connected with Dublin University. IF   MIF

H

Habbagan, Hobbikin *Mac Oibicín* (of Anglo-Norman, not of Gaelic-Irish origin). These names have been widely changed to the cognate Hopkins. As Hobagan it is listed in the 'census' of 1659 as a principal Irish name in Co. Longford.

Haberlin A German name in Ireland since early eighteenth century: it was fairly numerous in south Kilkenny and Waterford a century ago but is now rare.

Hackett *Haicéid*. Families of this name have been in Ireland since the Anglo-Norman invasion, mainly in Kilkenny and Kildare. A branch in Connacht became completely hibernicized and was known as MacHackett and also as Guckian. In Cos. Armagh and Tyrone Hackett has been used as a synonym of MacCahey, MacGahey and Gaggy from the sound of the Irish form *Mag Eachaidh*. IF

Hadden, Haddon An English name found in Ulster and Louth, occasionally used as a synomyn of Hadian.

Haddock, Haydock An English toponymic now found in Co. Armagh. From 1690 to 1800 the family was prominent in Co. Kilkenny.

Hade See Haide. This may be a Palatine name in Co. Carlow.

(O) Hadigan See Hedigan.

(O) Hadian See Hedian.

Hadnett A variant of Hodnett.

Hadsor This Anglo-Norman toponymic was prominent in Co. Louth and Dublin from its introduction in the thirteenth century until the main family was ruined through its adherence to the Jacobite cause. It survived till late eighteenth century but is now very rare.

(O) Haffey See Haughey.

Hafford See Harford.

Mac Haffy See Mahaffy.

(O) Hagan *Ó hÁgáin*. It is fairly well established that this name was originally *Ó hÓgáin* (from óg, young). It is that of an important Ulster sept: the leading family was of Tullaghogue (as Map). *Ó hAodhagáin*, also anglicized O'Hagan, is said to be a distinct sept of Oriel, but owing to proximity of Cos. Tyrone and Armagh, they are now indistinguishable. The Offaly name mentioned by Woulfe is now extinct or absorbed by Egan in Leinster. IF   MIF Map Tyrone. See Hogg.

(O) **Haggerty** A variant of Hegarty.

Mac Haghey See Haughey and MacCaughey.

(Mac) **Hague, -Haig** Forms of *Mac Thaidhg* found in Co. Cavan. See MacCague.

(O) **Haher** See Haier.

(O) **Hahessy** *Ó hAitheasa* (from *aitheasach*, victorious; not *aitheas*, distress). Originally of the Síol Anmchadha in Co. Galway; already by mid-seventeenth century it was well established in Co. Waterford. It is now rare. MIF

Haide, Hayde The origin of this name is uncertain. It is found in the same part of the country as Hayden and it is thought that it is an abbreviated form of that name. SIF 84. See Head.

Haier, Haher Former variants of Hehir in Clare, seldom used now.

(O) **Haigney** A variant of Heagney.

Haines See Haynes.

(O) **Hainey** See Heany.

Hairt A Scottish name associated with the Plantation of Ulster, quite distinct from the Irish (O) Hart.

Halden See MacCaldin.

Mac Hale *Mac Céile*. MacFirbis says this derives from one Cele Ó Maolfaghmair whose family were co-arbs of Killala (*céile* means companion). The form *Mac Eli* is used in the 'Annals of Loch Cé'. A Mayo sept. The Howells, early settled in the same area, were called *Mac Haol*, which was also anglicized as MacHale. Without the prefix Hale (numerous in Ulster) is an English locative name. IF   Map Mayo.

Hales See Hayles.

(O) **Halferty, Halverty** See Hilferty.

Halfpenny See Halpeny.

Hall An English locative name (dweller or worker at the hall) on record in Munster since the fourteenth century; it has become very numerous in Ulster since the seventeenth century.

Mac Hall A variant of MacCaul. Hall without the prefix Mac, numerous in Ulster, is English.

(O) **Hallahan, Hallighan** *Ó hAileacháin*. A Cork and Waterford family, often confused with Halligan. MIF

(O) **Hall(e)y** This is of dual origin: it is *Ó hAilche* in Cos. Waterford and Tipperary (where some Halleys are, however, really Mulhalls); and *Ó hAille*, a small Clare sept, whence Ballyally near Ennis. Map Clare and Tipperary.

Halliday App.

(O) Halligan *Ó hAileagáin.* An Oriel sept of Louth and Armagh. MIF

(O) Hallihy An earlier form of Hally.

(O) Hallinan *Ó hAilgheanáin* (perhaps *ailghean*, noble offspring). This name is seldom met outside Munster. It is on record in Cos. Waterford, Tipperary and Limerick in very early records. In modern times it has to some extent been absorbed by Hanlon and Allen. MIF 133.

(O) Hallion, Hallin *Ó hAilín.* (The personal name *Ailín* is of doubtful derivation: Woulfe gives *ail*, noble, rock). An Ormond name often absorbed by Allen.

(O) Hallissey *Ó hÁilgheasa* (*áilgheas*, eagerness). Almost exclusively of west Cork and south Kerry. Map Cork–Kerry.

(O) Halloran *Ó hAllmhuráin* (*allmhurach*, pirate or stranger from overseas). There are two distinct septs of this name (as Map) geographically not far apart. Bibl. IF   MIF   Map Clare and Galway.

Hally See Halley.

(O) Halpeny, Halfpenny *Ó hAilpine* (*alp*, lump). This is basically the same as Halpin, but each has a definite location: Halpeny mainly Co. Monaghan and Halpin mainly Co. Limerick. MIF

(O) Halpin *Ó hAilpin.* See preceding. Halpin is also wrongly used as a synonym of the Scottish MacAlpin which is of similar derivation. MIF

(O) Haltaghan See next entry.

Halton Woulfe states correctly that Halton is an English toponymic; but I have no doubt that the name in Breffny and Fermanagh, where it was formerly mainly found, is not English but a corrupt form of O'Haltahan, which is a variant of Hultahan.

(O) Halverty See Hilferty.

(O) Halvey *Ó hAilmhic* (*ailmhic*, noble son) in Cos. Galway and Mayo. In Leinster Halvey is a synonym of Holloway, an old Anglo-Irish name.

(O) Haly A variant of Healy formerly common in Co. Cork. The Halys of Co. Limerick claim to be Hanley. Haley is an English toponymic.

Hambery, Hambrogh See Hanbury.

(O) Hamill A branch of the Cenél Eoghain. Later mainly found in Armagh and Monaghan. Woulfe gives *Ó hÁdhmaill* deriving it from *ádhmall*, active (*?aidhmeamhail*) but the older word *admall* has exactly the opposite meaning. MIF   Map Tyrone. See next entry.

Hamilton This family came from Scotland with the Plantation of Ulster and became numerous and influential giving their name to the town of Manorhamilton in Co. Leitrim, which indicates how far from their original place of settlement the family influence spread. A few families so called are really Hamill. Bibl . IF   MIF

Hamlin This name, now very rare, was prominent in Co. Meath from the thirteenth to the eighteenth century. Hamlinstown in Co. Meath is named from the family, as presumably is also Hamlinstown in Co. Louth.

Hammond This name was in Ireland before the coming of the Normans, but it also borne by recent immigrants from England. It is occasionally a synonym of Hamill; also, but rarely, of MacCammon(d), *Mac Ámoinn,* which is a Co. Down name. See MacCalmont.

(O) Hampson, Hamsey *Ó hAmhsaigh.* The English name Hampson has superseded the older O'Hanson, that of a small sept of Co. Derry. An earlier anglicized form was O'Hampsey, which is still extant in north Ulster as Hamsey. MIF

Hampton This English toponymic occurs in mediaeval Irish records from the early fourteenth century; but its prevalence in Co. Down in modern times is due to seventeenth-century immigration.

Hamrogue, Hamrock See under Shamrock.

(O) Hanafin *Ó hAinbhthin* now spelt *Ó hAinifin* (*ainbhioth,* storm). This name belongs almost exclusively to Kerry, where it is numerous. Woulfe suggests that it is cognate with Hanvey of west Cork.

Hanagan See Hannigan.

(O) Hanahan *Ó hAnnacháin.* A Co. Limerick name, now much changed to Hannon.

(O) Hanahoe, Hanahy *Ó hEanchadha.* A north Mayo name, possibly cognate with Heanue. The family provided many mediaeval clerics in the diocese of Killala.

(O) Hanaty, Hannerty See Hennarty.

Hanbidge Bibl.

Hanbury, Hambery *Ó hAinmhire.* Woulfe suggests that the old personal name *Ainmire* means freedom from levity (*mire,* levity, madness). This name belongs mainly to Cos. Galway and Clare; Ansboro is a synonym of it found in the former; Hambrogh and Hambrock in Co. Mayo.

Hand An English name used, by pseudo-translation, for Claffey, MacClave, Glavy and Lavan, through confusion with the word *lámh,* hand.

(O) Handlon A variant of Hanlon.

Handrick See Henrick.

(O) Haneen, Hanheen *Ó hAinchín.* (The derivation from *ainghein,* unborn, is not accepted). A branch of the Síol Anmchadha in Clare and Galway: frequently changed to Hannon. A notable clerical family. IF 172.

(O) Hangley A form of Hanley in use in Co. Roscommon.

(O) Hanify, Hanfey Variants of Hanvey.

Hankard This is a local form of the Norman Tancred, elsewhere anglicized Tankard. Families of Hankard have been in south-east Cork since the sixteenth century and were known in Irish as *na hAncardaigh*.

(O) Hanley, Handly *Ó hÁinle* (*áinle*, beauty). An important Connacht sept. A branch migrated to Co. Cork. The distinguished family of Hanley in the Ormond country may be of different origin. Bibl. IF Map Roscommon. See Jago.

(O) Hanlon *Ó hAnluain* (possibly from *luan*, champion, intensified by *an*). One of the most important of the septs of Ulster. The present association of the name with west Munster is of comparatively recent inception. Bibl. IF Map Armagh.

Hanna Of Scottish origin, this name is very numerous in north-east Ulster. The Gaelic form *Ó hAnnaidh* is one of the few Scottish O names. MIF

(O) Hannahan See Hanahan.

(O) Hannavan *Ó hAinbheáin*. This is cognate with Hanvey of Oriel and is well known in Co. Monaghan but rare elsewhere.

Hannaway, Hanway Variants of Hanvey mainly found in south Down.

(O) Hanneen See Hanheen.

(O) Hannelly See Hanley.

Hannick, Hanwick I have not traced the origin of this name. As it is a Mayo name Woulfe's suggestion that it may be from *Ó hAilmhic* (see Halvey) is possibly correct.

Hannify, Hanify (the double N is more usual). A variant of Hanvey, found in Co. Galway.

(O) Hannigan *Ó hAnnagáin*. A scattered name of uncertain origin. Mainly connected with two widely separated areas, Cos. Waterford and Tyrone. MIF

(O) Hannon *Ó hAnnáin*. When not substituted for Haneen, as it frequently is in Connacht, this is a Munster name, chiefly found in Co. Limerick. IF MIF

(O) Hanrahan *Ó hAnracháin*. Woulfe makes this a variant of *Ó hAnradháin* (see Hourahan). The O'Hourahans are a notable Dalcassian sept. The name is spelt Handrahan in some south Tipperary districts. Map Clare.

(O) Hanratty, Hanraghty *Ó hAnrachtaigh* (*anrachtach*, unlawful). This is one of those names which are frequently mentioned in the Annals and are still predominantly located in their original habitat, viz. Oriel—now chiefly Louth and Armagh. Map Louth and Monaghan. IF

Hanrick See Henrick.

(O) Hanson See Hampson and Kitterick.

(O) Hanvey *Ó hAinbhith (ainbhioth,* storm). The principal sept of this name was located on the borders of Armagh and Down. Another was a little south of that. Minor septs were in Meath and west Cork. Map Down and Cork.

O Hara *Ó hEaghra.* An important dual sept located in Co. Sligo, the chiefs being O'Hara Boy *(buidhe)* and O'Hara Reagh *(riabhach).* A branch migrated to the Glens of Antrim. Bibl. IF   Map Antrim and Sligo.

(O) Haraghy, Harahoe See Harrihy.

(O) Haran, Harhan See Haren.

Harbin This has been used as a synonym of Herbert in Co. Clare. It is gaelicized as *Hoirbin.*

Harbinson App.

Harden A well-known English name used as the anglicized form of *Mac Giolla Deacair* in Oriel. See Hardy and Dockery.

Hardiman An English name meaning bold man used in Ireland for Hargadan, Harman, Hardman and Hardy.

Harding Families of this name settled in Tipperary and adjoining counties in the seventeenth century. Others of pre-Cromwellian origin came to Ireland as early as the fifteenth century.

Hardman This is distinct from Hardiman but is often confused with Harman. It is of two origins, both Old-English, viz. hard man and herd(s)man. Herdeman of Herdemanstown, Co. Meath, is on record since 1356.

Hardy This English name when found in Connacht usually stands for the Irish *Mac Giolla Deacair,* the early anglicized form of which— Macgilledogher—is now obsolete. *Deacair* is the Irish word for hard. Some Co. Galway Hardimans are now called Hardy. MIF   See Dockery.

(O) Hare *Ó hIr, Ó hÉir.* Hare is an English name but when properly O'Hare it is that of an Oriel sept. It is very rarely a variant of O'Hehir. MIF   Map Armagh. See also MacGarry.

(O) Haren This name has several origins. It is most numerous as *Ó hEaghráin* which belongs to Clare and Connacht, where it has the variants Haran and Harhan, the former particularly in Mayo. I am uncertain of the origin of the Harans of Fermanagh. In seventeenth-century documents they appear as *Ó hAráin* and as they were erenaghs of Ballymacataggart they are presumably a distinct sept. In Oriel the name is *Ó hEaráin* (see Heran). According to Woulfe Haran is also sometimes used for Harrahan, a corrupt form of Hanrahan; this can be regarded as rare; but it should be noted that Haren and Haran have frequently been changed to Horan. Map Clare.

Harford In Ireland since 1250, mainly Cos. Dublin and Kilkenny.

Ball in his 'Howth and its Owners' states that one of the Norse families which settled at Howth was Harford. If so the name was in Ireland before the Anglo-Norman invasion. Nevertheless, it is mainly of English origin, being formerly *de Hereford*. The synonym Hafford is fairly numerous in Westmeath. MIF

Mac Harg This Tyrone name is an earlier form of Maharg. See MacIlhagga.

O Hargadan *Ó hArgadáin* (the basic word is *argat*, mod. *airgead*, silver, indicating shining). This name is extant in Co. Sligo. In Co. Galway it has been generally superseded by Hardiman. MIF

Hargan A variant of Horgan found in Ulster.

(O) Harkin(s), Harkan *Ó hEarcáin* (*earc*, red). An erenagh family of Inishowen. This name is quite distinct from Arkins of Co. Clare. MIF   Map Donegal.

Harkness App.

Harland This name appears in the 1664 hearth money rolls of Co. Armagh and has since been continuously in that county and adjacent areas. It is an English toponymic (Yorkshire and Devon).

Harley This is a well-known English name; in Ireland it is also a synonym of Harrily, but it is sometimes changed to Hurley in west Cork.

Harman Occasionally a variant of Hardiman, but in Leinster it is the modern form of an English name derived from Old-German *hereman*, warrior. The form Harmon is mainly found in Co. Louth. Bibl. MIF

Harnedy, Harnett See Hartnett.

(O) Harney *Ó hAthairne* (possibly from *athardha*, paternal). This was formerly anglicized Haherny, now sometimes Hartney. The latter is confused with Hartnane. Originally of Co. Roscommon, Harney is still found in Connacht, but has also spread to Co. Tipperary.

Harold-Barry Bibl.

Harold *Harailt*. The Harold family, of Norse origin, was established in Ireland before the Anglo-Norman invasion in two places, as Map. The name is also an occasional synonym of Harrell, Hirrell and Hurrell. Bibl. IF   Map Dublin and Limerick.

(O) Haroughten An erenagh family in Co. Roscommon. See Harrington.

Harpur, Harper The Norman name *le Harpur* (the harper) occurs frequently in mid-Leinster records from the thirteenth century. In modern times Harpur has been mainly found in Co. Wexford. It is sometimes spelt Harper there, e.g. in the place-name Harperstown. Harper as an English name is numerous in Ulster, where it was introduced at the time of the Plantation of Ulster.

(O) Harraghan *Ó hArcháin*. A Co. Leitrim name.

(O) Harragher A synonym of Faraher.

(O) Harrahill *Ó hEarghail.* Formerly numerous in Co. Clare; also found in Co. Waterford.

(O) Harran, Herron *Ó hEaráin.* A Co. Donegal name quite distinct from Haren of Clare. According to Woulfe it is derived from *earadh,* dread, and was anciently of importance in Oriel.

Harrell See Arrell and Hurrell.

(O) Harrigan When found in south and west Munster this is usually a variant of Horgan. There was formerly a Leix sept of *Ó hArragáin* whose name was anglicized Harrigan.

(O) Harrihy, Harhoe *Ó hEarchaidh.* (Woulfe's derivation as noble warrior is not accepted by Celtic scholars). Harahy, so spelt, was formerly very numerous in the barony of Banagh, Co. Donegal. Harvey is substituted for this name in Fermanagh. In Mayo the variant *Ó hEarchadha* (see Horohoe) has become Harris and even Harrison.

(O) Harrily *Ó hEarghaile* (etymologically akin to O'Farrelly). A rare name as such in Donegal and Mayo, but in Donegal it is fairly numerous as Harley.

Harrington In Kerry this English toponymic usually stands for *Ó hIongardail,* formerly anglicized O'Hingerdell; but *Ó hArrachtáin* (Harroughten) is also called Harrington there and in Connacht. IF Map Cork.

Harris, Harrison These English names are usually those of immigrant families established under the Plantation of Ulster and since; but see also Harrihy, Henry and Horohoe.   **Harrity** See Herrity.

Mac Harry See Maharry.

(O) Hart *Ó hAirt.* Originally of Meath this sept was pushed westwards by Anglo-Norman pressure and attained prominence in its new territory (as Map). Hart is also a common English name brought in by the Plantation of Ulster. Bibl. IF   Map Sligo. See next entry.

(O) Hartigan *Ó hArtagáin.* Like O'Hart this is formed from the Christian name *Art.* The sept is Dalcassian, located in east Clare and north Limerick. IF

(O) Hartily, Hartley Hartley is a common English name, but in Ireland it usually denotes a family of *Ó hArtghaile* (*gal,* valour, with the forename *Art*) in south-east Leinster. Map Wexford.

(O) Hartin *Ó hArtáin.* A Co. Longford name found also in west Ulster. The English toponymic Harton is used as a variant.

(O) Hartnane This has been used as a synonym of Heffernan in Kerry. Woulfe gives also *Ó hEarnáin* (from *earna,* experienced) for which see Hernon.

(O) Hartnett, Harnet *Ó hAirtnéada.* This is mainly found now, as in mediaeval times, in south-west Munster. Hartnett is the usual spelling in Co. Cork, Harnett in Co. Limerick. The variant Harnedy is now rare. MIF   Map Cork.

(O) Hartney See Harney.

Hartpool Bibl.

(O) Hartry *Ó hAirtrí*. This rare name, originally of some note in Connacht, is now found in Co. Waterford and south Tipperary. Harty is sometimes substituted for it.

(O) Harty *Ó hAthartaigh* mod. *Ó hÁrtaigh*. (Woulfe's equation of this etymologically with Faherty—*faghartach*, noisy—is possible). Harty is a Munster name principally found in Cos. Tipperary and Cork. MIF   See Hearty.

Harvey This name, of English origin, is mainly found among Ulster settlers, though prominent also in Co. Wexford. Occasionally it is an anglicization of the small south Galway sept of *Ó hAirmheadhaigh*. Woulfe derives this from *airmheadhach*, having a herd of cattle, but Gaelic scholars dispute this: it may be from the old word *airmed*, a measure of grain. Bibl. IF

Harwood An English toponymic, so spelt in Munster; in Ulster it has sometimes been changed to Harrot and even Hart. Woulfe gives *Haróid* (i.e. Harold) as the form in Irish.

Haselden See Hazelton.

Haskin(s) See Heskin.

Haslam This English name is both a toponymic and a locative (dweller by the hazels). It first appears in Ireland in the person of army officers (not Cromwellian) in mid-seventeenth century and has since been closely associated with Cos. Leix and Offaly.

Haslip See Heaslip.

(O) Hassan *Ó hOsáin*. (Woulfe's derivation from *os*, deer, is possible). This name is distinct from Hession and Hishon and belongs to Co. Derry. Hasson, formerly associated with Co. Wexford, is of English origin. MIF

Hassard Bibl.

Hassett *Ó hAiseadha* (the suggested derivation from *aisid*, strife, is considered unlikely). A sept of Thomond, long prominent in Co. Clare, not to be confused with Blennerhassett, a planter family, though some in Kerry have become Hassett. MIF

Hastie, Hastings See under Hestin.

Hatch This is an English toponymic and also a locative name. It is in Ireland since the seventeenth century, first in Co. Meath, and for the past two hundred years closely identified with the adjacent part of Co. Louth. Bibl.

(Mac) Hatton See MacIlhatton.

(O) Haugh *Ó hEachach* (for derivation see MacCaughey). This belongs mainly to Co. Clare. It is spelt Hough in Co. Limerick.

(O) Haughan See Haughton.

(O) Haughey *Ó hEachaidh.* This name is associated both with Co. Donegal and Armagh. In the latter it is also called Haffey. With the Mac prefix it is a different name, normally anglicized MacGaughey. SIF 86.

(O) Haughian *Ó hEachaidhin.* An east Ulster name. Haughian has been sometimes changed to Hawkins, an English name fairly common in south-east Leinster. O'Donovan equates it with Houghegan.

Haughney See Aughney.

(O) Haughran An Offaly name often changed to Horan. Woulfe gives *Ó hEachráin.*

Haughton This English Quaker toponymic, quite common in Ireland as such, has also been used as an anglicized form of *Ó hEacháin,* Haughan; and even of *Ó hEachtair,* now Hoctor and earlier O'Haghtir, formerly an important family in north Tipperary. Woulfe equates the forename *Eachtair* with Hector. Bibl. MIF

Haven A Westmeath variant of Heaven.

(O) Haver(a)n, Havron *Ó hAmhráin.* Variants of Heffron.

(O) Haverty *Ó hÁbhartaigh.* Probably a variant of Faverty. Haverty is now almost exclusively found in a small area near Craughwell as Map. MIF   Map Galway.

(O) Havigan See Hevican.

(O) Havlin This is a Co. Donegal name. I have not discovered its form in Irish.

Hawe An English locative name sometimes used as a variant of Haugh.

Hawkins An English name sometimes used as a synonym of Haughan.

Hawthorn App.

Hay Norman *de la Haye* of Co. Wexford. In modern times this has widely become Hayes.

Hayburn See Heyburn.

Hayde See Haide.

(O) Hayden *Ó hEideáin.* This name of a Co. Carlow sept, sometimes anglicized as Headon, which is also that of a family of Norman origin settled in Co. Wexford but now very rare. MIF   Map Carlow. See Hedian.

Haydock See Haddock.

Hayes This name is very numerous in Munster. It is usually an anglicized form of *Ó hAodha.* Septs of that name belong to the counties indicated in Map. In Co. Wexford Hayes is Norman, i.e. *la Heise* or *de la Haye* as in England. IF   Map Donegal, Mayo, Meath, Monaghan and Tyrone. See also O'Hea.

Hayles A common name in England and Scotland sometimes used as a synonym of Healy and MacHale. As Hales as well as Hayles it has been in Co. Cork since early seventeenth century.

Haynes This English name is occasionally used for Hynes in Munster.

Hazelton An English toponymic found in Co. Armagh. Haselden in Co. Down is a synonym. Woulfe says this and Hazelwood are anglicized forms of *Mac Conchollchoille* but I have found no evidence of this.

Hazlett Twelve variant spellings (e.g. Heslitt) or synonyms (e.g. Heazley) of this locative name (hazel copse) are recorded, all in Ulster. It is numerous in that province, especially in Co. Monaghan, since the middle of the eighteenth century.

(O) Hea *Ó hAodha*. The name of a sept of the Corca Laoidhe where it is very seldom anglicized Hayes as it is elsewhere. Bibl. IF Map Cork.

Head(e) This is occasionally a surname of nickname type, but usually it is a locative name denoting dweller at the head of a valley or source of a stream. It appears as a 'principal name' in the 'census' of 1659 in Cos. Meath and Tipperary and in that century was of some note in Waterford and Co. Cork. Though of English origin, families of this name were largely Catholic and transplantation as papists under Cromwell no doubt accounts for their presence today in east Galway. References in seventeenth-century documents to Ballyhead in Co. Kildare (now Ballyhade) have no relation to the surname Head, but commemorate a family of Aide in that area. Ade is a diminutive of Adam.

Headon See Hayden.

(O) Heafy See Heaphy.

(O) Heagney See Hegney.

Heague *Mac Thaidhg* in Connacht. See MacTeige.

(O) Healihy See Healy.

(O) Healion A variant of Heelan.

(O) Healy, Hely This is *Ó hÉalaighthe* in Munster, sometimes anglicized Healihy, and *Ó hÉilidhe* in north Connacht, derived respectively from words meaning ingenious and claimant. Ballyhely on Lough Arrow was the seat of the latter. The Munster sept was located at Donoughmore, Co. Cork, whence was taken the title conferred on the Protestant branch. Bibl. IF   MIF   Map Cork and Sligo.

(O) Heanahan See Henaghan.

(O) Heaney, Heeney The principal sept of this name is *Ó hÉighnigh* in Irish, important and widespread in Oriel, formerly stretching its influence into Fermanagh. Hegney is a variant. Another family of the name in Ulster were erenaghs of Banagher in Co. Derry. Minor septs of *Ó hÉanna* (*Éanna*, old form of Enda), also anglicized

Heaney, were of some note in Clare, Limerick and Mayo up to the seventeenth century. MIF   Map Armagh. See Bird.

(O) Heanue *Ó hÉanadha*. This is seldom found outside Connemara where it is fairly numerous. It is probably an offshoot of the Mayo sept mentioned in the previous entry.

(O) Heaphy *Ó hÉamhthaigh*. This is listed as a principal name in Co. Waterford in the 1659 'census' and is still mainly found there.

(O) Hear A Co. Tyrone spelling of O'Hare.

Hearne A well-known English name used in Co. Waterford as a variant of Ahearne.

(O) Hearney See Harney.

Hearon Usually a variant of Hearn; occasionally Heeron is for Heerin.

(O) Hearty *Ó hAghartaigh*. Its equation by Woulfe with *Ó Faghartaigh* is conjectural but I have no authentic alternative to offer. This name belongs almost exclusively both now and in the past to the Oriel counties of Louth and Monaghan: it is not the same as Harty.

(O) Heary, Heery Woulfe gives *Ó hÍoruaidh* as the form in Irish. This is on record in the southern midlands in the fourteenth century as O'Hyry and in the sixteenth as O'Herrye. Never numerous, in modern times it has been found mainly in the Meath–Cavan area.

Heaslip This is the most usual of six variant spellings (Haslip, Hyslop etc.); it is derived from Old-English words meaning dweller in the hazel valley. In the seventeenth century it was mainly found in Munster, but it is now also associated with Co. Cavan. MIF

Heath This English locative name has been in Dublin continuously since 1589.

Mac Heath A variant of MacKeith.

Heatley Now mainly found in Belfast and Co. Armagh, this English toponymic was fairly numerous in Dublin from mid-seventeenth century until recent times.

Heaton This English toponymic, first established in Co. Offaly in mid-seventeenth century, is now mainly found in Ulster.

(O) Heaven *Ó hEimhín* (perhaps from *eimhidh,* swift). A rare Offaly name, changed to Evans elsewhere.

(O) Heavy *Ó hÉamhaigh*. This name, cognate with Heaphy, is found in all the provinces, but rare in Ulster. The centre of its main location is Athlone.

(O) Hederman *Ó hÉadromáin* (*éadtrom,* light, fickle). A west Clare family whose traditional connection with St. Senan and the Shannon estuary is interesting. MIF

(O) Hedian, Hadian *Ó hÉidín*. A Roscommon–Leitrim name sometimes confused with Hayden. The names are similarly derived though the septs are distinct.

(O) Hedigan, Hadigan *Ó hÉideagáin*. Now found in west Clare, but originally of Cos. Roscommon and Leitrim. Cognate with Mac-Gettigan.

(O) Hedivan *Ó hÉadamháin*. A Westmeath name often spelt Heduvan and sometimes changed to Hednan.

(O) Heelan A variant form of Hyland in Munster.

(O) Heenan *Ó hÉanáin*. Though sometimes an abbreviated form of Henaghan, it is correctly the name of a small sept located in the Roscrea area on the border of north Tipperary and Offaly. It is also found in Co. Down.

(O) Heeney See Heany.

(O) Heerin *Ó hUidhrín*. The name of an Offaly sept, first anglicized as O'Heryne and O'Heverine: the latter no doubt accounts for the fact that in modern times Heffron is found as a synonym of Heerin. This has led to confusion with Heffernan.

(O) Heery See Heary.

(O) Heever A synonym of Ivers, MacKeever and Howard. See also Hever.

(O) Heffernan *Ó hIfearnáin*. Though originally of Clare, this sept early established themselves on the Limerick–Tipperary border. Bibl. IF   Map Limerick.

(O) Heffron, Hefferan *Ó Éimhrín*. A branch of the Cenél Eoghain established in Mayo. Haveran is a variant in Ulster. MIF 142. See Heerin.

O Hegan A variant of O'Hagan found in Co. Armagh.

O Hegarty *Ó hÉigceartaigh* (*éigceartach*, unjust). Primarily an Ulster sept. There was also one of the same name in Munster, a branch of the Eoghanacht. Bibl. IF   Map Derry.

(O) Hegney, Hegeany, Heagney *Ó hÉignigh*. A small but once powerful sept of Oriel. The name is now rare and scattered; it has been much changed to Heaney.

(O) Hehir, Hegher *Ó hAichir* (*aichear*, bitter, sharp). The name of a Dalcassian sept which is numerous in Cos. Clare and Limerick; some are probably of Uí Fidhgheinte origin, rare elsewhere. IF   Map Clare.

(O) Helehan *Ó hAoilleacháin*. This is a variant of Whelahan, both names being derived from *faoilleach*, joyful. Helehan is mainly found in Co. Waterford.

(O) Hel(l)en West Cork form of Heelan.

(O) Helly A variant of Hely found in and near Sligo.

(O) Helverty See Hilferty.

(O) Hely See Healy.

Hempenstall, Hepenstal This Yorkshire toponymic has been in

Ireland since the seventeenth century, mainly in Co. Wicklow. SIF 88.

Hemphill This Scottish (Ayrshire) toponymic is on record in Ireland from 1630; the main family of the name was established in Co. Offaly early in the eighteenth century since when, however, it has been mainly found in Co. Derry.

(O) Hempsey, Hempson See Hampson.

(O) Henaghan, Henihan *Ó hÉineacháin* or *Ó hÉanacháin*. A sept of the Uí Fiachrach. See Bird. MIF Map Mayo.

(O) Henchy, Hinchy *Ó hAonghusa*. This is the Clare form of the name elsewhere called Hennessy. The modern Irish form *Ó hInse* conceals its derivation from the personal name Angus. Bibl. IF

Hendrick See Henrick.

Hendron, Henderson Of Norman origin, Hendron is peculiar to Co. Armagh. The English Henderson, cognate with Hendron, also found there, is widespread over the Ulster counties. Both are of comparatively late introduction in Ireland. MIF

Hendry This is usually of Scottish origin, Hendrie being a branch of the clan MacNaughton. It is not used as a synonym of Hendron though it, too, belongs now to Co. Armagh. Some Hendrys are properly Henry. MIF

Hendy An English name found in Co. Kildare. It is derived from an Old-English adjective meaning courteous.

Henebry Originally *de Hindeberg* and gaelicized *de Hionburgha*. This name in Ireland continuously since the thirteenth century. MIF Map Kilkenny–Waterford.

(O) Henery See Henry.

Henley This English toponymic is used as a synonym of Hennelly and also occasionally of Hanley.

(O) Hennelly This name, numerous in Mayo, is said to be a variant of Fennelly. Woulfe gives *Ó hIonnghaile* as the form in Irish.

(O) Hennerty This is said to be the Co. Cork form of Finnerty, but in fact it is a variant of Hingerty.

(O) Hennessy *Ó hAonghusa* (descendant of Angus). There are a number of distinct septs (as Map) of this well-known name, which is now very numerous in Munster. The Hennessys of Cognac descend from a Mallow family. IF   Map Cork, Dublin–Meath and Offaly.

(O) Hennigan This is a variant of Henaghan found in the same area (Co. Mayo).

Henning An English name now numerous in east Ulster. Bardsley says it is a variant of Hemming, which is of Danish origin.

(O) Henrick, Han(d)rick *Mac Annraic* (from a Norse personal name cognate with Henry). A branch of the MacMurroughs in Co. Wexford was so called. MIF

Henright A rare variant of Enright.

(O) Henrion This name belongs almost exclusively to Westmeath. Woulfe gives *Ó hIonnráin* as the Irish form, treating it as a variant form of Hanrahan.

(Mac) Henry Either *Mac Éinrí* a Síol Eoghain family, or *Mac Einri* (see Fitzhenry); or a variant of MacEniry. See also Hendry. The name MacHenry is now mainly found in south-east Ulster. Bibl; IF 136; Map Galway.

(O) Henry *Ó hInneirghe* (derivation as MacEniry). Unconnected with the foregoing but indistinguishable from it when both prefixes are dropped. IF   MIF   Map Derry–Tyrone.

Hensey A variant of Hennessy.

Henson See Hampson.

Hepburn See Heyburn.

Hepenstal See Hempenstall.

(O) Heraghty, Heraty *Ó hOireachtaigh*. Mainly of Galway, Mayo and Donegal. This is sometimes used synonymously with Geraghty (q.v.) for derivation.

Herald This rare English name has been used in Ulster as a synonym of Harold.

(O) Heran *Ó hEaráin*. An Oriel sept. Map Armagh. Heron, often a synonym of Heffron and Ahearne, is a different name. See Harron.

Herbert *Hoireabard*. This name came to Ireland soon after the Anglo-Norman invasion; the leading families, closely identified with Co. Kerry, came *temp.* Elizabeth I. Bibl.

Mac Herbert See Delamer.

Herdman An English occupational name now well known in Co. Antrim. Isolated references to it occur much earlier in Munster and Leinster, some as early as the fourteenth century.

Herley This is used as a synonym of Herlihy in Co. Cork and of Harley in Ulster.

(O) Herlihy *Ó hIarlatha (iarfhlaith,* underlord). A Ballyvourney erenagh family whose name is sometimes changed to Hurley. IF Map Cork.

(O) Hernon *Ó hIornáin*. A sept of the Uí Fiachra (formerly in the Aran Islands) presently found in Cos. Leitrim and Galway. In Munster Hernon is a short form of Heffernan, usually made *Ó hEarnáin* in Irish.

Heron An English name of nickname type, seldom of that origin in Ireland. See Heran and also MacElheron.

(O) Herr A corrupt form of Hehir.

(O) Herreran *Ó hEararáin*. This rather rare name belongs to Cos. Derry and Donegal.

Herrick This is an English name of Scandinavian origin. In Ireland it is a synonym of Erck. Bibl.

(O) Herrity A variant of Heraghty.

(O) Hertnon A variant of Hernon found in Co. Offaly, where it has also been changed to Hehernan. Hertnam is a corrupt form of Hertnon.

Hervey See Harvey.

(O) Heskin *Ó hUiscín*. A Connacht name. This is one of several which have been anglicized as Waters, though it is improbable that it is derived from *uisce,* water. It has also been occasionally anglicized Hoskins. See Askin.

(O) Heslin *Ó hEislin*. This was formerly *Ó hEisleanáin*, anglicized Heslenan. A Breffny sept of Mohill, Co. Leitrim. MIF

(O) Hession *Ó hOisín*. A north Galway and south Mayo name, sometimes strangely changed to Usher. See Hishon.

Hester The origin of this name, mainly found in Co. Mayo, has not been determined. Woulfe makes it a Gaelic-Irish name—*Ó hOistir*. There is an English name Hester derived from Anglo-Norman *estre,* street.

(O) Hestin *Ó hOistín*. A sept associated with the MacDermots of Moylurg, located in Co. Mayo; a branch migrated to Co. Limerick, where they are called Histon. Both have widely changed their names to the English Hastings which is numerous in Ulster, where Hastie is often synonymous.

Hetherington This English name was established in Co. Leix in the sixteenth century. It is now mainly found in Tyrone. One of the name was hanged as an Irish Catholic who ignored an order to transplant to Connacht in 1655.

Hetherman A variant of Hederman.

Heuston This may be a variant of either Houston or Hewson.

Hevaghan See Hevican.

(O) Hever *Ó hÍomhair* (from a Norse personal name). A Sligo sept of the Uí Fiachrach. See Howard.

(O) Heverin, Hevron Usual variants of Heffron in Mayo.

(O) Hevican, Havigan These are found in Cos. Galway and Roscommon, and are presumably variants of the Uí Fiachra *Ó hÉimheacháin,* more correctly anglicized Hevaghan.

Hewetson Bibl.

Hewitt An English name, being a diminutive of Hugh gaelicized as *Húighéad*. Though now regarded as of Ulster, practically all the early references to it, beginning in 1295, are to families in Munster or the city of Dublin. MIF

Hewlett A variant of Howlett.

Hewson, Heuson A numerous English name used in Ireland as a synonym of MacHugh. Bibl.

Hewston An Ulster form of Houston.

Heyburn The usual form in Ulster of the Scottish name Hepburn.

(O) Heyne *Ó hEidhin* (possibly from *eidhean*, ivy). A leading sept of Aidhne. This name is now usually made Hynes. Bibl. IF Map Galway.

(O) Hickey *Ó hÍcidhe* (*iceadh*, healer). A medical family of the Dál gCais. The name is now numerous in Co. Limerick and north Tipperary as well as in its place of origin, east and mid-Clare. Bibl. IF Map Clare.

Hickman An English name (servant of Hick, which is a pet-name of Richard) prominent in Co. Clare from the seventeenth century.

Hickson This English name has been closely associated with Co. Kerry since seventeenth century (before Cromwell).

(O) Hiffernan See Heffernan.

(O) Higerty An occasional variant of Hegarty.

(O) Higgins *Ó hUigín* (from an Old-Irish word akin to Viking, not from *uige*). A sept of the southern Uí Néill which migrated to Connacht. The O'Higgins father and son of South American fame came from Ballinary, Co. Sligo, not Ballina. Bibl. IF MIF Map Sligo.

Higginson App.

Highland A corrupt form of Hyland.

(O) Hilan Usually a variant of Hyland in Cos. Kilkenny and Kildare but it has been used for Filan in Westmeath.

(O) Hilferty *Ó hAilbheartaigh* (probably from *ilbeartach*, accomplished). A Donegal name. Halferty and Helverty are variants.

Hill This English name is numerous in north-east Ulster. In Kerry it is also the agnomen *an chnuic* (of the hill), cf. Glanny. Bibl; App.

(O) Hillan(d), Hillen Hillan is occasionally a variant of Hilan; but in Ulster, where they are mainly found, Hillan and Hillen are of English origin.

Hillas, Hillis Hillas is nearer to the original form Hillhouse, but Hillis is now much more numerous, being found mainly in Ulster; the older form Hillas is retained in Co. Sligo, where it is on record since mid-eighteenth century. Bibl.

Hillery Derived from the Latin *hilarius*, cheerful, this is an English name long established in Co. Clare. There is no basis for the statement that it is an anglicized form of *Ó hIrghile*, i.e. Hirelly, a very rare Donegal name. It is locally gaelicized as Helaoire. MIF

Hilliard An English name of German derivation which came to Ireland from Yorkshire in the seventeenth century. It has since been mainly associated with Co. Kerry. MIF

(O) Hilly, Hillee *Ó hItcheallaigh.* A variant form of Fihelly peculiar to north Kerry.

Hilton Now fairly numerous in Ulster and in Dublin, most families of this English toponymic name in Ireland were established here at the time of the Plantation of Ulster (*c.* 1609); but it is on record in Dublin in the previous century.

Hinan See Hynan.

Hinchin This name, of doubtful origin (possibly a corruption of the English Hinson), has been associated with north Cork and adjacent areas since the sixteenth century. It is also spelt Hinshion.

(O) Hinchy See Henchy.

Hines, Hinds See Heyne.

(O) Hiney, Hynie *Ó hEidhnigh* or *Ó hAdhnaigh* (possibly from *adhnadh, courage*). Originally Co. Galway, both these forms are now rare there; they are sometimes found in the midlands.

(O) Hingerdell See Harrington.

(O) Hingerty This is one of the anglicized forms of *Ó hIongardail* which has for the most part become Harrington. MIF

Hipwell This English toponymic is in Co. Leix since the mid-seventeenth century.

(O) Hirelly See under Hillery.

(O) Hirrell, Hirl *Ó hIrghil.* A Donegal name akin to O'Friel. See Harold.

Hishon The Co. Tipperary form of Hession.

(O) Hiskey *Ó hUisce.* One of the Connacht names which have been anglicized as Waters. Woulfe treats it as a corrupt form of *Ó hUarghuis* (Horish). See Waters.

Histon See Hestin.

Hoade, Hode There is an English name Hoade alias Hoath: however, O'Hode occurs in Co. Clare in the seventeenth century, and today in Co. Galway it is locally called *O hOdach* in Irish.

Hoare Bibl. See Hore.

Hobagan See Habbagan.

(O) Hoban *Ó hÚbáin.* A branch of the Cenél Eoghain settled in Mayo. From the seventeenth century it has also been associated with Co. Kilkenny. MIF

Hobart This aristocratic English name is sometimes used in Kerry and west Cork as a synonym of Herbert.

Hobbikin See Hopkins.

Hobson Derived from a diminutive of Robert, this English name is now numerous in Ulster though not confined to that province. Apart from a few isolated mediaeval references it first appears in Ireland in mid-seventeenth century. Hobbs, of similar derivation, is scattered and less numerous.

Hoctor See under Haughton.

Hodder This English name (meaning hoodmaker) was well established in Co. Cork in mid-seventeenth century, but is now rare.

Hodges See under Hodgins.

Hodgins This variant of Hodgeson (Hodge is a pet name of Roger) is one of the English names which has become very numerous since its establishment in Ireland in the seventeenth century. It is now much scattered throughout Leinster and Munster but rare in other provinces. Hodges (which, as well as Hodson, has been confused with Hodgins) is less numerous but is on record from late sixteenth century.

Hodnett (From *Odinet,* a diminutive of Odo). An English family who assumed the Gaelic patronymic MacSherry. Bibl; Map Cork.

(O) Hoey *Ó hEochaidh.* The O'Hoeys were of primary importance in Ulster till subdued by their kinsmen the MacDunlevys about the year 1300. There are, however, Hoeys in Ulster of planter stock. These are Huey, a derivative of Hugh. Hoey is also the name of a Meath sept. IF   MIF   Map Down. See MacGahey and Howe.

(O) Hogan *Ó hÓgáin (óg,* young). Three septs are so called: one is Dalcassian and one of Lower Ormond (sometimes regarded as the same); there is also one of the Corca Laoidhe. IF   MIF   Map Cork and Tipperary.

(O) Hogart *Ó hÓgairt.* Presumably an abbreviated form of Hogarty. In Antrim the variant form *Ó hOghairt* became Howard. The English name Hogarth is quite distinct.

(O) Hogarty This is a Co. Galway form of Fogarty, the F being aspirated giving *Ó hÓgartaigh.*

Hogg An English name numerous in Ulster used, unfortunately, also as an occasional synonym of O'Hagan.

Hoggan This name is usually found in or near Tyrone where it is a variant of Hagan not of Hogan.

Hoins A variant of Hynes and Owens in Tyrone and Fermanagh.

(O) Holahan See Hoolihan.

Holden Used erroneously as a later form of Howlin, it belongs to Cos. Kilkenny and Wexford. It is also the name of a recent English immigrant family. The English name Holden is of locative derivation denoting residence in the hollow valley. Howlin, a diminutive of Hugo is of Breton origin for which Woulfe gives *Húilín* as the Irish form. Carrigan says Holden is a diminutive of Hoel, Hoel being an early synonym of Walsh. MIF

Holey A spelling variant of Wholey. See under Whooley.

(O) Holian *Ó hÓileáin.* In Co. Galway, it has been changed to Holland. Holian may also be a variant of Hyland. MIF

Holland An English toponymic. In Co. Limerick it is an abbreviated form of Mulholland, and in Clare sometimes as synonym of Holohan. IF   MIF   See also Holian.

(O) Hollegan, Holligan *Ó hAllagáin*. A rare name, found in the midland counties. It is a variant of the Connacht name Halligan.

(O) Holleran A form of Halloran peculiar to Cos. Galway and Mayo.

Hollingsworth First appearing in Connacht in mid-seventeenth century, families of this English toponymic name later settled in Co. Wexford. Bibl.

Holloway, Holway See Halvey.

Holly This name in Ireland is seldom of English origin. In Kerry it is the anglicized form of *Mac Cuilinn* by translation. In Ulster it is an occasional synonym of MacQuillan. MIF

Hollywood A toponymic, possibly from Hollywood, Co. Dublin. The Anglo-Norman family so called early settled in Co. Dublin and Oriel and the name is still found in those localities.

Holmes The English name Holmes is not common in Ireland. The Scottish Holmes, which is found in considerable number in all the provinces, especially Ulster, can, like Thomson, be equated with several combinations of Mac and the Christian name Thomas, e.g. *Mac Thomáis* or *Mac Thómais*, which is also anglicized Mac-Combs and MacComish. In north Connacht Holmes has been used synonymously with Cavish.

(O) Holohan See Hoolahan.

Holt (from Old-English *holt*, a wood). The earliest reference I have met to the name in Ireland is in 1295. It appears several times in Co. Cork in the next century; later we find it in Ulster. It is now scattered. Its interest in Ireland lies in Joseph Holt, 1798 leader.

Homan (Bardsley gives the derivation as Howman, i.e. Hugh's man). Families of the name settled in Westmeath in the seventeenth century; later mainly Co. Cork.

(O) Honahan See Hounihan.

(O) Honan The west Clare family closely associated with Iniscathy, and later with Limerick, are *Ó hEoghanáin*. Elsewhere in Clare Honan is often a variant of Honeen. MIF

Hone The best-known family of this name came to Ireland from Holland. It may also be a form of Howen, *Ó hEoghain*, in Co. Fermanagh. O'Hones appear in the seventeenth-century hearth money rolls for Co. Monaghan.

(O) Honeen *Ó hUainín* (*uaine*, green). The derivation of this Thomond surname indicates the reason for the widespread use in Co. Clare of Greene as its anglicized form, which was formerly O'Huonyn. Honeen has been changed to Honan as well as Greene.

(O) Hooban A variant of Huban.

Hood *Ó hUid*. Hood is a well-known English name; but the O'Hoods, bards to the O'Neills, were of course Irish. Mahood is the same name, i.e. MacHood—Mac having been substituted for O. MIF Map Antrim.

(O) Hoolahan *Ó hUallacháin* (*uallach*, proud). Prominent septs so named belong to Thomond (Clare) and mid-Leinster. Seventeen variant spellings are recorded by the registrar-general including Oulihan and Whoolahan. Houlihan is usual in Munster, Holohan in Co. Kilkenny. In north Connacht Nolan is a frequent synonym. For connection of the name with Merry see MIF IF Map Offaly; See also Merry.

Hoolan Probably an Australian abbreviation of Hoolahan.

Hooley A variant spelling of Whooley in west Cork.

(O) Hooney *Ó hUainidhe*. Properly the name of a small sept of the Corca Laoidhe; but Hooney is usually met as a variant of the Clare name O'Honeen. IF Map Cork.

Hoonihan See Hounihan.

Hooriskey See Houriskey.

Hope The equation of this name with Hobbs is erroneous. Reaney and Weekley derive it from Old-English *hop*, a small enclosed valley, thus making it locative. It is now scattered, but from the fourteenth to the nineteenth century it was associated with Westmeath.

Hopkins In Connacht and Co. Longford, where it is fairly numerous, this English name is used as the modern form of the gaelicized Norman *Mac Oibicín*. In other parts of Ireland it is usually of English origin. MIF See Habbagan.

(O) Hora This is usually a variant of O'Hara (now almost peculiar to Co. Mayo) and sometimes of Horahoe. MIF

(O) Horaghy See Horohoe.

(O) Horahan See Hourahan.

(O) Horan *Ó hOdhráin* (*odhar*, dun-coloured). The name of this north Connacht sept is also widely used for Haren and to some extent for Hourihan. IF Map Cork and Mayo. See Haughran.

Hore Formerly *le Hore* not *de Hore*. An Anglo-Norman name meaning grey-haired or grizzled; *de Hóir* and *de Hóra* are used as the forms in Irish. It is among the Co. Wexford families in the old Forth rhyme, its epithet there being obstinate, and it is still essentially a Co. Wexford name. As Hoare it is mainly found in Co. Cork. Bibl; MIF See also Horohoe.

(O) Horgan *Ó hArgáin*. A Co. Cork name which takes the form Hourigan in Co. Limerick, and sometimes Arragan in south Waterford and Tipperary. This arises from the earlier Irish form *Ó hArragáin*. MIF Map Cork.

(O) Horish *Ó hUarghuis*. Woulfe quite inaccurately makes this 'cold choice': the component *gus* denotes vigour not choice. Horish is the anglicized form in the Clogher area; elsewhere in Ulster it is called Caldwell. MIF

(O) Horisky See Hourisky.

(O) Horkan A Mayo variant of Harkin.

Horner App.

Hornibrook This name, the origin of which I have not yet ascertained (presumably a toponymic), has been in Cork city and west Cork since early in the seventeenth century. It is very rare elsewhere.

(O) Horoho(e) *Ó hEarchadha*. This name, which is particularly associated with Swinford, Co. Mayo, has many variants and synonyms, e.g. Haraghy, Harroe, Hurroe, Horoe, Hore, and even Harris and Harrison. See Harrihy. MIF

Horrigan A variant of Horgan found in Cos. Cork and Kerry.

Horsey An Anglo-Norman name in Ireland since the thirteenth century. Its earlier form de Horsey has been made to look Irish by calling it O'Horsey, though in Irish *de Horsaigh* is used.

Hort Bibl.

Hosey This name is of dual origin: either O'Hosey, a variant of O'Hussey, or de Hosey, a Norman family settled in Meath. See Hussey.

Hosford An English toponymic of Cromwellian origin in Ireland, since found in considerable numbers almost exclusively in Co. Cork. MIF

Hoskin(s) Usually Hoskins is an English name distinct from Heskin.

(Mac) Hosty *Mac Oiste*, also *Mac Coiste*. The latter gives the anglicized form Custy found in Co. Clare. Hosty is a Mayo name. The family is said to be descended from a Welshman who lived in Co. Mayo in the thirteenth century and the name derived from Hodge, a pet form of Roger. MIF

Hough See Haugh.

(O) Houghegan *Ó hEochagáin*. This west Connacht name has unfortunately been now absorbed by the better-known Hogan and Geoghegan. See Haughian.

Houghton See Haughton. It has been gaelicized *de Hochtún*.

(O) Houlaghan See Hoolohan.

(O) Houneen See Honeen.

(O) Hounihan, Hoonahan *Ó hUamhnacháin* (*uamhnach*, terrible). A north Cork and Co. Limerick name.

(O) Hourahan Either a spelling variant of Hourihan, or *Ó hArracháin* of north Tipperary which is also a corrupt form of *Ó hAnradháin*. See Hanrahan.

(O) Hourican *Ó hAnnracháin*. This Co. Longford name is a synonym of Somers in the Granard area, seldom of the Munster Hourigan.

(O) Hourigan See Horgan. Woulfe mentions a Corca Laoidhe family of *Ó hOdhragáin* so anglicized.

(O) Hourihan(e) *Ó hAnradháin* (probably from *anradh,* warrior). A sept of west Cork, the leading family of which were erenaghs of Ross. See Hanrahan and Hourahan.

(O) Houriskey *Ó hUaruisce.* A corrupt form of *Ó hUarghuis.* One of the many names anglicized as Waters. See Horish.

Houston A well-known Scottish name very numerous in Ulster. It is sometimes a synonym of MacQuiston, and in Donegal of Mac-Taghlin. See MacCutcheon and MIF

Hovenden Now rare this name, originally de Offington or Ovington, is that of a family which settled in Tyrone under O'Neill at the end of the sixteenth century. They soon became hibernicized and at the time of the Plantation of Ulster they were classed as 'native'. A family of Hovenden was planted in Leix under Philip and Mary, but being Catholic lost those lands in the Cromwellian confiscations. In modern times the name is not confined to Ulster. Bibl. MIF

Howard This famous English name does duty for *Ó hÍomhair* in Clare where it was formerly O'Hure. MIF

Howe This well-known English name is, in Ireland, an occasional synonym of Hoey and of Hough.

Howell See under MacHale.

Howen See Hone.

Howlett *Húiléid.* An Anglo-Norman family in Leinster, now mainly found in Co. Wexford.

(O) Howley *Ó hUallaigh* (probably from *uallach,* proud). This name belongs to Connacht and Clare. The English toponymic Howley is very rarely the origin of the name in Ireland. MIF See Wholey.

Howlin See Holden.

Hoy A synonym of Hoey and Haughey.

Hoyle See MacIlhoyle.

(O) Hoyne The Kilkenny form of *Ó hEoghain* which elsewhere is Owens etc. **Huban** See Hoban.

(O) Huddy *Ó hUada.* A Munster variant of the Connacht name Foody.

Hudson This is one of the English names introduced in the seventeenth century which is much more numerous in Dublin than in Ulster. Bibl.

Huey See under Hoey.

Huggard A name of dual origin, viz. English (cognate with Howard) or Huguenot (French Hugard). As the latter it came to the north of Ireland; as the former it is on record in sixteenth-century Dublin, where two of the name were leading musicians; in Kerry it was established early in the eighteenth century and later became numerous there.

Mac Hugh This is a form of *Mac Aodha* very numerous in north

Connacht and west Ulster. There were two distinct septs of this name in Co. Galway: one was located near Tuam and the other, a branch of the O'Flahertys, in Connemara. IF   Map Galway.

Hughes A well-known English name very numerous in all the provinces except Munster. It is often also a synonym of *Ó hAodha*—see Hayes. App.

Hughey A variant of Huey.

Mac Hugo A branch of the Burkes of Connacht to be distinguished from MacHugh. See MacCooke.

Huleatt A variant of Hewlett associated with Co. Clare from mid-seventeenth century.

Hull App.

(O) Hulnane An east Cork variant of Cullinane.

(O) Hultaghan *Ó hUltacháin* (presumably from *Ultach*, Ulsterman). A Fermanagh family sometimes disguised under the name of Nolan. See Halton.

Hume Of dual derivation—Scottish toponymic and English from Old-Danish *hulm*. In Ireland it has become a Fermanagh surname, now more numerous in Antrim.

Humphries App.

(O) Huneen, Huonyn See Honeen.

Hungerford Coming from Wiltshire, England, in mid-seventeenth century, this family settled in west Cork, and the name has since become quite numerous there.

Hunt This is found in all the provinces: least in Ulster where it is of English origin and most in Connacht where it is used by pseudo-translation for several Irish names, viz. Feighney, Feighry and Fey. MIF 104.

Hunter An English name very numerous in north Ulster.

(O) Hure See Howard.

(O) Hurish See Horish.

(O) Hurley Woulfe gives *Ó hUrthuile* for this. An important Dalcassian sept, now scarce in Clare. Hurley of Co. Cork is numerous: there it is *Ó Muirthile* or *Ó Murghaile*, which is occasionally more phonetically anglicized as Murhilla and Murley. IF   Map Cork and Limerick. See Commane.

(O) Hurney *Ó hUrnaidhe*. This Irish form given by Woulfe is doubtful. The name was formerly numerous in the barony of Moycullen, Co. Galway.

Hurrell An English name denoting shaggy-haired (from Old-French *hure*) and possibly a form of *Ó hEarghaill*. See Arrell.

Hurst A common name in England, Hurst is often of different origin in Ireland, viz. a corrupt anglicized form of *de Horsaigh, recte* Horsey from the Norfolk place-name.

(O) Hussey *Ó hEodhusa*. A bardic family attached to the Maguires. In Kerry and Meath Hussey is a variant of de Hosey. Bibl. IF Map (O'Hussey) Fermanagh–Tyrone, (de Hussey) Meath.

(O) Hussian See Hession.

Huston A variant of Houston in Donegal.

Husty See Hosty.

Hutchinson See under MacCutcheon. App.

Hutton A Cumberland (England) name in Antrim and Armagh since mid-seventeenth century. App.

Hyde *de Híde*. As de la Hyde this name was early prominent in Leinster. A leading family of Hyde settled in Co. Kilkenny in the fourteenth century; later the name became prominent in Co. Cork where they were Elizabethan planters after the Desmond rebellion. Douglas Hyde, though born in Co. Roscommon, was of the Co. Cork family. IF 296.

(O) Hylan(d) *Ó hAoileáin*. Usually a form of *Ó Faoláin* (Phelan). It has become *Ó hAoileáin* in Connacht, where it is sometimes synonymous with Whelan. In England (but not in Ireland) Hyland is variant of Hayland. MIF   See Heelan.

(O) Hynan, Hinan *Ó hEidhneáin* (possibly from *eidhneán,* ivy). A rare name found in Cos. Limerick and Tipperary.

Hyndman App.

Hynes, Hynds See Heyne.

Hynie See Hiney.

Hyslip See Heaslip.

I

Ievers See Ivers.

Igoe See Jago.

Mac Ilcar, -Ilcharr* See MacElhair.

Mac Ilchon See MacConn.

Mac Ildoon If Woulfe is right in giving *Mac Mhaoldúin* as the Irish form of this rare Co. Armagh name, his derivation 'chief of the fort' can be accepted.

Mac Ildowney See MacEldowney.

Mac Ilduff *Mac Giolla Dhuibh* (*dubh,* black, i.e. black-haired). This is sometimes contracted to Duff in Co. Tyrone. Map Cavan.

Mac Ilee A variant of MacAlee.

Mac Ilgorm *Mac Giolla Ghuirm* (*gorm,* blue). A north-east Ulster name.

Mac Ilhagga *Mac Giolla Chairge*. This Gaelic form is given by Mac Giolla Domhnaigh. A Scottish name found in Cos. Antrim and Derry. MacElhargy, MacIlhargy and Maharg are variants of it. MIF

*See footnote on p. 96.

Mac Ilhair See MacElhair.

Mac Ilhatton *Mac Giolla Chatáin* (devotee of St. Catan). A north Antrim and Derry name, sometimes contracted to MacHatton. Mac-Clatton and Hatton and also made Macklehatton.

Mac Ilhenny See Kilkenny.

Mac Ilheron See MacElheron.

Mac Ilholm *Mac Giolla Choluim.** This north Fermanagh and west Tyrone name appears in the Annals as *Mac Giolla Chalma* and was first anglicized Macgillecolme. The usually accepted form, in Irish, given above, which denotes devotee of St. Columcille, may therefore be incorrect. MIF

Mac Ilhome See MacElhone.

Mac Ilhoyle See Coyle. This equation differs from that of Woulfe who regards MacIlhoyle as an anglicized form of *Mac Giolla Choille,* which is also made Woods by mistranslation. MIF

Mac Illesher *Mac Giolla Ghlais.* This Co. Fermanagh name is now nearly always anglicized Green(e) by partial translation (*glas,* green). Its synonym MacAlesher is occasionally changed to MacAlister. Fr. Livingstone says the correct Irish form is *Mac Giolla Laisir.*

Mac Ilmoyle, -Ilmeel See MacElmeel.

MacIlmurray See MacElmurray.

Mac Ilpatrick A variant of Gilpatrick.

Mac Ilrath, -Ilrea See Kilrea.

Mac Ilravy, -Elreavy The north Ulster form of *Mac Giolla Riabhaigh.* See Kilrea.

Mac Ilroy See Gilroy.

Mac Ilvany A variant of MacElvenna. See Mulvenna.

Mac Ilveen, -Elveen, -Kilveen *Mac Giolla Mhín* (*mín,* gentle). A Co. Down name. MIF

Mac Ilwaine, -Elwain *Mac Giolla Bháin* (*bán,* white). Properly speaking this is a Co. Sligo sept, but there it is anglicized Kilbane. In Ulster, where it is numerous, MacIlwaine may be the Scottish MacIlvaine or another form of MacIlveen. MIF

Mac Ilwee See MacElwee.

Mac Ilwraith See Kilrea.

Mac Inch See MacAninch.

Mac Inerney *Mac an Airchinnigh* (*airchinneach,* erenagh). One of the principal septs of Thomond, and one of the most numerous names in Co. Clare. There was also an erenagh family of Elphin, but there the name has often become Nerney. The synonym Kinnerk arose from the Co. Clare pronunciation which was almost MacInerkney. IF Map Clare.

---

*See footnotes on pp. 3 and 7.

Inglis See English.

Ingoldsby See Gallogly.

Ingram First settled in Co. Limerick in the seventeenth century, men of the name fought on both sides of the wars of that period. It is now mainly located in Ulster.

(Mac) Innes *Mac Aonghuis.* The Scottish form of MacGuinness. Angus and Anguish are cognate.

Mac In(o)ulty An occasional variant of MacNulty in Co. Clare.

Mac Inroe See MacEnroe.

Mac Intee See MacEntee.

Mac Inteer A Breffny form of MacAteer.

Mac Intyre See MacAteer.

Mac Ireavy See MacAreavy.

Ireland This name is said to have originated in England through early emigrants from Ireland called *de Irlande*, whose descendants returned as strangers. It is now fairly numerous in Cos. Armagh and Antrim. The surname Irish, of similar origin, formerly of Co. Kilkenny, now seems to be almost obsolete. MIF

Irons See Kenirons.

Irvine, Ervine Usually Irving in Scotland. Though much confused with Irwin, this Scottish toponymic is of different origin; seldom found outside Ulster where it was established in early seventeenth century, it is now numerous in Fermanagh and adjacent areas of that province. MIF 150; Bibl. See next entry.

Irwin, Erwin A sept of O'Hirwen (*Ó hEireamhóin*) did exist in Offaly, but nearly all Irwins are of planter stock in Ulster and in Co. Roscommon, their name, when not a synonym of Irvine, being derived from Old-English *eoforwine*, boar friend. Bibl. App. MIF

Itchingham See Etchingham.

Mac Iveagh A rare synonym of MacVeagh.

Ivers This can be the name of an English settler family in Co. Clare or more often the anglicized form of *Mac Íomhair*, see MacIvor. It is also occasionally for *Ó hÍomhair*; see Howard. MIF   See Evers.

Ivis In England this is for St. Ives, but in Ireland usually a corrupt form of Ivers.

Mac Ivor, -Iver *Mac Íomhair* (from a Norse forename). This is usually a synonym of MacKeever and is found in Tyrone and adjacent areas. MIF   See MacKeever.

Ivory This name, of French origin *(de Iverio)* has been closely identified with Co. Waterford since the Cromwellian soldier William Ivory settled there. Bibl. MIF

J

Jack This is usually derived from the pet name for John, but sometimes it is from the French *Jacques*. It occurs occasionally in early records in Co. Kilkenny, where possibly Jackstown commemorates it. In modern times it is quite numerous in Cos. Donegal and Tyrone as well as Belfast.

Jackman This English name was formerly fairly numerous in Co. Kilkenny, now Co. Waterford.

Jackson An English name numerous, especially in Ulster, since mid-seventeenth century. Bibl.

Jacob This Old-English name is in Ireland since the fourteenth century, though the well-known family of Cos. Wexford and Leix came in the seventeenth. MIF   See Jago.

Jaffrey See Jeffreys.

Jago Basically the same as Jacob, i.e. of Cornish origin. It was in Ireland in the sixteenth century as MacEgo and MacKigo *(Mac Iago)*. It has since been mainly found in Co. Cork. In Co. Roscommon and Longford, where they are a branch of the O'Hanleys, it is called Igoe. MIF

James This name is of dual origin in Ireland. It is an English name borne by a few comparatively recent immigrants and as such is found mainly in north-east Ulster. It is also an abbreviation of MacJames and Fitzjames, which, first formed from the Christian name of some members of one of the larger septs or more often Norman families, became in due course fixed as hereditary surnames. James is now fairly numerous in Cos. Carlow and Wicklow.

Jameson A Scottish name in Ireland since mid-eighteenth century. See Keamish.

Jardine App.

Jarvis See Jervois.

Jeffers, Jeffares According to Reaney this English name is a variant of Jeffreys (son of Jeffrey or Geoffrey). Both forms are on record in Ireland since the second half of the seventeenth century, Jeffers formerly mainly in Cos. Cork and Carlow and in Dublin, Jeffares in Co. Waterford. Jeffers is now numerous in Belfast and adjoining Ulster counties. When synonymous with Jeffreys, Jeffers may occasionally be for MacShaffrey. The rather similar Cromwellian name Jeffords (a variant of Gifford) has no connection with Jeffers. Jeffrey is now associated with Co. Cork.

Jeffreys See under Jeffers. For an alternative Irish origin of this English name see Shaffrey. Jeffreystown, Co. Westmeath, is called Ballyhaffray in a Fiant of 1569.

Jenkins App. See Shinkwin.

Jennings *Mac Sheóinín*. The Irish form is a Gaelic patronymic adopted by a branch of the Burkes of Connacht. Jennings is numerous also in Oriel where it is from a Norse diminutive of Jen or Jan. IF Map Galway-Mayo. See Kilmaine.

Jephson A leading Anglo-Irish family of Co. Cork, especially in the Mallow area, where they have been since the beginning of the seventeenth century. Bibl.

Jerety A variant of MacGeraghty in Westmeath.

Jermyn From *le Germain* (the German). In Ireland, mainly Munster, since the thirteenth century.

Jervois, Jervis On record in Ireland since early fourteenth century as Gervais (derived from Old-French forename). Since mid-seventeenth century it has been closely identified with Co. Cork.

Mac Jimpsey A variant of MacGimpsey.

Johnson Many of the Johnsons in Ireland, especially in Ulster, are of Scottish origin. This name in Ireland, however, is often a translation of MacShane and so a branch of the O'Neills. See MacKeown. It is much less numerous than Johnston, which is a British toponymic, but is also used synonymously with Johnston.

Johnston(e) Bibl; App. See previous entry.

Jolley, Joly This name is on record in Ireland since the sixteenth century. Both forms are derived from the French *joliffe*, festive. Bibl. MIF

Jones This, the most numerous surname in Wales and common in England, is also one of the most numerous settler names in Ireland. It is found in every county, especially in the larger towns. It has been gaelicized as *Mac Seóin*. Bibl; App.

Jordan *Mac Siúrtáin*. A Gaelic patronymic adopted by the d'Exeter family, one of those which acquired estates in Connacht after the Anglo-Norman invasion; that territory was later called MacJordan's country. The name is now numerous in all the provinces. IF Map Mayo.

Joy This is found in very early Irish records. In Connacht it is a variant of Joyce. In Munster, where it has close association with both Kerry and Waterford, it is of French origin.

Joyce *Seoigh*. A family of Welsh origin which became completely hibernicized; their territory (as Map) was called Joyce's country. They also became one of the 'Tribes of Galway'. IF Map Galway. See Cunnagher.

Joynt A Huguenot name (Fr. *le joint*—slim, graceful), formerly well known both in Cos. Limerick and Mayo.

Judge See Breheny.

K

Mac Kaig See MacKeague.

Kalshander See Alexander.

(O) Kanavaghan *Ó Connmhacháin.* This small sept is genealogically akin to the O'Haras; the name is now usually corrupted to Conway or Convey. Map Sligo.

Mac Kane, -Kain Variants of the Scottish MacKean but not of the Clare MacKeane.

(O) Kane, O Cahan *Ó Catháin.* As lords of Keenaght the O'Kanes were a leading sept in Ulster up to the time of the Plantation of Ulster. The name is still very numerous in its original homeland. Bibl. IF Map Derry-Tyrone. See also Keane.

(Mac) Kangley *Mac Ceanglaigh.* A Breffny sept of Co. Cavan. Sometimes anglicized Tighe by pseudo-translation (q.v.). Woulfe suggests that it may be a corruption of *Ó Coingheallaigh* (Quinnelly), but that has no connection with Breffny.

Kavanagh *Caomhánach.* A famous branch of the MacMurroughs. The name is said to have been adopted from the first Kavanagh having been fostered by a successor of St. Caomhan. The use of the prefix O with it is wrong. Bibl. IF Map Wexford.

Mac Kavanagh A variant of MacCavanna. See also Keaveney and Keevan. The name has no connection in any way with Kavanagh of Co. Wexford.

Mac Kay The name of a Scottish clan, some of whom settled in Ulster. Also, like MacKee, a synonym of *Mac Aodha.* IF See MacHugh and MacCoy.

(Mac) Keady *Mac Céadaigh. Céadach* was a personal name (from *céad*, hundred) popular with the O'Mores of Leix with whom the MacKeadys were associated. The name, however, is now rare in that country. The prefix Mac is usually dropped. Keady is now found mainly in Co. Galway. The name of the Corca Laoidhe sept *Ó Meicéidigh* has been corrupted to *Mac Céidigh* or *Mac Éidigh,* so Keadys in Co. Cork are mainly of that origin. MIF

(Mac) Keaghry, Keahery See Keighry.

Mac Keagney See MacKegney.

Mac Keague *Mac Thaidhg.* This Ulster name, which is cognate with MacTeague and MacTeige, the T being aspirated, has many variant forms, at least fourteen having been noted. Among those are Mac-Cague (with and without the prefix Mac) and even MacAig and Mac-Haigh.

(Mac) Keahan See Keehan.

Kealaghan, Ke(e)laghan *Ó Céileacháin.* (This like *Ó Céile*—see Keally —is possibly from *céile*, companion). An Oriel sept whose name has often been changed to Callaghan by attraction; it occurs with prefix Mac in Westmeath. Map Armagh. See Keelan.

(O) Keal(l)y, Keeley Each of these can be the anglicized form of several names: viz. *Ó Caollaidhe* (see Queally); *Ó Céile*, an ecclesiastical family in Meath and Louth; *Ó Cadhla* (see Kiely) and even *Ó Ceallaigh* (see Kelly). MIF   Map Leix. See previous entry.

Mac Keamish *Mac Shéamuis*. A gaelicized form of Jameson.

Mac Kean *Mac Eáin* (*Eáin* is a variant of *Eoin,* John). A well-known Scottish name, found in Cos. Donegal and Derry. See also under Muckian.

(Mac) Keane, Mac Cahan *Mac Catháin*. A family of west Clare who were co-arbs of St. Senan. Map Clare.

(O) Keane When this is not a variant of the Ulster O'Cahan it is *Ó Céin* of Munster which embodies the personal name *Cian*. Inevitably Keane has often been substituted for Kane. Map Waterford.

Keany A name of doubtful origin (the possibilities are considered in MIF   It is mainly found in Leitrim, Galway and Donegal.

Mac Kearney When Kearney is found in north Ulster it is usually *Mac Cearnaigh,* a branch of the Cenél Eoghain, and distinct from the name dealt with in the next entry.

(O) Kearney The anglicized form of two Irish surnames: (1) *Ó Catharnaigh* (warlike) of Kilcoursey, Co. Meath, now often Fox, the head of the family being known as 'The Fox'; and (2) *Ó Cearnaigh* (*cearnach,* victorious) which is the name of two septs now called Kearney (or Carney in Connacht), viz. of the Uí Fiachrach and of the Dál gCais; the latter migrated to Cashel. IF   Map Mayo and Tipperary.

(O) Kearon, Kearns See Kieran. The form Kearon is peculiar to Co. Wicklow.

Kearse, Kearsey, Kiersey Variant spellings of Kierse and Keirsey.

Mac Keary A variant of MacAree in Co. Monaghan.

(O) Keary, Keery *Ó Ciardha* (*ciar,* black or dark brown). A sept of the southern Uí Néill in north Leinster. Now widely anglicized as Carey. Keary is also an abbreviated form of Kilkeary.

Keating One of the earliest of the hibernicized Anglo-Norman families whose name was gaelicized *Céitinn*. They settled in south Leinster. The historian Dr. Geoffrey Keating was of Co. Tipperary. The name with the prefix Mac is associated exclusively with the Downpatrick area, where MacKetian is a synonym of it. The theory that Keating is derived from *Mac Eitienne* is improbable. Woulfe makes it a toponymic. The most acceptable suggestion is that it is from *Cethyn,* a Welsh personal name. Bibl. IF   See Keaty.

Keatley See Gately.

(O) Keaty *Ó Céatfhadha* (possibly from *céatfhaidh,* sense). A minor

Dalcassian sept, located near Limerick. Keaty has been frequently changed to Keating.

Keaveney *Ó Géibheannaigh* and *Mac Géibheannaigh*. Also and more correctly anglicized Geaveney, sometimes changed to Kavanagh. A sept of the Uí Maine still numerous in Connacht. MIF

(O) Keavy *Ó Ciabhaigh* (*ciabhach*, having long locks of hair). A rare name found in Cos. Clare and Galway.

Mac Kechnie *Mac Eacharna* in Scottish Gaelic according to Black. This is a branch of the Scottish clan MacDonald.

(Mac) Kedian, Keadian Forms of MacCadden found in Co. Roscommon. See Keating.

(Mac) Kee One of the many anglicized forms of *Mac Aoidh*, which in the form of MacKee is essentially a north-east Ulster name: there it is usually a variant of the Scottish MacKay. In Donegal it is numerous as Kee without the prefix Mac. Bibl. MIF

(O) Keeffe *Ó Caoimh* (*caomh*, gentle). Though driven by the Anglo-Normans from their original homeland in east Cork, this sept, which had given early kings to Munster, migrated only within the bounds of what is now Co. Cork and established themselves in the territory subsequently known as Pobal O'Keeffe. The name, which has spread widely through south Munster, is especially numerous in Co. Cork. IF   Map Cork.

Mac Keefry See MacKeighry.

Keegan Correctly *Mac Aodhagáin* but now usually corrupted to *Ó Caogáin*. Keegan is now numerous in two widely separated areas, viz. Cos. Wicklow and Dublin or Cos. Leitrim and Roscommon. See Egan.

(Mac) Keehan *Mac Caocháin* (*caoch*, blind). Well known in Co. Clare, rare elsewhere.

(O) Keelahan See next entry.

(O) Keelan Woulfe gives *Ó Caoláin*, treating it as an almost obsolete Meath name. It is, I suggest, an abbreviation of Keelahan, *Ó Céil-eacháin*, the name of an Oriel family formerly chiefs of Uí Breasail and still fairly numerous in that area alone. See Kealaghan.

(O) Keeley See Kealy.

Keeling This English name is in Ireland since the seventeenth century and all the earlier references to it relate to Dublin. It is quite distinct from Keelan, but is occasionally found as a synonym of Keeley.

(O) Keelty A spelling variant of Kielty.

Mac Keeman *Mac Shiomóin*. A gaelicized form of Fitzsimon found in Ulster.

Keena As this name is mainly found in Westmeath, I think Woulfe is mistaken in equating it with Keaney: I suggest MacKenna, but as yet have no conclusive evidence of this.

(O) Keenahan See Kinahan.

(O) Keenan *Ó Cianáin*. A Fermanagh family noted as historians to the Maguires. In Co. Offaly and other midland areas Keenan was formerly Kinahan. Woulfe says that in Co. Roscommon it is *Mac Cinín*, a modern form of *Mac Fhinghin* (fair offspring). IF

(Mac) Keeny See Keany.

(O) Keerican A Leitrim variant of Kerrigan.

Keery See Keary.

(O) Keeshan *Ó Ciseáin*. Woulfe's statement that this is an attenuated form of *Ó Ciosáin* (Kissane) may be correct: I have found no evidence to support or refute this. Keeshan is found in east Clare and north Tipperary. See Kissane.

(O) Keevan, Kevane *Ó Ciabháin* (derivation as Keavy). A sept of Corca Laoidhe, usually called Kevane in Kerry. A quite distinct origin is *Ó Caomháin* (*caomh*, mild). This is a sept of the Uí Fiachrach as Map. Keevan has been changed to Kavanagh in Kerry by absorption. MIF Map Mayo and Sligo.

(Mac) Keeveen An occasional variant of (Mac) Kevin in north Connacht. The name is found in Offaly and north Tipperary.

Keeveney See Keaveney.

Mac Keever, -Keevers *Mac Íomhair*. This mainly Oriel name is also anglicized MacIvor in Tyrone and adjacent counties. *Mac Íomhair* is generally thought to derive from the Norse personal name *Ivaar*, but it has also been stated that the Irish form, in Oriel at any rate, should be *Mac Éimhir*, from the forename *Éimhear* (Heber), a favourite with the MacMahons, of which great Co. Monaghan sept these MacKeevers claim to be a branch. MIF

(O) Keevey See Keavey.

(O) Keevlin *Ó Cibhlín*. Woulfe gives also *Ó Coibhleacháin*. The family were co-arbs of St. Feichin at Fore, Co. Westmeath. The name is now rare.

(O) Kegley See Quigley.

(Mac) Kegney, Keagney *Mac Éignigh*. This name has always been associated with Cos. Tyrone and Fermanagh.

Keheerin, Caheerin Variants of Mac Echern. For derivation see Aherne.

Keherney A Connacht variant of *Ó Catharnaigh* (Kearney) formerly *Mac Ceithearnaigh*. The head of this family was lord of a good part of the barony of Castlerea in Co. Roscommon.

Kehigan, Kihegan Variants of Keogan found in south Ulster.

(Mac) Kehilly *Mac Caochlaoich* (*coach*, blind—*laoch*, hero). Except in the Dunmanway area of Co. Cork where Kehilly is extant, this name has been changed to Coakley, which is also almost peculiar to Co. Cork. MIF

Kehir, Keher Variants of Cahir found in north Munster and east Connacht.

(Mac) Kehoe See Keogh.

Kei- See also Kie-.

(Mac) Keighan See Keehan.

(O) Keighron *O Cíocharáin* (*cíocharán,* hungry person). A small sept of east Galway, whose name is often wrongly made Kerrigan.

(Mac) Keighry *Mac Fhiachra* (*Fiachra* is an ancient personal name). A Co. Galway sept. The anglicized forms Keighry, Kehery and Keaghry are now very rare, as these have been absorbed by Carey. Another *Mac Fhiachra* sept, that of the northern Uí Néill, was called Mac-Keaghery and MacGeaghery in seventeenth-century records, but it appears to have become MacKeefry in Tyrone. MIF

Keightley An English name used as a synonym of Gately.

Mac Keigue An east Galway form of MacKeague.

(O) Keily See Kiely.

Keirsey, Kiersey *Ciarasach* and *de Céarsaigh.* This Norman toponymic came to Co. Waterford in the thirteenth century and has since been continuously there. It has no connection with de Courcy.

(Mac) Keith The name of a Scottish clan numerous in Ulster in the seventeenth century.

(O) Kelaghan, Kellahan See Kealahan.

Kell See Kells.

Mac Kell See Mackle.

Mac Kellan In Oriel this is a variant of MacKillan, elsewhere usually of MacCallion.

(O) Kelledy *Ó Callada* (*callaid,* crafty). An Oriel name fairly numerous in Co. Louth.

(O) Kelleher *Ó Céileachair* (companion dear). This Dalcassian sept migrated to Cos. Kerry and Cork in the fourteenth century. The name is sometimes abbreviated to Keller, which, however, is normally one of German origin. IF   Map Kerry.

Keller See previous entry.

Kellett Having obtained grants following the Williamite confiscations families of this name became fairly numerous in Cos. Cavan and Meath. It is a north of England toponymic.

Mac Kelloch See Killough.

Kellogg See under Killough.

Kells According to Reaney Kells and Kell are abbreviated forms of Old-Norse *ketill* (i.e. cauldron). Kells is seldom derived from any of the place-names in Ireland so-called, though there are a few examples of this in mediaeval records. In Scotland, however, it is a toponymic. These two surnames are mainly found in Ulster: Kells in Cos. Cavan and Monaghan, Kell in Antrim. Bibl.

(Mac) Kelly *Mac Ceallaigh.* A minor sept of east Connacht; now that the prefixes Mac and O have been so widely dropped from these names, it is indistinguishable from O'Kelly.

(O) Kelly *Ó Ceallaigh.* (The derivation of Kelly is uncertain; the most probable suggestion is that it is from *ceallach*, strife). The most important and numerous sept of this name is that of the Uí Maine. There are several other septs as indicated in Map. Kelly is the second most numerous name in Ireland. In 1890 less than one per cent of them had the prefix O but this has since been to some extent resumed. Bibl. IF Map Derry, Galway, Leix, Meath and Wicklow.

Kelso App.

Mac Kelvy *Mac Giolla Bhuidhe* (*giolla*, lad—*buidhe*, yellow). The name of this Donegal sept has many variants, e.g. MacElwee, MacCalvey, MacGilloway, MacGilvie, Kilvey. In Mayo it has become Kilboy. See Calvey.

Mac Kemmin A variant of MacKimmon. See Kimmons.

Kemmis A Monmouthshire name associated with Co. Leix since the late seventeenth century. Bibl.

Kemp This English name (Middle-English *kempe*, athlete) recurs in Irish records from the fourteenth century till the present day but has never been closely identified with any particular locality. It is now fairly numerous in Dublin and Belfast. See Campbell.

Kemple A form of the English toponymic Kemble found in east Galway.

(O) Kendillon A Co. Louth variant of Kindellan.

(Mac) Kendrick *Mac Eanraic* (*Eanrac*, an old German personal name meaning home-rule). In north-west Ulster the prefix is usually retained; in Munster the name has become Kenrick and Condrick. See Kenrick.

(O) Kendrigan *Ó Cinndeargáin.* (?*ceann*, head—*dearg*, red). Clare and west Connacht.

(Mac) Kendry A form of MacHenry found in north-east Ulster.

(O) Kenealy See Kinnealy.

Kenefick *Cinipheic.* This name, now associated with Co. Cork, came to Leinster in the early thirteenth century. It is taken from a Welsh place-name. MIF

Kenerney See Kinnarney. **Kenehan** See Kinahan.

Kenirons This name is found in north Tipperary and is occasionally abbreviated to Irons. I am still trying to discover its origin.

Keniry, Kinniry Variants of MacEniry found in Co. Clare.

Mac Kenna, Kennagh *Mac Cionaoith.* A branch of the southern Uí Néill, mainly located in Co. Monaghan where they were lords of Truagh; the name is now fairly numerous also in Leinster and Munster. Locally in Clare and Kerry the last syllable is stressed, giving the variants Kennaw, Ginna, Gna, etc. Bibl. IF Map Monaghan.

(Mac) Kennan This name when the prefix Mac is dropped can be confused with Kinnane, or if the Mac is retained with the Scottish Mac-Kinnon. It is, however, a distinct name, *Mac Fhionnáin (fionn,* fair) belonging to Oriel, quite numerous in Cos. Monaghan and Armagh. The 'census' of 1659 lists Kennon as a principal name in the barony of Ardee, Co. Louth.

(O) Kennane A spelling variant of Kinnane.

(O) Kenneally See Kinneally.

(O) Kennedy *Ó Cinnéide (ceann,* head—*éidigh,* ugly). An important Dalcassian sept of east Clare which settled in north Tipperary and spread thence as far south as Wexford whence came the family of President J. F. Kennedy. The Scottish Kennedys are by remote origin Irish Gaels. Bibl. IF   MIF   Map Tipperary.

(O) Kennellan, Kenlan Variants of Kindelan.

(O) Kennelly A south Munster name used as a variant both of Quinnelly and Kinnealy and occasionally of Connelly.

Kenney This is sometimes of English origin even, by coincidence, in the homeland of the Uí Maine Kennys where an English family settled; but usually it is from Mac or O Kenny.

Mac Kenniff A Co. Cavan name. See Cunniff.

Kenning See Kenyon.

Kennion A variant of Kenyon.

Mac Kenny An Ulster variant of MacKenna.

(O) Kenny *Ó Cionaoith.* The name of several distinct septs. The majority of the name today are of the Uí Maine sept. It is sometimes used as a synonym of Kinney and Kilkenny. Woulfe's derivation from *cionaodh* (firesprung) is conjectural. IF   MIF   Map Donegal and Galway. See Kenney.

Kenrick This and Kendrick are, according to Reaney, the Welsh *Cynwrig;* Weekley derives it from Anglo-Saxon *Coenric.* In Ireland the origin is usually Gaelic. See MacKendrick.

Kent *Ceannt.* Families of this name, derived from the English county, settled in Meath in the thirteenth century. IF

Mac Kenty A variant of MacEntee.

Kenure A spelling variant of Kinure.

Kenyon This is an English toponymic which, with Kenning, has been used as the anglicized form of *Mac Coinín*—see Cunneen. Woulfe states that Kenyon and also Kenning and even Keenan are sometimes anglicized forms of *Mac Fhinghin.* See Keenan.

Mac Kenzie A Scottish name: see MacKinney. Bibl.

Keogan *Mac Eochagáin.* This has been corrupted to *Ó Ceogáin,* with the result that in Cavan and Meath it is sometimes a variant of Cogan.

(Mac) Keogh *Mac Eochaidh.* The location of the three septs so called is indicated in the Map. Ballymackeogh in south Tipperary and Keogh's

Country in south Roscommon commemorate two of these. The sept of Co. Wicklow were hereditary bards to the O'Byrnes. These are now usually called Kehoe. IF   Map Limerick-Tipperary, Roscommon and Wicklow-Wexford. See p. 304.

(Mac) Keo(g)hane, Kohane *Mac Eocháin,* corruptly *Ó Ceocháin.* Peculiar to west Cork.

Mac Keon, -Keown The Irish forms are *Mac Eoghain* in Connacht, and *Mac Eoin* in east Ulster (both from Irish forms of John). Fr. C. J. Travers states that Keown is *Ó Ceotháin* in Co. Fermanagh. No less than seventeen variants and synonyms of MacKeown have been officially recorded—among these are Magone, MacCune, MacEwen, MacGeown and also Caulfield all in Co. Down, and Mackone in Co. Monaghan, while both Johnson by translation and Johnstone erroneously have been also so used. The main sept is of north Connacht with a branch in Co. Galway. The MacKeons of the Glens of Antrim are mainly descendants of Scottish Bissetts. IF   Map Roscommon-Sligo and Antrim.

(Mac) Keoneen *Mac Sheóinín* (i.e. little John). A gaelicized form of Jennings in use in Cos. Galway and Mayo. It is often corrupted to *Ó Ceóinín.*

Keppel See Capel.

Keppock See Cappock.

(O) Kerby See Kirby.

Kerdiff A variant of Cardiff.

(O) Kerevan A variant of Kirwan in Leix and Kilkenny. According to Woulfe, however, Kervan, alias Carvin, is a distinct name, viz. *Ó Cearbháin* which he says is derived from *cearbh,* stag (Latin *cervus*). See Kervon.

(O) Kerin, Kerins See Kieran.

(Mac) Kerley This is usually the anglicized form of *Mac Fhearghaile* (Carley) mainly found in Oriel; it is an occasional variant of Curley in Offaly.

(O) Kerlin, Kirlin Variants of Carolan found in Donegal and Derry.

(Mac) Kermode *Mac Dhiarmada.* This is MacDermot with the initial D in Irish aspirated, which occurs in Connacht. The use of Kermode as a synonym of Carmody is an error which arose from spelling not pronunciation.

(O) Kernaghan *Ó Cearnacháin* (*cearnach,* victorious). Now mainly found in Cos. Armagh and Antrim. MIF   Map Donegal.

(Mac) Kernan A variant usually of Kiernan in Co. Cavan and Fermanagh and occasionally of Kernaghan. Bibl.

(O) Kerney An Ulster variant spelling of Kearney.

Kerr A very numerous name in Ulster usually of Scottish origin; also a synonym of Carr, and in Donegal of Kerin. App; MIF

(O) Kerrane, Kirrane *Ó Cearáin*. Perhaps variants of *Ó Ciaráin* (Kieran) of Donegal. It is mainly found in Co. Mayo and adjacent areas. MIF

(Mac) Kerribly Map Mayo. See under Kirby.

(O) Kerrigan *Ó Ciaragáin*. (The root word is *ciar*, black or dark brown). A sept of the Uí Fiachrach located around Ballykerrigan. MIF Map Mayo. See Comber.

(O) Kerrin A variant of Kerin *(Ó Céirín)* in Donegal.

(Mac) Kerrisk *Mac Fhiarais* (*Fiaras*, Piers). A branch in Kerry of the O'Healys. The name is called Kierse in Clare.

Kervan, Kervon A variant of Kirwan in Munster.

Mac Kervey *Mac Cearrbhaigh* (probably from *cearrbhach*, gambler). A Fermanagh name, perpetuated in the place-name Mullaghmakervy

(O) Kervick, Kerwick See Kirby.

Kesham See Keeshan.

(O) Kessidy A variant of Cassidy found in Fermanagh.

Mac Ketian See under Keating.

(O) Kett *Ó Ceit*. The eponymous ancestor is believed to have been Ceat of Corcomroe. This name is well known in west Clare but rare elsewhere. Map Clare.

Kettle *Mac Coitil* (from a Norse personal name). Kettle is on record in Cos. Louth and Dublin since the early fourteenth century. MIF

Mac Kettrick See Kitterick.

(O) Kevane See Keevan.

(Mac) Kevany, Keveney Variants usually of Keaveney and sometimes of Coveney.

Kevelighan A variant of Kevlehan. See Kivlehan.

Keverney This has been used as a synonym of Kevany and Governey.

(O) Kevil(le) *Ó Cibhil*. Cos. Mayo and Roscommon. Woulfe says this is an abbreviation of Kivlehan, which seems not unlikely.

Mac Kevin See MacGiven.

Mac Kevitt *Mac Dhaibhéid*. Exclusively an Oriel name. Etymologically akin to MacDevitt.

(O) Kevlehan See Kivlehan.

Mac Kew A variant of MacHugh in Ulster.

Mac Key An Ulster variant of MacKee, not of Mackey.

Keyes An English name often used in Ireland for MacKee.

Keyse A variant of Keyes and Keys which have occasionally been used as corrupt forms of Casey.

Mac Kibbin *Mac Fhibín* (*Fibín* is a diminutive of Philip). A Down and Antrim name. As *Mag Fhibín* it is anglicized MacGibben.

Kickham An English family of comparatively recent introduction, but nevertheless hibernicized as exemplified in C. J. Kickham of Mullinahone, Co. Tipperary, IF

Kidd App.

Kidney A synonym, by pseudo-translation, of Duane, mainly found in Co. Cork.

(O) Kielty See Quilty.

(O) Kiely *Ó Cadhla* (*cadhla*, graceful). Much confused with Keeley and Queally. Kiely belongs mainly to Cos. Waterford and Limerick. MIF Map LImerick.

Mac Kieran *Mac Ciaráin*. A Co. Donegal name.

(O) Kieran, Kerin *Ó Ciaráin* and *Ó Céirín* (*ciar*, black or dark brown). The main sept of this name is of north Connacht, now fairly numerous in Co. Monaghan and Fermanagh; another small one was located in east Cork. It is often anglicized as Kearns. IF   Map Cork and Mayo. See Kerrane.

(Mac) Kiernan *Mac Thighearnáin* (*tighearna*, lord). This is basically the same as MacTiernan. The main sept is of Breffny; another is a branch of the O'Conors of east Connacht; while there was also a third in Fermanagh. The name, with and without the prefix Mac, is numerous today, the great majority of families so called being found in Cos. Cavan and Leitrim. In Fermanagh the name has become MacKernan and Kernan. IF   MIF   Map Cavan and Fermanagh.

Kierse See Kerrisk.

Kiersey See Keirsey.

(O) Kiervan A midlands variant of Kirwan. See Kerevan.

(Mac) Kiggins, Kiggan *Mac Uigin* (a diminutive of Hugo). A branch of the Joyces of Connemara; also of the Stantons of Mayo. It is peculiar to Galway and adjacent Connacht counties.

(O) Kihegan See Kehigan.

(Mac) Kilbane *Mac Giolla Bháin*. A sept of the Uí Fiachrach belonging to north Connacht. Often by translation of *bán* made White. Map Sligo.

(Mac) Kilboy See Kelvey.

(Mac) Kilbride *Mac Giolla Bhrighde* (devotee of St. Brigid). Kilbride is the Connacht form of this name, elsewhere anglicized MacBride and MacGilbride.

(Mac) Kilcarr See MacElhair.

(Mac) Kilcash *Mac Giolla Chais* (devotee of St. Cas). A rare name belonging to Co. Sligo. It has no connection with the woods of Kilcash in the well-known song. Kil is of course one of the commonest components of place-names: in Connacht it is used in the anglicized forms of *Giolla* surnames which begin with Gil elsewhere.

(Mac) Kilcawley ?*Mac Giolla Chalbaigh* (*calbhach*, bald). This name belongs in Cos. Sligo and Roscommon. Kilcowley is a variant.

(Mac) Kilchrist A variant of Gilchrist.

(Mac) Kilcline *Mac Giolla Chlaoin* (*claon*, deceitful). A Co. Roscommon

179

sept whose name has been widely abbreviated to Cline: Clynes is now the most usual synonym. MIF

(Mac) Kilcommon(s) *Mac Giolla Chomáin* (devotee of St. Coman). This name is mainly found around Athlone and east Galway.

(Mac) Kilcooley *Mac Giolla Chúille*. (Woulfe says that *Cúille* is an abbreviation of *Mochúille*, the name of a saint). It is found in Clare and Galway and sometimes shortened to Cooley.

(Mac) Kilcourse A Mayo name. See under Kilgore.

(Mac) Kilcowley See Kilcawley.

(Mac) Kilcoyle A variant of MacIlhoyle.

(Mac) Kilcoyne *Mac Giolla Chaoine* (*caoin*, gentle). Exclusively a Connacht name. Sometimes it is abbreviated to Coyne. IF

(Mac) Kilcullen See Kilgallen.

Kildare This is never a toponymic. See Kilderry.

(Mac) Kildea See Gildea.

(Mac) Kilderry A variant of MacElderry found in Co. Clare, where it has occasionally been corrupted to Kildare.

(Mac) Kilduff *Mac Giolla Dhuibh* (*dubh*, black). This is also anglicized as MacElduff, MacIlduff, Gilduff, Duff and, by translation, Black. Map Galway.

(Mac) Kildunn *Mac Giolla Dhuinn* (*donn*, brown). The name of a Sligo family, where it is sometimes abbreviated to Dunn. It is to be distinguished from Kilgunn, Gilgunn, etc. See Gunn.

(O) Kiley See Kiely.

(Mac) Kilfedder, Kilfeather *Mac Giolla Pheadair* (devotee of St. Peter). A Co. Sligo name. The prefix Mac is not now retained. Kilfedrick is a variant of Kilpatrick not of Kilfedder.

(Mac) Kilfillen A variant of Gilfillan.

(Mac) Kilfoyle See Gilfoyle.

(Mac) Kilgallen *Mac Giolla Chaillín* (devotee of St. Cailin). Numerous in Co. Mayo; it has become Kilcullen in Co. Sligo.

(Mac) Kilgannon *Mac Giolla Ghannáin*. Another of the many Co. Sligo names beginning with Kil. Gannan has not been identified.

(Mac) Kilgar, Killegar *Mac Giolla Gheáirr* (*geárr*, short). Perhaps a synonym of Kilgore.

(Mac) Kilgarriff See next entry.

(Mac) Kilgore The Irish form of the name of this north-west Ulster family is probably *Mac Giolla Gheáirr*, as Kilgar. Woulfe, however, suggests *Mac Giolla Ghairbh* (*garbh*, rough) hence Kilgarriff also, which is conjectural. He gives this conjecturally also for Kilcourse.

(Mac) Kilgrew This rare Connacht name is equated by Woulfe with Kilgore which can only be accepted with reserve. It is found in Co. Waterford as Killigrew and Kilgrove, Killigrew being an English place-name.

(Mac) Kilgunn See Gunn.

(Mac) Kileeny An occasional variant of Gilheany.

(Mac) Kilkeary *Mac Giolla Chéire* (devotee of St. Ciar). A rare Co. Kilkenny name.

(Mac) Kilkelly, Killikelly *Mac Giolla Cheallaigh* (devotee of St. Ceallach). This family were hereditary olavs to the O'Flahertys. The name is sometimes abbreviated to Kelly with resultant confusion as to its origin. MIF   Map Galway.

Kilkenny The tribes of: Archer, Archdekin, Cowley, Knaresborough, Langton, Lawless, Ley, Ragget, Rothe, Shee.

(Mac) Kilkenny *Mac Giolla Chainnigh* (devotee of St. Canice). A sept of the Cenél Eoghain group, now scattered. As Kilkenny the name is mainly found in north Connacht, and as MacElhinney and MacIlhenny in west Ulster. This surname has no connection with the town of Kilkenny except the similar derivation. MIF

(Mac) Kilkey *Mac Giolla Chaoich (caoch,* blind). A predominantly Co. Derry name. There it has not only Gilkie as a synonym but also Kielty. See Quilty.

(Mac) Killacky, Killahy *Mac Giolla Aithche,* the current form in Irish (from *faithche,* lawn) is not authentic. The suggestion that the root word is the forename *Eachaidh* is also doubtful. This small sept has always been located on the border of Offaly and north Tipperary, whence it has spread to the adjoining part of Co. Galway.

Killard See Killiard.

(O) Killeen *Ó Cillín.* (Woulfe considers *Cillín* to be a diminutive of *ceallagh,* strife, but this seems impossible). It belongs to the western seaboard counties. A branch was located at Ballykilleen, Co. Mayo; another was an erenagh family of Clonmacnois. It spread to Clare and Galway and thence to Offaly. MIF   Map Mayo.

(Mac) Killen *Mac Coilin.* (Colin is a Scottish forename). A galloglass family brought from Scotland by the O'Donnells, now mainly found in Oriel. MIF

(Mac) Killeran, Kilrane Variants of Gilleran, not of Killoran.

(Mac) Killerlean *Mac an Fhirléighinn (fear,* man—*léighinn,* of learning). Almost exclusively now a Co. Sligo name, and probably a branch of the O'Donnells of Tirconnell. MacNerlin is a synonym of it.

(O) Killian *Ó Cilleáin.* A Clare and Galway variant of Killeen. As Killion it is mainly found in Westmeath and Roscommon.

Killiard A rare Westmeath name. It is probably distinct from Gilliard of Co. Down, which is an English name of quite frequent occurrence in seventeenth-century army lists in Ireland. I have not ascertained the origin of either.

Killigraw See Kilgrew.

(Mac) Killilea *Mac Giolla Léith.* Woulfe derives this from *liath,* grey.

181

The name has always been associated with Co. Galway and adjacent areas. MIF

Killimet See Kilmet.

Mac Killop *Mac Fhilib*. A branch of the Scottish clan MacDonald numerous in Co. Antrim. Kellops and Killips are variants. MIF

(Mac) Killoran *Mac Giolla Luaighrinn* (from a saint of that name according to Woulfe). Of Co. Sligo. Gilloran is a variant of it in Co. Roscommon. MIF

Killough This is the Irish form of the Scottish MacKelloch, in Louth and Ulster since the seventeenth century. Kellough is an English toponymic distinct from Killough, and is presumably the original form of the American Kellogg. SIF 98.

(Mac) Killoughrey *Mac Giolla Luachaire* (devotee of St. Luachair). A west Clare name. MIF

Kilmaine This name, that of their home in Co. Mayo, was assumed by a Jennings family in France.

(Mac) Kilmartin See Gilmartin.

(Mac) Kilmary A variant of Kilmurray. See MacElmurray.

(Mac) Kilmet, Kilmaith *Mac Uilliméid* (son of Willimet or French *Guillemet*). This rare Westmeath name is now absurdly mistranslated Woods—*adhmad*, wood.

(Mac) Kilmore A form of Gilmore used in Co. Sligo.

(Mac) Kilmurr(a)y More usually MacElmurray or MacIlmurray.

(Mac) Kilpatrick *Mac Giolla Phádraig*. An older form of Fitzpatrick almost peculiar to Ulster. It is sometimes used synonymously with Kirkpatrick.

(Mac) Kilrain See Killeran.

(Mac) Kilrea A Co. Sligo form of *Mac Giolla Riabhaigh* (*riabhach,* brindled) elsewhere MacIlrea. MacIlwraith, the Scottish form of this name, is now very numerous in north-east Ulster. MIF

(Mac) Kilroy, Kilroe The latter, which is phonetically nearer the Irish form *Mac Giolla Rua* (*rua,* red), is peculiar to Roscommon. See Gilroy.

(O) Kilty See Quilty.

(Mac) Kilvant Fr. Paul Walsh gives the Irish form of this as *Mac Giolla Mhanntaigh* (*mantach* means gap-toothed, hence stammering). An old surname of Westmeath, now very rare.

Mac Kilveen, Kilvine See MacIlveen.

Kilvey See MacKelvey.

Kilwee A Sligo form of MacElwee.

(Mac) Kimm *Mac Shim*. The name of a branch of the Scottish clan Frazer mainly found in Co. Derry.

Kimmons, Kimmins An occasional variant of Cummins, in Cos. Monaghan and Armagh, where it is usually *Mac Coimín* not *Mac Shiomóin* which is Fitzsimons.

Kinagan, Kinagam, Kinningham Variants of Cunningham in Cos. Louth, Monaghan and Armagh.

Kinally See Kinnally.

(O) Kinahan *Ó Coinneacháin*. A sept located in the country south of Athlone. Kinahan in Ulster is usually one of the many variants of Cunningham. MIF

Kincaid, Kinkead This Scottish toponymic had become well established in several northern counties by mid-seventeenth century, especially Antrim and Derry. A branch settled in Co. Sligo. MIF

Kincart See Wright.

Kinch This is the Manx form of *Mac Aonghuis* (MacGuinness). It is found mainly in Cos. Wicklow and Wexford, but is not numerous.

Kinchella See Kinsella.

(O) Kindelan *Ó Caoindealbháin* (the words embodied in this name mean gracefully shaped). A Westmeath and Meath branch of the southern Uí Néill prominent in Spain. The name is now usually merged in Connellan. IF   Map Meath.

(O) Kindrigan See Kendrigan.

Kine See Kyne.

King Usually an English name; but it is also widely used as an anglicized form of several names by pseudo-translation (*rí*—king); viz. Conry, Conroy, Cunree in Connacht, MacAree and MacKeary in Oriel, and even sometimes of Gilroy and MacKinn. There is also a rare name *Ó Cionga*, now King, which belongs to Lough Ree. App. IF Map see Conry.

Kingerty A synonym of MacGinity.

Kingsley This English toponymic is used as a synonym of Kinsella.

Kingston Though this toponymic occurs in mediaeval Dublin records, it is now represented by an English family established in the Drimoleague area of west Cork in the seventeenth century and numerous there, so much so indeed that it was reported in 1885 that every one of the sixty pupils in the National School at Meenies was a Kingston! Occasionally by far-fetched mistranslation it is the anglicized form of the rare Co. Sligo name *Mac Clochaire* (MacCloughry). Bibl. MIF

Kinifeck See Kenerick.

Kininghan See Kinahan.   **Kinirons** See Kenirons.

(Mac) Kiniry A variant of MacEniry.

Kinkead See Kincaid.

(O) Kinlan An abbreviated form of Kindelan.

Mac Kinley, -Kinlay Usually this is the Scottish *Mac Fhionnlaoich* (fair hero) in Antrim; but sometimes it is for the Irish *Mac an Leagha* (see MacAlee). Bibl. MIF

Kinloch So spelt in Scotland, the country of its origin, where Black says it is from *ceann an locha,* head of the lake. It is now often Kinlough in Ulster. It is also the anglicized form of the very rare surname *Mac Conlocha* (hound of the lake).

Mac Kinn *Mac Fhinn (fionn,* fair). An early form of MacGinn, now rare, being changed to King.

Kinnally A north Tipperary name. I am uncertain whether it is a variant of MacAnally or Kineally.

(O) Kinnan Usually a variant of Keenan, not of Kinnane.

(O) Kinnane *Ó Cuinneáin.* A Thomond name, mainly found in north Tipperary, synonymous with Guinane, sometimes called Quinane. See Ginnane.

(Mac) Kinnarney, Kenerny A form of MacInerney found in Offaly.

(O) Kinnavane The Clare form of Canavan.

Mac Kinnawe, Kinneavy *Mac Conshnámha.* A Connacht name, now usually made Forde by mistranslation; actually the derivation is from *cú,* hound—*snámh,* swim. For Kinnawe in Kerry see MacKenna. IF   Map Leitrim (as Consnave).

(O) Kinneally *Ó Cinnfhaolaidh (ceann,* head—*faol,* wolf). Though dispersed from their original homeland in the barony of Connelloe people of this name are still quite numerous in south Munster. IF Map Limerick.

Kinnear Woulfe gives *Mac an Fhir* (son of the man . . .) as the Irish form. The early anglicized forms of this, MacEnir, MacInnire, etc., occur frequently in the sixteenth-century records relating to Co. Wexford, but it is unlikely that families of Kinnear in Ireland today are of that origin, as this name is mainly found in Ulster, where it is Scottish (a Fifeshire toponymic).

Kinneavy See Kinnawe.

(Mac) Kinneen A form of Cunneen found in Connacht. See Rabbitt.

Kinnegan See Kinagan.

Kinnerk, Kinnerney See MacInerney.

(Mac) Kinney *Mac Coinnigh.* This name is numerous in Tyrone and Antrim where some families so called are descendants of Scottish immigrants, MacKinney being a branch of the clan MacKinnon; in some cases, too, Scottish MacKenzies have become MacKinney. There is also an indigenous Irish sept of the name whose homeland was on the border of Tyrone and Fermanagh. Finally it should be noted that MacKinney has sometimes been used as a variant of MacKenna. MIF

Kinniff See Cunniff.

Kinnirey See Keniry.

Kinnole A variant of Conole.

Kinoulty A Co. Down variant of MacNulty also found in Co. Clare.

Kinsella *Cinnsealach*. One of the few Gaelic-Irish surnames without the prefix O or Mac, being taken from the ancient clan name *Uí Ceinnsealaigh* which became a territorial designation covering much of the north of Co. Wexford. This sept is a branch of the MacMurroughs. IF   Map Carlow-Wexford.

Mac Kinstry, -Nestry *Mac an Aistrigh* (*aistreach*, traveller). Of Scottish origin this name is seldom found outside Ulster.

Mac Kinty A variant of MacEntee.

Kinucane See Finucane.

Kinure See Gaynor.

(O) Kirby *Ó Ciarmhaic* (*ciar*, black or dark brown—*mac*, son). This has for the most part now become *Ó Ciarba*, which gives the pronunciation Kirby in its homeland (as Map). The branch in Co. Kilkenny retains the old sound in its anglicized form, viz. Kerwick, while in Co. Waterford Kervick is found. Kirby in Mayo, however, is the modern form of Kerribly, *Mac Geirble*. Bibl. MIF   Map Limerick.

Mac Kirdy A variant of MacCurdy.

(O) Kirivane A variant of Kirwan.

Kirk(e) Kirk families of British stock are numerous in Ulster and Louth; but in Munster it sometimes occurs as a synonym of Quirke.

Kirkpatrick A Scottish toponymic found in Ulster. See Kilpatrick. Bibl; SIF 99.

Kirkwood App.

Kirley See Kerley.

(O) Kirlin See Kerlin.

(O) Kirrane See Kerrane.

(O) Kirwan *Ó Ciardhubháin* (*ciar dubh*, black). One of the 'Tribes of Galway', of which only Kirwan and one other (Darcy) are of Irish origin. Members of the family have been noteworthy on the Continent as well as at Galway. IF   Map Galway.

(O) Kissane This is essentially a Kerry name; it belongs equally to Co. Cork, but there it has been changed to Cashman. The usual form in Irish in *Ó Ciosáin* but there is reason to believe that it should be *Ó Cíosáin*, the basic word being *cíos*, tribute or rent. Woulfe's derivation from *cas*, curly, and equation with *O Casáin* (for which see Cussane) is not accepted. MIF

Mac Kissock, -Kissack This Ulster name of Scottish origin in distinct from Cusack. In Scotland MacIsaac is a variant.

Kitchen See MacCutcheon.

Kitson An anglicized form of *Ó Ceit* (Kett) corrupted to *Mac Ceit*, found in west Clare.

(Mac) Kitterick *Mac Shitric*. Derived from a well-known Norse per-

sonal name, MacKetterick, MacKetrick and the variant Munketrick
belong to the Oriel counties, where strangely Hanson is found as a
synonym. The cognate Scottish MacKettrick on the other hand is
associated in Ireland with Co. Sligo. MIF

(O) Kivelle See Keville.

Mac Kiverkin A south Down name recorded as used synonymously
with MacGurran.

(O) Kivlehan *Ó Cibhleacháin*. A co-arb family of Fore, Co. Westmeath.
In modern times the name is found mainly in Cos. Leitrim and Sligo.

Klisham See Clisham.

Knally See Nally.

Knapp An English name (derived from Old-English *cnaepp*, a hillock)
in Ireland since late seventeenth century, mainly in Co. Cork.

Knaresborough This English toponymic is the name of one of the
'Tribes of Kilkenny'.

Knavin See Navin.

(O) Kneafsey *Ó Cnáimhsighe*. (According to Woulfe *Cnáimhseach* is a
woman's name). Also anglicized Crampsy and, by pseudo-translation, Bonar (*cnámh*, means bone). These names belong almost exclusively to Co. Donegal. MIF

Knee See Nee.

Mac Kniff A variant of MacNiff.

(Mac) Knight If of Irish origin this is *Mac an Ridire* (*ridire*, knight); see
Ruderry. MacKnight, if Scottish, is *Mac Neachtain*. Knight is a
common English name. MIF

Knightly This English name, derived from a place in Staffordshire, has
become fairly numerous in Co. Kerry, where it was established in the
seventeenth century.

Knipe This well-known Co. Armagh name is there and in Co. Cavan
since the mid-seventeenth century. It is derived from a north of England dialect word meaning ridge.

Knockton See Naughten.

Knott A form of the name Canute, distinct from Nott. There are occasional mediaeval references to these names in Ireland. Knott is found
mainly in Dublin since the seventeenth century. MIF

Knowd See Nowd.

Knowell, Knowles See Newell.

Knowlan(d) A variant of Nolan listed in the 'census' of 1659 as a principal name in Cos. Westmeath and Longford; it is still extant.

Knox App.

Koen A variant of Coen.

Kohane See Keohane.

Mac Kone A Co. Louth form of the Ulster MacKeown or MacKeon.

(Mac) Kough, Keough Midland spellings for Keogh.

Mac Kowge Map Galway. See Cooke.

Mac Krann A variant of MacCran in Co. Leitrim.

Krisham A synonym of Klisham and Clisham in Co. Galway.

(Mac) Kurdy A variant spelling of Curdy.

Mac Kusker, -Usker Variants of MacCusker in Co. Tyrone.

(O) Kyan This is the Wicklow form of *Ó Catháin* not a synonym of Kyne. MIF

Kyle According to Black this is a Scottish toponymic. It is often also described as an anglicized form of the Scottish *Mac Suile*. The principal families of this name came from Ayrshire to Co. Derry at the time of the Plantation of Ulster. MIF

Kyley See Kiely.

(O) Kyne *Ó Cadhain* (*cadhan*, wild goose). This is a Connacht name, to be distinguished from Kyan. IF   See Barnacle and Coyne.

L

(O) Lacken *Ó Lacáin* or *Ó Laicín*. This is a west Connacht name for centuries on record there, but now rare. It is sometimes mistranslated Duck (*lacha*, duck).

Lackey A Westmeath form of Lecky.

(de) Lacy *de Léis*. Though the vast O'Melaghlin territory acquired by the Norman de Lascy in the twelfth century was lost, some descendants of the de Lacy lords of Meath remained there. The de Lacys of Co. Limerick, who flourished in Munster and later distinguished themselves in military service abroad, were probably of different origin: the name first appears in the thirteenth century as *del Essé*, which became *de Lees* and eventually Lacy. There is also a Gaelic name *Ó Laitheasa* in Co. Wexford anglicized Lacy. It was originally *Ó Flaithgheasa* (from *flaith*, prince). Bibl. IF   Map Limerick.

Lade, Laide (Old-English dweller by the forest). The name occurs in the Co. Tipperary hearth money rolls of 1664–65 and is now found in Co. Kildare; it may also be an abbreviated form of MacGlade.

Laden A variant of Leyden found in Leitrim.

(O) Ladrigan See Landrigan.

Laffan An Anglo-Norman family established in the fourteenth century in Cos. Tipperary and Wexford. The derivation from *l'enfaunt* (anglicized Fant) is improbable; *La Font* is preferable. MIF

Mac Lafferty A variant of MacLaverty.

(O) Lafferty See O'Laverty.

(O) Laffey See Lahiff.

Lagan Used in Antrim synonymously with Logan.

Lahart See Laherty.

(O) Laheen *Ó Laithín*. Woulfe suggests that this is an abbreviation of *Ó Laithimhín*, i.e. *Ó Fhlaithimhín*. See Flahavan.

(O) Laherty Woulfe may be right in treating this as a variant of O'Lafferty (see Laverty), but it must be noted that Laherty and Lahart are almost peculiar to Cos. Kilkenny and Tipperary.

(O) Lahiff, Lahive *Ó Laithimh*. The earlier form was *Ó Flaithimh* (*flaitheamh*, ruler) giving Flahy, which is still extant in the same area as Lahiff, viz. Co. Clare. Flahive is found in Kerry. Laffey is a variant in Co. Galway. MIF

Lahy Used as a synonym of Lahiff (Clare) and Leahy (Kilkenny).

Mac Lain An occasional variant of MacClean.

Laing See Lang.

Laird This is the Scottish form of Lord which is found in the northern counties of Ireland in considerable numbers, but is of comparatively recent introduction.

Lalee A variant of Lawlee.

Lally See Mullally.

(O) Lalor, Lawler *Ó Leathlobhair* (*leath*, half—*lobhar*, sick person). The name of two early kings of Ulidia, whose family is extinct. Another, also important, and still numerous throughout Leinster, was one of the 'Seven Septs of Leix'. IF   Map Leix.

Lambe See O'Loane.

Lambert A numerous name of dual English origin, long settled in south-east Leinster and from the seventeenth century in Cos. Galway and Mayo. Bibl. See Lamport.

Lamont This is the name of a leading Scottish clan, a branch of which settled in Ulster. Lammon is a variant.

Lamport An old form of Lambert in Co. Wexford. The epithet traditionally attached to the old Forth family was 'dogged'.

Landers *de Londras*. This essentially Munster name, sometimes called Landry and Londra, derives from the mediaeval *de Londres*, which is still extant as London, though rare. For Glanders, an occasional synonym of Landers, see Gillanders. MIF

(O) Landrigan, Ladrigan Variants of Lonergan.

Mac Landrish See Gillanders.

Landry See Landers.

Landy From the Norman *de la Launde* (*launde*, a glade); this name has been found in Cos. Kilkenny and Tipperary since the thirteenth century. It is written phonetically in Irish as *Leaindí*. MIF

Lane In addition to English families of Lane settled in Ireland, we find the name used as the anglicized form of several Gaelic-Irish surnames—see Lehane, Lyne, Lyons. The majority of people called Lane are from Cos. Cork and Limerick. Bibl; IF

Mac Lane A variant of MacLean.

188

Lang A branch of the Scottish clan Leslie fairly numerous in north-east Ulster. Woulfe states that it is also the anglicized form of Ó *Lainn*, but if this Irish name is extant, except as Lyng, it is very rare.

(O) Langan Ó *Longáin* (probably from the adjective *long*, tall, not *long*, ship). As Langan this name survives in Co. Mayo. MIF Map Armagh. See Long.

Langford This English toponymic mainly associated in Ireland with south-west Munster, came to Ulster in the sixteenth century and was later established in Cos. Limerick and Kerry.

Langrishe See p. 304.

Langton One of the 'Tribes of Kilkenny'. Bibl.

(O) Lanigan Ó *Lonagáin*. The derivation is uncertain: Woulfe mentions several alternative possibilities. The name belongs mainly to Co. Kilkenny and adjacent areas. MIF

(O) Lannon A form of Lennon found in Co. Kilkenny.

Laphin Used for both Lappin and Laffan.

(O) Lappin Ó *Lapáin*. (Woulfe's derivation from *lapa*, fist, is conjectural). A Donegal sept now mainly found in Tyrone and Armagh. It is sometimes changed to Delap, which is used as a synonym for the Scottish Dunlop in Cos. Derry and Fermanagh. Delap is also on record in Connemara and Mayo. MIF

(O) Laracy See Larrissey.

Lardner The English name Lardner, found in Co. Galway, is there used as the anglicized form of Ó *Lorgnáin*, which is to be distinguished from Ó *Loirgneáin*, see Lerhinan.

Mac Lardy This name, that of a branch of the Scottish clan Mac-Donald, is now fairly numerous in Ulster, particularly Belfast.

(O) Largan Ó *Lairgneáin*. A minor Oriel sept. See Lerhinan.

Large A Norman adjectival surname (Fr. *large*, generous) in Ireland since 1285 but rare and scattered now.

(O) Larkin Ó *Lorcáin* (probably from *Lorc*, and old name denoting rough or fierce). The name of four distinct septs as indicated in Map. It is now numerous and is mainly found in its original locations. IF   Map Galway, Monaghan, Tipperary and Wexford.

Larminie Of Huguenot origin this name is now rare, but was formerly fairly numerous in Co. Mayo, where it was established in the early eighteenth century. MIF

Larmour, Larmer, Armour Three variants of the same occupational name (the armourer) of French origin, numerous in Ulster. It first appears in Ireland in mid-seventeenth century as Armorer and also took the form Armar.

Larner An English name used for Lardner in Co. Galway.

(Mac) Larney See Mullarney.

Mac Larnon *Mac Giolla Earnáin* (devotee of St. Earnan). The name of a sept of Iveagh, Co. Down; also a Scottish name. Variants are Mac-Lernon, MacLornan and MacClarnon. MIF

(O) Larrissey *Ó Learghusa* (*lear*, sea—*gus*, vigour). This sept originated in the barony of Carra, Co. Mayo, but the name has long been mainly found in Co. Kilkenny and adjacent areas. MIF

Mac Lary, -Clary Variants of MacAlary and MacCleary.

Lasty See Losty.

Latchford A Palatine name well known in Co. Kerry.

Latimer A name derived from the Latin *Latinarius*, which came to Ireland, mainly from Scotland, in the seventeenth century and has since been fairly numerous in Cos. Monaghan and Cavan.

Latouche A Huguenot family associated with Dublin since the end of the seventeenth century. Bibl.

Lattin This English name has been associated with Co. Kildare since the fourteenth century. Bibl.

Lauder See Lawder.

(O) Laugheran See Loughran.

Mac Laughlin Bibl. See MacLoughlin.

(O) Laughnane See Loughnane.

Laundy See Landy.

Lavallin This name, a form of the Welsh Llewellyn, once prominent in Co. Cork, is now very rare. Bibl.

(O) Lavan See Lavin.

Mac Lave See MacClave.

Lavelle *Ó Maolfhábhail* (*fáball*, movement). This, formerly more correctly anglicized Mulfaal, is the name of a north Connacht sept found also in Donegal, where it is sometimes corrupted to Fall. It is also disguised as Melville. MIF

Mac Laverty *Mac Fhlaithbheartaigh*. An Ulster name probably akin to O'Laverty.

(O) Laverty, Lafferty *Ó Laithbheartaigh*. Though racially distinct, etymologically this is the same as O'Flaverty, the initial F in the case of the Ulster sept being aspirated. The Four Masters describe the chief as 'the Tanist of Tyrone'. IF   MIF   Map Donegal and Tyrone.

(O) Lavery, Lowry *Ó Labhradha* (*labhraidh*, spokesman). This Ulster sept has three branches: Baun-Lavery, Roe-Lavery and Trin-Lavery (*bán*, white—*rua*, red—*tréan*, strong), the last being mistranslated Armstrong. IF   Map Antrim–Down.

Lavey This Westmeath name is presumably a local form of the Co. Longford Leavy.

Mac Lavin See Mullavin.

(O) Lavin *Ó Laimhín* or *Ó Lamháin*. Probably a modern contraction of *Ó Flaithimhín* (*flaitheamh*, ruler). A sept located in the Mac-

Dermot country. Their name has sometimes been changed to Hand by pseudo-translation. MIF   Map Roscommon. For MacLavin see Mullavin.

Lawder, Lauder An adjectival surname from *láidir* (strong), mainly found in Leinster but scattered. Bibl.

Law(e) An English name mainly found in north-east Ulster. Bibl.

Lawell A synonym of Lavelle.

Lawlee A Westmeath form of the English toponymic Lawley, which is found in Ulster and occasionally in Co. Cork.

Lawler, Lawlor See Lalor.

Lawless *Laighléis* (from the Old-English *laghles*, outlaw). This name, introduced into Ireland after the Anglo-Norman invasion, is now numerous in Cos. Dublin and Galway. It was one of the 'Tribes of Kilkenny' but has now no close association with that city. IF MIF   Bibl.

(O) Lawn *Ó Liatháin*. The Irish form of this name is the same as Lehane of Co. Cork. In Donegal it is the name of a sept of the northern Uí Fiachrach originating in Co. Sligo.

Lawrence, Laurence This English name is fairly numerous in Ireland since mid-seventeenth century, but is not closely identified with any particular locality. See St. Lawrence.

Lawson This English name is found in most Ulster counties since early seventeenth century.

Lawton A well-known English name used in Co. Cork as an anglicized form of *Ó Lachtnáin*. See Loughnane.

Mac Lea See MacAlee.

Leacy A variant spelling of Lacy.

Leader This surname was established in Co. Cork in mid-seventeenth century; by mid-nineteenth it had become very numerous, though it is now much less so.

(O) Leahy *Ó Laochdha* (*laochdha*, heroic). This name is very numerous in Munster but not elsewhere. It is basically distinct from Lahy though they have often been used synonymously. MIF   Map Cork, Kerry and Tipperary.

Leaky See Lecky.

(O) Leamy *Ó Laomdha* (perhaps *laomdha*, bent) and later *Ó Léime*. A sept of Upper Ormond, always closely associated with north Tipperary. MIF

Mac Lean See MacClean.

(O) Leane See Lyne. Map Kerry.

(O) Leany *Ó Laighnigh* (i.e. descendant of the Leinsterman). A rare Munster name.

Mac Lear A variant of MacAleer.

Mac Leary A variant of MacCleary.

(O) Leary *Ó Laoghaire.* (*Laoghaire* was one of the best-known personal names in ancient Ireland). A sept of the Corca Laoidhe established in Muskerry, of importance in all fields of national activity, especially in literature, and in the military sphere both at home and as Wild Geese. IF   Map Cork.

Leathem A Co. Armagh form of Latham.

(Mac) Leavy, Levy *Mac Con Shléibhe* (*cú,* hound—*sliabh,* mountain). This is the name of an old Co. Longford sept akin to the O'Farrells. It is only occasionally used as an abbreviation of Dunlevy. The prefix Mac is now very rarely retained. MIF   Map (as Conlevy) Longford.

Lecky A branch of the Scottish clan MacGregor, settled in Cos. Donegal and Derry in mid-seventeenth century; later also in Co. Carlow. Lackey and Leaky are variants.

(O) Leddan A Munster variant of Liddane.

Leddy See Liddy.

Ledger This is usually treated as synonymous with St. Leger, but in Co. Limerick it is a distinct Palatine name. There Ledger derives from the Old-German *leodegar,* people-spear. Legear is a variant spelling.

Ledlie Bibl.

Ledwich This family came to East Meath in 1200 and settled in Westmeath. The Dublin-born opera singer William Ledwidge changed his name to Ludwig, the reputed German original of the surname. There is no doubt, however, that Ledwich is found as an English toponymic. IF

Lee Lee is a very common name in England, and is numerous and widespread in Ireland where, however, it usually represents either of the two following: *Mac Laoidhigh* (which Woulfe derives from *laoidheach,* poetic) of Leix, or *Mac an Leagha* (son of the physician). See next three entries.

(Mac) Lee Of north Connacht. See previous entry, also MacAlee and MacKinley.

(O) Lee This is also the name of two distinct septs, viz. *Ó Laoidhigh* (often *Ó Laidhigh* in Connacht), the more important being a family of hereditary physicians to the O'Flahertys; the other is located in Cos. Cork and Limerick. IF   Bibl; Map Galway. See Leech.

Leech This name, derived from Middle-English *leche,* physician, is confused in Co. Galway with Lee, where it may also be *Ó Laoghóg* (see Logue). Bibl. MIF

(O) Leehan See Lehane.

(O) Leen, Leyne Kerry variants of Lyne.

Leeper This English name (meaning runner or jumper, not from leper as sometimes stated) is well established in Co. Donegal since mid-seventeenth century.

Mac Lees A variant of MacAleese.

Leeson The main families of this name came to Ireland in the seventeenth century. It may possibly also have been used for the rare O'Lishane which Woulfe says is a corrupt form of *Ó Gliasáin*. See Gleeson. MIF

Leevy A variant spelling of Leavy.

Lefanu One of the best-known of Huguenot names in Ireland. Bibl.

Lefroy A Huguenot name not found in Ireland before the eighteenth century. Bibl.

Legge Authorities on surnames differ as to the derivation of this English name which is found in Ulster. O'Donovan states that it was used as the anglicized form of *Mac Coise* (*cos*, foot or leg), as also was another English name, Foote (see Quish).

(O) Lehane, Leehan *Ó Liatháin* (probably from *liath*, grey). Lehane is now almost peculiar to Co. Cork, though it originated in Co. Limerick; another anglicized form of *Ó Liatháin*—Lyons—is more widespread. IF   Map Cork. See Lawn.

Mac Leheron See MacElheron.

Leigh An English name occasionally used as a synonym of Lee.

Leitch The Scots form of Leech. Very numerous in Ulster.

Leix The Seven Septs of Leix: O'Devoy, O'Doran, O'Dowling, MacEvoy, O'Kelly, O'Lalor, O'More.

Mac Lellan, -Clelland, -Leland Most families of these names in Ireland are of Scottish origin. The old Uí Fiachrach sept of *Mac Giolla Fhaoláin* in Co. Sligo appears to be almost, if not quite, extinct though possibly it survives as Gilfillan in Leitrim. MIF

(O) Lemasney See Lomasney.

Lemass From the French *le Maistre*. In Carlow and Dublin since the mid-eighteenth century. SIF

Lemon A numerous name in Ulster where it may be of English origin or an abbreviated form of MacLamond. See MacClement.

Lendrum A Scottish (Aberdeenshire) toponymic associated with Cos. Tyrone and Fermanagh since mid-seventeenth century.

Mac Lenaghan See MacClenaghan.

(O) Lenigan A variant of Lanigan; seldom of Lenihan.

(O) Lenihan, Lenaghan, Linehan *Ó Leannacháin*. A Co. Roscommon sept; another of Munster, which according to Woulfe is *Ó Luingeachán*, is now very numerous in Cos. Limerick and Cork. IF

(O) Len(n)ane See Linnane.

Mac Lennon, -Lennan Usually Scottish; it is certainly also a variant of MacLenaghan, and according to Woulfe also of MacAlinion and

MacAlonan. In Co. Galway he makes it *Mac Loineáin*, but as they were MacAlenan in the seventeenth century *Mac Ailgheanáin* is a preferable alternative.

(O) Lennon, Lennan *Ó Leannáin* (possibly from *leann*, a cloak or mantle; *leanán*, paramour, has also been suggested). This is the name of several distinct septs located respectively in Cos. Cork, Fermanagh and Galway. The last named is of the Sodhan pre-Gaelic stock. The Fermanagh family were erenaghs of Lisgoole. *Ó Leannáin* is also used as a synonym of Linneen (*Ó Luinín*), another Fermanagh erenagh family. Further confusion arises from the fact that these have been widely changed to the English name Leonard. IF   See also Linnegar.

Lenox Bibl.

Leo This old Anglo-Irish name is peculiar to Co. Limerick. Reaney says it derives from Latin *leo*, lion, while Woulfe makes it a locative —*lea*, meadow. Nicholls, however, has given me definite evidence that in Co. Limerick it is from *de l'eau*. Latin *de aqua*.

Leonard This well-known English name is used as an anglicized form of many Irish surnames, viz., Lennon, Linnane, Linneen, Lunny, Gilsenan, MacAlinion and Nannany. IF

(O) Lerhinan, Lernihan *Ó Loirgneáin*. A Co. Clare name to be distinguished from *Ó Lorgnáin* (Lardner) and *Ó Lairgneáin* (Largan). SIF 103.

Mac Lerney See under Mullarney.

Mac Lernon See MacLarnon.

Mac Leroy A south Down variant of Gilroy.

Leslie A Scottish toponymic established in Ireland early in the seventeenth century, prominent in Co. Monaghan. Bibl. See Losty.

(Mac) Lester In Ireland this is a variant of MacAlister. See Lister.

Lestrange This is the only form now in use of the Westmeath name *Mac Conchoigcriche* (border hound), formerly anglicized Mac-Enkegry. The adoption of the modern anglicized form may have been due to the existence in Westmeath of an English family called Lestrange who settled there in the sixteenth century. Map Offaly and Westmeath.

Lett Reaney derives this from the Latin *laetitia*, joy. The well-known Lett family of Co. Wexford is Cromwellian. Several centuries earlier de Leyt and Leth occur in Carlow and Dublin records, but these are of different origin. MIF

Levallin A form of the Welsh Llewellyn. See Lavallin.

Levens Woulfe gives *Mac Dhuinnshléibhín* (a variant of Dunlevy) for this Co. Louth name, which has been changed to Levinge and even Livingstone in some cases. As Living it is listed in the 'census' of

1659 as one of the principal Irish names in the barony of Ferrard, Co. Louth.

Levinge, Levin(e), Levingstone Bibl. See Levens and p. 304.

Levis This west Cork name is rarely a corrupt form of Mac Conlevy as suggested by W. F. Butler. It is usually of Huguenot origin.

Levitt See Lyvet.

Levy See Leavy.

Lewis This is of three origins: Scottish, English and Welsh. It is widely distributed in Ireland.

Ley One of the 'Tribes of Kilkenny'.

(O) Leyden See Lydon.

Leyhane A frequent variant of Lehane in Co. Cork.

Leynagh See Lynagh.

Leyne See Leen.

Mac Liammoir See Wilmore.

Mac Lice, -Lise An occasional variant of MacAleese.

(O) Liddane See Lydon.

(O) Liddy *Ó Lideadha*. A Dalcassian sept, formerly of considerable importance in Thomond. Found also in Co. Cavan as Leddy. MIF Map Clare.

Liffe See Elliffe.

Liffey An Offaly name: probably a variant of Liffe.

Lightfoot This English name is in Ireland since mediaeval times. As Lighterfoot it came to Ulster at the beginning of the seventeenth century.

Lillis A variant in Cos. Clare and Limerick of Lawless.

(Mac) Lilly *Mac Ailghile*. The name of a branch of the MacGuires of Fermanagh. It was formerly anglicized MacAlilly. The English name Lilly, alias Lely, is rarely found in Ireland. MIF

Limerick A toponymic taken not from the Irish city but from a French place. This rare surname is found in Co. Derry. MIF

Linagh See Lynagh.

(O) Linchy See Lynch and Lindsay. Map Antrim and Cavan.

(Mac) Linden See MacAlinden.

Lindsay The majority of Lindsays in Ireland descend from the great Scottish clan of that name; but in Ulster *Ó Loingsigh*, elsewhere anglicized as Lynch, has often been made Linchey and this in turn became Lindsay. To add to the difficulty in determining the origin of an Ulster Lindsay some families of MacClintock adopted that surname. Bibl. MIF

(O) Linehan See Lenihan.

Ling See Lyng.

(O) Linnane *Ó Linneáin* and *Ó Lionnáin*. A west Munster name much confused with Lennon. IF

(O) Linneen See Lennon.

(O) Linnegar A variant form of Linneen. Map Fermanagh.

Linnett See Lynott.

Linskey See Lynskey.

Linton An English toponymic used sometimes as an abbreviation of MacClinton. See Glendon.

Lipsett An anglicized form of the German *Lipsitz*. I have not ascertained when it came to Ireland but it is certainly quite numerous in Co. Donegal at least since the early eighteenth century.

Mac Lise See MacAleese.

Lisle See Lyle.

Lister This name in Ireland has four distinct origins: (1) an abbreviation of MacAlister; (2) in Ulster the Scottish *Mac an Leastair*, alias Fletcher; (3) an occasional synonym of St. Leger in Co. Kilkenny; (4) English, Lester (dyer) or de Leycester.

Liston An Anglo-Norman family in Co. Limerick since the thirteenth century. The name was originally *de Lexinton*.

Little This English name is used as a synonym by translation of Begg, Biggane, Beggane and Petty or Pettit.

Littleton This is synonymous with Little in Co. Down and so with Beggane.

Litton This English toponymic occurs in Co. Meath in 1420. It has been identified with the commercial life of Dublin continuously since 1692.

Livett See Lyvet.

Livingstone Numerous in Ulster. See Levens.

Lloyd Bibl. See Floyd.

(O) Loan(e) *Ó Luain* (*luan*, hound, hence warrior). The principal sept of this name is that of Oriel. The form Lamb(e), which results from a more than usually absurd pesudo-translation (*uan*, lamb), is now much more numerous than O'Loan: but some Lambes are of English descent. MIF   Map Monaghan.

Loch See Lough.

(O) Lochrane See Loughrane.

Locke This English name of dual derivation (locative, or of nickname type from lock of hair) is in Ireland since the sixteenth century, when it is on record as that of tenants and yeomen; but, though now fairly numerous, it has never been particularly identified with any specific area. In at least one well-known case (Joseph Locke, the singer) it has been used instead of O'Loughlin.

Lockhart App.

Loftus This English name, in Ireland as such since the sixteenth century, is very numerous in Connacht, where it is not English but almost always a synonym of Loughnane. Bibl; Map Mayo.

Logan This name is of several origins in Ireland: viz. Norman de Logan; Scottish Logan (syn. Lagan); and Gaelic-Irish *Ó Leogháin* as a variant of Lohan. MIF

(O) Loghlen See O'Loughlin.

(O) Logue, Loogue Logue is now almost exclusively a Donegal–Derry name and there it is *Ó Maolmhaodhóg* (formerly anglicized phonetically Mulvogue); it can also be *Ó Laoghóg,* which is strangely anglicized Leech in west Leinster, Connacht and Clare. MIF See Molloy and p. 304.

(O) Lohan, Loghan, Loughan *Ó Leocháin.* Originally of Westmeath this sept became established in Co. Galway. Duck is a synonym by mistranslation. MIF   See Chaff and Lacken.

(O) Lomasney *Ó Lomasna (lom,* bare—*asna,* rib). The variant form Lemasney has led to the erroneous belief that this Irish name is of French origin. Map Tipperary.

Lombard The first Irish Lombard came from Lombardy, in the thirteenth century. The word lombard subsequently came to mean banker. Lombardstown in Co. Cork is named from this family. MIF   Map Cork.

London, Londra See Landers.

(O) Lone See Loan.

(O) Lonergan, Londrigan *Ó Longargáin.* A family notable in the ecclesiastical sphere. It has many variants. IF   Map Tipperary.

(O) Loney A variant of Lunney but not of Looney.

Long Numerous in Munster and in Donegal, this may be *de Long* (Norman); Long (English); or *Ó Longáin* alias Longan. In Co. Cork, where the name is most numerous, they are an erenagh family of Garrane I Long in the parish of Moviddy and of Canavoy, called *Ó Longaigh* in Irish. Bibl. MIF

(O) Longan *Longáin.* A Co. Limerick co-arb family, notable as scribes, much confused with *Ó Longaigh.* (The basic word is believed to be *long,* tall, not *long,* ship). MIF   See previous entry.

Longfield One of the leading Anglo-Irish families in Co. Cork since mid-seventeenth century. Bibl.

(O) Looby See Luby.

(O) Loonan(e) *Ó Luanáin (luan,* hound, warrior; the primary meaning was light). This name is, or was, numerous in Co. Longford. Woulfe gives its location as Co. Donegal, but it is not found there unless Lambe of Inishowen is Loonan in disguise, which is doubtful.

Mac Loone A variant of MacGlone. Formerly peculiar to Glenties, Co. Donegal. The Fermanagh genealogies have *Mac Collúin.* MacAloon is well known there.

(O) Looney *Ó Luanaigh* (for derivation see Loonan). A Munster name mainly found in Co. Clare, quite distinct from Lunney and Lowney. MIF

(O) Looran, Loran Westmeath and Meath variants of Loughran.

Lord An English name (usually of the nickname type) in Dublin and Westmeath in mid-seventeenth century, subsequently mainly in Dublin. It is an occasional synonym of Kiernan and Tierney (*tighearna*, lord).

(O) Lordan *Ó Lórdáin.* A name belonging almost exclusively to Co. Cork: it is numerous in the western part of the county.

Lorimer App.

Mac Lorinan See MacLarnon.

(O) Lorkan, Lorkin Rare variants of Larkin. Bibl.

(O) Lorrigan A variant of Lonergan.

Mac Loskey A variant of MacCluskey.

(O) Losty *Ó Loiste.* This name has long been associated with Donegal. Variants are Lasty and Lusty, and also Lastly, which accounts for the fact that Leslie has been used as a synonym. MIF

Lough A variant of the Scottish toponymic Loch, in Ulster since the early seventeenth century.

(O) Loughan See Lohan.

Lougheed This is a variant of the Scottish Lochhead, which, according to G. F. Black, denotes head of the loch and he says is akin to Kinloch (in Gaelic *ceann an locha*).

Mac Loughlin *Mac Lochlainn* (from a Norse personal name). Of Inishowen; a senior branch of the northern Uí Néill. They lost their early importance as a leading sept of Tirconnell in the thirteenth century, but are still very numerous in their original homeland—Cos. Donegal and Derry—where usually their name is spelt MacLaughlin; MacLoughlin, also numerous, is more widespread. Minor septs in Connacht were akin to the MacDermots and the O'Connors. IF   Map Donegal. See also O'Melaghlin.

(O) Loughlin *Ó Lochlainn.* An important Dalcassian sept located in the northern part of Thomond. IF   Map Clare. See also Loughnane.

Loughman While I have not got quite conclusive evidence I have little doubt that this name is a corruption of Loughnan, which was the anglicized form of *Ó Lachtnáin* in Kilkenny and adjacent counties in the sixteenth century, as we know from the Ormond Deeds. The sixteenth-century Fiants actually have O Loughman in more than one case. Later the 1659 'census' lists Loughman as a principal Irish name in Co. Kilkenny and Queen's County (Leix). The name has been prevalent in those counties up to comparatively recent times.

(O) Loughnane *Ó Lachtnáin* (*lachtna,* grey). The name of several small Connacht septs; in Meath, where it may be classed as of Oriel, it has been often changed to O'Loughlin, thus hiding the identity of an old family there. Similarly it is disguised as Lawton in Co. Cork. IF   Map Mayo and Meath.

Mac Loughney See Maloughney.

(O) Loughney *Ó Lachtna*. A Mayo name now nearly always made Loughnane.

(O) Loughran *Ó Luchráin* (probably from *luchair*, bright). An Armagh family with a branch in Tyrone notable for many distinguished ecclesiastics. The name is still numerous there. Lutheran as well as Lochran are recorded as synonyms of it. MIF   Map Armagh. See Early.

(O) Loughrey *Ó Luachra*. Mainly found in Ulster. For confusion with Loughran and Early see MIF   See also Rush (*Ó Luachra*) and Deloughery.

Louth, Lowthe This was probably an Irish toponymic when found in Ireland in the mediaeval period; in later times it is usually an English one from the parish in Lincolnshire. The fact that the name is found in Co. Louth is coincidental. It has been in Leinster since the fourteenth century.

Louther, Luther Variants of Lowther found in the midlands, and Co. Waterford. Seldom for the German Luther.

Love Woulfe gives *Mac Ionmhain* for this and does not mention that Love is a well-known English name which came to Ireland in the seventeenth century. *Mac Ionmhain* is a modern attempt at translation into Irish. Love is a numerous name in Co. Derry. *Mac Graith* is said to have been sometimes so anglicized in Ulster, MacGrath being pronounced MacGraw in parts of that province. (*Grádh* is the Irish for love).

Lovell Woulfe's derivation of this name as a diminutive of love is wrong; it is from Anglo-French *lovel* (*lupellus*), wolf cub. It is on record at Clonmel as early as 1310 and has been closely associated with Kilkenny and neighbouring counties since the sixteenth century.

Lovett A Co. Kerry name cognate with Lyvet, of French derivation, meaning wolf cub. The Scottish Lovat (*Mac Lomhaid*) may be an alternative origin.

(O) Lowan A variant of Loane.

Lowe This well-known English name, quite numerous in Dublin and Ulster, is according to Woulfe also used as the anglicized form of the rare Irish *Mac Lughadha*. See MacLoy.

Lowney This exclusively west Cork name is traditionally believed to be *na Leamhna* (i.e. of the river Laune) a branch of the O'Sullivans.

Lowry See Lavery. According to Fr. Travers, Lowry in Ulster is often of Scottish origin.

Lowther This is a north of England toponymic. After the Plantation of Ulster it was established in Co. Fermanagh and gave its name to Lowtherstown, which later became Irvinestown. Bibl.

(Mac) Loy *Mac Lughaidh*. An Oriel name usually now without the prefix Mac. See MacCloy, with which it may be confused.

(O) Luby *Ó Lúbaigh (lúbach,* cunning). It was formerly spelt Looby, a form still found to some extent in the midlands. MIF   Map Tipperary.

Lucas An older form of Luke now numerous in all provinces except Connacht, this name is on record in Ireland as early as the fourteenth century; by the seventeenth it was well established in Co. Waterford before the Cromwellian upheaval, as a result of which further families of the name settled in various parts of the country. It is sometimes found as an abbreviated form of the Scottish Mac-Lucas.

(O) Lucey *Ó Luasaigh*. Woulfe says it was formerly *MacCluasaigh*. A Co. Cork name. The Norman de Lucy is probably now extinct. The Lucy family in Fermanagh are from Oxfordshire, England. MIF

Lucid This name, which is almost exclusively of Co. Kerry, is said to be a variant of Lucey. I have not found evidence of this. Woulfe's statement that it is Anglo-Norman and a derivative of Lucas, gaelicized *Lúiséid,* is more acceptable.

(O) Ludden An occasional variant of Lydon in use in Co. Galway and Mayo.

(O) Luddy *Ó Loidigh*. The north Cork form of Liddy. MIF

Ludlow This English (Shropshire) toponymic (originally de Lodelowe) occurs in Irish records as early as the fourteenth century, but was not permanently settled in Ireland till the seventeenth. Apart from Dublin it was mainly associated with Cos. Louth and Meath up to modern times but has now become scattered, being found also in Ulster and in Co. Cork.

Luke This is rarer and of later introduction than Lucas. It has been used as a synonym of the Scottish MacLucas. **Luff** See p. 304.

Lumley Though in most cases this is simply de Lumley (from an English place-name) the fact that *Ó Lomthaile* is on record in mediaeval Co. Cork is worthy of mention.

Lundergan See Londrigan.

Lundon A variant of London.

Lundy This now ranks as an Ulster name. Though historically associated with Derry through the association of the Englishman Robert Lundy with its famous siege, Lundy (Norman *de la Lounde*) occurs quite frequently in mediaeval records relating to Cos. Tipperary and Kilkenny. MIF

Lunn An English name found in east Ulster.

(O) Lunneen A variant of Linneen.

(O) Lunney *Ó Luinigh.* Though the territory Munterlooney is named from this family they are not called Looney but Lunney. MIF Map Tyrone.

Mac Lure See MacClure.

Mac Lurg See MacClurg.

(O) Lurigan A variant of Lonergan in west Clare.

Lush See next entry.

Lusk Lusk is an Irish mediaeval toponymic from the village of Lusk, Co. Dublin, now mainly found in north-east Ulster; it is quite distinct from Lush which is akin in derivation to Usher.

Lusty See Losty.

Luther See Lowther.

Lutheran See Loughran.

Luttrell Old-French *le lutrel* (the otter). One of the chief families of the Pale since the thirteenth century. Bibl; Map Dublin.

(O) Lydon Lydon, which belongs almost exclusively to Cos. Galway and Mayo, is the most numerous anglicized form of *Ó Loideáin.* Other forms of the name are Leyden in Connacht and Clare and Liddane mainly in Co. Clare. MIF

(O) Lyhane A variant of Lehane numerous in Kerry and west Cork.

Lyle Woulfe treats this name as Irish *Ó Laoighill.* If this is so it is very rare as such. Normally it is a variant of Lisle, a locative name (French *de l'isle*). It came to Ireland from south-west Scotland early in the seventeenth century and has become fairly numerous in Ulster, especially in Cos. Derry and Antrim. Lisle also occurs among the Huguenot immigrants settled in Belfast in the eighteenth century.

Lynagh, Leynagh *Laighneach* (the Leinsterman). Formerly peculiar to Cos. Galway and Mayo this name is now scattered. It is sometimes used as a synonym of Lynam and vice versa. Nicholls states that the Lynaghs of Meath and Kildare are a branch of the Berminghams. MIF

(O) Lynan, Lynam *Ó Laigheanáin.* Originating in east Leinster where one branch were erenaghs of Ferns, another in Co. Carlow, families of this name were later established in north Leinster. The variant spelling Lynham arises usually from an attempt to make this Irish surname appear English—Lyneham is an English toponymic found in Co. Meath in the fourteenth century. MIF

Lynch This is of dual origin. The Norman *de Lench* is the more numerous and important, being predominant among the 'Tribes of Galway'. The Gaelic *Ó Loingsigh* (*loingseach,* mariner) giving Lynch and Linchy, is the name of several small but distinct septs, see Map. Bibl; IF 213; Map Antrim–Down, Cavan, Clare, Cork and Tipperary. See also next entry.

(O) Lynchehan *Ó Loingseacháin*. The Mac prefix is also used. This name is now almost always contracted to Lynch. Map Donegal and Tyrone.

Mac Lynchy A variant of MacGlinchey in Donegal.

Lyndon See under Glendon.

(O) Lyne *Ó Laighin*. In the form Lyne this name is nearly always that of a family of Co. Kerry where Lyons is often substituted for it. It is spelt O'Leane in the Map (Kerry) Leane being a variant of Lyne in that county. O'Donovan was of the opinion that the Kerry sept is *Ó Laoghain* in Irish. The Co. Cork medical family of the name may be distinct. See Lyons. IF

Lyness A north of England name numerous in Co. Armagh in the seventeenth century and now mainly in Antrim and Down. It is sometimes used as a synonym of MacAleenan.

Lyng, Ling Apart from a few O'Lynns of Ulster who become Lyng, this name belongs to Cos. Kilkenny and Wexford. It is an English toponymic which appears among the Cromwellian 'adventurers' who acquired lands in Co. Tipperary. Whether the Kilkenny Lyngs are descended from that family or, more probably, are *Ó Floinn*, formerly called Fling in Co. Waterford, has yet to be finally determined.

Lynham See Lynam.

Lynigar See Linnegar.

(O) Lynn *Ó Fhloinn*, now usually made *Ó Loinn*. This is the northern form of *Ó Floinn* (Flynn) and is the name of a sept located near Lough Neagh. IF Map Antrim.

Lynott *Lionóid*. One of the powerful Cambro-Norman families established in Mayo in the thirteenth century. MIF

(O) Lynskey *Ó Loinscigh*. A form of *Ó Loingsigh* (Lynch) peculiar to Mayo and Galway.

Lyons Though this is an English name, few people so called in Ireland are of English stock. It is used as the anglicized form of *Ó Laighin* (elsewhere usually Lyne) in Co. Galway and of *Ó Liatháin* (see Lehane) in Co. Cork. The Scottish Lyon is distinct but often confused with Lyons. Bibl. IF Map see O'Leane, O'Lehane and O'Lyne.

(Mac) Lysaght *Mac Giolla Iasachta*. An offshoot of the O'Briens of Thomond. Woulfe gives the meaning of *giolla iasachta* as strange youth, but *iasachta* always conveys the idea of 'loaned' so the family tradition that the first of the name was a fourteenth-century O'Brien transferred for some purpose to another north Clare sept is probably not without foundation. The name is fairly numerous in Clare and Limerick but very rare elsewhere apart from Dublin. The variant spelling Lysaught is found in America. Bibl. IF MIF Map Clare.

Lyster Bibl. See Lister.

Lyvet An Anglo-Norman name in Ireland since the thirteenth century, mainly in Leinster, not Mayo; now very rare.

M

Mack Originally only a temporary abbreviation of a Mac name, in some cases it has become a surname, e.g. for MacEnroe in Tyrone. In Co. Clare Mack represents MacNamara in speech but the full name is normally retained for formal and legal purposes.

Mackeen This form is used sometimes for MacKeane in Co. Clare.

(O) Macken *Ó Maicín, Ó Macáin* (from *mac* son, hence youth). The Corca Laoidhe sept of this name is nearly extinct, but that of Co. Mayo is still fairly numerous. MIF   See next entry.

(Mac) Macken, Mackin *Mac Maicín* (for derivation see previous entry). The name of this Oriel sept is spelt Mackin in Co. Monaghan where it is mainly found, though Macken is used in Louth. MIF Map Monaghan.

(O) Mackesy *Ó Macasa.* (According to Woulfe this is indirectly derived from *Maghnus* Manus). It is sometimes quite erroneously made MacKessy and MacKissy as if a Mac name. Map Limerick.

(O) Mackey *Ó Macdha.* An Ormond sept: Ballymackey near Nenagh, indicates their location. This name is sometimes used erroneously for MacKee and MacKay. MIF   Map Tipperary.

(O) Mackle ?*Ó Machail.* Formerly anglicized O'Mackell; so it appears in the hearth money rolls for Co. Armagh (1664). It is since mainly found on the west side of Lough Neagh. Though properly an O name Mackle has sometimes become MacKell and is occasionally a synonym of MacGill in Co. Down. It is not to be confused with MacCahill which is now usually made MacCall and MacCawill.

Macklehatton See MacIlhatton.

Macklemoyle See MacIlmoyle.

Mackworth See under Worth.

(O) Madden *Ó Madáin*—earlier form *Ó Madadháin* (see Introduction p. ix for derivation). One of the principal septs of the Uí Maine. The Maddens retained their lordship of their territory in east Galway even under the Norman de Burgo supremacy. They are still numerous there. A branch settled in Co. Kildare where an English family of the same name also settled.* Bibl. IF   MIF   Map Galway.

Maddock, Maddox A Welsh name now indistinguishable from the Irish *Mac Mhadoc,* a branch of the MacMurroughs in Co. Wexford,

---

*The Madden Brassil mentioned in MIF   was in fact Brassil O'Madden, Brassil being a very common Christian name among the O'Maddens of east Galway. (I have to thank Mr. P. J. Kennedy for this correction.)

formerly MacVaddock, as well as Maddock or Maddox. The droll synonym Mayduck occurs in Co. Down. MIF

(O) Madeen A variant of Madden in Cos. Galway and Mayo.

(O) Madigan *Ó Madagáin.* A branch of the O'Maddens, settled in Clare and Limerick, where they are numerous. IF

Madill, Madell Now mainly Co. Monaghan, formerly Co. Cavan. Possibly a variant of Madole; but more probably from the Old-French *madle,* variant of *masle,* male.

Madole, Medole Forms of MacDowell in use in Oriel and Antrim, now rare.

Maffett See Moffat.

Magaghan See MacGahan.†

Magan See MacGann.

Magarry See MacGarry.

Magauran See MacGovern.

Magaw See Megaw.

Magawley See MacAuley.

Magee See MacGee.

Mageean See MacGeehan.

Magennis See MacGuinness.

Mageown This Oriel name is cognate with MacKeown but regarded as distinct. Mageown is also used as a synonym of MacGowan. MIF

Mac Magh, Mac Maugh See MacMath.

(O) Ma(g)han, Maughan *Ó Macháin.* Variants of Mohan of Kilmacduagh, Co. Galway. Frequently changed to Mahon.

Maghery *An Mhachaire* (of the field). This is one of the few cognomina taken from place of residence which finally became hereditary surnames. It is on record in Co. Limerick at least as early as 1309. It takes the form Field in Co. Armagh.

Magill See MacGill.

Magilligan See MacGilligan.

Magilloway See MacGilloway.

Magilly See MacQuilly.

Maginn See MacGinn.

Maginnity See MacGinty.

Maginver See Gaynor.

Maglamery A variant of Montgomery in Co. Down.

Maglin(n) See MacGlynn.

Magner *Maingnéir.* This name appears in Co. Cork as Magnel in the thirteenth century and has been continuously associated with that county since. Castlemagner was formerly Magnelstown. MIF

†A number of other names beginning with Mag will be found under G as MacG names.

Magonagle See MacGonagle.

Magone See MacKeown.

Magournahan See Gordon.

Magourtey See MacGourkey.

Magowan See MacGowan.

Magrane See MacGrane.

Magrannill See MacRannell.

Magrath See MacGrath.   **Magree** See MacGrae.

Magreece A variant of MacCreesh.

Magreevy See MacGreevy.

Magrudden See Groden.

Maguigan See MacGuigan.

Maguire See MacGuire.

Magunshenan A form of MacGilshenan, formerly common in Co. Tyrone. Woulfe says it has been corrupted to *Maguinnsionnáin* in Irish.

(O) Mahada, Mahady *Ó Moithide*. A rare name found in Cos. Longford, Roscommon and Westmeath.

Mahaffy A Scottish Gaelic name—*Mac Dhuibhshíthe* (from *síoth*, peace, making black-haired man of peace)—also anglicized MacAfee, MacHaffy and MacFie. In Ireland these names mainly belong to Co. Donegal. SIF 108.

Maharg See MacIhagga.

Maharry A variant of MacCarry used in Ulster.

Maher Now the more usual spelling of Meagher.

Mahew See Mayo.

Mahon Much used for Mohan, and for Mahan, occasionally for MacMahon. Bibl. See Maghan and Mohan.

Mac Mahon *Mac Mathghamhna*, mod. *Mac Mathúna* (*mathghamhan*, bear). The name of two septs, both of importance. That of Thomond descends from Mahon O'Brien, grandson of Brian Ború. MacMahon is now the most numerous name in Co. Clare. In later times the majority of the many distinguished men of the name were from the Co. Monaghan, where MacMahons are numerous today, though less so than in Thomond. Bibl. IF   Map Clare and Monaghan. See Matthews. See p. 304.

(O) Mahony *Ó Mathghamhana* (for derivation and modern form see MacMahon). A well-known sept of west Munster where people of the name are still mainly found. Bibl. IF   Map Cork.

Mahood See Hood.

(O) Mainey, Meany See Mooney.

Mainwaring See Mannering.

Mairs See Meares.

Major Though occasionally on record in Ireland in the Middle Ages, this English name was not established in Ireland until the seventeenth century; it is now found in most of the Ulster counties. MIF

(O) Malady See Melody.

Malaniffe See Mullanphy.

Malbury, Malborough See under Mulberry.

Malcolm An Irish (Ulster) name as *Ó Maolcholuim* (St. Columcille); also that of a Scottish clan.

Malcolmson App.

Malet In modern times Malet is a name of Huguenot origin mainly associated with Co. Cork, but it is of interest to note that it occurs several times in mediaeval Hiberno-Norman records. Reaney gives four different derivations, three French and one English.

(O) Maliffe *Ó Maoldhuibh* (black chief). A family of the Uí Maine. The name is rare but extant in north Co. Galway. It is also written Miliffe and Mealiffe.

(O) Malinn, Millynn *Ó Maoilfhinn* (fair chief). This family originated in the Clones, Co. Monaghan area. It is now much confused with Mallin and Mullin. MIF

Malise *Mac Maoil Íosa* (servant of Jesus). This distinguished name is now very rare in Ireland, but survives in Scotland where it is also called Mellis.

Mallagh *Mailleach*. A sept of the Scottish clan MacGregor, found in north-east Ulster. Woulfe wrongly identified it with O'Malley. though it may have been sometimes used as a synonym through ignorance.

(O) Malla(g)han *Ó Maolacháin*. A variant of Molohan in east Ulster.

O Malley, Mailey *Ó Máille*. One of the best-known septs of north Connacht. O'Malley is one of the few O names from which the prefix was seldom dropped. In Mayo, however, it is also called Melia. The famous sixteenth-century Grace O'Malley typifies par excellence the maritime prowess of this sept. Bibl. IF   Map Mayo.

(O) Mallane A variant of Mullane (*Ó Maoláin*) in west Cork, quite distinct from Mallan, which is a variant of Mallon.

(O) Mallarky See Mullarkey.

(O) Mallon, Mallin *Ó Mealláin* (*meall,* pleasant). A branch of the Cenél Eoghain located in Tyrone where their territory was known as 'O'Mellan's Country'. They were hereditary keepers of the Bell of St. Patrick. Now numerous in Co. Armagh. MIF

(O) Mally See O'Malley.

(O) Malmona See Moss.

(O) Malone *Ó Maoileoin* (devotee of St. John). This sept has been closely associated with Clonmacnois until recent times. The name, now scattered, is numerous in Clare where it is pronounced Maloon and is probably really Muldoon. IF   MIF   Map Offaly.

(O) Maloney A variant spelling of Molony.

(O) Maloughney *Ó Maolfhachtna* (devotee of St. Fachtna). A north Tipperary family many of whom are now called Molony and Mac-Loughney.

Malseed This name is found in Co. Donegal; it is probably of Dutch origin.

(O) Manahan, Manihan *Ó Mainchín (manach,* monk). A sept of the Corca Laoidhe, usually anglicized Mannix, still mainly found in south-west Cork. Mannix is sometimes used for Minogue in east Clare. IF   MIF

Mac Manamon The Mayo form of MacMenamin.

Mac Manamy See MacMenamy.

Manarry See Menarry.

Manasses A form of MacManus in use in Tyrone.

Manaway See MacMenamy.

de Mandeville *de Móinbhiol.* A Norman family which came to Ireland in the twelfth century and settled in Antrim, later being established in Cos. Tipperary and Waterford where the name became Mansfield. K. Nicholls states that in the sixteenth century the Norman family of de Maydewell of Ballydine, Co. Tipperary, altered their name to Mandeville which their descendants still use. MIF   See MacQuillan.

Maneely, Mineely Composite forms of MacNeilly.

Manellis See MacNelis.

(O) Mangan *Ó Mongáin (mongach,* hairy). There are three septs of *Ó Mongáin*: one in north Connacht (sometimes Mongan there); the second is of Ballymongane, Co. Limerick; the third, an erenagh family always called Mongan, is of Termonomongan, Co. Tyrone. IF   MIF   See Mingane.

Manihan See Manahan.

Manley, Mannelly When found in Co. Cork this is *Ó Máinle* and often pronounced Mauly there. See Monnelly. Manley is also a well-known English name.

Mann This is numerous in Ulster where it is usually of Scottish origin (an abbreviation of Magnus). It has, however, been used in Belfast as a variant of Mahon. Mann occurs in mediaeval Co. Meath records, there presumably of English origin.

Mannering A well-known English name from the place-name Mainwaring. It has been used as an anglicized form of *Ó Manaráin,* also called Marrinan and Manron.

Mannice See Minnis.

(O) Mannin, Mannion *Ó Mainnín.* An important sept in the Uí Maine country, but descended from the pre-Gaelic Sodhan race. IF Map Galway.

Manning An English name numerous in Co. Cork and Dublin sometimes used as a synonym of Mannin.

Mannix See Manahan. O'Mannis was an alias of MacManus, not of Mannix.

(O) Manny *Ó Maine*. This name has apparently no connection with Uí Maine. It is now almost peculiar to Westmeath; possibly it may be an offshoot of the O'Meany sept of Thomond.

Manogue A variant of Minogue in Cos. Clare and Limerick.

Manron See under Mannering.

Mansergh Named from a place in Cumberland this name is in Cos. Cork and Tipperary since mid-seventeenth century.

Mansfield Bibl. See Mandeville.

Manton *Ó Manntáin* (*manntach*, toothless). Co. Waterford. Mantan and Mintaun are also found in Co. Galway. See Mountain. Manton is also an English toponymic.

Mac Manus *Mac Maghnuis*. (The forename Manus is from the Norse, ultimately Latin, *Magnus*.) The main sept of this name is a branch of the Maguires; the other is akin to the O'Connors of Connacht. Bibl. IF   Map Fermanagh and Roscommon. See Mayne.

Mapother An English toponymic, formerly Maypowder, associated with Co. Roscommon since 1613.

Maqueeney See MacQueeney.

O Mara See O'Meara.

(O) Maragan See Merrigan.

Maree See under Marry.

Marisco Bibl.

(O) Markahan *Ó Marcacháin*. This fine Dalcassian name has now been widely changed to the English Markham in its homeland, Ballymarkahan, in east Clare. Map Clare. See next entry for derivation.

(O) Markey *Ó Marcaigh* (*marcach*, rider). The sept of O'Markey has always been closely identified with Oriel, especially Cos. Louth and Monaghan. It has sometimes been changed by translation to Ryder; but Ryder is mainly found in north Connacht where it stands for Markahan. MIF

Mark(s) Mark and Markes are basically synonymous, but the latter was found in the seventeenth century in Co. Leix and elsewhere, whereas Mark, of later introduction, belongs almost exclusively to north-east Ulster, where, when not of English origin, it is an abbreviation of Markey.

Marlborough A Co. Clare name apparently not of English origin: probably a corrupt form of *Ó Maoilbhearaigh*. See Mulberry.

(O) Marley, Marrilly *Ó Mearlaigh*. Originally an Oriel name, and still there to some extent, it is now mainly found in Cos. Donegal and Mayo. Marley as a variant of Marlay is the name of an English family who settled in Co. Longford in 1675. MIF

Marmion A Norman name in the Pale from 1302. Also a synonym of Merriman in modern times.

Marnell This name has been closely associated with Kilkenny since 1550. The townland of Marnellsmeadows now forms part of that town. The family became hibernicized. The name was originally Warnell, a derivative of Warner. MIF

(O) Marriga *Ó Meardha*. An east Cork and west Waterford name. See Merry.

(O) Marrinan, Marnane *Ó Maranáin*. See Murnane and Mannering.

(O) Marron *Ó Mearáin* (probably from *mear*, quick, lively). Certainly a sept of Co. Monaghan. The prevalence of the name Marren in Co. Sligo should also be noted. MIF   Map Armagh and Monaghan.

Marry A Co. Louth name: origin uncertain, possibly cognate with Merry. Marry alias Maree is found in north Connacht. Though *Ó Mearadhaigh* in Irish this is quite distinct from Merry of Co. Waterford.

Marsh An English name of obvious derivation (not to be confused with Morris) which came to Ireland in the seventeenth century and was prominent in the ecclesiastical (Protestant) life of the country.

Marshall An occupational name of Norman origin found in Ireland in considerable numbers from early mediaeval times to the present day; not identified with any particular area, though more numerous now in Ulster than elsewhere. Bibl.

Martell See Mortell.

Martin, Martyn This is one of the most numerous surnames in Ireland, as it is also in England and Scotland. One family of Martins are included in the fourteen 'Tribes of Galway', having come to Ireland at the time of the Anglo-Norman invasion. The name is also used as an abbreviation of Gilmartin. In Tyrone Martin, formerly Mac-Martin (*Mac Máirtín*) is the name of a branch of the O'Neills. O'Martin (*Ó Martáin*) was an established name in Westmeath in the sixteenth century. Bibl. IF

Marum I do not know the origin of this name: Carrigan in his 'Diocese of Ossory' says it is Irish—*Ó Marum* which appears conjectural. The family settled in Co. Kilkenny about 1690 and among its distinguished members was Dr. Kieran Marum, Bishop of Ossory.

Mason An occupational English name, in Ireland since the thirteenth century; now fairly numerous in all the provinces except Connacht, but mainly the descendants of comparatively recent immigrants.

Massey One of the leading Anglo-Irish families of Co. Limerick. Bibl.

Mac Master *Mac an Mháighistir* (son of the master). A Breffny sept,

209

a branch of the MacKiernans now usually anglicized Masterson. MacMaster in Antrim and Down is of Scottish origin. MIF Map Longford.

Masterson When not for MacMaster, as in foregoing, this is the name of an English family settled in Co. Wexford since the sixteenth century. MIF   Map Wexford.

Matchett App.

Mateer A syncopated form of MacAteer.

Mac Math A branch of the Scottish clan Matheson, in Ulster since mid-seventeenth century. In Co. Monaghan the variant MacMeath also occurs. MacMagh, MacMaugh are variants. See MacMawe.

Mather(s) Mathers is now the usual form of this name in Ulster, though it originated in Yorkshire, England, as Mather, and that is the form in which it first appeared in Ireland. Mather is the more numerous in the other provinces and is on record in Dublin since the first half of the seventeenth century. By the end of that century it was well established in Co. Armagh. Mathers has to some extent been changed to Mathews in Co. Down. The obsolete English word *mather*, from which the surname is derived, means mower.

Matheson See MacMath.

Mathew A family of repute of English origin. Fr. Theobald Mathew, of temperance fame, was of Thomastown in south Tipperary. Bibl.

Matthews This English name, numerous in Ulster and Louth, is used also as a synonym of MacMahon there.

Mattimoe, Milmoe *Ó Maolmhuaidh* (derivation as Molloy). A minor sept of the Silmurray located in Co. Roscommon. Millamoe and Mallimoe are intermediate forms in the transition from Milmoe to Mattimoe. MIF

Maturin A Huguenot surname.

Maude An aristocratic English family, a branch of which settled in Co. Kilkenny in the seventeenth century. This name is also found among the Irish speaking people of Connemara.

Mac Maugh See MacMath.

(O) Maughan A variant of Maghan and Mohan. MIF

Maume Usually a misspelling of Maune.

Maun(e), Mawn *Mághún*. (Woulfe states that this is from Mayon, a Norman diminutive of Mathew). In both variants it occurs in the records of many counties but is nowhere numerous. In Mayo it is a variant of (O)Maughan.

Maunsel, Mansell A name of Norman origin closely associated with Cos. Limerick and Tipperary since early seventeenth century, but on record there and in Co. Wexford as early as the thirteenth century. Bibl. MIF   **Mavitty** A syncopated form of MacVitty.

(Mac) Mawe *Mac Máighe* (from Maheu, an old form of Mathew).

This is an Irish patronymic assumed by a family of Condon. May is sometimes a synonym of this. MacMawe is sometimes used for MacMath. MIF

Mawhannon A synonym of Buchanan in Ulster.

Mawhinney This Antrim name, alias MacWhinney and MacQueeney, is said to be an anglicized form of *Mac Shuibhne,* a variant of Mac-Sweeney. It is distinct from MacWeeney, though that has sometimes been used synonymously with MacQueeney. MIF

Mawhittey A syncopated form of MacWhitty.

Maxey A variant of Mackessy.

Maxwell A Scottish name very numerous in Ulster, sometimes used as a synonym of Mescall. Bibl.

May The English name May has several different derivations. In mediaeval Westmeath we find May an Irish sept, viz. *Ó Miadhaigh,* which survives as Mea as well as May. This is derived from *miadhach,* honourable. MIF   See Mawe.

Maybury An English name numerous in Co. Kerry, rare elsewhere so spelt; Mayberry is found in Ulster. It came to Kerry with Petty and Orpen, *q.v.*

Mayduck See Maddock.

Mayers See Meares.

Maynard Bibl.

Mayne This English name disguises MacManus in Co. Fermanagh, but is usually that of a settler family in or near Co. Antrim.

(Mac) Mayo *Mac Máighiú.* Though this is a Mayo name it is not taken from the name of the county, but is derived as MacMawe. Mayhew and Mahew are variants. MIF

Maziere A Huguenot name in Co. Cork.

(O) Mea See May and Mee.

Meacle This name appears to be peculiar to Connemara. I have not discovered its origin.

Meade The earlier forms of this, e.g. Miagh—*de Midia* in Latin and *Midheach* in Irish—indicate that this well-known family came originally from Meath. They were a leading family in Cork city and county from the early fourteenth century. Meade is also an English name. Bibl; MIF

(O) Meagher, Maher *Ó Meachair (michair,* kindly). This important sept is akin to the O'Carrolls of Ely. Unlike so many Irish septs, they were not driven from their homeland (as Map) after the Anglo-Norman invasion. Bibl. IF   Map Offaly and Tipperary.

(O) Meally This is properly a synonym of Melly but is often used for O'Malley.

(O) Mealue See Millea.

Mealiffe See Maliffe.

(O) Meany This form of *Ó Maonaigh* (see Mooney) originated in Thomond and is mainly now found in Cos. Clare and Kilkenny.

O Meara, Mara *Ó Meadhra (meadhar,* merry). This well-known sept, which has produced many distinguished men and women, gave its name to the village of Toomevara, which locates their homeland. This is one of the few O names from which the prefix was never very widely dropped. IF   Map Tipperary.

Meares Woulfe treats this as synonymous with the Thomond name (O) Meere. Mears, however, is best known in Dublin and the midland counties where it is of English origin, as are the variants Mair, Mairs and Mayers found in Ulster.

(O) Mearn An occasional variant of Marron in Oriel.

Mearns This is usually Scottish but it can be for Mearn.

Mac Mearty See MacMerty.

Meath See MacMath.

Mac Mechan A Co. Down variant of MacMeekin.

Medill See Madill.

Medole See Madole.

Mee *Ó Miadhaigh (miadhach,* honourable). This is called Mee in Roscommon and Mea in Mayo. Mee is occasionally used as a synonym of both Meehan and MacNamee in south Down. MIF

(O) Meegan *Ó Miadhagáin* (derivation as Mee). Almost exclusively a Co. Monaghan name which has been changed to Meehan in Louth. MIF

(O) Meehan *Ó Miadhacháin* (derivation as Mee). This is the name of at least two distinct septs (as Map); it is now equally distributed throughout the four provinces. The Leitrim sept is said to have originated as a branch of the MacCarthys of Munster, but it is of long standing in Connacht where Ballymeehin in the parish of Rossinver locates it. Fr. Livingstone states that the family of O'Meehan (*Ó Míotháin*) were erenaghs of Devenish. IF   Map Clare–Galway and Leitrim. See previous entry and Mehegan.

Meeke App.

(Mac) Meekin *Mac Miadhacháin* (derivation as Mee). Numerous in Antrim and Down where it is confused with Meighan and Meegan. MIF

(Mac) Meel See MacElmeel.

(O) Meenagh A variant of Minnagh. Meenagh is also used as a synonym of Thornton by pseudo-translation (*muineach,* thorns).

(O) Meenaghan This is the normal anglicized form of *Ó Muimhneacháin* in Co. Mayo. For derivation see Minnagh. Formerly Minaghan was sometimes so used, *O Mionacháin* is distinct and belongs to Co. Roscommon, being (according to Woulfe) a modern form of *Ó Manacháin* (see Monaghan).

(O) Meenan *O Mianáin* (*mian*, goodwill). Almost exclusively of Co. Donegal and adjacent areas. MIF

(O) Meeney *Ó Maonaigh*. See Mooney. IF   Map Sligo.

(O) Meere *Ó Midhir* (*meidhir*, mirth). The name of a Co. Clare family, erenaghs of Drumcleeve, sometimes corrupted to the English Myers. *De la Mere* (of the marsh) occurs in mediaeval records, but has little or no relevance in treating of the name Meere in modern times. *Ó Meidhir* is a variant.

Megarry A variant of Magarry.

Megaw An Ulster form of MacCaw or MacGaw.

Megraw, Megrath Forms of MacGrath used in Ulster.

Meguigan A syncopated form of MacGuigan.

Mehaffy A form of Mahaffy usual in Co. Monaghan.

Meharg A variant spelling of Maharg. See MacIlhagga.

(O) Mehegan *Ó Maothagáin* (*maoth*, soft). A Co. Cork family, of Castlemehigan near Crookhaven. The name has been altered to Meehan in some cases, as has the Co. Sligo *Ó Maotháin* which is now indistinguishable from Meehan (*Ó Miadhacháin*).

(O) Mehody See Mahedy.

(O) Meighan This is usually a variant form of Meehan, but is also sometimes used for Mehegan and Meekin. IF

Meiler See Meyler.

(O) Melaghlin *Ó Maoilsheachlainn* (devotee of St. Seachlann, i.e. St. Secundinus). The name of one of the royal houses of Ireland now almost entirely superseded by the form MacLoughlin. IF   Map Westmeath.

Melamby See Mullanphy.

Melay See Millea.

Meldon A synonym of Muldoon.

Meldrum Derived from a Scottish place-name, this name has been in Ulster and north Connacht since the Plantation of Ulster early in the seventeenth century.

(O) Melia See O'Malley.

(O) Melican *Ó Maoileacháin*. An attenuated form of *Ó Maolacháin* (Molohan). A west Clare name.

Mellan, Mellon Forms of *Ó Mealláin*. See Mallon. Bibl.

(O) Mellerick *Ó Maoilgheiric* (probably devotee of St. Cyriacus). Though in modern times this name is associated with Co. Cork it originated in north Connacht. MIF

Mellott See Millett.

Mellin A variant of Malinn.

Mellis See Malise.

Mellowes It is very doubtful whether this is a Gaelic-Irish name: there is an English name Mellows. In any case the form in Irish would be *Mac Maoil Íosa* (servant of Jesus), not *Ó Maoil Íosa*, only the former being found in mediaeval records. MIF

(O) Melly *Ó Meallaigh* (*meall*, pleasant). Though belonging to north Connacht and Donegal, this name is quite distinct from O'Malley.

(O) Melody *Ó Maoiléidigh*. (See Kennedy for derivation). The main sept of this name was located in north Clare on the Galway border. There was another in the Westmeath–Offaly area of which Mulleady, Moledy and Malady are variants. MIF   Map Clare.

Melville A rare name of Norman origin now mainly found in Ulster. It is sometimes used as a synonym of Mulvihil and of Mulfaal.

Melvin See Mulvin and Bleheen.

Menaght A contracted form of MacNaughten found in Co. Down.

Mac Menamin *Mac Meanman*. This name, originally of Tirconnell and still found there, is spelt MacManamon in Mayo. MIF   Map Donegal. See Merriman and next entry.

Mac Menamy *Mac Meanma* (*meanma*, high spirits). A form of Mac-Menamin found in Co. Tyrone. It is MacManamy in Co. Roscommon, where MacManaway is also probably a local form.

Menarry *Mac Naradhaigh* (probably from *nárdach*, modest). An Oriel name more numerous now than the older anglicized forms MacNary or MacNeary.

Mac Menim An abbreviated form of MacMenamin found in Co. Tyrone.

Menogher A syncopated form of MacNogher.

(O) Menton The usual form of *Ó Manntáin* in Munster; sometimes spelt Mentin and Mentane. See Manton.

Meran A variant of Marron.

Mercer This occupational name is numerous in Antrim and Down. It was well known in Leinster in mediaeval times. See next entry. Bibl.

Mercier A variant of Mercer used in Offaly and other midland counties. Both are derived from the French *mercier*, merchant. As *Le Mercier* and *Le Mercer* it occurs quite frequently in mediaeval Irish records.

Meredith A Welsh name (meaning magnificent) established in Ireland in the sixteenth century; now fairly widespread.

Mergagh *Meirgeach* (*meirgeach*, rusty, freckled). One of the several cognomina used by the Co. Cork sept of O'Hingerdell. See Harrington.

Mergin A rare variant of Bergin.

(O) Merlehan *Ó Méirleacháin* (*méirleach*, rebel or felon). A rare Westmeath name.

Mernagh Probably from *méaranach*, deft, rather than *meirtneach*, dispirited. A Co. Wexford cognomen; probably that of a branch of the MacMurrough–Kavanagh sept. MIF

(O) Mernin *Ó Méirnín*. This name is found in fair numbers in Co. Waterford and east Cork but is very rare elsewhere.

Merrick Of triple origin: a Welsh name in Connacht from the thirteenth century and gaelicized *Mac Mibhric*; in west Waterford and adjoining areas probably *Ó Mearadhaigh* (alias Merry); or occasionally an English name. MIF

(O) Merrigan Woulfe gives *Ó Muireagáin* for this name, variants of which are Maragan, Murrigan, Murricane and Morgan; originally of Westmeath and Longford, now scattered.

Merriman An English name. The origin of it as a synonym of a Gaelic surname is uncertain. *Mac Giolla Mheidhre* is only a humorous semi-translation of merryman used by Brian, the poet, whose family was probably an off-shoot of the MacNamaras, but possibly O'Houlihan. The equation with MacMenamin is improbable. MIF 178. See also Marmion.

Merry *Ó Mearadhaigh, Ó Meardha* (both are from adjectives meaning lively). The strange use of Holohan (in various spellings) synonymously with Merry in Co. Kilkenny is of long standing; it occurs frequently in sixteenth-century records as well as in those of a later date. Bibl. MIF   Map Tipperary and Waterford.

Mac Merty, Mearty Variants of MacBrearty in Donegal.

(O) Mescal *Ó Meiscill*. This name is found in a number of variant spellings, e.g. Miskell, mainly in Co. Clare and adjacent parts of Cos. Galway and Limerick, and to a lesser extent in the Waterford area. Miskelly is not one of the variants referred to. MIF

Metcalf This English name is in Ireland since early seventeenth century. It was called Medcalf in Yorkshire whence it came.

Mey See May.

Meyer This name, sometimes called Meyers, is usually of native origin when found in the west of Ireland, viz. *Ó Meidhir* (see Meere); as a foreign name it has three different origins, English, French and German.

(Mac) Meyler *Maoilir, Mac Maoilir*. The name of a Welsh family in Ireland since 1200. Map Wexford.

Michael This English name, formerly more numerous, has been to some extent changed to Mitchell. It is also a synonym of Mulvihil in Connacht. For Scottish Michaels see next entry.

Mac Michael A branch of the Scottish clan Stewart.

Mick This is a Palatine name, not an abbreviation of Michael.

Midleton One Cromwellian 'adventurer' of this name got extensive lands in Co. Kerry; but it was found in that county in the previous century and occurs earlier still in mediaeval records.

(O) Mihan A variant form of Meehan occasionally found in Ulster.

Mihill An abbreviate anglicized form of some Irish name embodying the forename *Micheál*, e.g. *Ó Maoil Mhichil* (see Mulvihill) and *Mac Giolla Mhichil* (see Elmeel). Mihill is mainly found in Co. Derry.

Miles This name, when not an anglicized form of *Ó Maolmhuire* (see Mullery) is derived either from Latin *miles*, a soldier, or from the personal name Milo. Miles and Myles are scattered, but the variant Moyles is mainly found in Co. Mayo. These are gaelicized as *Milidh* and *Milis*. MIF

Miley See Millea.

Milford An English name used in Mayo as a synonym of Mullover.

Milhair See Mulcair. **Milholland** U.S. variant of Mulholland (q.v.).

Miliffe See Maliffe.

Mac Millan *Mac Maoláin*. The name of a Scottish clan which has become numerous in Ulster. It has been there used also as a synonym of MacMullan.

Millane See Mullane.

Millar, Miller An English name very numerous in Antrim and adjacent counties. App.

(O) Millea This name has always been associated with Kilkenny and adjacent south-eastern counties since the sixteenth century when it first appears in Irish records. Miley is a comparatively modern synonym of it. Melay and Mealue have also been noted as such. Woulfe treats it as a Connacht name—*Ó Maol Aoidh* (devotee of St. Aodh or Hugh)—but there this is anglicized Mullee which has now often become Mulloy by absorption. As Millea is not an English name the Gaelic form may be the same as that given by Woulfe for Connacht.

Millerick See Mellerick.

Millett Mellot and Mylotte are two of several variant spellings of this name: these are all derived from *miles*, soldier. From the early fourteenth century families so called were associated with the Ormond country, but from the seventeenth their habitat has been mainly Co. Mayo and with east Galway where they were called MacMyloyd. MIF

Milliffe See Maliffe.

(O) Milligan, Milliken *Ó Maoileagáin*. An attenuated form of *Ó Maolagáin* (Mulligan). This name is numerous in Antrim and south Derry where it originated. MIF

Millin, Millynn See Malinn.

Millington This English toponymic appears occasionally in mediaeval Irish records; from mid-seventeenth century it occurs frequently in scattered locations. It is rare now except in Dublin, with which city it has a long connection.

Millmoe See Mattimoe.

Mills This English name, numerous in Ulster, may be an agnomen, *an Mhuilinn* (of the mill), elsewhere.

Milne From Old-English *milyen,* worker at the mill. Coming from Scotland, this name has been in Dublin since early eighteenth century.

(O) Milroy See Mulroy.

Mimnagh See Minnagh.

Minch See under Minchin.

Minchin A very old name in England (derived, like Mincing Lane, from Middle-English *minchen,* a nun) but unconnected with Ireland before the Cromwellian period when it became firmly established in the Roscrea area of Offaly and north Tipperary. Minch, a name associated with Co. Kildare, may be an abbreviation of Minchin or a variant of Minnish, i.e. *Mac Naois*; see Minnis.

Mineely See Maneely.

(O) Mingane *Ó Muingeáin.* An attenuated form of *Ó Mongáin.* A Kerry name now rare due to its having been absorbed by the better known Mongan.

(O) Minihan(e) See Moynihan.

Miniter *Minitéir.* One of the few Norman names established in Co. Clare. See Viniter.

Mac Minn *Mac Minne.* The name of a branch of the Scottish clan Menzies numerous in Ulster.

Minnagh *Muimhneach* (Munsterman). Mainly found in Co. Tyrone, Minnagh is occasionally synonymous with Kennedy in Donegal.

Minnion This name appears as that of yeomen farmers in Co. Meath in 1600. It has since been found in small numbers in Carlow and adjacent counties.

Minnis, Mannice These are two of several east Ulster forms of Mac-Neece and MacNish which, as *Mac Naois,* are variants of *Mac Aonghuis,* itself a variant of *Mag Aonghuis.*

(O) Minogue, Minnock *Ó Muineóg.* Woulfe's derivation from *manach,* monk, is not generally accepted but it is to some extent corroborated by the fact that Mannix and Monaghan are used as synonyms of it. It is an east Clare sept, which spread across Lough Derg from Ballyminogue to north Tipperary. MIF   Map Clare.

Minorgan A syncopated form of MacNorgan of Co. Carlow, both now very rare.

Mintaun, Mintaine See Manton.

Minteer An example of *Mac an* becoming Man or Min: in this case *Mac an tSaoir,* see MacAteer.

Miskell See Mescal.

217

Miskelly Naturally apt to be confused with one of the variants of Mescal: Miskelly, however, now an Antrim name, is seldom found in Munster and is normally a syncopated form of MacScally. MIF

Missett The Missetts were one of the leading families in Cos. Kildare and Meath from the time of the Anglo-Norman Conquest till the seventeenth century when they espoused the Jacobite cause. Since then they have gradually died out and the name is now very rare.

Mitchell *Mistéil*. This well-known English name is long established and very numerous in all the provinces except Munster. In Connacht it is often a synonym of Mulvihil. IF

Mitton, Mythen An English toponymic found in Co. Wexford since early seventeenth century.

Moakley See Mohilly.

Moan(e) See Mohan.

(O) Moany An Ulster variant of Mooney.

Mockler, Moclair The modern form of the French *Mauclerc* on record in Co. Tipperary since 1210; still numerous there. It has been gaelicized as *Móicléir*. MIF

Moen, Mone, Mowen Oriel variant spellings of Moan. See Mohan.

Moffat A Scottish toponymic numerous in Ulster since early seventeenth century. It has six variant spellings, e.g. Maffett, Mefatt etc.

Mogan See Mugan.

(O) Mohan *Ó Móchám*. In Connacht, where there are two septs of the name (as Map), it has been widely changed to Mahon. Mohan with its variant Moan, is actually now more numerous in Co. Monaghan. Mohan is occasionally used for the Norman *de Mohun*. MIF Map Galway and Sligo.

(O) Mohedy A variant of Mahady.

(O) Moher *Ó Mochair* (*mochar*, a place overgrown with brushwood). From the earliest records up to modern times this name is almost exclusively of west Waterford and east Cork. A few families of the name are found in Co. Clare. MIF

Mohery See Early.

(O) Mohide *Ó Muichide*. A rare name found in Cos. Cork and Tipperary.

(O) Mohilly, Moakley *Ó Mothlaigh* (*mothlach*, shaggy). A Co. Cork name.

Molamphy Also spelt Melampy etc. See Mullanphy.

(O) Molan *Ó Mothlacháin* (derivation as Mohilly). Of Munster, especially Co. Tipperary. Sometimes written Moland, which is an English name. MIF See Molohan.

(O) Moledy See Melody.

de Moleyns A distinguished name of Norman origin, occasionally used as a pretentious synonym of Mullins.

Mollan An occasional variant of Mullan in Co. Down.

(O) Mollarky See Mullarkey.

(O) Molline This Co. Monaghan name is now almost obsolete having been absorbed by Mullen.

(O) Molloy, Mulloy *Ó Maolmhuaidh*. (The adjective *muadh* denotes big and soft as well as noble). An important sept of Fercal in mid-Leinster. Molloy is also an anglicized form of *Ó Maolaoidh* see Millea. Apart from five variant spellings, such as Maloy and Mulloy, Molloy has been officially recorded as a synonym of Mulvogue (Connacht), Logue (Co. Donegal), Mullock (Offaly), Mulvihill (Kerry) and Slowey (Co. Monaghan) while Maloy has been used for MacCloy in Co. Derry. Bibl. IF   Map Offaly and Roscommon.

(O) Molohan In the Leitrim–Longford area this may be either *Ó Mothlacháin* (see Molan) or *Ó Maolacháin* (Mallaghan). In Co. Clare it is called Mollahan. It has become Mulligan in some places.

(O) Molon(e)y *Ó Maoldhomhnaigh* (servant of the Church). A well-known Dalcassian sept. In Co. Tipperary Maloughney has become Molony in some cases; there too the Molumby family of the Corca Laoidhe has been changed to Moloney. IF   MIF   Map Clare.

Molphy A form of Murphy used in Westmeath.

Molseed A variant spelling of Malseed.

(O) Molumby Woulfe treats this as a distinct name, *Ó Maolchomadh*, of south-west Cork (see Moloney) but it is also one of several variants of Mullanphy.

Molyneux A Norman name which in Ireland, when not of that origin, either stands for Mulligan or, in Kerry (the only county where Molyneux is at all numerous) it is said to be *Ó Maol an Mhuaidh* by Woulfe and others and so cognate with Molloy. Bibl.

Monaboe A composite form of MacNaboe.

(O) Monaghan *Ó Manacháin* (*manach*, monk). A numerous name mainly found in the counties adjoining the original homeland of the sept (as Map). It is also numerous in Fermanagh where it is said to be of Oriel origin. IF   Map Roscommon. See Minogue and Monks.

Mac Monagle, -Monigal *Mac Maongail* (wealth valour). One of the more numerous names in Co. Donegal with which county it has always been closely associated. The prefix Mac is usually, but not always, retained.

(O) Monaher *Ó Manachair* (monk dear). An old Offaly surname.

Monckton Bibl.

Monday A far-fetched synonym of MacAloon used in Cos. Fermanagh and Derry. See MacGloin.

Mone See Moen.

Money A variant of Mooney in north-east Ulster.

(O) Mongan *Ó Mongáin*. This is basically the same name as Mangan. IF MIF Map Mayo. See also Warburton.

(O) Mongey, Mungay *Ó Mongaigh* (derivation as Mongan and Mangan). A Co. Meath name.

Mongney See Montgomery.

(O) Mongovan See Mungavan.

Monks An English name used as a synonym of Monahan and of Mac-Evanny, these being derived from the basic word *manach*, a monk.

(O) Monnelly, Monley *Ó Maonghaile* (derivation as Monagle). A Mayo surname of which Munnelly, Mannelly and even the English name Manley are variant forms. It appears as O'Monillea and Monylla in sixteenth-century records relating to Mayo.

Monroe, Munroe *Mac an Róthaich*. A Scottish surname adopted by some O'Mellans and some Milroys. Bibl.

Mons This east Galway name (origin there not yet determined) is synonymous with Monds and Munds of Cos. Sligo and Roscommon.

Monsell See Maunsel.

Montagu(e) This Norman toponymic (*de Montaigu*) has been used as a synonym of MacTague especially in Cos. Tyrone and Armagh.

Montane See Mountain.

Monteith A Scottish name introduced at the time of the Plantation of Ulster, now quite numerous in Tyrone and adjacent areas.

Montgomery A toponymic of French origin. The mediaeval Hiberno-Norman Montgomerys of Co. Cork are probably extinct. The well-known families of Ulster are of seventeenth-century introduction. A modern gaelicization of this name is *Mac Iomaire*, which is also used for Ridge. Synonyms of Montgomery reported from Louth and adjacent counties are Goonery, Maglammery, Mongney and even MacGivern. Bibl. MIF

Montmorency Bibl.

Moody An English adjectival name (meaning brave or impetuous) found quite frequently as Mody in Irish records as far back as 1297. Since 1600 it has been found mainly in Ulster and also in Offaly. It has been gaelicized as *Ó Muadaigh*. MIF

(O) Moohan A variant of Mohan in and near Co. Donegal.

Moolick See Mullock.

(O) Moonan *Ó Muanáin*. The Oriel form of the Munster Moynan. MIF

Moon(e) This has been used synonymously with (O) Mohan and de Mohun and it is not closely identified with any particular area.

(O) Mooney *Ó Maonaigh.* According to Prof. M. A. O'Brien this is from *moenach,* dumb; Woulfe gives *maonach,* wealthy. Mooney is widely distributed, being of several distinct septs. That of Co. Sligo uses the form Meeney. Meaney or Mainey is the Munster form. IF Map Donegal and Offaly.

Moore A well-known English name much substituted for the Irish O'More. It is widespread throughout Ireland, but really numerous only in Co. Antrim and Dublin. Bibl. IF

Moorehead A numerous name in east Ulster; it is a variant of the Scottish Muirhead.

(O) Morahan *Ó Murcháin* (for derivation see Morchoe). A sept of east Offaly, sometimes called Morrin but now usually contracted to Moran. Morgan and Markan are other names sometimes used as anglicized forms. A second sept of this name, in Co. Leitrim, usually retains the spelling Morahan but Morrin is sometimes found there also. MIF   Map Kildare.

MacMoran See next entry.

(O) Moran Apart from MacMorran of Fermanagh, which has inevitably been changed to Moran, there are a number of distinct septs of *Ó Moráin* and *Ó Moghráin* whose name is anglicized Moran. Four of these are of Connacht—in which province the name is much more numerous than elsewhere—originally located (a) at Elphin (akin to the O'Connors), (b) in Co. Leitrim (of the Muintir Eolais), (c) in Co. Mayo at Ardnaree, (d) in Co. Galway, a minor branch of the Uí Maine. The Leitrim families are also called Morahan, as is the fifth to be enumerated, viz. that of Offaly, where Morrin is a synonym. Bibl. IF MIF

(O) Morchoe *Ó Murchadha* (*murchadh,* sea warrior). The chief of the O'Murphys uses that form of the name. Map Wexford.

Mac Mordie See MacMurdy.

O More *Ó Mórdha* (*mordha,* majestic). The leading sept of the 'Seven Septs of Leix'. This name is now almost invariably changed to Moore. Bibl. IF   Map Leix. See p. 304.

Moreland See under Murland.

Morell A Huguenot name.

Morey This is sometimes found as a synonym both of Moore and Moriarty.

Morgan A Welsh name numerous in Oriel as well as in Dublin and Belfast. It is also used as the anglicized form of several Irish surnames. See Merrigan and Morahan. Bibl.

(O) Moriarty *Ó Muircheartaigh* (*muircheartach,* navigator). Of the same stock as the O'Donoghues and the O'Mahonys, this sept has always been intimately associated with Co. Kerry. Bibl. IF

Map Kerry. For another name with the same form in Irish see Murtagh.

Morkan This is found as a variant of Morohan in Co. Offaly.

Morley See Morrally.

Mac Morney See Murney.

(O) Moroney Properly *Ó Maolruanaidh*, now often corrupted to *Ó Murruanaidh*. This Clare name has spread to Kerry. See Mulrooney. IF

Morphy A variant of Murphy formerly not unusual in Cos. Kerry and Cork.

(Mac) Morran See under Moran.

(O) Morrally, Morley *Ó Murghaile* (sea valour). A Mayo name for which the English surname Morley is now almost always used. It must be clearly distinguished from the Munster Murley. (See Hurley).

Morrin A Huguenot name in Ulster. For O'Morrin see Morahan and Moran.

Morris One of the 'Tribes of Galway'. This family is of Norman origin (*de Maries* and *de Marisco*). Morris is also sometimes used for Morrissey and even Fitzmaurice. Bibl; App; IF

Mac Morris, -Morish *Mac Muiris* is the Irish form of Fitzmaurice of Co. Kerry. It is also an Irish patronymic adopted by the Prendergasts. IF   Map Mayo.

Morrison An English name numerous in Ulster. See Bryson.

(Mac) Morrisroe *Mac Muiris Rua* (red Morris). Almost exclusively of Co. Roscommon.

Morrissey This name can be Irish *Ó Muirgheasa* (*muir*, sea—*geas*, action) or Norman *de Marisco*. The complications arising in connection with it and with Morrison are discussed in IF and MIF

Morrough This may be an abbreviation of MacMurrough or a synonym of Morrow.

Morrow Without the prefix Mac, Morrow is now more common in Ulster than in England whence it originated. In Fermanagh, however, it is usually for MacMorrow. See next entry.

Mac Morrow This, in the homeland of the sept (see Map) where the name MacMurrow is numerous, is *Mac Muireadhaigh* (which is from *muireadhach*, mariner) formerly anglicized MacMurry. They are a branch of the O'Rourkes. IF   Map Leitrim.

Mac Morry A variant of MacMorrow in Co. Leitrim.

Mortagh A variant of Murtagh. It has been used synonymously with Mortimer in Mayo.

Mortell, Martell *Mairtéil*. This name is on record in Co. Tipperary and adjacent parts of Cos. Limerick and Cork continuously since the thirteenth century. It is of dual derivation: from the Latin personal name *Martellus* and from the Old-French *martel,* hammer. MIF

Mortimer This English name, by origin a French toponymic, is on record in Co. Meath as early as 1382. In Connacht it has been used as a synonym of MacMurty. See Mortagh.

Morton An English toponymic, in Ireland continuously since the thirteenth century. Mainly now found in Ulster and Dublin.

Moss This English name is a partial translation of *Ó Maolmóna* (*móin,* gen. *móna,* moorland or turf bog). This is correctly anglicized Mulmona and Malmona in Fermanagh and Donegal.

Motherway An east Cork name gaelicized *Modartha.* Mothersoll, strangely supposed to be derived from 'my mother's soul', was well known in Donegal in the eighteenth century. Another similar sounding name in Ulster is Motherwell which came from Scotland in the seventeenth century.

Motley This name, of English origin, formerly Motlowe and Mutlowe, is in Ireland since the fourteenth century; it appears among the Co. Wexford Papist proprietors of the seventeenth century and for some time after that was prominent in Waterford and the eastern counties of Leinster, but is now much reduced in numbers.

Moughan A variant of Mohan and occasionally of Vaughan.

Moughty Woulfe lists this name with no particulars, giving *Ó Mochta* as the form in Irish. *Mochta* is an old Irish word for mighty. O'Moght and O'Mought occur in the Elizabethan Fiants in Westmeath and Tyrone.

Mountain This can be a modern form of the Norman *de la Montagne* or of *Ó Manntáin* (see Manton). It is fairly numerous in Co. Waterford.

Mountcashell See Cashell.

Mowen See Moen.

(O) Moy *Ó Muighe.* An indigenous Donegal surname. There is also an English name Moy which came to Ireland at the time of the Plantation of Ulster. MIF

Mac Moyer(s) See Weir.

(O) Moylan *Ó Maoileáin.* The name of a Munster sept whose early location has not been determined. It is now found mainly in Cos. Clare, Cork and Tipperary. MIF

Moyle The frequent occurrence of Moyle in mediaeval records arises from its use as an epithetal surname, i.e. *maol,* bald. For Moyles see Miles. MIF

(Mac) Moyler See Meyler.

Moylett A form of Millett in Co. Mayo.

Moyna(gh) A variant of Minnagh.

(O) Moynihan *Ó Muimhneacháin* (*Muimhneach,* Munsterman). Although there was a small sept of this name, sometimes changed to Munster, in Mayo, families so called belong almost exclusively to south-west Munster, Moynihan being very numerous on the borders of two counties, as in Map. Minihan, another form of the name, is found mainly in Cork. MIF   Map Cork–Kerry.

(O) Muckian, Muckeen *Ó Mochaidhean.* Owing to similarity of sound when the prefix O is dropped this essentially Co. Monaghan name has often been changed to MacKean. In mediaeval times the sept held a leading position in the barony of Cremorne in Co. Monaghan.

Muckle This name, found in Co. Down, is presumably a contraction of Mucklebreed, but may also be a variant of Mackle.

Mucklebreed A crude phonetic anglicization of *Mac Giolla Brighde.* See MacBride.

(O) Muckley, Mulclahy *Ó Maolchluiche** (*cluiche,* game). Originally of Co. Sligo where Inishmulclahy locates them, families of this name are now mainly found in Munster, where the better-known Mulcahy has largely displaced Mulclahy or Mulclohy. Stone by pseudo-translation (*cloch, cloiche,* stone) has also been substituted for it.

Mugan, Muggane There is an isolated case on record of synonymous use, but this provides no basis for Woulfe's statement that Mugan is a form of Magann, i.e. MacGann. Mugan and its variant Mogan belong almost exclusively to Connacht. Whether they are synonyms of Moughan or constitute a distinct name, *?Ó Mógáin,* has not been finally determined.

Muggevan A variant of Mungevan.

(O) Mulberry *Ó Maoilbhearaigh* (devotee of St. Barry). A Co. Derry name. This may· be the origin of the name Malborough or Marlborough found in Co. Clare.

(O) Mulbrandon A Co. Claré form of Mulrennan.

Mulbride, Mulbreedy See Mulready.

(O) Mulcahy *Ó Maolchathaigh.* This name is derived from St. Cathach, not from *cathach,* warlike. It is numerous throughout Munster. In Co. Down Cahy, Caughey and MacCahy have been used for Mulcahy. IF   Map Tipperary.

(O) Mulcair *Ó Maoilchéire* (devotee of St. Ciar). Now mainly Co. Limerick formerly also of Co. Galway where Mulhare is a variant. Earlier variants were Mulkerry etc. MIF

(O) Mulchrone *Ó Maolchróin* (*crón,* swarthy). This name belongs to Co. Mayo and is seldom found elsewhere.

(O) Mulclohy See Muckley.

(O) Mulconry *Ó Maolchonaire.* (The identity of the Conaire here

*For names beginning with Mul *(Maol)* see footnote p. 40.

perpetuated is unknown). A famous Silmurray family of chroniclers to the kings of Connacht. The name is often abbreviated to Conry and sometimes corrupted to Conroy. Bibl; IF 90; Map Roscommon.

(O) Mulcreevy, Mulgrievy *Ó Maolchraoibhe*. An Oriel sept whose name and been widely changed to Rice. The now obsolete O.E. word for branch is *rhìs*. IF MIF   Map Armagh-Down.
See Mullgrew.

(O) Mulderrig *Ó Maoildeirg* (red chief).* A Mayo name often changed to Reddington, Reid and Ruttledge.

(O) Mulderry *Ó Maoldoraidh.* Formerly important in Tirconnell, now very rare. Probably Muldrew and Muldragh are variants in Ulster.

(O) Muldoon *Ó Maoldúin* (*dún*, fort). The name of three distinct septs. The most important is that of Ulster; another is of Co. Clare (now probably called Malone); and the third of Uí Maine in Co. Galway. MIF   Map Fermanagh.

(O) Muldowney *Ó Maoldomhnaigh.* Akin to Moloney (q.v. for derivation) but found mainly in Ulster. In the Newry area Downey, Gildowney, MacDowney, MacGilldowney and Muldowney have all been officially recorded as used synonymously. MIF

(O) Mulfall Map Donegal. See Lavelle.

(O) Mulgannon A rare Co. Clare name.

(O) Mulgeehy *Ó Maolghaoithe*. A Donegal name which has been almost superseded by Wynne or occasionally by Wyndham, due to the word *gaoth*, wind, embodied in the surname.

(O) Mulgrew, Grew The earlier anglicization O'Mulcreevy is nearer to original Irish *Ó Maolchraoibhe*. Mulgrew is mainly found in Co. Tyrone and the rarer abbreviation Grew in Co. Armagh. There is also an English surname Grew, derived from Old-French *griu,* crane. MIF

(O) Mulhall *Ó Maolchathail* (devotee of St. Cathal). Formerly anglicized Mulcahill. Map Leix. See Halley.

(O) Mulhane An occasional variant of Mullane found in Kerry.

(O) Mulhare See Mulcair.

Mulhartagh See under MacCartney.

(O) Mulhatton *Ó Maolchatáin* (devotee of St. Catan). A rare Tyrone name.

(O) Mulhern The Ulster form of Mulkerrin.

(O) Mulholland *Ó Maolchalann* (devotee of St. Calann). The name of several septs located as indicated in Map. That of Loughinsholin, Co. Derry, is the one which is of most interest as they were keepers of the Bell of St. Patrick, and they only are numerous now. The other two—of Demifore, Westmeath, and of the Uí Fidhgheinte—were

*See footnote on p. 40.

important in early mediaeval times, but the name is rare now in those localities. IF   MIF   Map Derry, Donegal, Limerick and Meath.

(O) Mulhooly See Mulooly.

(O) Mulkeen See Mulqueen.

(O) Mulkere A variant of Mulcair found in Co. Galway.

(O) Mulkerrill *Ó Maolchairill* (devotee of St. Caireall). This east Galway name has been changed to Mulkerrin. MIF

(O) Mulkerrin *Ó Maoilchiaráin* (devotee of St. Kieran). A Co. Roscommon family who were erenaghs of Ardcarne and produced many notable ecclesiastics. In the neighbouring county of Galway Mulkerrin has superseded Mulkerrill. MIF

Mac Mulkin *Mac Maolchaoin*. This name is found in Mayo, Tyrone and Fermanagh. See Mulqueen.

(O) Mullahan The Co. Clare form of Molohan.

(O) Mullahy *Ó Maolaithche* (which according to Woulfe means votary of regeneration). A Mayo sept.

(O) Mullally *Ó Maolalaidh.* (Woulfe derives this conjecturally from *aladh,* speckled). An important branch of the Uí Maine. The name has been contracted to Lally. As such it holds a distinguished place in the records of the Wild Geese. Bibl. IF   Map Galway.

Mac Mullan See MacMullen.

(O) Mullan *Ó Maoláin* (*maol,* bald, hence tonsured). Mullan is now indistinguishable from Mullen, Mullins, Mellon and (Mac) Mullen in many parts of the country, being very numerous in all the provinces except Munster, for which see Mullane. It can definitely be assigned historically to two areas as in Map. Bibl. IF   Map Derry and Galway.

(O) Mullane This is the Munster form of O'Mullan; it is often now called Mullins especially in Co. Clare where Millane is another variant. IF   Map Cork.

(O) Mullaney *Ó Maoileanaigh.* The derivation from St. Seanach is disputed (see MIF   ). The location of the sept is indicated by the place-name Ballymullany on the Roscommon–Sligo border as in Map.

Mullaniffe A north Connacht variant of Mullanphy.

(O) Mullanphy *Ó Maolainbhthe, Ó Maolanfaidh* (chief of the storm).*
The name has a number of variant spellings beginning with Me— . and Mo—as well as Mu. It is seldom met outside north Tipperary. Map Tipperary.

(O) Mullark(e)y *Ó Maoilearca* (devotee of St. Earc). This family migrated from Tirconnell to Connacht early in the seventeenth century and are now almost exclusively found in Cos. Sligo, Mayo and Galway. MIF

(O) Mullarney Foley (NL. MS. G841) gives some reason to believe that this is *Ó Maolshathairne*. Woulfe gives *Ó Maoilearna*. It has been changed to MacLarney in the midlands. The very similar names MacLerney and MacAlearney found in Co. Monaghan are *Mac Giolla Earna*.

(O) Mullavin *Ó Maoiléimhin* (devotee of St. Evin). A Westmeath name, occasionally changed to MacLavin.

(O) Mulle(a)dy, Mulleda Variant forms of Melody. Map Westmeath.

(O) Mullee See under Millea.

Mullen This is used as a variant of Mallon and Mellon as well as MacMullen in Ulster and sometimes of Mullane and Millane in Munster.

Mac Mullen, -Mullan *Mac Maoláin* (*maol*, bald). These are very numerous in Antrim and Down where they are usual forms of the Scottish MacMillan used in Ireland.

(O) Mullerick A variant of Mellerick.

(O) Mullery, Mulry These are the anglicized forms of *Ó Maolmhuire* (devotee of B. V. Mary) found in Roscommon and neighbouring parts of Connacht; Mulry is also an anglicized form of the Mayo name *Ó Maolruaidh,* see Mulroy. MIF

Mullett This name, found in Co. Wexford, is said to be a variant of Millett.

Mulley A variant of Mullee.

(O) Mulligan *Ó Maolagáin* (probably a diminutive of *maol*, see Mac-Mullen). An important sept in Donegal, much reduced at the time of the Plantation of Ulster and now found more in Co. Mayo and Monaghan. IF   MIF   Map Donegal. See also Molohan, Mulqueen, Diamond and Baldwin.

(O) Mullihan A variant of Molohan.

Mullins The Clare and Cork form of *Ó Maoláin*. See Mullane and de Moleyns. *Ó Mothláin* of Silmurray is also anglicized as Mullins.

Mullock, Mulock *Mac Míoluic*. This old east Connacht family appears in sixteenth- and early seventeenth-century records as MacMoleg, MacMullicke, etc. In Leitrim and Roscommon it is also called Moolick. According to family tradition this name is derived from Meelick, a place in east Galway with which they were associated. Woulfe's derivation from the personal name Milo is more probable. Bibl.

(O) Mullooly *Ó Maolghuala*. (Woulfe's derivation from a word meaning glutton is not accepted; *guala*, shoulder, is more likely). An old family in Cos. Longford and Roscommon.

(O) Mulloon This form is on record in Co. Clare. See Malone.

(O) Mullover *Ó Maolfhoghmhair* (*foghmhar,* harvest). Mullover, the older phonetic anglicization of this name, is now almost obsolete. Milford is the present synonym. Palmer is also occasionally so used. Map Mayo.

(O) Mullowney A Connacht form of Molony.

(O) Mulloy See Molloy.

(O) Mulmohery Map Cavan–Leitrim. See Early.

(O) Mulmona See Moss.

Mulogue A variant of Mullock.

Mulpatrick See under Patrick.

Mulpeters *Ó Maolpheadair* (devotee of St. Peter). Originally of Co. Cork, later Leix and Offaly.

(O) Mulqueen(y) Woulfe differentiates between Mulqueen, which he makes *Ó Maolchaoin* (gentle chief), and Mulqueeny *Ó Maolchaoine* (servant of St. Caoine), though stating correctly that both are of Thomond where they are synonymous, and instancing O'Mulqueen of Ballymulqueeny in that connection. I think, however, they are without doubt variants of the same name, *Ó Maolchaoine*. The name is sometimes unaccountably changed to Mulligan in west Clare. The variant Mulkeen is found in Mayo. MIF   Map Clare.

(O) Mulrain See Mulrine.

(O) Mulready *Ó Maoilbhrighde* (devotee of St. Brigid). A small sept of the Uí Maine. MIF   Map Roscommon.

(O) Mulreany *Ó Maoilréanna*. A corruption of *Maoilbhréanna,* the Donegal form of *Maoilbhréannain*. See Mulrennan.

(O) Mulreavy *Ó Maoilriabhaigh* (*riabhach,* brindled or swarthy). This name belongs to Co. Donegal.

(O) Mulrennan, Mulrenin *Ó Maoilbhréanainn* (devotee of St. Brendan). The head of this important family was chief of Clanconnor and held a leading position in the retinue of the kings of Connacht. MIF   Map Roscommon.

(O) Mulrine A Donegal name. The Irish form is presumably *Ó Maoil Riain*. Mulrain and Mulroyne are variants found in Connacht and some Ulster counties. These are distinct from the well-known Munster sept of O'Mulryan.

Mulroe A variant of Mulroy in Cos. Galway and Sligo.

(O) Mulrooney *Ó Maolruanaidh*. A once powerful sept subjugated by the Maguires; in Fermanagh the name is still found in small numbers. In Co. Galway it has been changed to Moroney. Map Fermanagh, Galway. See Rooney.

(O) Mulroy, Mulry *Ó Maolruaidh* (*maolruadh,* red chief*). A sept of the Uí Fiachrach in Mayo whose name is also anglicized Milroy and has sometimes been changed to Munroe. Also an old family in Co. Longford. MIF   Map Longford and Mayo. See Mullery.

(O) Mulryan *Ó Maoilriain*. In modern times this name has been abbreviated to Ryan (today the tenth most numerous surname in Ireland) and the vast majority of Ryans are really Mulryans. With its variants Mulrine, Mulroyne etc. the name survives in Cos. Galway and Leitrim far west of its original homeland. This is possibly a distinct but little recorded sept. IF See Intro. p. xvi. Map Tipp.

(O) Mulshinoch *Ó Maoilsionóg*. This name belongs almost exclusively to Cos. Cork and Kerry. Though it is rare it has a number of variant spellings, e.g. Mullsheenogue and even Multinock. MIF

(O) Multilly See Flood.

(O) Mulvanaughty *Ó Maoilbheannachta*. This old Co. Leitrim name has been corrupted to Mulvanerty and even Mulvanerton, or is made Blessing by translation of the Irish word *beannacht* embodied in the surname.

(O) Mulvan(n)y, Mulvenna These may be distinct families. Mulvenna is certainly *Ó Maoilmheana* and is essentially of north Ulster; Dr. O'Raifeartaigh derives this from the river *Meana* now Main. Mulvany may also possibly, as Woulfe says, be *Ó Maolmhaghna* of Donegal. Mulvany, however, is now mainly found in Leinster, and I see no reason to doubt that it is *O Maoilmheana* there also. In Ulster Mulvenna is sometimes used synonymously with MacIlvenna. MIF Map Derry.

(O) Mulvey, Mulveagh *Ó Maoilmhiadhaigh* (*miadhach,* honourable). The main sept has long been important in Co. Leitrim. Mulvey of Co. Clare is, according to Woulfe, of different stock, *Ó Maoilmheada* in Irish. Bibl; MIF   Map Clare and Leitrim.

(O) Mulvihill, Mulville *Ó Maoilmhichil* (devotee of St. Michael). Now much scattered but formerly a sept of note in Connacht. The name has been changed to Mulville and Melville in Clare and Galway and to Mitchell in Ulster. IF   MIF   Map Roscommon.

(O) Mulvin *Ó Maoilmhín* (*mín,* gentle). A rare name found in east Leinster.

(O) Mulvogue *Ó Maolmhaodhóg* (devotee of St. Mogue). Formerly numerous in Connacht and Donegal, now rare.

Munday See Monday.

(O) Mungovan *Ó Mongabháin* (*mongbhán,* white hair). A west Clare family.

Mac Munigal A variant of MacMonagle.

Munkettrick See MacKitterick.

Mac Munn A Scottish name found in Co. Donegal.

(O) Munnelly See Monnelly.

Munroe See Monroe and Mulroy.

229

Munster See Moynihan.

Murchison, Murchie A Scottish name. Woulfe gives *Mac Murchaidh* as the Irish form and relates it to Murphy. See MacMurphy.

Murdoch A Scottish name, numerous in Ulster, used occasionally as a synonym of Murtagh.

Mac Murdy A Co. Cavan variant of *Mac Muircheartaigh*; see Mac-Brearty. MacMordie is another spelling found in Ulster.

(O) Murilly, Murhila, Murley *Ó Murthuile*. This Co. Cork name has generally become Hurley, but Murhilla, etc. are still found in west Cork. IF

(Mac) Murland Woulfe gives *Mac Murghaláin* (*murghal*, sea valour). This is not the origin of Moreland, which is an English name of obvious derivation (dweller on the moorland). Both are associated with Co. Down.

(O) Murnaghan *Ó Muirneacháin* (*muirneach*, lovable). An Ulster name which is quite distinct from the Munster Murnane.

(O) Murnane *Ó Murnáin*. This Thomond name, now in Cork, is also anglicized Marrinane and Marnane. The mediaeval form Iwarrynane shows how it became Warren in some places. MIF

Murney An occasional synonym of Murnane. See Gilmore.

(Mac) Murphy *Mac Murchadha*. MacMurphy was formerly numerous in Armagh and Tyrone but the prefix Mac has been almost entirely dropped. This is probably the origin of the majority of the Murphys in Ulster. See next entry.

(O) Murphy *Ó Murchadha* (for derivation see Morchoe). Murphy is the most numerous name in Ireland and is that of three different septs as indicated in Map. The resumption of the prefixes O and Mac, which is a modern tendency with most Gaelic–Irish names, has not taken place in the case of Murphy. Bibl. IF   Map Cork, Roscommon and Wexford.

Murray, Murry Apart from Scottish Murrays, we have *Ó Muireadhaigh* formerly O'Murry of Uí Maine; *Mac Giolla Mhuire* (Mac-Elmurray or Gilmore); and *Mac Muireadhaigh* (MacMurray) very numerous in Co. Donegal. IF   MIF   App; Map Down (MacMurray) and Roscommon (O'Murray). See Murrihy.

(O) Murrican, Murrigan See Merrigan.

(O) Murrihy *Ó Muirighthe*. A Clare name sometimes changed to Murray. Woulfe says it is a corrupt form of *Ó Muireadhaigh* (Murray).

(O) Murrin, Murran *Ó Muireáin*. A family of the Uí Fiachrach, whose name has been changed to Moran. For MacMurran see MacMorran.

Mac Murrough *Mac Murchadha*. This name is famous in mediaeval Irish history, not always happily. It is now rare. The sept was subdivided and became Kavanagh, Kinsella, Hendrick and Mernagh. IF   Map Wexford.

Murtagh *Ó Muircheartaigh* (*muircheartach,* navigator). Though Irish in origin in Leinster, this name in Ulster is sometimes Scottish and a synonym of Murdoch. In Co. Roscommon it is a Mac name first anglicized MacMoriarty. IF   Map Meath.

Murtha A variant of Murtagh found in Co. Meath and adjacent areas of Louth and Cavan.

Mac Murtry See under MacBrearty.

Mac Murty See MacBrearty.

Musgrave This name from Westmoreland, introduced at the time of the Plantation of Ulster, later became prominent in Co. Waterford.

Mustey See MacStay.

Mutloe See Motley.

Myers See under Meere.

Myhill See Mihill.

Myhan See Mihan.

(O) Mylan A variant spelling of Moylan in Co. Clare.

(Mac) Myler See Meyler.

Myles See Miles.

Mylotte See Millett.

(O) Mynihan A Kerry, particularly Killarney, form of Moynihan.

Mythen See Mitten.

N

Naan See Nawn.

Mac Nabb *Mac an Abbadh* (*abbadh,* abbot). The name of a Scottish clan, some families of which settled in Ulster.

Mac Nabney Little is known of this Co. Down name. A yeoman called MacNebna appears in a Co. Longford Fiant of 1601. MacNabney would be a likely modern form of this, but I have no evidence to indicate that they are in fact connected.

Mac Naboe *Mac Anabadha.* (Woulfe derives this from *anabaidh,* premature.) Many families of this Breffny sept in Cos. Cavan and Longford are now called Victory by pseudo-translation as if *Mac na buadha.* MIF

Mac Naboola *Mac Con na Búille* (the hound of Boyle). A north Connacht name mainly found in Co. Sligo. The English name Benbo (meaning archer) has strangely been used as a synonym of it. MIF

Mac Naghten See MacNaughton.

(O) Naghten, Naughton *Ó Neachtáin.* (*Neachtáin,* a well-known personal name, may derive from the word meaning bright or pure). There are two septs of this name in the west (for location see Map). There are several variants including Nocton, Knochton and Natton, and the English name Norton is also so used. IF   MIF   Map Clare and Galway-Roscommon.

Nagle *de Nógla*. This is the Co. Cork form of *de Angulo*, see Nangle. Woulfe suggests that the supposedly obsolete MacNogly—*Mac an Óglaigh* (son of the soldier) of Co. Sligo may have survived as Nagle. Bibl. IF

Mac Nair A branch of the Scottish clan MacNaughton found in Ulster.

Nallen An Offaly name. Woulfe says it is *Mac Nailín* in the spoken language.

(Mac) Nally, Mac Anally *Mac an Fhailghigh* (*failgheach*, poor man). Without the prefix Mac this name now is found mainly in Mayo and Roscommon; with the Mac it belongs to Oriel. Woulfe says that the Mayo Nallys are of Norman or Welsh origin and acquired a Gaelic name. This is unlikely in the case of the MacNallys of Ulster as there they are often called *Mac Con Ulaidh* (son of the hound of Ulidia, i.e. eastern Ulster). In the 'census' of 1659 it appears as Mac-Anully, MacEnolly, MacNally and Knally, all in Oriel or in counties adjacent thereto. IF

Mac Nalty *Mac Conallta* (*cú*, hound—*allta*, wild). In its homeland, north Connacht, and in adjacent parts of Ulster, the prefix Mac is usually dropped. MacAnalty is a variant of it.

Mac Nama *Mac Conmeadha* (*con*, gen. of *cú*, hound—*Meadha* is a place-name). A Leitrim name now usually made Conway.

Mac Namara *Mac Conmara* (hound of the sea). The most important sept of the Dál gCais after the O'Briens to whom they were marshals. Bibl . IF   Map Clare. See Mack.

Mac Namee *Mac Conmidhe* (hound of Meath). This family was notable as poets and ollavs to the O'Neills. MIF 188; Map Tyrone.

(Mac) Nanany A rare Co. Roscommon name for which Leonard has been used as a synonym. Woulfe gives *Mac Conanaonaigh* (hound of the fair) as the Irish form.

Nangle *de Nógla*. The name of those of the Norman *de Angulos* in Connacht and Leinster who did not become Costelloe was anglicized Nangle. Bibl . IF   Map Meath.

(Mac) Nanny A Roscommon variant of MacEneaney.

Nannery A curious variant of MacNeary found in north Connacht and Co. Longford.

Napper Though this name occurs occasionally in mediaeval Irish records it did not become prominent till a branch of the well-known west of England family settled in Meath early in the seventeenth century. The name is a variant of Napier (from the French word meaning a maker of tablecloths). SIF

Nary See Neary.

Nash *de Nais*. This English locative name (from *atten ashe*) has become hibernicized in Cos. Limerick and Kerry. Bibl. IF

Nason An English (Warwickshire) name, probably of Dutch origin. Apart from one student of Dublin University, born Co. Derry 1623, I have found no reference to this name in Ireland earlier than the end of the seventeenth century. After that the family became well established in the eastern end of Co. Cork. They were numerous there (but not elsewhere in Ireland) in the eighteenth and nineteenth centuries but the name has now become rare.

Natton See Naghten.

Mac Naugher See MacConnor.

Mac Naught A Donegal form of MacKnight. Sometimes it is an abbreviated form of MacNaughton.

Mac Naughton This name is Scottish and is quite distinct from O'Naughton. Bibl. See Naghten.

Mac Naul See MacAnaul.

(Mac) Naulty, Nolty. See Nalty.

(Mac) Navin See Nevin.

(O) Nawn, Nahane *Ó Náthan*. Originally an ecclesiastical family of Co. Donegal, it has long been located in and near Co. Fermanagh. Nahane has been found in Co. Cork, possibly as an offshoot of the Ulster family, but more probably there it is a corruption of Nihane. See Nyhan.

Naylor The first Naylors came to Dublin early in the seventeenth century as a result of their relationship to the famous Richard Boyle, 1st Earl of Cork. The name was quite numerous a century ago in Cos. Limerick and Offaly as well as Dublin, but is now less so.

Mac Nea(gh), -Nay See under MacNee.

Neagle A variant of Nagle.

(Mac) Neale This is a branch of the Scottish clan MacNeill (see MacNeill). Neale without the prefix Mac is an English name which was formerly much used for Neill.

(O) Nealon A variant of Neylan.

(Mac) Nealy See Neely.

Mac Neany See MacEnaney.

Neaphsy See Kneafsey.

Mac Neary See Menarry.

(O) Neary *Ó Náraigh* (possibly from *nárach*, modest). A north Connacht name. Bibl. MIF

Neazer See Bovenizor.

Mac Nee *Mac Niadh* (*niadh*, champion). A branch of the Scottish clan MacGregor. It is also used as a variant of the quite distinct Connacht MacNea(gh), MacNay, *Mac Néidhe* (also from *niadh*, champion).

(O) Nee, Needham *Ó Niadh* (for derivation see MacNee). In Co. Galway this preserves the correct anglicized form Nee, but in Mayo it is sometimes called Needham. There was also a co-arb family of the name in Co. Limerick, now Neville. MIF

Neecy See Kneafsey.

(O) Neehan A variant (phonetically preferable) of Nyhan.

Neef See Denieffe.

Mac Neela See next entry.

(Mac) Neely Confusion arises in connection with this name because it is used as a variant of MacNeilly in Co. Antrim, but it is properly that of a Co. Galway sept, viz., *Mac Conghaile*, also anglicized Conneely. Another Connacht name, MacNeela, tends to become MacNeely by absorption, but in fact it is distinct, being that of the Uí Fiachrach sept *Mac Conghaola* derived from *cú*, hound—*Gaola*, a Co. Galway place-name, mod. Gowla.

(O) Neenan *Ó Naoidheanáin* (*naoidhean*, child). A west Clare name, often changed to Noonan.

Neeson *Mac Aonghusa*, which is often anglicized MacNeece. Neeson occurs in both Tyrone and Monaghan seventeenth-century records as O'Neason. MIF

Mac Neice, -Neese *Mac Naois*. An Ulster surname akin to MacGennis, MacGuinness and Neeson.

Mac Neight A form of MacKnight in north-east Ulster.

Mac Neilage A variant of MacNelis.

(O) Neilan See Neylan.

Mac Neill *Mac Néill*. A galloglass family from the western isles of Scotland, in Antrim and Derry since early fourteenth century. A branch settled in Mayo. MIF   See MacGreal.

(O) Neill *Ó Néill*. In addition to the famous O'Neills of Ulster there were septs of the name in Thomond (see Nihil), Decies (Co. Waterford) and Carlow. The main family of the O'Neills, dominant in Tyrone up to the collapse of the Gaelic system in the seventeenth century, descend from the famous Niall of the Nine Hostages. A branch known as Clandeboy *(Clann Aoidh Bhuidhe)* settled in Co. Antrim in the fourteenth century. The name is numerous throughout Ireland, especially in Tyrone and Antrim. For fuller treatment of the O'Neills see IF   Map Antrim, Down, Tyrone, Carlow and Waterford-Tipperary. For derivation see Neilson.

Mac Neilly *Mac an Fhilidh* (*fileadh*, poet). An ancient Irish sept of Antrim. This name is also anglicized MacAnilly. MIF   See under MacNellagh and Neely.

Neilson, Nelson Derived from *Njall*, the Norse form of the Irish *Niall*. The name came to Ireland from Scotland and is numerous in Dublin and Ulster since the early seventeenth century. It is gaelicized as *Mac Neighill*.

Mac Neish, -Nish A sept of the Scottish clan MacGregor. Sometimes a synonym of MacNiece.

Mac Neive, -Nieve A form of *Mac Conduibh* used in Co. Roscommon. See Cunniff.

(O) Neligan *Ó Niallagáin*. This sept originated in the south-east of the country, and Ballynelligan is near Lismore, but for centuries the name has been mainly in Cos. Cork and Kerry. MIF

Mac Nelis, -Nellis *Mac Niallghuis* (*gus*, vigour, with forename). With the Mac this name is peculiar to Tirconnell, without the prefix it is found in adjacent areas. MIF   Map Donegal.

Mac Nellagh, -Nello This name is found in Co. Longford. Woulfe equates it with Connelly as well as with MacNeilly. Nelly, without the prefix Mac, is found in Co. Clare. The MacNellys, also called Mac-Neilly, were a sept of Clanrickard in Connacht.

(Mac) Nelly See previous entry.

Nelson App. See Neilson.

Mac Nerlin See Killerlean.

Nerney, Nerheny, Nertney, Nirney North Connacht forms of MacInerney.

Nesbitt An English toponymic of pre-Cromwellian introduction, numerous in Cavan and adjoining counties. Bibl.

(Mac) Nestor *Mac an Aghastair* formerly *Mac Girranadhastair* (short man of the halter). A sept attached to the O'Loughlins of the Burren, notable as clerics. Bibl; Map Clare.

Mac Nestry See MacKinstry.

Netterville, Netterfield This Anglo-Norman family was formerly of importance in the Pale but the name is now rare. Map Meath.

Neville This aristocratic English name is used for *Ó Niadh* (see Nee) in Co. Limerick and occasionally for Nevin in Co. Clare. The Nevilles of Cos. Kilkenny and Wexford are of English (ultimately French) origin. MIF   Map Limerick.

(Mac) Nevin *Mac Cnáimhín* (*cnámh*, means bone, but derivation from this is conjectural). Formerly Knavin. A sept of the Uí Maine notable both as poets and physicians. The name, usually as Nevin without the Mac, is now found in all the provinces, Navin in Mayo. MIF Map Galway.

Newcom(b)e, Newcomen The earlier form Newcomen, a name of note in Dublin in the seventeenth century, came to Ireland at the end of the sixteenth century. In the last century Newcombe was mainly found in Co. Mayo, where it is said to be the anglicized form of *Ó Niadh* (see O'Nee).

(O) Newell *Ó Tnúthghail* (*tnúth-gal*, envy valour). A small sept of north Kildare. Ulster Newells (numerous in Co. Down) are for the most part of English origin. Another English name is also used as an anglicized form, viz., Knowles. MIF

Newenham The first of this family in Ireland came from England to Dublin in mid-seventeenth century; soon after that they settled in Co. Cork where they became prosperous and fairly numerous in the eighteenth century (two were members of the Irish parliament). The name is still well known in Co. Cork.

Newman This is one of the more numerous surnames of English origin found in Ireland, but, unlike most of those, it is rare in Ulster. It is frequent in Anglo-Irish records, occurring as early as the thirteenth century in Co. Dublin. Since the mid-seventeenth century it has been mainly found in Co. Cork, and to a considerable extent also in Co. Meath. The very similar Newnan is an occasional variant of Noonan.

Newsom The name of a well-known Quaker family in Cork. It is an English toponymic.

(O) Neylan, Neilan *Ó Nialláin* (for derivation see under O'Neill). A Thomond sept seated at Ballyally near Ennis, who spread into Connacht. IF   Map Clare.

Niblock This name, which appears in the hearth money rolls (1664) for Co. Antrim, is now fairly numerous there and in other parts of Ulster but not elsewhere in Ireland. I do not know its origin.

Mac Nicholas *Mac Niocláis.* The name of a gaelicized branch of the Norman de Burgos, sometimes corrupted to Clausson. The appearance of MacNicholas in the 1659 'census' as a principal name in Co. Waterford is due to its being mistaken for Fitznicholas. MIF   Map Tyrone.

Mac Nicholl, -Nickle *Mac Niocaill.* A Co. Tyrone name. Nicholls and Nicholson are occasional synonyms of it, but these are usually names of seventeenth-century or more recent immigrants, as is Nicholl without the prefix Mac.

Mac Nieve See MacNeive.

Mac Niff The Co. Leitrim form of Cunniff.

(O) Nihan See Nyhan.

(O) Nihill A form of O'Neill in Co. Clare often written *Ó Neighill* in Irish. The sept which was located in the barony of Bunratty was of the Thomond, not of the Ulster O'Neills.

(O) Nilan, Nieland See Nylan.

Mac Ninch See MacAninch.

Nipe See Knipe.

Mac Nish See MacNeish.

Mac Niven See Nevin.

(Mac) Nix *Mac Niocais.* An Irish patronymic assumed by some families of Woulfe in Co. Limerick. The two names were used synonymously up till recently.

Nixon This English name is numerous in Ulster since it was established in Co. Fermanagh at the time of the Plantation of Ulster (1609). It later became established also in Co. Wicklow. Bibl. MIF

Noakley, Nockley See Nohilly.

Noble Norman-French *le noble* (which means well-known as well as noble). This name is in Ireland continuously since the thirteenth century. It is recorded in the 1659 'census' as a principal surname in Co. Fermanagh. It is now numerous in Ulster.

Noblet(t) This Huguenot name (from the French adjective *noble*) is now found mainly in Ulster.

Nochtin, Nocton See Naghten.

(Mac) Nocker, Noctor, No(g)her See MacConnor.

(O) Nohilly *Ó Neothallaigh* or *Ó Neothaille*. A north Connacht name. Noakley is a variant.

(O) Nolan, Knowlan *Ó Nualláin* (*nuall*, shout). In early times holding hereditary office under the Kings of Leinster, the chief of this sept was known as Prince of Foherta, i.e. the barony of Forth, in the present county of Carlow where the name was and still is very numerous. A branch migrated to east Connacht and Co. Longford. In Roscommon and Mayo Nolan is used synonymously with Holohan (from the genitive plural); and in Fermanagh as an anglicized form of *Ó hUltacháin* (Hultaghan). There was also a sept of the name of Corca Laoidhe which is now well represented in Co. Kerry. IF   Map Carlow.

(O) Noonan, Nunan *Ó Nuanáin*, formerly *Ó hIonmhaineáin* (*ionmhain*, beloved). A Munster name mainly found in Co. Cork, where they were co-arbs of Tullylease and later lords of Muskerry-Noonan. IF Map Cork. See Neenan.

(O) Noone *Ó Nuadháin* (for possible derivation see O'Nowd). A sept of the Uí Fiachrach traditionally descended from Niall of the Nine Hostages, now numerous throughout Connacht. MIF   Map Sligo.

Mac Norgan See Minorgan.

Norman This name is now mainly found in Dublin. In the seventeenth and eighteenth centuries it was closely associated with Ulster, especially Co. Derry. It occurs occasionally in the thirteenth-century records in midland counties. Norman by derivation means man from the north rather than from Normandy.

(Mac) Normoyle, Normile *Mac Confhormaoile* (hound of Formoyle). A Clare name found also in Co. Limerick. MIF

Norris *Noiréis*. This name has several derivations, the most usual being Anglo-French *noreis*, northerner (in Ireland implying Norseman). Though it occurs in mediaeval records it is essentially of Elizabethan origin in Co. Cork; it is now fairly numerous in all the provinces except Connacht. MIF   See Nurse.

North See Ultagh.

Northridge This name, closely associated with Co. Cork since early eighteenth century, is said to be a synonym of Norris, but it is certainly derived from some north ridge in England.

Norton See Naghten.

Notley, Nutley These, probably derived from one of several place-names in England, are synonyms in Ireland since the seventeenth century and, apart from Dublin, mainly associated with Co. Leitrim.

(O) Nowd *Ó Nuadhat*. This name is found in Wicklow and Kildare. It is also spelt Knowd. *Nuadha* was the name of an ancient sea-god, which is a possible derivation.

Nowlan See Nolan.

Nugent *Nuinseann*. One of the hibernicized Norman families *(de Nogent)*. Members of the main branch in Co. Westmeath were found on both sides in the ever recurring wars with England; that of Co. Cork, which was located near Carrigaline, formed a sept with a chief in the Irish fashion. The latter were originally *de Winchedon*. Bibl; IF   Map Cork and Westmeath. See also Gilsenan.

Mac Nully, -Nulla See MacAnulla.

Mac Nulty *Mac an Ultaigh* (*Ultach*, Ulsterman). In Meath it is usually without the Mac, but in Louth, where it is numerous, the Mac is generally retained. IF   Map Donegal.

(O) Nunan See Noonan.

Nunn An English name closely identified with Co. Wexford since mid-seventeenth century.

Nurse, Nourse Synonyms of Norris. When so used the probable derivation is Old-French *norrice*, nurse.

Nutley See Notley.

(Mac) Nutt *Mac Nuadhat*. Fairly numerous in Ulster. For derivation see O'Nowd.

Nuttall Bibl.

Nuzam A variant spelling of Newsom in Cos. Wicklow and Wexford.

(O) Nyhan, Nihane *Ó Niatháin*. This family is on record in west Cork since 1295 and is still well known there. The form Nyhan, which has led to the current mispronunciation as *Nye*han, is of recent introduction: Nihane has the stress on the second syllable—Ne-haan. It has no connection with the Donegal name Nahane. See Nawn. MIF

Nyland, Nilan Forms of Neylan used in Co. Galway.

(O) Nynane A variant of Neenan.

O

Oakes See Darragh.

Oates A synonym by pseudo-translation of Quirke. (*Coirce* means oats).

Obins, Obbyns This, like its synonym Aubin, derives from Latin *albanus,* white. The family came to Ulster early in the seventeenth century and have since been closely associated with Co. Armagh.

Odell An English name, formerly Odle and quite incorrectly written O'Dell, connected with Co. Limerick since the mid-seventeenth century. Bibl. MIF

Odlum An English name of German derivation, an earlier form being Adlam, associated with Co. Offaly since the mid-seventeenth century. MIF

Offington See under Hovenden.

Ogan, Oogan These are synonyms of Wogan, in Cos. Louth and Dublin.

Ogilvie See under Gilbey.

Ogle Bardsley, quoting Yonge, gives the derivation as from the Icelandic name *Ogvalid.* Though from the time of its introduction in the Cromwellian period it has been mainly associated with Co. Louth, it is now mainly found in Ulster.

Oliffe An American and French variant of MacAuliffe and formerly also in Cork.

Olis, Olice, Olasagh *Eolgasach* (which means knowledgeable, but it is doubtful whether this is the derivation of Olis). Very rare but extant in Cos. Leitrim and Roscommon. Their territory was Muintir Eolais, Co. Leitrim, the chiefs of which assumed the name *Mac Raghnaill.* The Fiants record the name as Olase in Co. Wexford, 1566.

Oliver An Anglo-Norman name in Co. Louth since early fourteenth century. It is numerous in Ulster, but the best known families of the name came to Co. Limerick from England in the seventeenth century. Bibl.

Olligan A synonym in Co. Kildare of Halligan.

Ollive See Oliffe.

Olus See Olis.

Onions Used as a synonym of Oonihan and Union.

Oolahan A variant of Hoolahan in the midlands.

Oonihan See Hounihan and Unehan.

Oonin, Oonan A variant of Houneen, sometimes corrupted to Union, which is not an English name.

Orahoe A Co. Longford variant of Horohoe.

Orchard This English name, of obvious derivation, now mainly found in Ulster, occurs in Co. Wexford as a synonym of Archer. In south Tipperary Augher has been recorded as synonymous with Orchard.

Organ A south Tipperary variant of Horgan.

Ormond *Ó Ruaidh* (*ruadh*, red). The fact that this sept is found in the Ormond country is coincidental. *Ó Ruaidh* is also anglicized Roe. MIF   Map Cork-Waterford.

Ormsby The name of a Lincolnshire family which settled in Co. Mayo at the end of the sixteenth century and has since been mainly identified with north Connacht. Bibl.

Orpen This English name (derived from Old-English *eorp*, swarthy) has been in Co. Kerry since mid-seventeenth century. Bibl.

Orr A Scottish toponymic in Ireland since the seventeenth century; it has since been prominent in north-east Ulster. MIF

Osborne First settling in Cos. Waterford and Tipperary about 1550, families of this name became both influential and numerous, as the large number which appear in testamentary records, etc. testify. It is now found in all the provinces.

Mac Oscar A variant of MacCusker in north Ulster.

Mac Ostrich *Mac Osraic*. This family is said to be a branch of the Scottish clan Cameron but is not officially recognized as such. In Ireland the name is associated with Co. Cork.

Oswell An English name, also called Oswald, assumed by a branch of the *Ó hEodhusa* (Hussey) family in Ulster.

Ounihan, Onahan See Hounihan and Unehan.

Ouseley Bibl.

Ovens A locative name from Old-English *ofen*, furnace, found in Co. Fermanagh.

Mac Owen See Owens.

Owens This Welsh name is used in Ireland as a synonym of MacKeown, for which MacOwen and Owenson are other occasional substitutes. Owens is also equated with Hynes and Hinds in Ulster, but not in Connacht. IF

P

Mac Padden, Padine *Mac Páidín* (*Páidín*, a diminutive of Patrick). An Irish patronymic adopted by some families of Barrett and also of Staunton in Connacht. This is liable to be confused with MacFadden, which occurs in the same area and was written MacPadin in the seventeenth century. It has also been used as the gaelicized form of Patterson and Pattison. IF   See also MacFadden.

Page This English name, in Ireland since the sixteenth century, and in a few isolated cases earlier, is well known in east Galway as well as in Ulster, where it is gaelicized as *Mac Giolla*.

Pagnam, Pegnam Synonyms of Pakenham used in Cos. Leitrim and Fermanagh.

Paisley A Scottish toponymic (Renfrewshire). It is fairly numerous in Ulster since the first half of the seventeenth century. Some families of the name were Quakers.

Pakenham This distinguished family came to Ireland in the sixteenth century and have since been established in Co. Westmeath. Bibl. IF

Paine See Payne.

Pallas *Pailís.* The Irish word *pailís,* a palisade, derives from Old-French *palis,* a stake. However, the first to come to Ireland, in the fifteenth century, was a Lombardy banking family originally called de Palatio. The name is mainly associated with Oriel.

Pallin Since the time of John Pallin, a Cromwellian 'adventurer', this name has been found in small numbers in Dublin and in some midland counties.

Palliser Bibl.

Palmer This is essentially an English name of Norman origin *le paumer,* the palmer or pilgrim. As such it is on record in Ireland since the thirteenth century. For its occasional use as the synonym of an Irish name see Mullover. Bibl. MIF

Panneen This is said to be a synonym of Fanning in Co. Limerick.

Parish See Parris.

Parker *Paircéir.* Derived from the Old-French *parquier* (parkkeeper) it is on record in Ireland since mediaeval times and is prominent in the 1659 'census', appearing as 'tituladoes' in all the provinces. Most Irish Parkers of the present day, who are mainly found in Ulster, are more recent immigrants.

Parke(s) App.

Parkinson An English name in east Ulster since mid-17th century.

Parle, Parill This name, derived from a diminutive of Peter, is on record in Co. Wexford since the sixteenth century and is still, apart from a few families in Co. Clare, almost exclusively found there. The Parles of Co. Clare are probably descended from the Parrells who occupied the island of Islandeady from the fifteenth to the seventeenth century. MIF

(Mac) Parlon Parlon and Parlone are found in Co. Offaly. See Partlan and Parnell.

Parnell This name is one of the many derivatives from Peter. It is famous in Ireland both in politics and literature since the family came from Cheshire early in the seventeenth century. The branch to which Charles Stewart Parnell belonged was established in Co. Wicklow, but the name is otherwise chiefly associated with Co. Longford and Dublin. In the Roscrea district some Parlons changed their name to Parnell. Bibl. IF

Parogan, Parrican, Patrican, Patchy These are local corruptions of Fitzpatrick found in Co. Dublin.

Parris An English name of dual derivation (from Paris, the city, and an abbreviation of Patricius). Rare in Ireland but associated with Youghal, Co. Cork, from early fourteenth century and later found also in Leinster. Parish is a variant of it—from Paris—not from the word parish. Pharis is a synonym of Farris not of Parris.

Parsons This name is best known as that of an Anglo-Irish family of note settled at Birr (Parsonstown) at the end of the sixteenth century. The Gaelic name *Mac an Phearsain* (MacPherson in Scotland) has occasionally been abbreviated to Parsons. IF

(Mac) Partlan, Parlan *Mac Parthaláin*. In Ulster this name, which is that of the Oriel sept, notable as poets and scribes, is much confused with the Scottish MacFarlane. Bartley is a synonym. MIF   Map Armagh.

Partridge An English name (taken from the bird) which came to Ireland under the Cromwellian régime. It is not closely identified with any particular part of the country. In some cases it has been changed to Partrick and Patrick.

Patrick Most people of this name are of Scottish origin. Patrick or MacPatrick is a sept of the clan Lamont. It does, however, occasionally occur as Patrick in mediaeval Anglo-Irish records and later as an abbreviated form of Mulpatrick, i.e. *Ó Maolphádraig* (devotee of St. Patrick), a Longford sept, now almost extinct, or even of Fitzpatrick. MIF

Patten, Pat(t)on See Peyton.

Patterson, Pattison These English names are very numerous in Ulster. In Co. Galway they are absurdly used as synonyms of Cussane (the English word path is *casán* in Irish). Bibl. See MacPadden.

(Mac) Paul A synonym of MacPhail, MacFall. The English surname Paul is quite distinct.

Pay See Pey.

Payne The antiquity of this English name in Ireland is evident from its frequency in the fourteenth-century records and from the fact that the Tudor Fiants mention no less than six places called Payneston in five Leinster counties and in Tipperary. In later times it has been mainly found in Dublin. See Pyne.

Payton See Peyton.

Peacock This English name is now found in all the provinces. It is on record in Co. Meath since the beginning of the fifteenth century.

Mac Peake *Mac Péice* (*péic* is not an Irish word; probably from Old-English *peac*, a thickset man). The prefix Mac is always retained in its homeland, Cos. Derry and Tyrone. Elsewhere, without the Mac, it can be of English origin. MIF

Peard This family was established in Co. Cork in the seventeenth century and has been closely associated with that county since. See Peart.

Pearse See Pierce.

Pearson (son of Piers). Introduced mainly in the seventeenth century this name became very numerous in Leinster in the eighteenth century and is now found in many parts of the country.

Peart Distinct from Peard. The main family came from Newark-on-Trent in the eighteenth century, but the name as Peart is on record in Co. Kilkenny in 1659. Peart possibly a variant of Perrot; Peard is a form of pear-head.

Pedlow (From French *pied de loup*). Now numerous in Cos. Armagh and Antrim, but of comparatively recent introduction.

Peebles This Scottish toponymic is used as a synonym of Peoples in Ulster.

Peery See under Perry.

Pegnam See Pagnam.

Pelly Several derivations, both English and French, have been suggested for this name. In Ireland it is mainly found in Cos. Galway and Roscommon. It was well established in Co. Galway when in 1656 the main family was among the transplanted 'papists'. MIF

Pembroke This Welsh toponymic, which occurs in mediaeval Irish records, became permanently established in Cos. Kerry and Kilkenny in the seventeenth century.

Pender, Pendy, Pinder These are abbreviated forms of Prendergast.

Penn For connection with Co. Cork see Bibl.

Pennefather This English name (from penny father), which has Pennyfeather, Panfare etc. as variants, is of Cromwellian origin in Ireland. It has been prominent among the Anglo-Irish landed gentry in Munster and Leinster. Bibl.

Penny This name was in Dublin as early as 1296. The numerous Pennys of Co. Cork are comparatively recent immigrants.

Penrose This name derives from Penrose in Cornwall, where the family originated; they moved to Yorkshire, and thence to Ireland (Cos. Waterford and Wicklow, where they were prominent as Quakers) at the end of the seventeenth century.

Pentheny, Pentony First appearing in Co. Meath in the twelfth century families of this name have since been continuously settled in Cos. Meath, Louth and Dublin. The earlier form of this name was (de) Repenteny, being formed from a place in France. The abbreviated forms Penteny etc. came into use at the end of the fourteenth century. It is not therefore an English toponymic. Bibl.

Peoples In Irish this Donegal name is *Ó Duibhne* which is also anglicized Deeney. Its resemblance in sound to the Irish word *daoine* (people) gave rise to this example of absurd pseudo-translation. MIF

Peppard A Norman family identified with Co. Louth from 1185. The Co. Wexford Peppards are a branch of that family. Pepper is a synonym of it. MIF   Map Louth-Meath.

Perdue The name, derived from the words *par Dieu,* of a Huguenot family first settled in the Youghal area of Co. Cork.

Perrill See Parle.

Perrot This name, a derivative of Peter, was in Munster in the sixteenth century and now belongs mainly to Co. Cork. Irish Perrots do not descend from the famous English Lord-Deputy, Sir John Perrot.

Perry An English name well known in Munster from the first half of the seventeenth century; now mainly found in Ulster. Pirrie, of similar derivation (pear-tree) is a synonym there. Pery and Peery, of which Peere is an earlier form, appear in the Plantation of Ulster and as a Cromwellian immigrant. In its various forms the name, mostly as Perry, has since been found in all parts of Ireland, in some cases as that of later settlers.

Persse The name (a variant of Pearse) of a landed family established in Co. Galway in 1700, previously in Co. Kildare.

Peters See MacFeeters.

Petit See Petty.

Pettigrew This name came to Ulster in the seventeenth century being that of one of the Huguenot immigrant families. They first settled in Co. Tyrone. The name is now numerous in Belfast and adjacent areas particularly in the form Petticrew. Some of these are probably settlers from Scotland, where the name appears as early as 1296. It is derived from the French *petit cru* meaning small growth.

Petty This is basically the same as Petit or Pettitt, which is a much more numerous name. The Petits were early settlers in Meath. The principal Petty family was established in Co. Kerry by the famous Sir William Petty in the seventeenth century. Little, by translation, is a synonym in Co. Wexford.

Pey, Pay Probably from St. Pega. Mainly of Co. Kilkenny: five of the name, outlawed as Jacobites, were all from Co. Kilkenny.

Peyton, Payton, Patton In Donegal, where these names are mainly found, they are anglicized forms of *Ó Peatáin* (probably another diminutive of Patrick) which is on record at Ballybofey as far back as 1178. Elsewhere Patton and Payton are English toponymics. Bibl. MIF   Map Donegal.

Mac Phail Sometimes a form of MacFall, and mainly of Scottish origin. MacPhail is also Manx, cognate with Quayle. See Veale.

Phair, Fair One of the adjectival surnames, in this case a translation of *fionn*. It is scattered and not numerous.

Pharis See under Parris.

Mac Pharlon A variant of MacParlan.

Mac Phelimy, -Philemy *Mac Feidhlimidh* (son of Phelim). This name is mainly associated with Co. Tyrone.

(O) Phelan *Ó Faoláin (faol,* wolf). One of the principal septs of the southeast. Before the Norman invasion their chief was Prince of the Decies. In west Ulster it is *Ó Fialáin* a distinct bardic family. IF   Map Kilkenny and Waterford.

Mac Phelim An abbreviated form of MacPhelimy.

Phibbs An Irish variant of the English Phipps (Phip a pet name for Philip), mainly associated with Co. Sligo, especially in the eighteenth century.

Philan See Phylan.

(Mac) Philbin *Mac Philbín* (a diminutive of Philip). The name of one of the hibernicized branches of the Connacht Burkes which formed a sept of the Irish type. O'Donovan says there were two branches, one in Mayo and one in Co. Galway. MIF   Map Mayo.

Phillips In modern times this English name has to some extent taken the place of Philbin. With the prefix Mac it is found in Cavan and Monaghan and there it is usually a branch of the Scottish clan MacDonnell of Keppoch.

Phylan, Fyland These are usually variants of Phelan in use in Westmeath and north Offaly. Phylan, Philan and Fyland are extant in Offaly and adjacent areas where they are definitely for *Ó Faoláin*. Phylan may also be a distinct name, viz., *Ó Fialáin* a bardic family of Ulster, now rare and called Phelan.

Piatt A Huguenot name.

Picken(s) A Scottish toponymic (Aberdeenshire) in Co. Cavan since the seventeenth century.

Pidgeon, Fidgeon Corrupt forms of MacWiggin found in Co. Monaghan. See MacGuigan.

Pierce, Pearse *Piaras, Mac Piarais.* An Anglo-Irish name mainly found in east Leinster. The Pierces or MacPierces of Kerry, who played an important part on the Irish side in the Desmond wars, were a branch of the Fitzmaurices. Bibl IF

Pigot, Piggott (From the Old-French personal name *Pic*). Well known in Ireland since the sixteenth century this name has been located in many parts of the country and has been conspicuous on both sides in the centuries-long struggle between Ireland and England. The Co. Cork Pigots were originally Becket. MIF

Pike See Pyke.

Pilkington This English toponymic is not specially identified with any particular area in Ireland. It first appears in Co. Louth early in the fifteenth century and later, in the Cromwellian period, in Cos. Kilkenny and Meath, while in the nineteenth century it was fairly numerous in Co. Clare. Bibl.

Pillion This name, of uncertain derivation, is now mainly found in Co. Offaly. It first appears in Cork in early eighteenth century.

Pim Prominent in Quaker records, this name came to Ireland in mid-seventeenth century and has since been identified with Co. Leix as well as Dublin.

Pinder See Pender.

Pindy See Prendeville.

Pinkerton App.

Piper An English occupational name; occasionally a synonym of Peppard.

Piphoe, Phypoe Of frequent occurrence in mediaeval Irish records but now very rare. Bibl.

Pirrie See Perry.

Plant This English name, of dual origin, is on record in East Anglia in 1262; it appears in Ireland in the seventeenth century and subsequently became identified with two areas, Cos. Longford and Wicklow.

Plover An anglicized form of MacPhilbin found in Co. Mayo. *Pilibín,* i.e. little Philip, is the Irish word for plover.

Plummer This English (Wiltshire) family first settled in Co. Cork in the seventeenth century and later became well known in Co. Limerick. The name is of the occupational type. Basically Plummer (plumber) and Plumer (dealer in plumes or feathers) are of different derivations but formerly they were used as variants.

Plunket(t) *Pluincéid.* Of French origin, this family came to Ireland at the time of the Anglo-Norman invasion and became one of the most distinguished in Irish history. IF   Bibl; Map Meath.

Pockrich Derived from the English place-name Puckridge this name has been well known in Co. Monaghan since mid-seventeenth century.

Poe The best known families of this name in Ireland are of Cromwellian origin and belong to Cos. Tipperary and Kilkenny. It was, however, in Co. Tyrone earlier in the seventeenth century. Bibl.

le Poer The earlier form of Power. Bibl.

Pogue, Poak, Poke These names are synonyms of Pollock, which is very numerous in north-east Ulster. They appear in the Antrim hearth money rolls of the 1660's.

Polan(d) See next entry.

(Mac) Polin *Mac Póilín* (a diminutive of *Pól,* Paul). This name, which belongs to Cos. Armagh and Down, is there sometimes called Poland. The latter, however, is mainly found in Co. Offaly. MIF

Pollard An English name usually denoting close-cropped head, but sometimes a derivative of Paul. The main family came to Ireland in the fourteenth century and settled in Co. Westmeath at the place now called Castlepollard.

Pollexfen Bibl.

Pollock Bibl. See Pogue.

Ponsonby An influential Anglo-Irish family for two centuries from mid-seventeenth, when they acquired estates in Kerry and Kilkenny. That of the latter branch, whose head became Earl of Bessborough, was very extensive. Bibl.

Poots App.

Poole Bibl.

Pope Though mainly of seventeenth-century introduction this name was in Dublin in the sixteenth. It was numerous in Co. Waterford a century ago but is less so now.

Porteous, Portis This Scottish name, of legal connotation, first appears as Portesse and Portas in the person of an army officer in 1563 resident in Queen's County (Leix). The family settled in Co. Kilkenny where the name is still found. It is also in Ulster.

Porter Though essentially English in origin there are few names which occur more widely in every kind of Irish record relating to all the provinces, except Connacht, from the thirteenth century to modern times. It is numerous now, especially in Ulster. App; MIF

Potter This appears as *le Poter* in Dublin in the thirteenth century and is now found in small numbers in all the provinces. MIF

Powderley My suggestion that this is an Irish toponymic from Power-lough in Co. Meath is supported by the fact that references to the surname since 1750 are nearly all to Co. Meath or Louth. I have not met it earlier than that date.

Powell This Welsh name *(Ap Howell)*, found in small numbers in all the provinces, is also an occasional synonym of Guilfoyle.

Power *de Paor*. One of the most completely hibernicized of the names introduced at the time of the Anglo-Norman invasion, it is now among the fifty most numerous Irish names, being found mainly in Waterford and adjoining counties. The *de* in the Irish form should be *le,*—the poor man, consequent on a vow. Bibl. MIF   Map Waterford.

Power-O'Shea Bibl.

Poyntz See Punch.

Pratt This English name, in Co. Cork before the Cromwellian immigration, is now numerous in the south-east. Bibl.

Prendergast *de Priondragás*. One of the powerful families which came to Ireland at the time of the Anglo-Norman invasion. They are still found mainly in the places of their original settlement (as Map). Some of those in Mayo assumed the name Fitzmaurice. IF
Map Mayo and Tipperary. See next entry.

Prende(r)ville This family, of Norman origin, is in Kerry since the thirteenth century. The name has been abbreviated to Pendy and even Pindy, as also has Prendergast.

Prenty A variant of Prunty.

Prescott First on record in Meath in the fifteenth century, families of the name became established in Co. Kilkenny early in the seventeenth century. It is now mainly found in Dublin and Belfast. The derivation is from Old-English words meaning priest's cottage.

Preston A distinguished name in Ireland since the family became established here at the end of the thirteenth century. Bibl. IF MIF
Map Meath.

(O) Prey, Pray *a Préith, Ó Préith* (colloq.) According to Prof. M. A. O'Brien this name is of Pictish origin. It belongs to Co. Down. Prey has been recorded in Co. Armagh as a synonym of Dupré. MIF 319.

Priall, Pryell This name is recorded after 1800 in Mayo and Clare. It occurs twice in Co. Tipperary hearth money rolls, 1666. Its origin is uncertain: possibly from the French *Prille*.

Price Welsh *Ap Rhys*. In Ireland since the fourteenth century but not specially associated with any particular locality. Price is sometimes a synonym of Bryson.

Pringle An abbreviated form of the Scottish toponymic Hoppringle: it first appears in Co. Down in the mid-seventeenth century, later mainly in Cos. Tyrone and Armagh.

Prior *Mac an Phríora*. The Priors of Cavan and Leitrim are usually of this Gaelic-Irish stock: elsewhere they may be of Anglo-Norman origin, especially those who appear in mediaeval records. Friar and Fryar are variants of this in Oriel, Friary in Co. Longford and Freer in south midlands. These are derived from Old-French *frere,* friar, but *Príor* in Irish denotes prior not friar. MIF

Pritchard See Uprichard.

Proctor Coming from the north of England as soldiers, families of this occupational name settled in Cos. Armagh and Donegal in midseventeenth century. The name occurs occasionally in mediaeval records relating to Co. Antrim.

Proudfoot Though rare now this name occurs frequently in Irish records relating to Cos. Cork and Meath from the end of the thirteenth century. Those of Meath predominate later. The place-name Proudfootstown locates these.

Prout (Norman *prout*, proud). In Ormond since the thirteenth century, but rare now. The older anglicized form Proud is still extant.

(O) Prunty, Pronty *Ó Proinntigh (proinnteach,* bestower, generous person). This east Ulster name is better known to the world as Brontë, a variant assumed by the father of the well-known authoresses. MIF

Pryell See Priall.

Punch *Puinse*. This name of Norman origin (derived from Pontius) was first established in Co. Kildare *c.* 1290 and later associated with

Munster. Its older form Poyntz is in Armagh but did not come there till the seventeenth century. MIF 199.

Purcell *Puirséil.* (French *pourcel,* little pig). This Anglo-Norman family is one of those which became completely hibernicized. They distinguished themselves in the wars of the seventeenth century and later as Wild Geese. Bibl. IF   Map Tipperary.

Purdon Families of this name, an English toponymic, were established in Cos. Clare and Limerick early in the seventeenth century; later a branch went to Co. Cork. MIF

Purdy The older form of this name, Purdue, gives a clue to its derivation, *Pour Dieu.* It has been fairly numerous in north-east Ulster since the seventeenth century.

Purtill In Ireland Purtill is not, as has been stated, a form of the English Porthill: it is a variant of Purcell found in Cos. Clare and Tipperary. MIF

Pyke, Pike Alternative derivations are from the tool, the fish or the Scandinavian *pik,* a tall thin person. It appears at Youghal in 1393 and in later centuries was found also in Cos. Waterford and Tipperary. It is one of those Anglo-Irish names which has had little connection with Ulster, though occasionally used there as a synonym of MacPeake.

Pyne This name is sometimes confused with Payne (which is *paganus*). Pyne is analogous with pine-tree. It has been located mainly in Co. Cork and is on record since 1599, mainly, but not entirely, as Protestant gentry. MIF

Pyper, Piper In Co. Limerick, where it has now become rare, this is a Palatine name. It is more numerous in Ulster, but there it is of English occupational origin.

Q

Qua This name is on record in Co. Armagh in 1660 and is still there. The form in Irish is uncertain; Qua is possibly an abbreviation of MacQuaid or MacQuey. See Quee.

Mac Quaid, -Quade *Mac Uaid* (son of Wat). A well-known name in Co. Monaghan and adjacent areas. Without the prefix Mac this name is found in Co. Limerick. IF   MIF

Quail, Quayle See Queale.

Quain See Quane.

Qualey A variant of Queally.

Qualter *Mac Ualtair.* A syncopated form of MacWalter in use in north Galway and Mayo for this branch of the Connacht Burkes. MIF

(O) Quane, Quan *Ó Cuain* (from the forename Cuan not from St. Cuan).

This family originated in Co. Sligo, but for the past three centuries it has been mainly associated with Co. Waterford. MIF

Quaney A Roscommon variant of Queeney.

Quarry (Old-French *quarré*, squarely built). A Huguenot name in Cos. Cork and Waterford. In Ulster, however, it is an abbreviation of the Scottish and Manx MacQuarrie, *Mac Guaire* (*guaire*, noble).

Mac Quatter(s) See Waters.

Mac Quay See MacQuey.

(Mac) Queale Usually Manx *Mac Fhail*; it may also be a form of *Mac Céile* in Connacht. Quail, now the usual spelling, is mainly found in Louth and east Ulster. MIF   See MacPhail.

(O) Queally *Ó Caollaidhe*. In addition to that of Co. Kilkenny (as Map) there was an important sept of O'Queally in north Clare. The confusion which has inevitably arisen between Queally, Keally, Keeley, Kiely, etc. is discussed in MIF   Map Kilkenny.

Quearney, Querney A Co. Leix name. Richard Foley's suggestion that it is a by-form of Ahern is conjectural.

Quee A Co. Antrim name, possibly for the Scottish MacQuey.

(O) Queelty See Quilty.

Mac Queen *Mac Shuibhne* (derivation as MacSweeney). The name of a Scottish clan: fairly numerous in Ulster. Without the Mac, Queen is an occasional synonym of Quinn in Oriel.

(O) Queenan *Ó Cuineáin*. (Woulfe says this is an attenuated form of Conan). This name is almost peculiar to Cos. Sligo and Roscommon. It is distinct from Kinnane. Cunnane is an occasional variant in Connacht.

Mac Queeney This is used synonymously with MacWeeney in Co. Roscommon and occasionally with Mulqueeney in Co. Clare, as also is Maqueeney. Its use as a variant of Mawhinney is rare. For Irish form see MacQueen.

Quemerford A variant of Comerford now almost obsolete.

Quentin See Quinton.

Mac Question, Quiston See MacCutcheon.

Mac Quey, -Quay Scottish forms of *Mac Aodha* (MacKay).

Quick A well-known English (Devon) name. It is sometimes used as a synonym of Quirke in Co. Cork.

(O) Quiddihy See Cuddihy.

(O) Quigg *Ó Cuaig*. This is the correct Irish form of the Derry sept of O'Quigg. Quig(g) has been used as an abbreviated form of Quigley, which has also the variant Twigley. Fivey, found in Co. Down, is another synonym mistakenly arising from the Irish word *cúig* (five). Quigg belongs mainly to Co. Derry but is also found in Co. Monaghan. MIF

Mac Quiggin *Mac Guaigín.* This Ulster name is now frequently anglicized as MacGuiggin. See also MacGuigan.

(O) Quigley *Ó Coigligh.* (Woulfe says it is derived from *coigeal,* denoting a person with unkempt hair, which is conjectural.) This sept of the Uí Fiacrach is now dispersed and the name is found throughout Ireland. It is most numerous in Donegal and Derry. In Co. Wexford it is called Cogley, while Kegley is used in Meath. IF   Map Mayo. See Quigg.

Quigney A Clare name, possibly a corruption of Quigley.

(Mac) Quilkin *Mac Uilcín.* In Connacht, where the prefix is no longer used in the anglicized form, this name is that of a branch of the Stauntons of Mayo now usually called Culkin or Culkeen. It is fairly well known in Co. Galway. Brian Merriman's mother was of that family. When found in north Ulster as MacQuilkin this may be a synonym of MacKellican, a branch of the Scottish clan MacKintosh.

(O) Quill *Ó Cuill.* Families of this ancient bardic Kerry sept are also found in Co. Cork. The name has been mistranslated Woods (*col,* genitive *cuill,* means hazel). MIF   Map Kerry.

Mac Quillan *Mac Uighilín.* This is the name taken by the Cambro-Norman family of Mandeville which developed into an Irish sept, and became lords of the Route. It spread to Oriel and adjacent counties where it is reported as having been changed to MacCullen— whence even Cullen—and also occasionally to MacWilliam. Bibl. IF   Map Antrim. See MacCollin.

(O) Quillenane A form of Cullinane found in Cos. Clare and Waterford.

Mac Quilliams A variant of MacWilliams in Co. Derry.

(O) Quilligan *Ó Cuileagáin.* This Thomond name, which is possibly an attenuated form of Colgan, is equally well known in its variant form Culligan. SIF   Map Clare.

Mac Quilly *Mac an Choiligh* (presumably from *coileach,* cock). This Co. Roscommon name, and its variants MacGilly and Magilly *(Mag Coiligh)* which are in use in Co. Monaghan, have been extensively changed to the English name Cox. Fr. Livingstone states that Cox in Fermanagh is *Mac Giolla.* The MacQuillys of Co. Roscommon were an erenagh family. Sometimes the Irish form *Ó Coiligh* is found. Map Roscommon. IF

Quilter Norman *le cuilter* (maker of quilts). This name has long been associated with north Kerry since the mediaeval period. The derivation from cutler is erroneous.

(O) Quilty *Ó Caoilte.* Quilty is mainly found in Munster, especially in Co. Limerick; the same name, as Kielty and Keelty, is more usual in Connacht. Kielty, Keeltagh, and O'Kielt are also sometimes used in Down and neighbouring Ulster counties as synonyms of Small (supposedly from *caol*, slender) and Woods (equally erroneously from *coillte*, woods). MIF

(O) Quinane A variant of Kinnane.

(O) Quinlan *Ó Caoinleáin.* The Munster (mainly Co. Tipperary) form of *Ó Caoindealbháin,* which in Leinster, where the sept originated, was usually anglicized as Kindellan and has now often been absorbed by the more common names Connellan or even Conlan. They were of the southern Uí Néill, the senior line of the descendants of Laoghaire, king of Ireland in the time of St. Patrick. IF   See next entry.

(O) Quinlevan A Clare form of *Ó Caoindealbháin.* Woulfe gives gracefully shaped for *caoindealbhain.* See previous entry.

(O) Quinlish, Quinlisk *Ó Cuindlis.* A name now of north Tipperary, the older forms Conliss and Cunlish belong historically to Connacht where they are still found. MIF

(Mac) Quin(n) *Mac Cuinn.* A Kerry name distinct from O'Quinn. MIF

(O) Quin(n) The most numerous surname in Tyrone and very numerous in all the provinces, it is that of four distinct septs as in Map. Properly Quinn in Irish is *Ó Cuinn,* from the personal name *Conn;* but in Ulster it is often *Ó Coinne,* more correctly anglicized Quinney. IF   Map Antrim, Clare, Longford and Tyrone.

Quinnell Woulfe says this is an abbreviated form of Quinnelly. Reaney says Quinnell is an English name and dates from the eleventh century and is derived from Old-English words meaning woman-war. It was formerly well known in Cos. Cork and Tipperary.

(Mac) Quinnelly *Mac Coingheallaigh,* also *Ó Coingheallaigh* (faithful to pledges). A west Cork name.

Mac Quinney This is a variant of MacWhinney or Mawhinney.

(O) Quinney *Ó Coinne.* The Ulster name Quinney is now rare. *Ó Coinne* is also anglicized Cunny which is quite numerous in Co. Sligo, but sometimes changed to Quinn. According to Woulfe it derives from the forename *Coinneach* alias Canice or Kenny. Map Tyrone.

(Mac) Quinniff See Cunniff.

Quinton, Quentin The usual derivation of this surname is from the French St. Quentin. It has been in Ireland in small numbers since the fourteenth century, but is not closely identified with any particular locality.

(O) Quirke *Ó Cuirc* (possibly from *corc,* heart). The name of one of the leading septs of Clanwilliam for which a number of synonyms have been used, e.g. Kirke, Quick, Oates, the last by mistranslation— *coirce* means oats. MIF   Map Tipperary.

Mac Quinter See Whirter.

Quish, Cush *Mac Coise* (the derivation from *cos,* leg, denoting a courier, is conjectural). This name, found in Cos. Limerick and Cork, is distinct from O'Quish. The latter, as O'Coishe is recorded in the sixteenth century Fiants as of Leix and as Quish is now in south Tipperary.

Mac Quiston See MacQuestion and Houston.

Mac Quitty *Mac Faoithigh.* Also anglicized MacWhitty and White or MacWhite.

(Mac) Quoid, Coyd Variants of MacQuaid found in north-east Ulster.

R

Rabbitt(e) This apparently English name is hardly ever of English origin in Ireland: *coinín* being the Irish for rabbit it does duty for Cunneen, Cunneeny, Conheeny, Cunnane and Kinneen in Clare, Galway Mayo and Offaly.

Rackard This is a modern form of MacRickard, which itself is the name of a branch of the Butlers and possibly also of the Kavanaghs. It belongs mainly to Co. Wexford. MIF

(O) Ractigan, Radigan variants of Ratigan in north Connacht.

Radford An English toponymic, in Co. Wexford continuously since the sixteenth century. **Radwell** See page 304.

Mac Rae A rare synonym of MacCrea. See Rea.

Rafe See Ralph.

(O) Rafferty *Ó Raithbheartaigh,* mod. *Ó Raifeartaigh.* Though etymologically this (from *rath bheartach,* prosperity wielder) is distinct from *Ó Robhartaigh* (from *robharta,* full tide) anglicized O'Roarty, these two names have been treated as one, at least since the fifteenth century. As co-arbs of St. Columcille on Tory Island Roarty is now mainly Co. Donegal while Rafferty is of Co. Tyrone and Co. Louth. IF MIF   Map Donegal.

(O) Rafter, Raftiss *Ó Reachtabhair (reacht,* decree). A small sept of Co. Kilkenny. The form Raftiss is due to the local pronunciation of slender R in the now extinct south Leinster dialect of Irish. Rafter is an occasional variant of Raftery in Co. Mayo. MIF

(O) Raftery *Ó Reachtaire* (earlier form *Ó Reachtabhra : reacht,* decree). A Connacht sept mainly associated with Co. Mayo.

Ragget *(le ragged,* untidy). One of the 'Tribes of Kilkenny'.

(O) Raghteen *Ó Raichtín.* Formerly widely used for Raftery in Co. Galway; to be distinguished from Raghtneen but presumably of the same origin.

(O) Raghtigan See Ratigan.

(O) Raghtneen See Roughneen.

Raher See Fraher.

(O) Rahill, Rhall, Rall Breffny forms of *Ó Raghaill.* See Ryle and Reighhill.

(O) Rahilly *Ó Raithile*. This well-known Munster family originated as a branch of the Cenél Eoghain in Ulster but has long been closely associated with west Munster, the poet Egan O'Rahilly for example was a Kerryman. IF   Map Kerry.

Rainey An English name numerous in Ulster. Also a variant of Reaney.

Raleigh See Rawley.

Rally A name mainly found in Cos. Offaly and Westmeath where it is a synonym of Raleigh. Possibly, as Woulfe suggests, it stands also for Reilly there.

Ralph, Rafe Rolfe is used as a synonym of Ralph though they are, in fact, derived from two different forenames. As Rauf it appears at Drogheda in 1311. It is now mainly found in east Leinster. Rafe has been used synonymously with Reap in Co. Mayo.

Ralston A variant of Rolston.

Ram This English name, of obvious derivation, prominent in Co. Wexford in the seventeenth and eighteenth centuries, is now almost obsolete.

Ramsey App.

(O) Ranaghan A variant spelling of Renehan both in Munster and Oriel.

Randles A variant of Reynolds.

Rankin (a diminutive form of Randolph). In Derry and adjacent counties, where it is numerous, Rankin is a Scottish name, that of a branch of the clan Maclean. It came to Ireland with the Plantation of Ulster at the beginning of the seventeenth century. The mediaeval MacRancan family of Westmeath is no longer extant. MIF

Mac Rann A variant of MacCrann.

Mac Rannall *Mac Raghnaill*. (*Raghnal* is equated with Reginald). Its synonym, the English name Reynolds, often with prefix Mac in Ulster, has to a very large extent displaced the older MacRannall. The chief of the name was called MacGrannill of Moynish, a form of the name which survives as Grannell in Co. Wexford. Bibl. IF   Map Leitrim. See Olis.

Rapenteny See Penthony.

Ratchford A Wexford variant of Rochford.

Rath A rare toponymic still extant in east Leinster, especially in Co. Louth. It is also an occasional abbreviation of MacIlwraith found in Co. Derry.

Rathborne Bibl.

(O) Ratigan *Ó Reachtagáin* (*reacht*, decree). This appears as an O name since the fifteenth century, though in twelfth-century charters it is given the prefix Mac. The family were co-arbs of St. Finnen in Co. Roscommon. Variants are Ractigan, Rattican, Rhatigan, etc. MIF Map Roscommon.

Ratty An occasional abbreviation of Hanratty, or of Radcliffe, both being reported in the Dublin area.

Raughter See Rafter.

(O) Raverty The Oriel form of Rafferty.

Ravey A variant spelling of Reavy.

(O) Rawe An Antrim name, the Gaelic form of which is uncertain. See Reeves and Rea.

Rawl See Reighill.

Rawley, Raleigh A toponymic of English origin. The family was established in the late sixteenth century in Co. Limerick, where Rawleystown, formally Ballinrawley, locates them. There is evidence to suggest that the de Rallye, alias de Rolly, who was described in 1307 as of Any, Co. Limerick, was their ancestor. Rawley has occasionally been used as an anglicized form of Rahilly. MIF See Rally.

Ray In Ireland this can be a corrupt form of Reavey, or a variant of Rea and of Wray. The English name Ray is cognate with Roy.

Raycroft See Roycroft.

Raymond A variant of Redmond, mainly found in Cos. Cork and Kerry.

Rea See MacCrea, Reagh, Reavy and Wray: Rea and also Raw have been used synonymously with all these names. The great majority of people called Rea are of Co. Antrim or adjacent areas, where the name is frequently an abbreviation of MacCrea. Bibl. MIF See Ray.

Read See Reid.

Ready This is used as a synonym of both Reidy and Reddy, the former mostly in Munster. With prefix Mac it is a synonym of MacCready.

Reagh *Riabhach* (grey or brindled). An adjectival surname which took the place of a hereditary surname. It is nowhere numerous.

Real See Ryle.

(O) Reaney *Ó Raighne* (a form of Reginald). The name of an old Westmeath family where the place-name Clonyrina *(Cluain Uí Raighne)* indicates their location. Reaney is also an English name, usually spelt Rainey as such. MIF

Reap, Reapy *Ó Réabaigh*. Reap, also called Rape, belongs exclusively to Co. Mayo. Reapy is found also in Co. Galway. See Ralph.

(O) Rearden See Riordan.

(Mac) Reavey See MacGreevy.

(O) Reavey *Ó Riabhaigh* (for derivation see Reagh). The name of a Co. Down family.

Reckle See Reighill.

Recraft See Roycroft.

(O) Redahan *Ó Roideacháin* in Mayo. Rodahan or Rodaughan and Rudican are variants found in Co. Longford and Redican in Clare. For its Leitrim form see Roddy. MIF

(O) Reddan *Ó Roideáin*. An attenuated form of *Ó Rodáin*, see Rudden. A Dalcassian sept. The main family were hereditary stewards to the O'Briens in east Clare. MIF   Map Clare.

Reddington An English name much used as a synonym of Mulderrig and occasionally of Redehan.

(O) Reddy *Ó Roidigh*. An attenuated form of *Ó Rodaigh* (see Roddy). This name is mainly associated with Co. Kilkenny where Reddysland indicates the location of the family. MIF

(O) Redican See Redahan.

Redmond *Réamonn*. A Hiberno-Norman family of importance throughout Irish history. They are associated almost entirely with south Wexford. The branch of the MacMurroughs in the north of that county, some of whom adopted the name Redmond whose chief was called Mac Davymore, are quite distinct from the MacRedmonds. Bibl. IF   Map Wexford.

Mac Redmond *Mac Réamoinn*. The name of a branch of the Burkes in Connacht now found in Offaly. Map Galway.

Mac Reedy See MacCready.

(O) Reen A variant of Ring in west Cork. **(O) Reehil** See Reighill.

(O) Reenan *Ó Rianáin*. An Oriel name.

Mac Reery See Mac Creery.

Reeves, Ryves This name formerly disguised *Ó Rimheadha* (O'Rive), the name of an ancient but now apparently extinct Co. Down family for which no other anglicized form survives, unless it be O'Rawe. The many Reeves families now in Ireland are of English origin, some of whom have been in the country since early seventeenth century.

(O) Regan *Ó Riagain*. *Ó Réagain* is used in Co. Waterford. There are three septs of this name as indicated in Map. That shown as of Leix was in early times one of the 'Tribes of Tara'. The eponymous ancestors of the Thomond sept were akin to Brian Boru. The third was akin to the MacCarthys. IF   MIF   Map Clare, Cork and Leix.

Rehan An American synonym of Crehan.

Rehill See Reighill.

Reid, Reade This English name is very numerous in Ulster. When not that of a settler family, in Ireland it is used as a synonym by semi-translation of Mulderrig (*dearg*, red) but also occasionally by abbreviation of Mulready. As an English name it has three derivations including the colour red. App.

(O) Reidy *Ó Riada* (possibly from the old word *riad*, driving or career). The head of this Dalcassian sept was at one period in mediaeval times known as King of Aradh in the present Co. Tipperary. They were forced to migrate westwards and are now mainly found in Clare and Kerry. MIF   Map Tipperary.

(O) Reighill *Ó Raghaill*, now often *Ó Reighill*. A Fermanagh name also called Reckle there. Rehill, Reehill and Rahill are variants found in Cos. Longford and Cavan. Woulfe's statement that these are etymologically the same as the Kerry name Ryle may perhaps be correct, but they seem to have no genealogical connection with the Kerry sept.

(O) Reilly *Ó Raghailligh.* One of the most numerous names in Ireland, especially so in Co. Cavan. The prefix O has been widely resumed in the anglicized form. The head of this important sept was chief of Breffny O'Reilly. Bibl. IF   Map Cavan-Meath.

(O) Reiny A form of *Ó Raighne* found in west Cork. See Reaney.

(O) Relehan *Ó Roileacháin.* Originally an Antrim family, now peculiar to Co. Kerry and west Cork.

Rellis I presume this name, found in Wexford and some other Leinster counties, is a variant of *Mag Riallghuis,* which is anglicized Grealish in Connacht.

Renan This is an abbreviated form of Mulrennan found in Co. Donegal.

(O) Renehan, Ronaghan *Ó Reannacháin (reannach* has two meanings: sharp-pointed and starry). Of the anglicized forms the former is found in Co. Cork, the latter in Co. Monaghan, being long associated with Oriel. The synonym Ferns occurs in Offaly (from the similarity of the word *raithneach,* fern). MIF

Rennick, Renwick, Rennix This name came from Cumberland. The earliest of the name in Ireland was a soldier who got a lease in Co. Kildare in 1585. Later families of the name settled in Cos. Monaghan and Meath.

Rennie Usually a Scottish name but sometimes an Ulster variant of Rainey.

Rentoul Bibl.

Reville Apart from occasional references in mediaeval records, Reville does not appear regularly in Ireland until the seventeenth century. Since then it has been definitely a Co. Wexford name. It is numerous in England where it is of French origin.   MIF

Reyney See Reaney.

Reynolds Bibl. See MacRannall.

Rhatigan See Rattigan.

Rhea A form of Rea of Donegal found in America.

Riall See Ryle.

Ribbon A Connacht name for which *Ó Ruibín* is used in Irish. Woulfe suggests that this may be an erroneous form of *Mac Roibín.* See under Gribben.

Rice, Rhys The Rices of Munster are of Welsh origin, *Ap Rhys;* those of Oriel are *Ó Maolchraoibhe* the anglicizing of which as Rice is puzzling. IF   See page 225 above.

Richardson Bibl; App.

Richey See Ritchie.

Richmond App.

Rickard See Rackard.

Riddell An English name numerous in Ulster. It was also found in the Claddagh, Galway, as *Riodal*. See Ruddle.

Ridge More than one English family called Ridge settled in several parts of Connacht from the early seventeenth century; their descendants multiplied and the name is now quite common in Co. Galway and adjacent areas where they are often called *Mac Iomaire, iomaire* being the modern Irish word for ridge. MIF

Ridgeway This family came to Ireland in connection with the Plantation of Ulster under which they obtained large estates in Cos. Tyrone and Cavan. Branches of the family later settled in Co. Leix and Co. Waterford. The name is now rare in Ulster but well known in various parts of Leinster and Munster. MIF

Mac Rifferty, Riverty See Crifferty.

(O) Rigney *Ó Raigne* (a variant of *Ó Raighne*). It is closely associated with Garrycastle both now and traditionally. MIF   Map Offaly.

(O) Riney *Ó Raighne*. The form of the foregoing peculiar to Kerry. The personal name from which the surname is formed is cognate with Reynolds.

(O) Ring *Ó Rinn* (possibly from *reann*, spear). The main sept of this name was and is located in east Cork. MIF   See Rinn and Rynne.

Ringrose More than one derivation has been put forward for this name, which came to east Clare from Yorkshire early in the seventeenth century. MIF

(Mac) Rinn *Mac Bhroin* (*bran*, raven). This is a Co. Leitrim name to be distinguished from Ring. MacCrann is a synonym.

(O) Riordan, Rearden *Ó Riordáin*. This numerous sept belongs exclusively to Munster. The earlier form *Ó Rioghbhardáin* reveals its derivation from *riogh bhard*, royal bard. IF   Map Cork.

(Mac) Ritchie This name, a Scottish diminutive of Richard, is frequently found with the prefix Mac. It is numerous in north-east Ulster.

Roan In Ireland a variant of Rowan especially around Athlone; the English name Roan is derived from the French town Rouen.

(O) Roark See Rourke.

(Mac) Roarty *Mac Robhartaigh*. In modern times the form *Mag Robhartaigh,* anglicized Groarty, is more usual. For derivation see under Rafferty. Map Donegal.

(O) Roarty See under Rafferty.

(Mac) Robb A branch of the Scottish clan MacFarlane, mainly found in north-east Ulster.

Mac Robbin See Gribben.

Roberts This name is found in all the provinces but is rare in Connacht.

When of Scottish origin it is frequently met in Ulster with the prefix Mac. Bibl.

Robertson App.

Robinson This English name has in comparatively recent times become very numerous in Ireland, especially in Ulster.

Robson App.

Roche *de Róiste* (French *roche*, rock). A completely hibernicized Norman name originally established in Munster and Wexford, now widespread. There are sixteen places called Rochestown in Ireland, six in Co. Wexford, two each in Cos. Cork and Kilkenny. Bibl. IF MIF   Map Cork.

Rochford I quote a note received from Mr. K. Nicholls: 'An Anglo-Norman family widespread in the Middle Ages but afterwards principally in Meath and Kilkenny. A branch of the Meath family joined the Cromwellian cause and are commemorated by the village of Rochfordbridge. The Rochfords of Co. Cork were in fact de Ridlesfords: their adoption of the name Rochford arose from mistaken reconstruction of a Gaelic form'. There were several of these, very dissimilar, in the annals, etc., e.g. *Rastabhard, Risibard*. See Roughneen.

Rock A partial translation of *Mac Conchairrige* (see Carrig) used in west Leinster and Galway. Elsewhere it is usually of English origin.

Rockett This name has a very long association with Co. Waterford, John Rocket being Mayor of that city in 1393. Rockets Castle near Carrick-on-Suir was known as Rocketscourt in the sixteenth century. This is distinct from the Huguenot name Rocquet and, as K. Nicholls has shown, is in fact a corruption of Rockell which was originally de la Rochelle.

(O) Rodden *Ó Rodáin* (*rod*, strong). Rodden is a Donegal name to be distinguished from Reddan. It takes the forms Roden and Rudden in Co. Cavan. In Donegal Rodden and Rudden are also for *Mac Rodáin*, usually anglicized MacCrudden.

(O) Roddy *Ó Rodaigh*. Of Co. Leitrim, particularly associated with Fenagh. O'Roddy of Donegal, another erenagh family, is thought to be of different origin. MIF   See next entry.

(O) Rodehan *Ó Rodacháin*. The earlier form of O'Roddy: the basic word in these names is *rod*, strong. MIF   See also Redehan.

Roe This name has several origins; it is a synonym of *Ó Ruaidh*—see Ormond; it may be English, synonymous with Rowe; or an abbreviation of MacEnroe; or an epithet, i.e. *ruadh* (red). MIF   Map Waterford.

(O) Rogan *Ó Ruadhagáin* (the basic word here is probably *ruadh*, red). An Oriel sept formerly of considerable importance. It is well known also in Co. Leitrim. MIF   Map Armagh.

259

Rogers, Rodgers These English names usually stand for MacRory, especially in Ulster. They are numerous throughout the country, less so in Munster than elsewhere. There were five of the name among the Cromwellian 'adventurers'. Bibl.

(O) Rohan This is *Ó Robhacháin* in Munster and *Ó Ruadhacháin* in Ulster. Rohan is now mainly found in Cos. Kerry and Cork. MIF See Roughan.

(O) Rolan *Ó Rothláin*. This name is now generally anglicized Rowland or corrupted to Rowley, which, however, in north-east Ulster is of English origin. MIF   Map Mayo.

Rolfe See Ralph.

Rolston, Roulston An English toponymic fairly numerous in Tyrone and Antrim. The main family (spelt Rolleston) settled in Co. Armagh, *temp.* James I.

(O) Ronahan See Renehan.

(O) Ronan, Ronayne *Ó Rónáin*. (The well-known personal name *Rónán* may be from *rón*, a seal.) Several small septs of the name (as Map) are now almost extinct. The principal one in east Cork is still numerous. Bibl; MIF   Map Cork, Dublin and Mayo.

(O) Roney A variant of Rooney mainly found in Co. Down.

(O) Roohan See Rohan.

Rooke An English name (from the bird) used as an occasional synonym of Rourke.

(O) Rooneen, Roonian *Ó Rúnaidhin*. This name which is closely associated with north Leitrim and south Donegal, has often been absorbed by Rooney. O'Donovan records the Irish form in Co. Sligo as *Ó Rúnaighean*.

(O) Rooney *Ó Ruanaidh*. Originating in Co. Down, where Ballyroney locates them, this name is now numerous in all the provinces except Munster. In west Ulster and north Connacht Rooney is often an abbreviation of Mulrooney. IF   Map Down. See previous entry.

(O) Ronoo *Ó Ruanadha*. A Co. Galway variant of Rooney.

(O) Rorke See Rourke.

Mac Rory *Mac Ruaidhrí.* The true MacRorys belong to Tyrone and Derry, descended, according to Douglas Hyde, from the Three Collas. MacRory was also frequently an ephemeral surname concealing the ancestral patronymic; in such cases, where it survived, it often became Rodgers or Rogers. Bibl. IF   Map Derry.

Rosborough Bibl.

Rose A scattered English surname, the best known family being that settled in Co. Limerick in mid-seventeenth century. The name appears occasionally in Irish records as early as the fourteenth century. It has several derivations mainly from the shrub or flower.

Roseman, Rosemond Originating in Germany, this name came to Ireland from England in the seventeenth century and became established in Cos. Cavan and Leitrim. I have found no early reference to it. (De Rosmyn of Kells, 1305, is not relevant).

(O) Rosney *Ó Rosna.* A rare Corca Laoidhe name which is extant in Co. Kerry.

Ross The name of a Scottish clan which is numerous in Ulster. In Dublin and Cork it may be of English origin. The patronymic MacAndrew was for a period adopted by some Scottish families of Ross in Ireland. Bibl.

Rossiter An English toponymic, gaelicized as *Rosaitear.* One of the earliest English families to be established in Ireland. They became and still are numerous in the Co. Wexford barony of Forth; but nowhere else. Bibl. MIF   Map Wexford. **Rothwell See p. 304.**

Rothe *Rút.* Becoming established in Co. Kilkenny in the fourteenth century the family was counted among the 'Ten Tribes'. The name, which is from a Norse word meaning red, has in modern times been changed to Ruth and Routh. It is now rare. IF 299; Map Kilkenny.

(O) Roughan This is the usual anglicized form of *Ó Ruadhacháin* in Co. Clare. See Rohan.

(O) Roughneen, Raghtneen *Ó Reachtnín.* A Mayo name, where Rochford has sometimes been used for it. Ronayne is occasionally used as a synonym of Roughneen. See Raghteen.

(O) Rouine, Rowine *Ó Ruaidhín.* Akin to Ruane this name belongs to south Connacht.

Roulston See Rolston.

Rountree, Roantree This, also spelt Roundtree, and, having regard to its derivation, more correctly Rowantree, is fairly numerous in Cos. Cavan and Armagh. It occurs in Oriel as early as 1376.

(O) Rourke *Ó Ruairc.* One of the two great septs of Breffny. The family is not of Norse origin though Ruairc is from a Norse personal name. Irish exiles of the name were prominent in Russia, Poland, Austria and France. Bibl. IF   Map Leitrim.

Routh See Rothe.

Rowan This is sometimes a synonym of Ruane, sometimes of Rohan, or may be of English origin (from the tree). It is widely distributed throughout Ireland but nowhere numerous. MIF

Rowantree See Rountree.

Rowe See Roe.

(O) Rowine See Rouine.

Rowland, Rowley See Rolan.

(O) Rowney A variant of Rooney in Co. Down.

Rowsome Originally a Quaker name in Ireland; it is seldom found outside Co. Wexford.

Roy This English name, derived from French *roi*, king, is not numerous in Ireland where it is usually an abbreviation of MacIlroy.

Royan See under Ruane.

Roycroft An English name (from rye croft) well known in Co. Cork since the seventeenth century, where it also takes the forms of Raycroft and Raecraft.

Roynane A variant spelling of Ronayne.

Royse A well-known Anglo-Irish name in Co. Cork and Limerick since the beginning of the seventeenth century. It is of Norman origin akin to Rose.

(O) Ruane *Ó Ruadháin* (*ruadh*, red). A sept of the Uí Maine. The variant Royan is found in the same area—Gortyroyan near Ballinasloe is *Gort Uí Ruadháin* in Irish. Royan, however, has inevitably been sometimes changed to Ryan by absorption, notably in Co. Mayo, as also have Rouine and Ruane. MIF   Map Galway.

Ruby Derived from the French *de Roubaix*, this name is in Co. Cork since the seventeenth century.

Ruckle See Ruttle.

Rudd An English name, derived from Anglo-Saxon *rud*, meaning red, which came to Ireland in the first half of the seventeenth century and has since then been closely identified with Co. Wexford.

Rudden See Rodden.

Mac Ruddery *Mac an Ridire* (*ridire*, knight). An Irish patronymic adopted by a branch of the Fitzsimons family of Westmeath. This was sometimes translated MacKnight.

Ruddle, Ruddell The former spelling is used in Cos. Limerick and Kerry, the latter in Co. Armagh. The earliest references are to Leinster in the thirteenth century. Woulfe equates it with Riddell, calling it an English toponymic. If so it was originally de Ryedale. In Co. Limerick Ruddle is occasionally a synonym of Ruttle.

Ruddy See Roddy.

Rudican See Redahan.

Rudkin Bibl.

Ruine See Rouine.

Rule A Scottish toponymic found in Co. Donegal. Occasional early references are scattered.

MacRum See MacCrum.

Rumley Bibl.

(O) Runian A variant of Rooneen.

(O) Rush This is *O Ruis* in Oriel. As such it is chiefly found in Co. Monaghan. More numerous, however, is Rush in Mayo where it is of quite different origin, being the name of a sept of the Uí Fiachra called *Ó Luachra*, normally anglicized Loughry, but made Rush by supposed translation—*luachair* is the Irish for rush. In mediaeval records de Russhe is also found, whence the modern English surname Rush. There are four words *ros*, genitive *ruis*, in Irish: the most usual is that meaning a wood. MIF **See Loughry.**

Russell (from an Old-French word denoting a red-haired person). Though of English stock the many Russells who have distinguished themselves in Ireland have all been true Irishmen both in the military and cultural spheres. The name, on record since the Anglo-Norman invasion, is now numerous in Ulster and Leinster. Russell is also an anglicized form of the Huguenot Rossel. App. IF   MIF

Ruth See Rothe.

Rutherford App.

Rutledge An English name common in Tyrone and Fermanagh since the seventeenth century; it is strangely used as a synonym of Mulderrig in Mayo.

Ruttle A Palatine name in Co. Limerick. Ruckle is a variant of this.

(O) Ruvane Families of this name belong to south Mayo. I have not discovered its origin: it may possibly be a variant of Ruane.

Ryall See Ryle.

(O) Ryan *Ó Maoilriain* is the correct form in the homeland of the great sept of Ryan, formerly Mulryan; but it is now usually abbreviated to *Ó Riain*, which is properly the name of a small Leinster sept. Ryan is by far the most numerous name in Co. Tipperary having almost four times the population of the next in order (O'Brien and Maher). For a note on the derivation of Ryan see Introduction, pp. xvi–xvii. Bibl. IF   Map Tipperary (Mulryan), Carlow (O'Ryan). See Ruane.

Ryder For the use of this English name in Ireland see Markey and Markahan.

Ryland Bibl.

(O) Ryle, Riall Woulfe gives the form in Irish as *Ó Raghaill* and considers this to be an abbreviated form of *Ó Raghailligh*, O'Reilly, which is conjectural: its equation with the Kerry Rahilly would seem possible. Ryle is the usual spelling in Kerry, where the name is mainly found. MIF   See Rahill and Reighill.

(Mac) Rynne A Clare name, probably from *Mac Bhroin* of Connacht, not from Ring of Co. Cork. See Rinn.

Ryves See Reeves.

S

Sadlier, Sadleir This occupational name is usually of Cromwellian origin in Ireland, but it is on record both in Dublin and in Co. Cork nearly a century earlier.

Sage An occasional synonym of Savage.

St. Clair Now usually made Sinclair.

St. John, Singen This family is in Co. Tipperary since the thirteenth century and to a considerable extent became hibernicized: one of the name was transplanted as an Irish papist from St. Johnstown, Co. Tipperary, in 1656, while two of the Co. Wexford branch were bishops of Ferns in the thirteenth century. The name is still fairly numerous in south Tipperary.

St. Lawrence The St. Lawrence family has been at Howth since 1177. The name is also found in east Clare. Bibl. MIF

St. Leger Of Norman origin, this family has been in Ireland since the fourteenth century. Some branches became hibernicized, especially in Co. Kilkenny, where the name has often been made Sallenger. Bibl. See Ledger.

Salkeld This Cumberland family is occasionally on record in Ireland from mediaeval times and has since been found in Dublin and Co. Wicklow, but never numerous.

Sall See Saul.

Sallenger See St. Leger.

(Mac) Sally *Mac Salaigh*. An earlier form of Solly.

Salmon, Sammon In Connacht Salmon is an anglicization, by translation, of *Ó Bradáin*, which retains the earlier form Bradden in Donegal and Leitrim. The English name Fisher is also occasionally so used. Sammon is the variant in use in Co. Clare. Salmon is also a name of English origin, and as such it is fairly numerous in Co. Leix and north Kilkenny, where it was established in the sixteenth century. MIF

Sampson This English name appears fairly frequently in mediaeval Irish records from early fourteenth century both in Leinster and Munster. It was prominent in Co. Limerick after the Cromwellian upheaval, but is now scattered.

Sand(e)s, Sandys Except in an isolated instance in Co. Limerick where this name was temporarily substituted for Shaughnessy, it is that of a family of English origin (derived from the word sand) which settled in Co. Kerry in the late sixteenth century. The spelling Sands is now the most usual, but this is found mainly in Ulster, where families so called are for the most part immigrants of a later date. Bibl. MIF

Sanfey See Feddis.

Sankey Bibl.

Santry *de Seantruibh*. One of the few Irish toponymics; mainly found in Co. Cork.

(O) Sarahan A variant of Sorahan.

Sargent See Sergeant.

Sarsfield *Sáirséil*. Branches of this family settled in Cos. Cork and Limerick in the twelfth century as well as in Co. Dublin; the famous

Patrick Sarsfield was of the Dublin branch. Bibl. IF   Map Dublin.

Saul *de Sál.* Of Norman origin this name, now rare, was formerly mainly associated with Cos. Tipperary and Waterford. MIF

Saunders Bibl.

Saunderson Bibl; App.

Saurin A Huguenot name from the Norman *de Sauvergne.* Occasionally it occurs as a synonym of Sorahan and Soden.

Savage *Mac an t-Sábhaisigh* is the Irish form used by the Four Masters. The great family of Savage of the Ards was planted there in 1177. They became hibernicized and from the fifteenth century onwards men of the name were prominent on the Irish side in the wars against England. A branch settled in Co. Kilkenny. Bibl. MIF   Map Down. See next entry and Sage.

(O) Savin *Ó Sabháin.* A small south Munster sept whose name has now been usually changed to Savage.

Sayers An English name of dual origin long associated with Co. Kerry. It has been gaelicized as *Saoghar.* It may also be for Sears, *Mac Saoghair,* there. Families of the name are also fairly numerous in north-east Ulster.

Scaddan This name is now very rare, surviving as Scadding and in the place-name Scadanstown near Clonmel, but it is of frequent occurrence in mediaeval records in Cos. Tipperary and Kilkenny. The derivation is obscure; in spite of its Gaelic appearance it does not appear to be of Irish origin. MIF

(Mac) Scahill *Mac Scaithghil* (probably from *scaith geal,* bright flower). This was sometimes made an O name but both prefixes, Mac and O, are now discarded. The MacScahill sept was located in east Galway and the name is now found there and in Co. Mayo in small numbers. MIF

Scales This is not a toponymic but a locative name (meaning dweller at the huts) of Anglo-Norman origin, in Co. Limerick since the fourteenth century, and still found in Co. Clare. Schoales, found in south Ulster, is a variant.

(O) Scallan *Ó Scealláin.* Derived from a word meaning kernel. This name was formerly very numerous in Co. Wexford and is still there. The place-name Scallanstown in Co. Meath is misleading as this is really Ballyscanlon. Scallan is distinct from the northern Scullin, though the latter has taken that form in Fermanagh.

(Mac) Scally *Mac Scalaidhe.* (The derivation is possibly the same as Scully). Traditionally and by present location this name belongs to Cos. Roscommon and Westmeath. Sometimes it is found with the prefix O in Irish. MIF   See Miskelly.

(Mac) Scanlan *Mac Scannláin.* Once prominent in Co. Louth, this name with prefix Mac is now rare. The place-name Ballymascanlon near Dundalk commemorates it. See Scallan.

(O) Scanlan *Ó Scannláin* (for derivation see Scannell). There were several septs of this name (as Map), the most important being of west Munster. There are no less than eight place-names embodying the surname in different parts of Ireland. The numerous Scanlans of Co. Clare mostly belong to the Connacht sept. Further north Scanlans are really as a rule Scannells. Bibl. IF   Map Cork, Fermanagh and Galway.

(O) Scannell *Ó Scannail.* (The early meaning of the word *scannal* is contention, not scandal). Properly a sept of north-west Ireland, it has become Scanlan in Co. Sligo, where Scanlans are really as a rule Scannells. IF   Map Sligo.

(O) Scarry, Scurry These anglicized forms of *Ó Scurra,* an east Galway Sodham sept, and *Ó Scoireadh,* of Waterford and Kilkenny, have been confused in modern times. MIF

Schoales See Scales.

Schofield A north of England toponymic found in east Galway distinct from, but sometimes confused with, Scuffle.

(O) Scollan, Scollin The Leinster form of the name called Scullin in Ulster.

Schaill See Scahill.

Scollard An English name in Kerry since the sixteenth century. Though synonymous with Scholar it is a locative, not an occupational, name.

Mac Scollog *Mac Scolóige.* This is still extant in Co. Monaghan, but elsewhere changed to Farmer by translation.

Scott One of the most numerous of British names in Ireland, it is mainly found in Ulster and Dublin. App.

Scriven An English name of Norman origin (from *escrivan,* writer) in Dublin in the late seventeenth century, but since mainly associated with Co. Cork.

Scuffle This curious form of the English name Scovell (originally a French toponymic) is found in west Connacht. See Schofield.

(O) Scullin, Scullane, Scullion, Skoolin *Ó Scolláin.* A Derry erenagh sept of Ballyscullion whose name has sometimes been changed to Scully; it is not a variant of Scallan. It is very rare outside Ulster. MIF

(O) Scully *Ó Scolaidhe* (student). Under Anglo-Norman pressure this Westmeath sept migrated to Munster, but nevertheless the name is numerous in central Leinster. IF   Map Tipperary.

Scurlock See Sherlock.

(O) Scurry See Scarry.

Seale An English locative name (dweller at the hall, Old-English *sele*) now fairly numerous in east Leinster.

Sealy As Sealy is mainly on record in Kerry and Cork it is probably there a variant of Shally (cf., Shealy in Co. Clare). Elsewhere it, like Seely, is of English origin (Old-English *saelig*, happy, blessed).

Sears When found in Kerry this is an anglicized form of *Mac Saoghair*; elsewhere it is an English name, being a variant of Sayers. See Searson and Sayers.

Searson When not of English origin this is *Mac Saoghair* not *Ó Saoraidhe*. See Seery.

Seaver (Derived from an Old-English word meaning sea-passage). This name first appears in Ireland in the first half of the seventeenth century in Cos. Armagh and Monaghan.

(O) Seery *Ó Saoraidhe*. A small sept of Westmeath also called Freeman and Earner. But according to Woulfe the derivation is from a Norse personal name not from *saor*, free.

Segrave *de Saograobh*. A prominent family in the Pale since the fourteenth century. Bibl; Map Dublin.

Segrue See Sugrue.

Seix See under Sisk.

Selenger See St. Leger.

Semple This is derived in Scotland from the adjective simple and in England from the French St. Pol. It has been in Ulster since the mid-seventeenth century. MIF

Sergeant An English occupational name frequent in mediaeval Irish records, now common in Co. Armagh and adjacent areas.

Seward The name of an English family, formerly called Seaward, settled in Co. Cork in mid-seventeenth century. It has no connection with *Ó Suaird* (Swords).

Sewell This scattered name is usually an English toponymic: it appears in mediaeval records as de Sewell; occasionally it is the anglicized form of the rare *Ó Súilligh* (quick-eyed).

Sexton *Ó Seasnáin*. The phonetic anglicized form Shasnan is still extant but is rare. The name Sexton is intimately associated with Limerick. It is rarely of English origin in Ireland. MIF   Map Limerick. See Tackney.

Seymour Several families of this name came to Ireland from England in mid-seventeenth century. It is now quite numerous in Cos. Cork and Tipperary as well as in Dublin and Belfast. It is usually a French toponymic (St. Maur) but in some cases may be from Seamer in Yorkshire. See Emo.

Shackleton One of the best known Quaker families in Ireland. The Shackleton school at Ballitore, Co. Kildare, was famous in the eighteenth century. Bibl. MIF

Mac Shaffrey The Irish form *Mac Seafraidh* is also used for Jeffries, Jefferson etc. In 1659 it was listed (as MacGeoffery) among the principal surnames in Co. Longford. It is now mainly found in Cos. Donegal and Derry.

(O) Shally, Shalvey, Shalloo, Shallow *Ó Sealbhaigh (sealbhach*, having possessions). These are only four of the ten or more anglicized variants of this name. It is that of a Corca Laoidhe sept which spread to other parts of Munster. Shalloo is the Clare form. It has been widely changed to the English name Shelley. MIF   Map Cork.

Shamrock Rather surprisingly this is an English toponymic, rare as a surname in Ireland. It has been used synonymously with Hamrock, which is also an English toponymic, gaelicized as *Hamróg* and reanglicized as Hamrogue. It occurs in the sixteenth-century Fiants of Cos. Cork and Waterford in the place-name Hamrockstown.

(O) Shana(g)her *Ó Seanachair* (probably *sean*, old—*cair*, dear). Little is known about this name beyond the fact that it is found in Co. Roscommon and seldom elsewhere.

(Mac) Shanaghy *Mac Seanchaidhe* (storyteller). A north Connacht family now called Fox by pseudo-translation.

(O) Shanahan *Ó Seanacháin.* (The basic word is *sean*, old). A numerous Dalcassian sept whose name is sometimes contracted to Shannon; now widespread throughout Munster. IF   Map Clare.

(Mac) Shane *Mac Seáin.* The name is thus equivalent to Johnson. In Ulster and Louth the MacShanes are a branch of the O'Neills. The Westmeath family of Shane were a branch of the O'Farrells; in Kerry the surname MacShane was assumed by the Fitzmaurices, but these families appear to be now extinct. Map Tyrone.

Shanessy A Co. Limerick form of Shaughnessy.

Shanks App.

(Mac) Shanley *Mac Seanlaoich (sean*, old—*laoch*, hero). A prominent sept of east Connacht, whose chief was known as MacShanley of Dromod. IF   Map Leitrim.

Shannon In addition to *Ó Seannacháin* (see Shanahan) Shannon can be *Ó Seanáin* (see Shinane) and *Mac Giolla t-Seanáin* (see Giltenan). Shannon is fairly numerous in all four provinces. IF   See also Sheenan.

(O) Shanny *Ó Seanaigh (sean*, old). A Co. Clare name also found in Co. Roscommon.

(O) Sharkett *Ó Searcóid.* A Roscommon name genealogically distinct from Sharkey, though the two are sometimes used synonymously and are probably both derived from *searc* (love).

(O) Sharkey *Ó Searcaigh (searcach*, loving). Originally of Co. Tyrone this name is now found in other counties of Ulster and Louth also. MIF

Sharman See Shearman.

Sharpe This well-known English name has been used as an anglicized form of *Ó Géaráin* in Donegal. The adjective *géar* means sharp. See Guerin.

Sharrig The Co. Cork form of Sharry.

(Mac) Sharry *Mac Searraigh*. A Breffny sept mainly found in Leitrim and adjacent counties. In Co. Roscommon it has been made Foley from *searrach*, a foal. This in its secondary connotation, flighty, may be the derivation of the name. MacSharry is sometimes used as a synonym of MacSherry. For O'Sharry see p. 304.

(O) Sharvin See Sherwin.

(O) Shasnan See Sexton.

(O) Shaughnessy *Ó Seachnasaigh*. A leading sept of the southern Uí Fiachrach said to be descended from Daithi the last pagan king of Ireland. They were located in the barony of Kiltartan. Bibl. IF MIF   Map Galway.

Shaw This name, that of a branch of the Scottish clan Mackintosh, is on record in Ulster since the sixteenth century, but most families so called came at the time of the Plantation of Ulster and subsequently. It is found in all the provinces but is still more numerous in Ulster than elsewhere. The first of the Dublin family to which George Bernard Shaw belonged was an officer in the army of William III. Bibl. IF

(O) Shea, Shee *Ó Séaghdha*, mod. *Ó Sé* (*séaghdha*, hawklike, secondary meaning—stately). Primarily a Kerry sept, but (as Shee) it is notable as the only Gaelic-Irish name among the 'Tribes of Kilkenny' to which county and Co. Tipperary a branch of the sept migrated in the thirteenth century. IF   MIF

(O) Sheahan See Sheehan.

(O) Shealy A Clare form of Shally.

Sheane See page 304.

Sheares An English name of dual derivation, in Co. Cork since the late seventeenth century.

(Mac) Shearhoon *Mac Séarthúin*. This patronymic was adopted by the Prendergasts of Kerry. *Séarthún* is one of several Irish variants equivalent to Geoffry.

Shearman, Sharman This English occupational name was in Dublin early in the seventeenth century and before 1700 was established in Co. Kilkenny where it is still found.

(O) Shee See Shea.

(Mac) Sheedy *Mac Síoda* (silken, soft spoken). A branch of the

269

Macnamaras—the two names have sometimes been used synonymously. It is never translated Silke as *Ó Síoda* is. Map Clare.

(O) Sheedy *Ó Síoda*. See Silke.

(O) Sheehan, Sheahan *Ó Síodhacháin*. (The obvious derivation from *síodhach,* peaceful, is not accepted by some Celtic scholars). The Dalcassian sept which spread southwards accounts for the majority of Sheehans who are now very numerous in Cos. Cork, Kerry and Limerick. Formerly also there was an Uí Maine sept of this name which, however, is rarely found in Connacht today. IF Map Limerick.

(Mac) Sheehy *Mac Síthigh*. (Woulfe derives this from *síthe* genitive of *síoth* peace; but the word *sítheach,* eerie, seems more probable). A gallowglass family from the Scottish clan MacDonald settled in Munster. *Ó Síthigh* is in use in parts of Munster but *MacSíthigh* is the correct form. Bibl. IF Map Limerick.

(O) Sheekey (Gaelic form uncertain: probably an Ulster variant of Sheehy). It appears in Co. Monaghan in the sixteenth century and is still extant in Oriel.

(O) Sheenan *Ó Síonáin*. Woulfe considers this to be a variant of *Ó Seanáin*. See Shinane. It is, however, the name of a Co. Tyrone sept to be differentiated from the southern, Synan. It has to some extent been absorbed by Shannon in Co. Monaghan.

Sheera See Shera.

(O) Sheeran, Sheerin *Ó Sírín*. A sept of the Donegal–Fermanagh area whence the name has spread as far southwards as Co. Leix. Syron of Co. Mayo is presumably a branch of this. The Co. Cork sept of *Ó Sírín* appears to be extinct. MIF

Mac Sheffry See Shaffrey.

Sheilds See Shiel.

Sheldon This distinguished Catholic and royalist English family first came into prominence in Ireland in the person of Dominic Sheldon, a colonel in the army of James II. In the previous generation another Sheldon had settled in Co. Tipperary. The name is now rare outside Ulster.

Shelley, Shelloe See Shally.

Sheppard, Shepherd This English name, which first appears as le Shepherd in Cos. Dublin and Kildare in the thirteenth century, occurs frequently in Irish records from the sixteenth till the present time. It is now fairly numerous in all the provinces except Connacht. Its connection with Ulster is of much later date than with Leinster and Munster.

(Mac) Shera, Sheera *Mac Séartha*. This name was assumed by a branch of the Fitzpatricks, *Séartha* being an Irish equivalent of Geoffrey. It is to be distinguished from MacSherry.

(O) Sheridan *Ó Sirideáin.* Mainly famous as a literary family. It originated as an erenagh family in Co. Longford. Bibl. IF MIF Map Cavan–Longford.

Sherkin An O'Driscoll agnomen (probably from Sherkin Island) which became a permanent surname.

Sherlock, Scurlock *Scurlóg.* This name, of early English origin, is generally taken to mean short-haired, but Reaney says it is fair-haired. One of the important families established in Ireland after the Anglo-Norman invasion, the Sherlocks became completely hibernicized. The place-name Scurlocktown in Cos. Meath and Westmeath indicates the centre of the area in which they settled. MIF

Sherman See Sharman.

Sherrard An English name closely associated with Derry since the seventeenth century. MIF

(Mac) Sherry *Mac Searraigh,* also *Ó Searraigh* (possibly from *searrach,* foal). This Ulster sept must not be confused with MacShera. The name MacSherry, i.e. son of Geoffrey, was also adopted as an Irish patronymic by the Hodnett family of Co. Cork, whence the place-name Courtmacsherry. MIF 217; Map Armagh and Cork. See MacSharry.

Sherwin This is sometimes a variant of Sharvin or Sharvan, i.e. *Ó Searbháin,* a Co. Roscommon sept now almost extinct there (*searbh* means bitter). Sherwin is also an English name well known in Ulster and Dublin. MIF

Sherwood This English toponymic, in Ireland since early seventeenth century, is now fairly numerous in all provinces.

(O) Shevlin *Ó Seibhleáin* (possibly from *sibhal,* swift). Of the two septs so called, that of Offaly appears to be extinct; that of the Uí Fiachrach in Mayo and later in Donegal is now also found in Co. Monaghan. MIF

(O) Shiel, Shields *Ó Siadhail.* The derivation from *siadhail,* sloth, is doubtful. A family of hereditary physicians mainly located in north-west Ulster, with an Offaly branch. IF MIF Map Donegal.

Shier See Shire.

Shinagh One of the many synonyms of Fox. See Shinnagh.

(O) Shinane *Ó Sionáin.* A west Clare name now widely changed to Shannon and spelt *Ó Seanáin* in Irish.

(O) Shine *Ó Seighin.* (Woulfe's derivation from a word meaning wild ox is not accepted; it is probably from Old-Irish *seigéne,* small hawk). A Munster name mainly located in Cos. Cork and Kerry. MIF

Shinkwin This is a variant of Jenkin, gaelicized as *Sinicín* or *Sinchín,* found in Co. Cork. MIF

Shinnagh *Sionnach* and *Ó Sionnaigh.* Also anglicized Shunagh and

271

Shunny, it is mainly found in Cos. Mayo and Galway and used there synonymously with Fox. *An Sionnach* (the Fox) was the epithetal designation of the chief of the *Ó Cathernaigh* sept, see Kearney.

(O) Shinnick *Ó Sionnaigh* (possibly from *sionnach*, fox). This is almost exclusively a Co. Cork name where, however, its origin may be confused with Shinkwin. Shinnock has been recorded as a synonym of Shinnagh.

Shinnock See under Shinnick.

Shinnors An Anglo-Norman name cognate with Skinner found in north Tipperary and Limerick.

Shipsey In west Cork since the early eighteenth century. Though probably of English origin it is very rare in England. It may well be a corruption of Shipside, the derivation of which denotes residence at a sheep slope or pasture. MIF

Shire A Palatine name in Co. Limerick. Formerly Shier, a form still in use there.

Shirley Bibl.

Shirra See Shera.

Shivers A Co. Tyrone variant of Chivers.

Shivnan I cannot give the origin or derivation of this Connacht name. Richard Foley held that it is a corrupt form of Shevlin.

Short An English name fairly numerous in Ulster and Dublin. See MacGirr.

Shortall *Soirtéil* (also written *Seartal*). The Shortalls settled in Ireland in the thirteenth century and became one of the principal hibernicized families in south Leinster. MIF   Map Kilkenny.

Shorten For the past 200 years this has been exclusively a Co. Cork name. In the seventeenth century it was in Co. Wexford. Woulfe regards it as a variant of the well-known Shorthall. That may possibly be so in Co. Wexford but not in Co. Cork.

Shouldice Though a Palatine name formerly in Co. Limerick, Shouldice and its variants Sholedice and Sholdis are now mainly found in north Leinster and east Ulster.

(O) Shovelin A variant of Shevlin.

Shoye An older variant of Joyce.   **Shreenan** See Sreenan.

(O) Shryhane See Strahan.

Shugrue See Sugrue.

Shunny See Shinagh.

Sibbery An Old-English toponymic formerly found in Co. Leitrim.

Sides See Sydes.

Sigerson This name of Norse origin has been in Ireland since the sixteenth century. It is now mainly found in Kerry. It has been gaelicized as *Mac Siogair*. MIF

Siggins *Sigín*. Of Anglo-Saxon origin this name has been in Co.

Wexford since the thirteenth century. Families so called were among those which became completely hibernicized. MIF

Silke This English name is used in east Galway for Sheedy, i.e. as the anglicized form of *Ó Síoda* (the Irish word *síoda* means silk) but not of MacSheedy.

Simington A Scottish toponymic in mid-Ulster since the Plantation in 1609.

Simms Well known in Antrim since the early seventeenth century, this name has also a close association with Donegal. MIF

Simpson App.

Sinclair The name of a Scottish clan well known in Ulster. Bibl.

Siney, Syney I have not yet discovered the origin of this name. It does not appear in works on British surnames. It is recorded among the gentry of Co. Meath in 1610 and has since been associated with Cos. Kildare and Offaly.

Singen See St. John.

Singleton Families of this name acquired estates in Cos. Louth and Monaghan at the time of the Williamite confiscations, but it is also on record in the Oriel area as early as 1387. A branch settled in Co. Cork which Woulfe says was sufficiently gaelicized to be called *Ó Sionduile*.

Sinnott From Old-English words meaning victory-bold; it is gaelicized *Sinóid*. This family has been prominent in Co. Wexford since the thirteenth century. Bibl. MIF   Map Wexford.

Sinon See Synan.

Sirr Bibl.

Sisk For the past 200 years this name has been closely associated with east Cork. Its origin is uncertain. It has been suggested that it is a modern variant of the mediaeval surname Seix (*saghas*) of Cos. Kilkenny and Kildare (which is now almost extinct) but I have no evidence of this.

Sitlington Bibl.

Skeffington This English toponymic is in Ireland since the coming of Sir William Skeffington, the terrorist deputy in 1534. Francis Sheehy Skeffington on the other hand, murdered by an insane British officer in 1916, was a pacifist.

(Mac) Skehan *Mac Sceacháin* (probably from *sceach,* briar). This name belongs to the Oriel counties of Monaghan and north Louth where it has often been changed to Thornton. It is also well known in north Tipperary. Woulfe says the prefix in use there is O not Mac. In fact this is one of those names with which the prefix is seldom if ever retained in the anglicized form. MIF

Skelly The Oriel form of Scally.

Skelton This English toponymic is on record in Dublin as early as

1403; it was established in Co. Leix in the sixteenth century (the home of the main family was Skeltonrath) where it was prominent until their close association with the Jacobite cause brought about their ruin after 1691. The name is still found in Dublin and is fairly numerous also in north-east Ulster.

Skerett Formerly Scared, an abbreviation of Huscared, which is a corrupt form of *Huscarle* (house care). One of the 'Tribes of Galway' prominent in the affairs of that city till late in the seventeenth century. Bibl; IF

Skerry See Scarry.

Skiddy *Scideadh,* i.e. a Norse-Gael from the Scottish island of Skye. This family formed a sept in Co. Cork on the Irish model and was also closely identified with Cork city from 1360. Bibl. IF

Skillen, Skilling This name is fairly numerous in Co. Down. It is of Norse origin and there is no justification for equating it with *Ó Scealláin* (Scallan).

Mac Skimmins Cummins, as well as Miskimmins, has been used as a synonym of this north-east Ulster name.

(O) Skinnion *O Sgingin.* An erenagh and learned family originally of Co. Roscommon, a branch of which were ollavs to the O'Donnells up to 1392. Some of the name in Co. Cavan became Delahyde. MIF

Skoolin See Scullin.

Skuse This name was established in west Cork in the mid-seventeenth century. Probably of Cornish origin.

Slacke Bibl.

Slamon This name has been used synonymously with Slevin in Co. Offaly.

Slane, Slaney *de Sláine.* One of the few Irish toponymics.

Slater, Slator, Sleater This occupational name, which has both an English and a Scottish background, is of Cromwellian origin in Cos. Longford and Louth. It has now become numerous, especially in Dublin.

(O) Slattery *Ó Slatara, Ó Slatraigh* (*slatra,* strong). Of Ballyslattery in east Clare. The name has now spread to the adjacent counties of Munster, MIF   Map Clare.

(O) Slavin, Slevin *Ó Sléibhín* (presumably derived from *sliabh,* mountain). The name of a branch of the Cenél Eoghain in Ulster; an old ecclesiastical family in Fermanagh. Some families of the name settled in Co. Westmeath in the seventeenth century. MIF

Sleeth This name, now rare, was formerly numerous in Oriel. Reaney says it is derived from the adjective sly, but Weekley makes it slade (i.e. valley).

(Mac) Sleyne, Sliney *Mac Sleimhne.* This is an Irish patronymic assumed by the Norman family of FitzStephen of Co. Cork. Sliney and Slyne are modern variants of it. MIF

(O) Sloan(e) *Ó Sluagháin (sluagh,* hosting or army). An old and well-known east Ulster name of Cos. Armagh and Down, now numerous also in Antrim. It is found in Co. Mayo as Sloyan. MIF

(Mac) Slowey, Sloy *Mac Sluaghaidh* (derivation as Sloan). A west Ulster name. It has become Molloy in Cos. Cavan and Monaghan through the elision of the C in Mac and aspiration of the S. MIF

Sloyan, Slyne See Sloan and Sleyne.

Small A form, by translation, of Begg, numerous in Co. Galway. It is also widely used for Kielty and variants in Ulster. Many of the name, however, are of English origin. See Quilty.

Smallen A variant of Smollen for which *Ó Smealláin* is used.

Smiddy A form of Smithwick or Smithers found in Co. Cork and peculiar to Ireland.

Smiley See Smylie.

Smith, Smyth When not the name of an English settler family, Smith is usually a synonym of MacGowan, nearly always so in Co. Cavan. See also O'Gowan. Bibl; App.

Smithwick Though the Smithwicks of Co. Cork are Cromwellian, those of the Carlow–Kilkenny area were established there earlier in the seventeenth century. MIF

(O) Smollan, Smullen *Ó Smolláin.* This Oriel name is also found in fair numbers in the midland counties of Leinster.

Smylie Coming from Scotland to Co. Tyrone early in the seventeenth century this name, also spelt Smiley etc., has since become fairly numerous in the other northern counties.

(O) Snee *Ó Sniadhaigh.* The name of a distinguished Mayo sept still extant there, mainly around Swinford. Celtic scholars are uncertain of the derivation of this name. MIF

Snoddy This is a Scottish name (Snoddie) found in Ulster. There is a branch of the family in Co. Carlow.

Snow Woulfe treats this as an epithetal name—*An tSneachta*—but the great majority of families of Snow descend from settlers under the Plantation of Ulster.

Soden Established in Co. Sligo in the mid-seventeenth century this name later spread to Co. Cavan and adjacent parts of Meath, where it has occasionally been used synonymously with Saurin. Soden, formerly Soudan in England, is a surname of the nickname class derived from the word sultan. MIF

(O) Solan *Ó Sochlacháin (sochlach,* renowned). Formerly anglicized Solahan. This name is mainly found in Co. Mayo. MIF

(Mac) Solly *Mac Soilligh.* An Oriel name which has now become rare. It appears in the Monaghan hearth money rolls of the seventeenth century with the prefix O. Map Louth.

(O) Somahan *Ó Somacháin* (*somachán*, soft innocent person). The English name Somers or Summers has now almost entirely superseded the older form. Map Sligo. See Somerville.

Somers, Summers These names when found in Leinster are usually of English origin; for Connacht see previous entry. In Ulster Somers is occasionally a synonym of MacGovern *Mag Shamhráin—samhradh* is summer in Irish.

Somerville Though well known in Co. Cork, this is mainly found in Ulster where Sumeril is a variant. Somerville is also an occasional synonym of Somahan. See also Summerly. Bibl.

(O) Soolivan A variant of Sullivan.

(O) Sorahan, Soran *Ó Soracháin* (*sorcha*, bright). Almost exclusively of Cos. Monaghan and Cavan. MIF

Mac Sorley *Mac Somhairle* (from a Norse personal name). A branch of the Scottish clan MacDonald, this was one of the earliest galloglass families to settle in Ulster. MacSorley is also of the clans Cameron and Lamont. The name is now found in Tyrone and Antrim. MIF

Sothern This name, now rare, is of antiquity in Ireland being frequently on record in Meath and adjacent counties from the beginning of the fourteenth century. It is also spelt Southern which indicates its derivation. Bibl.

(O) Soughley, Suckley *Ó Sochlaigh*. This Ulster name is of the same derivation as the Connacht Solohan. See Solan.

(O) Soulaghan A variant of Sullahan; very seldom of Solohan.

Soutar An old English name (meaning shoemaker) in Ireland since the fourteenth century.

Southwell Bibl.

Sowney A name of the agnomen type used by a branch of the MacCarthys in Co. Cork. It is written *Samhnaí* in Irish. My suggestion that it is a corruption of *na Samhain* (the beginning of the winter season during which troops were quartered) is not fully accepted.

Mac Spadden *Mac Spáidín* is the form given by Woulfe with no particulars. I do not know it except as a rare Co. Down name also anglicized MacSpedding. Spedding, however, is English in origin.

Spaight Derived from the Middle-English word *speight*, woodpecker, this name has been closely associated with Limerick and Co. Clare since the mid-seventeenth century. MIF

Spain A scattered surname originally bestowed on someone who returned from Spain.

Sparling The name is of dual origin in Ireland. It is now mainly found in Co. Limerick where it is Palatine. It was, however, in Waterford at least fifty years before the advent of the Palatines and there it was of English origin.

Mac Sparran *Mac an Sparáin* (*sparán*, purse). This name, fairly numerous in Cos. Derry and Antrim, is of Scottish origin (a branch of the clan MacDonald). In its homeland it is spelt MacSporran. MacAsparran is an occasional variant in Ulster.

Sparrow This is derived from the Old-English *spearwa*, i.e. sparrow, flutterer. It has been in Ireland since mid-seventeenth century, mainly in Co. Wexford.

Spedding Bibl. See MacSpadden.

Speed See Foody.

Speer(s) This can be for Spear(s) (spearman) or Spier(s) (watchman), English names of different derivation, numerous in Ulster, but little known before the eighteenth century.

(O) Spellane See Spillane.

(O) Spellissey *Ó Spealghusa* (possibly from *speal*, scythe—*gus*, vigour). A Co. Clare name.

Spelman *Ó Spealáin*. This name, anglicized (O)Spillane elsewhere, is Spelman in Connacht being a sept of the Uí Fiachrach unconnected with that of Munster. MIF   Map Sligo.

Spence The name of a branch of the Scottish clan MacDuff numerous in Cos. Antrim and Down.

Spenser This English name has occasionally been used as an anglicized form of *Mac Spealáin*. See MacSpillane. Bibl.

Spiers See Speers.

(Mac) Spillan(e) *Mac Spealáin* (derivation as O'Spillane). This family is, however, quite distinct from *Ó Spealáin* (O'Spillane). Spollan and Spollin, rarely retaining the prefix Mac, are numerous in Co. Offaly. Older anglicized forms were Spalane and Spalon.

(O) Spillane, Splaine *Ó Spealáin* (*speal*, scythe). A sept of Eliogarty (as Map) whence they migrated to south-west Munster. MIF   Map Tipperary.

Spollane, Spollen Variants of Spillane.

Spotswood Bibl.

Spratt App.

Spread Bibl.

Spring This family has been prominent in Co. Kerry since they came there from England in the sixteenth century. The surname is of the nickname type. MIF

Sprott A Co. Down variant of Spratt.

Sproule In Cos. Donegal and Derry since early seventeenth century; now mainly located in Co. Tyrone. Sprowle and Sprool are variants. MIF

Spruhan This name, formerly numerous in Co. Kilkenny, is probably a local variant of Sruffaun.

(O) Sreenan This name is quite well known in Co. Monaghan. Woulfe suggests *Ó Srianán* as a possible Irish form.

Sruffaun *Ó Sruthâin*. A southern branch of the Strahan family. Also called Bywater in Co. Waterford by semi-translation (*sruth*, stream).

Stacey A derivative of Eustace in Cos. Wicklow and Wexford.

Stack *Stac*. This English family, in Kerry since the thirteenth century, became determined enemies of England. The name is derived from the English word stack. IF   Map Kerry.

Stacpoole *Galldubh*. This Irish form (*gall*, foreigner—*dubh*, black) was also sometimes used for Stapleton. *De Stacapúl*, indicating a Welsh toponymic, is preferable for Stacpoole. The family is on record in the Pale since 1200; from the end of the sixteenth century it has been mainly associated with Co. Clare. MIF

Stafford An old and powerful Anglo-Norman family, deriving their name from the English town. MIF   Map Wexford. See Mac-Stocker.

Stamers Bibl.

Stanford A prominent Anglo-Irish family since the end of the sixteenth century. Mainly found in Co. Cavan. See Stankard.

Stankard This English toponymic has been long established in Co. Galway and Mayo. Ballystangford, near Claremorris, locates them and indicates the earlier form of the name.

Stanley This famous English name, a toponymic, is on record in Ireland since the thirteenth century, mainly in Cos. Louth and Meath. It is now fairly numerous in both Leinster and parts of Munster.

Stapleton A Hiberno-Norman family, some branches of which adopted *Mac an Ghaill* (son of the foreigner)—anglicized Gall and Gaule—as an Irish patronymic: they settled in Cos. Kilkenny and Tipperary and are mainly located there now. MIF   See Stacpoole.

Starkey This well-known Dublin name (of English adjectival origin meaning stiff) is in Ireland since the fourteenth century.

Starr A Cromwellian family now fairly numerous in north Tipperary. It is also in Ulster, frequently spelt Starrs there. The name is of the nickname type.

Starrett Of Scottish origin this is well known in Co. Donegal and adjacent Ulster areas. The variant Sterritt is also numerous in Belfast.

Staunton, Stanton *de Stonndún*. One of the earliest English names in Ireland. The most important branch settled in Mayo and are still numerous in Connacht. See MacEvilly.

Stawell Bibl.

Mac Stay *Ó Maoilstéighe*. MacStay is a corruption of the earlier anglicized form O'Mustey. The name belongs to Co. Down.

Steacey See Stacey.

Steele App.

Steen App.

Stenson This form of the English and Ulster Steenson (i.e. a variant of Stevenson) is almost peculiar to north Connacht, especially Co. Sligo.

Stephens This name has several origins: viz. Norman Fitzstephen; Irish *Mac Giolla Stiofáin* (devotee of St. Stephen); and planter English. Apart from Dublin it is mainly found in Mayo, where it is MacStephen, akin to Jordan. MIF

Stephenson This family of Co. Limerick, though Elizabethan planters, became hibernicized and were prominent as patrons of Gaelic literature. See Stevenson.

Sterling App.

Stevenson A numerous name in Ulster, where the variants Stephenson, Steenson and Stinson are also well known. It is occasionally a synonym of the Anglo-Norman FitzStephen. Bibl. See Stenson.

Stewart, Stuart This Scottish name is one of the most numerous non-indigenous names in Ireland. More than 90 per cent of the families so called are located in Ulster. Bibl; App.

Stinson See Stenson and Stevenson.

Mac Stocker *Mac an Stocaire* (trumpeter). Several families of this Ulster name assumed that of Stafford as early as the seventeenth century.

Stokes In Ireland since the fourteenth century. There were many distinguished persons of the name in the nineteenth century, especially in the field of Irish literature and science. IF

Stone This English locative name, nowhere numerous in Ireland, has been used as a synonym of Clogherty and Mulclohy by quasi-translation (*cloch,* stone). See under Muckley.

Stoney A locative name from Yorkshire. In Ireland since the end of the seventeenth century but seldom on record except as Anglo-Irish landed gentry in north Tipperary. Bibl.

(O) Storeen, Storan *Ó Stóirín*. Co. Limerick family, moved to Connacht in the Cromwellian transplantation, but still found in Limerick as well as Galway.

Storey An English name of Old-Norse origin. Several different families of Storey came from England in the seventeenth century and became of note in Co. Tyrone. The name, which occurs in sixteenth-century Fiants, is now fairly numerous in Ulster and Dublin.

Stout Bibl.

(O) Strahan, Strain *Ó Sruitheáin* (*sruth,* stream). A Donegal erenagh family, also called Shryhane. Strain is a Co. Down variant. MIF Map Donegal.

(O) Stranahan *Ó Sranacháin.* This belongs to Co. Down and is seldom found elsewhere.

Stritch An old English name meaning street, now quite hibernicized. It is closely identified with the city of Limerick. MIF

Mac Stravick *Mac Srabhóg.* Of Tyrone and adjacent areas. It appears as MacStravoge in the Co. Tyrone hearth money rolls of 1664.

Strong App.

Stuart See Stewart.

Studdert An Anglo-Irish name well known in Co. Clare since 1669. It is derived from the words stud herd, i.e. keeper of horses. In England it usually takes the form Stodart. Bibl.

Styles An English locative name found in Co. Wexford.

Suckley See Soughley.

(O) Sugrue *Ó Siochfhradha* (from a Norse personal name). Shugrue is a variant and phonetically more correct. It is seldom found outside its homeland (as Map). MIF   Map Kerry.

(O) Sullahan *Ó Súileacháin* (probably from *súileach,* quick eyed). A surname of the midlands and south Ulster now almost entirely changed to Sullivan.

(O) Sullivan *Ó Súileabháin.* (While there is no doubt that the basic word is *súil* (eye) there is a disagreement as to the meaning of the last part of the name). This is the most numerous surname in Munster and is third in all Ireland. Originally of south Tipperary, the O'Sullivans were forced westwards by the Anglo-Norman invasion where they became one of the leading septs of the Munster Eoghanacht. There were several sub-septs, of which O'Sullivan Mor and O'Sullivan Beare were the most important. Bibl. IF   Map Cork–Kerry.

(O) Summaghan, Summers See Somahan.

Summerly An anglicization of *Ó Somacháin* (Somahan) in Connacht, sometimes changed to Somerville in Co. Galway.

Sunderland A Yorkshire toponymic associated since early eighteenth century with Co. Wexford, where it is sometimes used synonymously with Sutherland.

Supple *Suipéal.* The first of this name, then de la Chapelle, came to Ireland with Strongbow in 1172. Since then it occurs very frequently in records relating to Cos. Limerick and Cork. MIF

Surgenor There are five different spellings of this occupational English name in Ulster where it has been since the seventeenth century.

Surtill A variant of Shortall.

Sutor, Sutter See Soutar.

Sutton *de Sutún.* A toponymic, possibly from the Irish place-name, prominent in Cos. Wexford and Kildare since the thirteenth century.

Swan See under Swayne.

Swanton This English toponymic, introduced into west Cork in the seventeenth century, has since become very closely associated with that area, though little known elsewhere in Ireland. It was notable among the Wild Geese. MIF

Swayne From 1288 throughout the mediaeval period this name occurs frequently in records relating to several counties of Leinster. The English name is derived from the Norse *swein* (servant); but it has been claimed that in some cases Swayne is a synonym of Sweeney. It does not appear to have been used synonymously with the more numerous Swan, found in Antrim and other parts of Ulster. MIF

(Mac) Sweeney, Swiney *Mac Suibhne* (the word *suibhne* denotes pleasant, the opposite of *duibhne*). Of galloglass origin it was not until the fourteenth century that the three great Tirconnell septs of MacSweeney were established; more than a century later a branch went to Munster. Bibl. IF   Map Donegal, Cork and Kerry.

Sweetman *Suatman* has been used as the Irish form. This family of Norse origin was established in Ireland in the twelfth century. Bibl. IF   Map Kilkenny.

Sweetnam An English toponymic from Swettenham, sometimes used as a variant of Sweetman and found in Co. Cork.

Swift This name appears in mediaeval Anglo-Irish records, but the famous Swift family came from England early in the seventeenth century. For the Swifts of Mayo see Foody. MIF
See Fodaghan.

Mac Swiggan *Mac Suigin.* Black says this is a Galloway name of Irish origin, probably from the Norse *Swegen* or *Swen.* It is mainly found in Co. Tyrone. The suggestion that it is a variant of MacSweeney is untenable.

Mac Swine See Sweeney.

Switzer A Palatine name.

Swords In mediaeval times this was often an Irish toponymic from the Co. Dublin village. More recently it has been found as a synonym of Clavin by mistranslation (*claidheamh,* sword), or as an anglicized form of the rare *Ó Suaird* of Leix and Offaly. MIF

Sydes, Scythes An English locative name (Old-English, dweller by the slope) seldom found except in Co. Kilkenny and adjacent areas. The variant Sides is found in Dublin.

Symons See Fitzsimons.

Synan, Synon *Sionnán.* A well-known Co. Cork name associated with Doneraile and its neighbourhood since the thirteenth century. It was formerly also spelt Shynan, but as even in early records it is given without the prefix O, the suggestion that it is the Gaelic *Ó Síonáin* cannot be finally accepted without definite evidence. It is almost certainly of Norman origin. Bibl; MIF

Synge In England, whence it came in the seventeenth century, this name is often written as it is pronounced—Sing. It is not identified with a particular place, but is notable in Ireland in the ecclesiastical and literary sphere. Bibl. MIF

Synnott See Sinnott.

Syron See Sheeran.

Sythes See Sydes.

T

Taaffe, Taa *Tath.* This family of Welsh origin (meaning son of David) who came to Ireland in the thirteenth century, soon became one of the most influential in the country. A branch settled in Connacht. Bibl. IF   Map Louth, Sligo.

Tackaberry See Thackaberry.

Tackney This name is found in Cavan and some adjacent counties where it is a synonym of Sexton, not of Tagney or Taheny.

(O) Tagan, Teegan *Ó Tadhgáin* (probably from the forename *Tadhg, Teigue*). This name belongs to Cos. Kildare and Leix. The place-name Ballyteegan is near Mountmellick.

(Mac) Taggart See MacEntaggart.

Mac Taghlin *Mac Giolla tSeachlainn* (devotee of St. Seachlainn or Secundinus). Co. Donegal. See Houston.

Tagney A variant of Tangney.

Mac Tague See Mac Teigue.

(O) Taheny The name of a Co. Roscommon family. Possibly a variant of *Ó Teitheacháin*. See Teahan.

Tait See Tate.

Talbot *Talbóid.* Unique among Hiberno-Norman families in that the senior branch has been in continuous possession of the Malahide estate for almost 800 years. Talbots have played an important part in Irish history. The name is now mainly found in or near Dublin. Bibl. MIF   Map Dublin.

Tallant, Tallent This English name is in Cos. Carlow and Dublin since the sixteenth century. Authorities on British names differ as to its origin. In Ireland it may be a corruption of Tallon.

Tallon *Talún.* A Hiberno-Norman family formerly influential in the Pale. The name is seldom found outside Leinster. Tallonstown is in Co. Louth. MIF   Map Carlow.

(O) Tally *Ó Taithligh* (*taithleach*, peaceable). As the name of a Co. Fermanagh family it is now very rare. They were erenaghs of Devenish, formerly *Mac Taichligh*. Tally as an occasional synonym of Tully occurs in Co. Longford. MIF

(O) Talty *Ó Tailtigh*. The name of a west Clare sept which has no connection with the Ulster sept of Tally though the names are probably etymologically cognate. MIF

(Mac) Taminy, Tamney See Timpany.

Tancred See Tankard.

Tandy A form of the Christian name Andrew, Tandy is in Ireland since the fourteenth century, mainly in Co. Meath. MIF

(O) Tangney *Ó Teangana*. A well-known Kerry name, very rare elsewhere. Tradition connects it with the MacElligotts. Tangley is probably a variant. MIF

Tankard Numerous and prominent in Leinster in mediaeval times Tankard is now very rare. Tancred is used as a synonym, though often of different derivation: Tankard is maker of tankards, Tancred from Old-German *tancrad* (thought counsel). See Hankard.

Tanner An Anglo-Norman occupational name in Ireland since mediaeval times and now fairly numerous, but not closely associated with any particular area.

(O) Tannian *Ó Tanaidheáin* (probably from *tanaidh*, thin). A Co. Galway name seldom met elsewhere. MIF

(Mac) Tansey *Mac an Tánaiste* (tanist or heir presumptive). Of Sligo and north Roscommon. The Irish synonym *Ó Blioscáin* arose in modern times from a misconception. MIF

Tarleton Coming to Ireland from Liverpool about the year 1600 the Tarleton family settled in Co. Offaly and have since become fairly numerous there. The name is very rare elsewhere in Ireland.

(O) Tarmey A Connacht form of Tormey.

(O) Tarpey *Ó Tarpaigh* (*tarpach*, sturdy). This sept originated in Co. Sligo and is now found also in other Connacht counties. *Ó Tarpaigh* is also a sept of Corca Laoidhe (west Cork) where it is anglicized Torpey. MIF   Map Sligo.

Tarrant An English name, used in Co. Cork with Thornton as the anglicized form of *Ó Toráin*. See Torrens.

Tarry A variant of Terry.

(O) Tarsnane *Ó Tarsnáin*. The origin of this west Clare name is obscure. MIF

(Mac) Tarsney See Torsney.

Tate App.

(O) Taugher A variant of Tougher in Mayo.

Taulty A variant of Talty.

Tavey See MacAtavy.

Mac Tavish See MacCavish.

Taylor *Táilliúir*. This English occupational name (which is not used as a synonym of any Gaelic-Irish name) is well known in Ireland since the fourteenth century and is now very numerous both in Ulster and in Dublin. Bibl. MIF

(O) Teagan See Tagan.

Mac Teague See MacTeige.

(O) Teahan *Ó Téacháin*. Woulfe suggests that this is an abbreviation of *téitheacháin*, fugitive. It is almost exclusively a Kerry name. As Tehan and Teehan it is found in Cos. Tipperary, Leix and Kilkenny. MIF 229.

Teefy This name occurs in the 1664 hearth money rolls for Tipperary in which county and adjacent parts of Clare and Limerick it is still found. It is possibly the Munster form of the Uí Fiachrach Tuffy (*Ó Toghdha*).

Teeling *Taoilinn*. Though not a numerous name it is that of a remarkable landed family, the leading branches of which have remained consistently Catholic and pro-Irish throughout the centuries. It was established in Co. Meath shortly after the Anglo-Irish invasion. MIF

Mac Teer, -Tier Abbreviated forms of MacAteer.

(O) Teevan The Irish form *Ó Téimheáin* is conjectural. Of Cos. Monaghan and Fermanagh, this is not the same name as Tivnan of Co. Sligo. MIF

(O) Tegan See Tagan.

(Mac) Teggart(y), Teg See MacEntaggart.

(O) Tehan See Teahan.

(O) Teheny See Taheny.

Mac Teige, -Tigue *Mac Taidhg*. This name has many variant spellings, It is not that of an actual sept, except in Co. Galway where MacTeiges are a branch of the O'Kellys, but arose from the perpetuation of an ephemeral surname formed from the Christian name *Tadhg*, Teigue. It is chiefly found in Mayo and Donegal. MIF   See Tighe, MacCaig, MacKeague and Montague.

Telford App.

Tempany See Timpany.

Tempest The English family of Tempest has been prominent in Ulster and Louth since 1640. *Mac Anfaidh*, used as the Irish form of this name, is a modern attempt at a translation. MIF

Tempseton App.

Tenneny, Tinnenny These names in various spellings were found in Cos. Cavan and Leitrim, where Tinnelly is also found. I have not ascertained their origin. It seems probable that they are both anglicized forms of the same Gaelic-Irish surname, possibly Timpany.

Tenpenny See Timpany.

Terence See Turley.

Mac Ternan *Mac Tighearnáin* (*tighearna*, lord). A Breffny sept whose name is usually spelt MacTernan in Leitrim and Tiernan outside Connacht. IF

Terry (French *Terri* from Old-German *Theudoric*, people rule). This Anglo-Norman family was closely associated with the city and county of Cork from the thirteenth century. Terry is also used for *Mac Toirdealbhaigh*—see Turley. Bibl. MIF

Tesky A Palatine name in Co. Limerick.

(O) Tevlin *Ó Teibhlin*. Possibly cognate with Shevlin. This name belongs to Co. Cavan and north Meath. MIF

(O) Tevnan A variant spelling of Tivnan.

Tew An English toponymic formerly well known in Co. Waterford and Co. Meath, on record in Ireland since the sixteenth century.

Thackaberry Families of this west of England name came to Co. Wicklow in mid-seventeenth century and their descendants are still there and in Co. Wexford. It is also spelt without the H—Tackaberry, which is nearer the form in which it first appears in Ireland, viz., Tacabray.

Thomas This name is now fairly numerous throughout Ireland but is principally found in Dublin and Belfast. It is mainly of comparatively recent English introduction, but in some cases may be an abbreviation of the mediaeval MacThomas. In Irish records up to the end of the sixteenth century references to MacThomas and FitzThomas are numerous, but in nearly every case these were ephemeral cognomina applicable to members of such well-known families as the Fitzgeralds.

Thom(p)son Though of comparatively recent introduction this is the second most numerous purely non-Irish name in Ireland. It is mainly found in Ulster. Without the intrusive P, Thomson is Scottish. See Holmes and MacCavish.

(O) Thoran *Ó Toráin* (*tor*, lord). See Tarrant and Torrens.

Thorn(e) Occasionally a variant form of Thoran, and also found as an abbreviated form of Thornton. Thorn is itself an English name.

Thornhill An English toponymic found in Cos. Cork and Limerick from mid-seventeenth century.

Thornton This English name has been used in Ireland as a synonym of Drennan, Skehan, Meenagh and Tarrant. Some Thorntons were Elizabethan planters in Co. Limerick.

Thulis, Toolis See Tolan.

Thunder A name of Norse origin found in Cos. Louth and Dublin from mediaeval times.

(O) Thynne *Ó Teimhin* (*teimhe*, dusk or gloom). A north Clare name formerly anglicized O'Tyne; it has no connection with the English Thin or Thynne. MIF   Map (O'Tyne) Clare.

Tidings See Toorish.

Mac Tier See MacTeer.

(Mac) Tiernan See MacTernan. Bibl.

(O) Tierney *Ó Tighearnaigh* (*tighearna*, lord). There were three septs of this name, in Donegal, Mayo and Westmeath, but it is now scattered. It is much confused with Tiernan in Mayo. In southern Ulster this is usually of different origin, viz., *Mac Giolla Tighearnaigh*, which was formerly also anglicized MacIltierney. Bibl. IF   Map Mayo.

Tiffeny According to authorities on English surnames this is derived from *Theophania* (Epiphany) but as in Ireland it is only found in any numbers in Co. Leitrim, I suggest that it is a variant of Tivnan there.

Tiger This has been recorded as a synonym of MacEntaggart in Co. Dublin. The English name Tiger is from an Old-German word meaning people-spear.

(O) Tighe, Tigue, Teague *Ó Taidhg*. There were four distinct septs of *Ó Taidhg*, but the name is now indistinguishable from MacTeague or Tighe, which is also a synonym of the English Tye. This explains the Irish synonym Kangley (*ceangal*, tie). MIF

Mac Tigue See MacTeige.

Tilly Normally a variant of Tully; Woulfe says it is also a variant of Tally.

(Mac) Timlin *Mac Toimilin*. The name of a family of Cambro-Norman origin, derived from a diminutive of Thomas. They formed a sept in the Irish fashion in the barony of Tirawley, Co. Mayo. The name was recorded as Tomilin in 1641. MIF

Timmons *Mac Toimin* (another diminutive of Thomas). A branch of the Barretts of Tirawley (Co. Mayo). In Cos. Wicklow and Carlow Timmons, formerly Timon, is *Ó Tiomáin*. MIF

(O) Timon See Timmons. In Mayo, however, Timon or Tymon has almost replaced Timmons.

(O) Timoney *Ó Tiománaidhe* (driver). This name belongs to southern Donegal and adjoining parts of Tyrone, Fermanagh and Leitrim. MIF

Timothy This English name has been used in Cos. Roscommon and Galway for Tumelty.

(Mac) Timpany *Mac an Tiompánaigh* (tympanist, musician). Variants of this now rare Co. Down name are Tempany and Tenpenny; MacAtamney has been used as a synonym in Co. Derry. MIF

Tiney, Tinney, Tyney Variants of MacAtinney in Donegal.

Tinnelly See under Tenneny.

Tinsley An English toponymic mainly found in Ulster where Townsley, another English toponymic, is sometimes used synonymously. I think the statement that it is a variant of Kinsella can be disregarded.

Tipper This name, of English origin, borne by one of the best-known Gaelic scribes of the early eighteenth century, has been found in Co. Kildare (in the baronies of Naas and Salt) since 1300 and is still extant.

Tirry See Terry.

Tivnan, Tinan See Tynan.

(O) Toal *Ó Tuathail*. Though the name is the same in Irish, this Co. Monaghan sept is to be distinguished from O'Toole. IF

Tobin *Tóibín*. A Norman family St. Aubyn, which became completely hibernicized. Bibl; IF   Map Kilkenny-Tipperary.

Todd App.

To(g)her See Tougher.

(O) Tohill *Ó Tuathail* (for derivation see Toole). The name of this Co. Derry sept, whose location is indicated by the parish of Desertoghill, was formerly anglicized O'Tuohill. O'Donovan found it as Toghill a century ago; it is now Tohill. MIF

(O) Tolan(d), Toolan *Ó Tuathaláin*. (This also is derived as O'Toole). In Ulster, the province of its origin, this is usually called Toland; in Mayo, whither many of the sept went with the O'Donnells, it is Tolan. In Achill it has become Thulis. MIF

(O) Tole A form of O'Toole used in Co. Down.

Toler The name as Toller appears in a list of Co. Leitrim tories in 1692 and this is probably an anglicized form of *Ó Talchair*. For derivation see Tolleran. Toler, better known as an Anglo-Irish name, first appears in the seventeenth century in Co. Tipperary and was fairly prominent in the eighteenth. As such it derives from the French *tollère*, tax-gatherer.

(O) Tolleran *Ó Talcharáin* (*talchar*, obstinate). This name is now rare but was formerly well known in north Connacht. Map Mayo.

(O) Toman *Ó Tuamáin*. Originally of Co. Tyrone, this name is still found in the areas lying to the east of that county. As Tooman it is found in Co. Roscommon.

(Mac) Tomulty See Tumelty.

Tone (Old-English *tun*, enclosure—later village). This famous Anglo-Irish name is not on record in Ireland before the sixteenth century. It is mainly associated with Dublin. IF

(O) Toner, Tonry *Ó Tomhrair* (from a Norse personal name). This family of the Cenél Eoghain possessed territory on the banks of the Foyle and later moved into Co. Derry. It has always been numerous in Ulster, particularly now in Cos. Armagh and Derry. MIF Map Donegal.

Tonge An English name of various derivations mainly found in Co. Wexford since the seventeenth century. MIF

(O) Tonra A Mayo form of Toner, Tonry.

(O) Tooher See Tougher.

(O) Toohill A form of O'Toole found in south Munster.

(O) Toohy A variant spelling of Tuohy found in Munster.

Tooke See Tuke.

(O) Toolan See Tolan.

(O) Toole *Ó Tuathail* (*tuathal,* people mighty). This is one of the great Leinster septs. Originally of Co. Kildare they moved to Co. Wicklow after the Anglo-Norman invasion and held their own there for 500 years. There was also a branch in Mayo where, according to Hardiman, there was also a distinct sept, an offshoot of the O'Malleys. Bibl; IF   MIF   Map Wicklow.

Toolis See Thulis.

(O) Tooman See Toman.

(O) Toomey See Twomey.

(O) Toorish *Ó Tuaruis(c)*. This is actually a corrupt form of Houriskey or Horish, but as *tuairisc* means tidings the name was understandably 'translated' Tidings, also spelt Tydings.

Toppin(g) According to Bardsley Toppin and Topping are variants of the English name Turpin. It appears in the hearth money rolls of Co. Armagh in 1664 and is still to be found there. An isolated reference to it occurs in 1409 in Co. Kilkenny.

Toran See Thoran.

Torkington See Turkington.

(Mac) Torley See Turley.

(O) Tormey *Ó Tormaigh* (from a Norse personal name). From the earliest recorded times it has belonged to Co. Longford and adjacent parts of Westmeath and Cavan. MIF

(O) Torney *Ó Tórna*. This name is mainly found in Ulster but it is also a synonym of, if not cognate with, Dorney of Cos. Cork and Kerry, where Abbeydorney is named from Torney not Dorney. MIF

(O) Torpey See Tarpey.

Torrens, Torrance The Latinized form of the English Brook(s) of Derry and Antrim. One family of Torrens in Co. Derry, however, is said to be of Swedish origin. It is also an anglicized form of *Ó Toráin*. MIF See Thoran.

Torrie A variant of Terry in Co. Waterford.

(Mac) Torsney, Tarsney Synonyms of MacAtasney, mainly found in Co. Sligo.

Tosh An abbreviated form of the Scottish Mackintosh found in northeast Ulster.

Tothill See Tuthill.

Totten App.

Tottenham An Anglo-Irish family in Ireland since about 1630 and established in Co. Wexford later in that century; prominent in the political life of the country in the eighteenth century, often on the popular side. Bibl.

(O) Tougher, Tooher *Ó Tuachair,* earlier form *Ó Tuathchair* (people dear). This is the name of two distinct septs, one of the Ely-O'Carroll territory, and the other, which originated in Ulster, of north Connacht. In both locations the name has become Toher, Tooker and even Tucker. SIF 148.

(O) Touhy See Tuohy.

(O) Tourish See Toorish.

(O) Towell A Co. Waterford form of O'Toole.

(O) Towey This is *Ó Toghdha* (*toghdha*, chosen) in Connacht; elsewhere Towey may be a variant of Tuohy. MIF   Map Mayo.

Townley A toponymic from Lancashire on record in Cos. Louth, Cavan and Dublin since the sixteenth century. The best known family of that name is that of Townley Hall, near Drogheda.

Townsend, Townshend Closely associated with Co. Cork since its establishment there in mid-seventeenth century. Bibl.

Townsley See Tinsley.

(O) Toye A variant of Towey in north Connacht and west Ulster. Toye is also an English name.

(O) Tracey, Treacy *Ó Treasaigh* (*treasach*, war-like). The name of two septs of importance (as Map); it is now fairly numerous in every province. According to Fr. Travers there is a distinct sept of *Ó Treasaigh* in Fermanagh. IF   Map Galway and Leix.

Trainor See Traynor.

Trant A family of pre-Norman origin, always associated with Co. Kerry. *Treamhant*, the form in Irish, recalls the original Tramant. Bibl. MIF   Map Kerry.

Travers Bibl. See Trower.

(Mac) Traynor, Treanor *Mac Thréinfhir* (*tréan*, strong—*fear*, man). This well-known Oriel name is sometimes anglicized more phonetically as MacCrainor, but with the usual form Traynor the prefix Mac is obsolete. IF

(O) Treacy See Tracey.

(O) Trehy, Trahy Variants of Trohy and Trihy. **Trent** See Trant.

Trench A Huguenot name which came to Ireland in the first half of the seventeenth century and is recorded in many parts of the country, notably Cos. Galway and Leix, but is nowhere numerous. Bibl.

Trevor A distinguished English name adopted by some families in Co. Leitrim as the anglicized form of *Ó Treabhair*. See Trower.

Tribes of Galway See Galway.

Tribes of Kilkenny See Kilkenny.

Trim *de Truim*. One of the few Irish toponymics.

Trimble App.

Trodden, Trudden *Ó Treodáin*. This name is mainly of Oriel. It is also an English name.

(O) Trohy, Troy *Ó Troighthigh* (*troightheach*, foot soldier). Originally a Clare sept which early migrated to south Tipperary. There was also an

Anglo-Norman family de Troy from whom Troyswood in Co. Kilkenny was named. IF   Map Tipperary.

Trolan, Trowland These are but two of a dozen variants of this name. It appears in the hearth money rolls of the 1660s for Co. Derry and subsequently frequently there and in Co. Tyrone. In one case it is called O'Trolan. I have not found a form in Irish, possibly it is *Ó Truailleáin* (*truaill* has several meanings, including sheath or scabbard). Practically all persons of the name were Catholics and I think the suggestion that it is derived from the French *Trouillon,* a Huguenot name, can be rejected.

(O) Trower *Ó Treabhair* (*treabhair,* secondary meaning skilful). The name Trower belongs to Co. Leitrim. It has to some extent been absorbed in that area by Travers, which there is Gaelic-Irish but elsewhere that of an English immigrant family.

Troy See Trohy.

Truell A landed gentry family in Co. Wicklow since the early seventeenth century. It is possibly a toponymic from Trowell in Notts., England, but more probably from the French Truelle.

(O) Tubridy, Tubrit *Ó Tiobraide* (*tiobraid,* a well). This Co. Clare name occurs in several early manuscripts like the Book of Lecan. By the sixteenth century it had become Tubrid. MIF

Tucker This English name, often met in mediaeval Anglo-Irish records, has been used as a synonym of O'Tougher.

(O) Tuffy A rare synonym of Towey.

Tuite *de Tiúit.* An important Hiberno-Norman family. The name, now as formerly, is mainly confined to Leinster. Map Westmeath.

Tuke This old English name of Norse origin, never numerous, is on record in various parts of Leinster since early seventeenth century. Chooke and Tooke are variants. Bibl.

(Mac) Tully, Mac Atilla *Mac an Tuile.* This is said to be a corrupt form of *Ó Maoltuile.* Both were used for the celebrated medical family who were hereditary physicians both to O'Reilly and O'Connor. The name has been anglicized as Flood (*tuile,* flood). IF   Map (MacAtilla). Cavan-Longford.

Tumany See Timoney.

(Mac) Tumelty *Mac Tomaltaigh,* also *Ó Tomaltaigh* (perhaps from *tomaltach,* bulky). The Connacht sept of this name is now almost extinct, except in the barony of Moycarn, Co. Roscommon; there remains the sept of Oriel, especially the part of it where Cos. Monaghan, Down and Louth meet. MIF

Tumpane A form of Timpany found in Co. Tipperary.

(O) Tunney *Ó Tonnaigh* (*tonnach* has several meanings: billowy from *tonn,* wave; also glittering). A branch of the Cenél Conaill located on the border of Cos. Sligo and Donegal. It is now found more in Mayo.

(O) Tunry See Tonry.

(O) Touhill See Toohill.

(O) Tuohy *Ó Tuathaigh (tuathach* in this case means ruler). A sept of the Uí Maine formerly of south Galway now mainly found in Co. Clare. MIF 233; Map Galway.

Turk Either for MacTurk *(Mac Tuirc),* a Scottish name found in Antrim, or more often an abbreviated form of Turkington.

Turkington An English toponymic closely associated with Co. Armagh since the seventeenth century.

(Mac) Turley, Torley *Mac Toirdealbhaigh.* Mainly found in Cos. Armagh and Down. This name is also occasionally anglicized Terence and Terry, the forename Turlough, from which the surname is derived, being equated with Terence. IF

Turner Of dual origin, English and Scottish, this numerous occupational name is widely distributed in Ireland, where it has been since the fifteenth century. In Scotland it is an abbreviation of Macinturner *(Mac an tuirnéir).*

Turtle App.

Tuthill, Tuttle, Tothill An English toponymic. Families of the name acquired properties under the Cromwellian and Restoration settlements in Co. Limerick and other parts of the country. Bibl. MIF

Tutton See Totten.

Tutty Mainly a Cromwellian name, but occasionally a synonym of Tuohy. MIF

Twamley An English toponymic in Co. Wicklow since about 1700.

Tweedy This Scottish name, spelt Tweedie in Scotland, is that of a branch of the clan Frazer; it is in Ulster since the early seventeenth century. Bibl. MIF

Twigg, Twigley See Quigg.

Twiss A locative English name signifying dweller by the bend in the road. It was established in Co. Kerry before the Cromwellian immigration and has since become quite numerous in that county.

(O) Twohig A variant of Tuohy found in Co. Cork.

(O) Twohill See Toohill.

(O) Twomey, Toomey *Ó Tuama.* A well-known west Munster name. The spelling Twomey is usual in Co. Cork and Kerry; Toomey in Co. Limerick. IF

Tydings See Toorish.

Tye A variant of Tighe.

Tymon See Timon.

(O) Tynan *Ó Teimhneáin.* (Woulfe's derivation from *teimhean,* dark or grey, must be accepted with reserve). In addition to the main sept shown in the Map there was another in Connacht where the name is made Tivnan. MIF   Map Leix.

(O) Tyne See Thynne.

Tyney See Tiney.

Tynte Bibl.

Tyquin A rare Offaly name, derivation not yet ascertained.

Tyrrell *Tirial*. Among the earliest of the Anglo-Normans to settle in Ireland the Tyrrells became one of the most prominent of the 'Old-English' Catholic families. The village of Tyrrell's Pass is called from them. Bibl. MIF   Map Westmeath.

U

Ultagh (*Ultach,* Ulsterman). An agnomen of some branches of Mac-Donlevy who left Ulster. It has been changed to North in Westmeath.

Unehan, Ounihan *Ó hOnchon*. (Woulfe's explanation of this as denoting leopard is not accepted). The name is now almost obsolete; it may survive under the alias of Donegan which has been recorded as a synonym of it in Co. Carlow. See also Hounihan.

Uniacke *Doinngeard*. Families so called are closely identified with Co. Cork, especially Youghal, since the fourteenth century. Some of them used the name Garde as a synonym. The origin of Uniacke and its etymological association with Garde are not finally agreed. Bibl. MIF

Union See Oonin.

Uprichard Welsh *Ap Richard*. Closely associated with Lurgan, Co. Armagh. Pritchard, a synonym of it, is also found there and in other parts of Ulster. Though fairly numerous now, neither is of any antiquity in Ireland.

Upton An English toponymic found in Co. Cork and Co. Antrim. Castle Upton in the latter commemorates the first permanent settler in 1598. Later the name came to Munster with Cromwell.

Urell, Uriell See Yourell.

Mac Usker See MacKusker.

Ussher *Uiséir*. Of Norman origin this family has been in Ireland since the fourteenth century and has produced a number of distinguished men. Bibl. MIF   See also Hession.

V

(Mac) Vaddock *Mac Mhadóc*. A branch of the MacMurroughs whose territory was anciently known as MacVadog's Country. MIF   Map Wexford.

Vady An abbreviated form of MacAvaddy.

Vahey In Mayo this is *Mac a' Bheatha* (*bioth,* life, gen. *beatha*) which, sometimes made MacVeigh there, is distinct from the main sept of that name in Ulster. MacEvey, with stress on the last syllable, is a variant of MacVahey, but this spelling has inevitably resulted in its being changed to the better known MacEvoy in some cases. The use of Vahy as a synonym of Fahy in Connacht further confuses the origin of the name. See MacAvey and MacVeagh.

Vail, Vale See Veale.

Valentine A family of this name (derived from Latin *valens*, strong) came from England in mid-seventeenth century and it has since become fairly numerous in Wicklow and adjoining counties.

de Valera A Spanish toponymic. MIF

(Mac) Vallelly This name has always been closely associated with Co. Armagh. The older anglicized form, found in the Armagh and Monaghan hearth money rolls and other seventeenth-century records, is MacIlvallelly, clearly indicating a surname of the *Mac Giolla* type. See Varrelly.

Vally Woulfe gives *Mac an Bhallaigh* (*ballach*, freckled). Vally, however, has been used as an abbreviated form of Vallelly, see previous entry.

Mac Vanamy A variant of MacMenamin used in north Connacht.

Vance (derived from an Old-English word meaning a marsh or fen). This name came to Ireland in the early seventeenth century and has since become numerous in Ulster. Bibl.

Vandeleur Of Dutch origin; prominent in Co. Clare since 1660.

Mac Vann, -Vean North Connacht forms of *Mac Bheathan*, i.e. the well-known Scottish and Ulster name MacBean.

MacVanny A variant of MacEvanny in Mayo and adjacent areas.

Vargus A variant of Fergus.

Varian The Gaelic poet of the name used the form *Ó Bhiorráin*. Varian has been associated with Co. Cork since mid-seventeenth century. I have not discovered its origin.

(Mac) Varrelly I give Woulfe's form of this in Irish without comment, viz. *Mac an Bhearshúiligh* (sharp-eyed man). This essentially west Connacht name which has a number of variant spellings—Varily, Varley, etc.—is quite distinct from Vallelly though they have been used synonymously. Varrelly has been reported also as an occasional variant of Farrelly. MIF

Vaugh A Leitrim name used as a variant of Waugh; but as it sometimes appears as MacVaugh there it may also be for MacVeagh.

Vaughan This is a common Welsh name (from *fychan*, little) and as such it has been in Ireland since early sixteenth century; but the majority of Vaughans in Ireland are either of families of Mohan or Maughan, or, according to O'Donovan, are *Ó Beacháin*, a Clare name whence the place-name Ballyvaughan. IF

Mac Vay, -Veigh Variant spellings of MacVeagh.

Mac Veagh, Veigh *Mac an Bheatha* (*bioth,* gen. *beatha,* life). A numerous name in east Ulster where it is widely spelt MacVey and has to some extent been changed to MacEvoy. MIF Map Armagh.

Veale A Norman name frequent in mediaeval records. It is gaelicized in Co. Waterford as *de Bhial* (*de* for *le*). Its variant Vail has been officially reported as synonymous with MacPhail in the same county but it was probably an isolated case due to error. Its synonym Calfe shows its derivation. Bibl; MIF

Veitch This Scottish name (as Veitch from 1331, earlier La Vache, etc.) is prominent in Cos. Fermanagh and Cavan since the end of the seventeenth century.

Veldon A variant of Weldon.

Verdon *de Bheardún.* One of the great Hiberno-Norman families of Leinster, later greatly reduced like all those of that origin which took the Catholic and Irish side in the wars of the seventeenth century. Bibl. MIF Map Louth.

Vereker Of Dutch origin, this name has been established in Cos. Limerick and Cork since the early seventeenth century. Bibl. p. 368.

Vergus A variant of Fergus.

Verling This name (the Anglo-Saxon *Feorthling*) has for many centuries been associated with Co. Cork. Bibl.

Mac Verry, -Varry *Mac Fearadhaigh* (for derivation see MacAree). Cos. Down and Armagh.

Vesey An English name of French derivation which has no less than twenty-eight variant forms in England. In Co. Mayo, where it is fairly numerous, it is said to be a synonym of MacVeagh, but if so this is rare.

Mac Vey See MacVeagh.

Mac Vicar, -Vicker *Mac an Bhiocaire* (son of the vicar). Though there was a branch of the MacMahons of Oriel so called, MacVickers in Ireland are mostly of Scottish descent. The name is rare outside Ulster. MIF

Vicars Scottish family prominent in Leix since mid-16th cent. Bibl.

Vickery This English name is quite distinct from MacVicker, though ultimately of the same derivation, viz. Latin *vicarius,* agent. Since its introduction in the mid-seventeenth century it has become fairly numerous in Co. Cork but is rare elsewhere.

Victory See MacNaboe.

Vigors A Co. Carlow family, the first of whom came to Ireland early in the seventeenth century. The name is of French derivation and means strong. Bibl.

Villiers See page 304.

Vincent This English name was well established in Cos. Limerick and

Dublin by mid-seventeenth century. It has been used in Co. Derry as a substitute for MacAvinchy. Bibl.

Viniter A rare Norman name (from *le vineter*, vintner) to be distinguished from Miniter, which is the name incorporated in Ballyviniter, Co. Cork.

Mac Vitty *Mac an Bhiadhtaigh* (for derivation see Beatty). Mainly Co. Antrim, but nowhere numerous. MIF

Vogan A variant of Wogan in Cos. Cavan and Armagh.

W

Waddell App.

Wadding *Uaidín*. A distinguished Anglo-Norman family, the Waterford branch of which produced a number of notable ecclesiastics. Wadden is an occasional variant. Bibl. MIF   Map Wexford.

Waddock A variant of Vaddock.

Wade In the Oriel counties MacWade is a corruption of MacQuaid; elsewhere Wade is of dual derivation—Old-English *waddan*, to go, and Norman-French *wade*, ford—and has been found in all the provinces since the thirteenth century. MIF

Wafer, Weafer This is derived from the Old-English *waferer* (maker of eucharistic wafers, not from weaver). It is in Ireland since the thirteenth century; from the sixteenth mainly in Co. Wexford. MIF

Wagh See Waugh.

Waldron (from the Old-English forename *Waleron*). As *Mac Bhaildrin*, Waldron is a branch of the Costello family in Connacht; as *Mac Bhalronta* it is an Irish patronymic assumed by the Wellesley family. *De Bhaldraithe* is the Irish form now used. MIF

Walker This is one of the English names which, though little known in Ireland in mediaeval times, has become very numerous in northeast Ulster and in Dublin. Walker is an Old-English word for a fuller. Bibl.

Wall, Wale Norman *de Valle* gaelicized as *de Bhál*. This is one of the hibernicized Norman families, the many branches of which were settled in the country between Limerick and Waterford. The Connacht branch, which in the Composition Book of Connacht is treated as an Irish sept with a recognized chief, were known as Faltagh. *An Faltach* was also used for the head of the Co. Limerick family. IF   MIF   Bibl; Map Limerick.

Wallace (Norman *le Waleis*, The Welshman). The name of a Scottish clan; also occasionally a synonym of Walsh.

Waller This English name has been well known in Cos. Limerick and

Tipperary since the regicide Sir Hardress Waller settled in the former county in the seventeenth century.

Wallis A variant of Wallace. Bibl.

Walpole This English (Norfolk) toponymic is seldom found in Irish records before the eighteenth century when it was prominent in Queen's Co. (Leix); in the nineteenth it had become quite numerous in Co. Leitrim, but is rare now.

Walsh *Breat(h)nach* (Welshman) which is re-anglicized also as Brannagh, Brannick etc. A name given independently to many unconnected families in different parts of the country and now the fourth most numerous of all Irish surnames. It is sometimes spelt Welsh, which is the pronunciation of Walsh in Munster and Connacht. Bibl. IF   Map Wexford.

(Mac) Walter Bibl. See Qualter.

Walton This English toponymic has been in Ireland since the thirteenth century, but is not now associated with any particular area.

Wandesford Bibl.

Warburton This English surname was assumed by a Co. Tyrone blind harper called Mongan, whose son became Protestant bishop of Limerick in 1806. The family settled in Offaly. Bibl. MIF

(Mac) Ward Ward is a common English name, but nearly all Irish Wards are *Mac an Bháird* (son of the bard), the name of two noted bardic septs. That of Co. Galway is of Sodhan origin. Bibl. IF Map Donegal and Galway.

Ware Two English families of this name settled in Co. Dublin and Co. Cork in the sixteenth century, the former notable as that of Sir James Ware, the antiquary. MIF

Waring This name has appeared continuously in Irish records since the end of the thirteenth century. First established in Co. Meath, it later became closely associated with Co. Kilkenny and also Co. Down. It is now mainly found in the latter area. It is derived from the Norman-French personal name Guarin, later Warin. Waring is not cognate with Warren, though confused with it: Waringstown, for example, is properly Warrenstown.

Warke An English toponymic fairly numerous in Cos. Donegal and Derry since mid-seventeenth century.

Warner An English name of dual Old-French derivation in Co. Cork since mid-seventeenth century.

(Mac) Warnock *Mac Giolla Mhearnóg* (devotee of St. Mearnog). First anglicized MacGillavearnoge, this is an old Co. Down name cognate with, but distinct from, the Scottish MacIlvernock. MIF

Warren According to Reaney this is not a locative name as one would expect but a toponymic, *de la Varenne,* thus ultimately of French origin. This family settled in the Pale, some branches becoming hibernicized. Warren is also used as a synonym of Murnane in Co. Kerry—q.v. for explanation of how this arose. *Bharain* is the form of the name used in Irish by those of the name who are not *Ó Murnáin*; MIF   See Waring.

Washington Bibl.

Waters In addition to being the name of English settler families Waters is also a synonym of several Gaelic-Irish surnames, e.g. Hiskey, Whoriskey, Toorish etc. As will be seen on observing the various synonyms of this name, the Irish word *uisce* (*water*) does not in fact form part of any of them. The English name Waters is derived from water as well as Walter; from the personal name Walter comes also the form Watters or MacWatters which is numerous in north and east Ulster. K. Nicholls states that Waters of Co. Cork is a later form of the Norman *de Auters,* established there from 1190. Bibl. MIF

Watkins This English name (Watkin is a diminutive of Walter) came to Ireland mainly in the seventeenth century, but it occurs occasionally a century earlier, e.g. in a Fiant of 1578 where a list of 'pardons' to soldiers in O'Flaherty's country (west Connacht) is given.

Watson With a Scottish background this is an anglicized form of the Scottish *Mac Bhaididh*—MacWhatty, MacWatt or MacQuatt. It is also of English origin—son of Wat (Walter). It is very numerous in north-east Ulster.

Watt The name is a diminutive of Walter; it is numerous in north-east Ulster.

(Mac) Watters See Waters.

Wauchope Bibl.

Waugh A name belonging to the Scottish border, derived from Old-English *walh* (foreigner) cognate with Irish *gall*. Coming to Ireland in mid-seventeenth century it has since been found in small numbers in all the provinces.   MIF   **Weadock A variant of Vaddock.**

Webb Families of this name have been in Ireland since mid-seventeenth century. It is fairly numerous now in Dublin and Belfast. The extent to which it has been distributed over Leinster in the past is exemplified by the following figures showing the birthplaces of 37 Webbs who were students of Dublin University between 1660 and 1843: Dublin and Cork 7 each, Westmeath 6, Meath 4, Limerick and Offaly 3 each, Kilkenny and England 2 each, Longford, Leix and Tipperary 1 each.

Webster Though this English name (meaning weaver) is not closely associated with any particular area, it is numerous in Leinster and Ulster and is on record in Ireland as such since mid-seventeenth century.

Mac Weeney *Mac Mhaonaigh* (*maonach* has two meanings—wealth and dumb). A sept of Moylurg, Co. Roscommon, now mainly found in the adjoining Co. Leitrim. MIF

Weir, Weer *Mac an Mhaoir* (*maor,* steward). First anglicized Mac-Moyer, this Co. Armagh family is to be distinguished from another Co. Armagh sept name *Mac Giolla Uidhir* (see MacClure) formerly MacGillaweer, hence occasionally Weir. In Co. Westmeath Weir is a mistranslation of *Ó Corra* (*corra,* edge), or sometimes of English origin. Weir is also a Scottish name which was introduced into Ulster at the time of the Plantation. MIF   See also Wyer.

Welby This name is now exclusively found in Co. Galway, mainly in Connemara, where it is called *Bheilbi* by native speakers of Irish. I have yet to ascertain when they went there. It is unlikely that there is any connection between them and a customs official of the name at Carrickfergus in 1666.

Weldon *de Bhéalatún.* An Anglo-Irish family settled in the Pale since the fourteenth century; also called Veldon and Belton. In Co. Fermanagh they may be of Irish origin from *Ó Maoldúin,* which is called Meldon as well as Muldoon. MIF

Wellesley This family was established in Meath in 1174. Some of them became hibernicized; others, like the famous Duke of Wellington did not. Some again used Wesley as a synonym, including one Catholic Bishop of Kildare. MIF   See Waldron.

Wells Though now mainly found in north-east Ulster, where it is numerous, this English name (which is both locative and toponymic) was on record in Munster and Leinster as early as the thirteenth century.

Welsh See Walsh.

Wemys See Weymes.

Wesley In Ireland this is an abbreviated form of Wellesley except when it relates to the Wesleyan branch of the Protestant Church.

West Bibl.

Weston This Anglo-Norman toponymic occurs frequently in Irish mediaeval records. Most of the families so called now in Leinster and Ulster descend from more recent immigrants; some were settlers at the time of the Plantation of Ulster (*c.* 1609.)

Westropp An English toponymic, the name of an Anglo-Irish family in Cos. Limerick and Clare since mid-seventeenth century. IF

Mac Wey See MacQuey.

Weymes This and Wymes are forms of the Scottish toponymic Wemyse found in Leinster as early as the fourteenth century, but now very rare. The variants Wims, Wyms and Wymbs are extant in north Connacht.

Mac Whannon See Bohannon.

Wharton In Ireland this is chiefly found in Co. Kerry and there it has no connection with the English name Wharton, but is a corruption of some Irish surname, possibly *Ó hArrachtáin*. Faughton is a synonym of Wharton in Co. Kerry.

(O) Whearty *Ó Faghartaigh*. (Woulfe gives *faghartach* for this which he says means noisy). Originally of the Uí Fiachrach in Co. Mayo this form is now found in Co. Louth and Westmeath.

Wheeler This English occupational name is in Ireland since 1603, when one John Wheeler was dean of Christchurch, Dublin. The family was established in Co. Kilkenny soon after and was prominent among the Protestant landed gentry of that county and Leix (Queen's Co.) for two centuries. One branch, however, in Co. Kilkenny later suffered as Papists under the Cromwellian régime. The name Wheeler has since become fairly numerous in Co. Limerick, perhaps there of different origin.

(O) Whelan *Ó Faoláin* (*faol*, wolf). A variant form of Phelan numerous in the country between Co. Tipperary and Co. Wexford. Whelan is also sometimes an abbreviation of Whelehan and occasionally a synonym of Hyland. Whelan is rare in Ulster: for its provenance there see under Phelan. IF

(O) Whelehan *Ó Faoileacháin* (perhaps from *faoileach*, joyful). A Westmeath name. Helehan is a Munster variant.

Whelton A very numerous name in west Cork where it was formerly often written Houlton and is probably a corrupt form of Houlahan, also numerous in the same area.

Mac Whinney See Mawhinney.

Mac Whirter This Scottish name, found in Cos. Armagh and Antrim, is from the Scottish Gaelic *Mac Cruitéir* (son of the harper). It is that of a sept of the clan Buchanan and has MacQuirter as a variant form. Woulfe's equation of it with MacArthur is erroneous.

Mac Whiston See MacCutcheon.

Whitaker This name (formerly Whiteacre) has been associated with Cos. Meath and Louth since the fourteenth century. MIF

White An English name numerous in every province since the fourteenth century, for which *de Faoite* is used in Irish. White, by translation of the words *bán* and *geal* often replaces Bane, Bawn, Galligan and Kilbane. Bibl; App; IF   Map Down and Sligo.

Mac White *Mac Faoitigh*. MacQuitty and MacWhitty are occasional variants.

Whitehead, Whitelock See Canavan.

Whiteside App.

Whitesteed See Aghoon.

Whitla An Ulster form of the English Whiteley.

Whitley Bibl.

Whitmore An English toponymic in Dublin in the seventeenth century and since associated with Co. Wexford.

Whitney *de Fuitnigh*. This name is not numerous, but has been found in east Leinster since the fourteenth century. It is derived from an English place-name.

Whittle An English toponymic numerous in Co. Waterford as early as 1650, now more so in adjacent Leinster counties.

Whitten Formerly also written Whitton, this is on record in Dublin from 1577; it later became established in Co. Armagh and is now numerous also in other parts of Ulster.

Whitty This Old-English name (originally Whitey) has been closely associated with Co. Wexford since the thirteenth century. MIF

Mac Whitty See MacWhite.

Wholey See under Whooley.

(O) Whoolehan See Holohan.

Whooley, Wholey Whooley is not a synonym of Howley (though Wholey occasionally is) but an agnomen of some O'Driscoll families of Clonakilty, Co. Cork, where it has become a surname. It is presumably from *uallach,* boastful. MIF

Whoriskey *Ó Fuaruisce*. This name has been anglicized as Waters and Watters in Co. Donegal. See the cognate Houriskey and Waters. MIF

Wickham An old form of this name, Wycomb, is on record in Ireland since 1335. Though one Wickham was a prominent Cromwellian official, the majority of the name were identified with the Irish cause, being among those transplanted to Connacht or outlawed as Jacobites. Apart from the city of Dublin the name Wickham has for the past two centuries been mainly found in Co. Wexford.

Wickstead See Wixted.

Wier See Weir.

Mac Wiggin, Wigan These are two of the many variants of MacGuigan.

Wiggins Usually, especially in Fermanagh, a variant of MacWiggin; it is also an English name of Breton origin.

Wilde A locative name (Old-English *atte wilde*). The famous family did not settle in Ireland till the beginning of the eighteenth century; the connection with Mayo dates from 1750. As de Wylde it appears occasionally in mediaeval times. IF   MIF

Wiley See Wylie.

Wilhair, Wilhere, Woolhare. Occasional synonyms of MacElhair.

Wilkinson Bibl; App.

Williams This Welsh name, quite numerous in all the provinces of Ireland, has not been used as the synonym of any Irish surname. Bibl.

Mac William(s) *Mac Uilliam*. This numerous north Ulster name (usually with terminal S) is not a variant of Fitzwilliam (which is a rare name found in south-east Leinster) but is that of a branch of the Scottish clan MacFarlane. MacWilliam has also been used as a synonym of MacQuillan in Co. Down.

Williamson Despite its English appearance this name is usually Scottish in origin. It is numerous in Ulster.

Willis App.

Willmore Better known now as *Mac Liammóir*. It is on record in Co. Tyrone in the sixteenth century. MIF

Wilmot An aristocratic English family in Ireland since the end of the sixteenth century; a branch settled in Co. Kerry in 1614.

Wilson This is by far the most numerous English surname in Ireland; it is mainly found in Ulster. App.

Wims See Weymes.

Windle An English name (from wind hill) mainly found in Co. Limerick, where it was established in the second half of the seventeenth century: it is spelt Wingle in the Glin area of the county. Woulfe says that Winkle, found in south Galway, is a variant of the same name.

Mac Winey A variant of MacWeeney in Co. Leitrim.

Wingfield Bibl.

Winkle See Windle.

Winston Though now mainly found in Dublin this name was in Co. Waterford from 1573, and was prominent there in the next century, one member of the family being sheriff of the city and two being attainted as Jacobites. There have been Winstons in Waterford ever since. Another family of the name has a long association with Co. Roscommon.

Winters This well-known English name is used in Co. Tyrone as a synonym of MacAlivery, *Mac Giolla Gheimhridh—geimhreadh* means winter.

Winthrop Bibl.

Wisdom This English name has been used in Co. Louth as a translation of *Ó Céile*. See Kealy.

Wise See Wyse.

Wiseman This English name has been in Ireland since the sixteenth century and has since been mainly associated with Co. Cork.

Wixted, Wickstead This English toponymic is found in Offaly and Tipperary since the mid-seventeenth century.

Woffington An English toponymic formerly well known in Dublin. MIF

Wogan *Úgán* (Welsh *Gwgan: gwg*, frown). An important family since they first came to Ireland in 1295, both at home and as Wild Geese. Bibl. MIF   Map Kildare.

Wolfe See Woulfe.

Wolohan See Woolahan.   **Wolsey** See p. 304.

Wood An English name distinct from Woods but often confused with it. Woods is approximately ten times more numerous than Wood. Bibl.

Woodcock Woulfe's equation of this with the Irish *Mac Con Choille* is not accepted. It is English in its origin, of dual derivation (nickname, and toponymic for Woodcot). In Ireland it became established in Co. Kilkenny in the Cromwellian period, but was well known in Co. Cork earlier than that. It is now mainly found in Dublin.

Woodlock An English name of frequent occurrence in Dublin and south of Ireland records since the thirteenth century. It was formerly closely associated with Co. Waterford, but is now rare.

Woodman An occupational name (le Wodeman) associated with Co. Louth since the fourteenth century. *Mac Giolla Choille* is the Irish equivalent.

Woods This is a numerous name throughout Ireland, especially in Ulster. Some families of Woods in Ireland are English in origin, but the name also does duty for MacIlhoyle, MacEnhill, Quilty, Quill, Quilly and Kilmet, the Irish for wood being *coill* which, however, is not a component part of any of these names except MacEnhill. See also Cox.

Woolahan, Wolohan Forms of Holohan found in Cos. Kilkenny and Wicklow.

Wooley Woulfe mentions Wooley, colloquially called *a Bhula* in Irish, as a synonym of Woulfe. This therefore is to be distinguished from Whooley.

Woolhare See Wilhair.

Worth This English locative name, derived from Old-English *werdh* (homestead), occurs frequently in seventeenth- and eighteenth-century Munster and Leinster records, but is now very rare. It has no connection with MacWorth which is a corruption of Mackworth, a parish in Derbyshire.

Woulfe *de Bhulbh*. The Woulfes were among the earliest of the Norman settlers but never formed a sept on the Irish model. Bibl. IF Map Kildare and Limerick. See Wooley and Nix.

Wrafter See Rafter.

Wray This is sometimes a synonym of Rea and MacCrea, but usually it is the name of Elizabethan settlers in Ulster. The name is now mainly found in Cos. Derry and Donegal. Bibl. MIF

Wrenn This English name is occasionally used as a synonym of both Ring and Rynne. MIF

Wright This English name is numerous in Ulster and also in Dublin. The synonym Kincart, found in Co. Mayo, arises from a phonetic anglicization of *Mac an Cheairt* which is an attempt by Irish speakers to gaelicize Wright (*ceart* means right).

Wrinne, Wrynn A variant of the Leitrim name Rinn.

Wrixon A form of the English Wrightson well known in Co. Cork since the end of the seventeenth century.

Wyer In Westmeath this is *Mac an Mhaoir*. It is often confused with Weir there but is basically distinct from it. MIF   See Weir.

Wylie, Wiley An English toponymic which came to Ireland at the time of the Plantation of Ulster at the beginning of the seventeenth century and is now numerous, especially in Co. Antrim. There are some families of the name in Co. Clare who use the form *Ó hUallaigh* in Irish: they may be of different origin. MIF

Wymes See Weymes.

Wyndham This aristocratic English name is an occasional synonym of Mulgeehy. In the Co. Galway gaeltacht it is called *Gaoithín*. See Wynne.

Wynne This is akin to the Welsh Gwynn; it is also a synonym of several Irish names which contain the sound gee (*gaoithe*, of wind), e.g. MacGee, Geehan, Mulgeehy. MIF

Wyse A distinguished family which came to Ireland at the time of the Anglo-Norman invasion and have since been prominent in Waterford city and county. It has been gaelicized as *de Uidheas*, properly *le Uidheas* for *le Wise*, the wise man. Bibl. MIF   Map Waterford.

Y

Yago See Jago.

Yarner Bibl.

Yarr This name is in Ireland since the second half of the seventeenth century as that of a Quaker family and this association continues throughout the eighteenth century, mainly in Co. Antrim. It is now quite numerous in the Belfast area. I have not ascertained its derivation; it may be an abbreviation of some name like Yarrow. Yore was fairly numerous in Co. Meath a century ago and is still found in that part of the country, but its connection with Yare and Yarr is conjectural.

Yeats, Yates The famous literary and artistic family of Yeats, which had formerly been in Dublin, settled in Co. Sligo at the end of the seventeenth century. There are a number of families of Yates and Yeates elsewhere unconnected with them. The name means dweller by the gate. Bibl. IF

Yore See under Yarr.

Yorke In Ulster this is of English origin; in Connacht and west Leinster it is the modern form of the obsolete MacEngarky, or MacIngarke (*Mac Conchearca,* hound of Cearc).

Young A very numerous name especially in Ulster. It is occasionally a translation of the epithet *óg.* Bibl; App.

Yourell This name has for centuries been associated with Co. Westmeath, though originating a little further east as a toponymic, viz. *de Oirghiall* i.e. of Oriel. It is also spelt Eurell and Uriell. SIF 155.

Z

Zorkin This, the only Irish surname having an anglicized form beginning with Z, is a rare variant of Durkan.

ADDENDA

Boyle The famous Boyle, Earl of Cork, was of an old English (Hertfordshire) family.

Bridgeman The main Bridgeman family in Co. Cork came from England (Gloucestershire) in the seventeenth century.

(O) Corby This west Cork name is distinct from MacCorby.

(O) Devine This branch of the MacGuires was a leading sept in Fermanagh in the fifteenth century, since found mainly in Tyrone.

Early Some families of this name in Co. Roscommon are of Silmurray not of Breffny origin.

Feighan In Oriel Fagan, Fegan, Fahan, Feighan and Feehan are numerous and much confused; probably these all derive from *O Faodhagain.* See p. 102.

(Mac) Glennon Another name similarly anglicized is *Mac Giolla Fhianain,* an Ui Maine sept also anglicized Gillinan.

Gonne This may also be a variant of Gawne, the Manx form of MacGowan.

MacKeogh The former Irish spelling of this name in Munster was *Mag Ceoch* or *Mac Ceoch,* which was retained while Gaelic survived there as the vernacular.

Kermode The normal name of MacDermot in the Isle of Man.

Langrishe An English name (locative and toponymic) prominent in Co. Kilkenny since mid-seventeenth century.

Logue In Connacht the synonyms Leoge and Lougue (i.e. *O Loaghog*) are also found, but the name is only numerous in Ulster.

Luff A rare and wuite modern surname of unusual derivation; beginning as MacLoughlin (q.v.) first the prefix *Mac,* and later the terminal *lin,* were dropped leaving just Lough. In the English surroundings of the family at the time the word lough (cf. rough, tough) was locally pronounced *luff,* not *loch* as in Ireland. Luff is now the official registered form of the name of that branch of the MacLoughlins who habitat has for the past fifty years been Jersey and Norfolk.

MacMahon MacMahon of Truagh was the leading sept of Oriel.

Mulholland An American variation of Mulholland. See Mulholland.

O More the transplantation of the remnants of this sept to Kerry after their subjugation in Leix may account for the frequency of the name Moore there now.

Rothwell, Radwell Came from England to Meath in mid-seventeenth century, now quite numerous in Co. Wexford; quite distinct from the Huguenot Rothell.

(O) Sharry An Ulster sept distinct from MacSharry.

Sheane Usually a variant of MacShane; sometimes an abbreviated form of Sheehan.

Vance The dieivation of this name as given on page 293 is applicable only to the Vances of southern England. Those of the name who have been in west Ulster since the early 17th century came there from Scotland (where the form Vans is also used) and were originally Norman de Vaux. Bibl.

Villiers Of Scottish origin; prominent in Co. Leix since the sixteenth century. Bibl.

Wolsey, Woolseley These English surnames though often confused are of two distinct derivations, Woolseley being a Staffordshire toponymic and Wolsey from O.E. wulfsige (wolfvictory) and also a nickname. It was established in Ulster in the early seventeenth century and later in some other parts of Ireland. Wolsey is now fairly numerous in Ulster but rare elsewhere.

Appendix I

Appendix D of *More Irish Families* (p. 282) gives a list of the commonest English and Scottish surnames found in modern Ireland, each having an estimated present population of 4,000 or more. Many of the families bearing these names are of comparatively recent introduction; all of them, however, except MacLean, occur in the 'census' of 1659. Some, of course, like Smith, Murray and Clarke, to take three from the half dozen most numerous, are, in Ireland, as often as not Gaelic names in disguise. Those of them which were then sufficiently numerous to be described in that document as 'principal names' are given below with the county or counties in which they so appear (N.B. The returns for Cos. Cavan, Galway, Mayo, Tyrone and Wicklow and part of Co. Sligo are not extant).

Bell, Antrim.
Black, Antrim, Derry.
Boyd, Antrim.
Browne, 6 Leinster, 2 Munster and 4 Ulster Cos.
Burns, Antrim.
Campbell, Antrim.
Clarke, Dublin.
Craig, Antrim.
Crawford, Antrim.
Davis, Dublin.
Donnellson, Antrim.
Eccles, Antrim.
Ferguson, Antrim.
Graham, Antrim, Fermanagh.
Hill, Antrim.
Hughes, Dublin, Louth, Westmeath.
Irwin, Fermanagh.
Johnston, Fermanagh.
Jones, Louth.
Kerr (Carr), Down, Meath.
King, Westmeath.
Millar -er, Antrim.
Morris, Cork, Tipperary.
Murry, Murray, 9 Leinster, 1 Connacht, 1 Munster and 6 Ulster Cos.

Reid, (Read), Antrim, Derry.
Russell, Antrim, Cork, Dublin, Limerick, Meath, Tipperary.
Scott, Antrim, Fermanagh, Offaly.
Smith, 6 Leinster, 1 Connacht, 4 Munster and 4 Ulster Cos.
White, 5 Leinster, 1 Connacht, 5 Munster and 4 Ulster Cos.
Wilson, Antrim.
Young, Antrim.

There are a number of other Scottish and English surnames now numerous in Ulster most of which, though not sufficiently well established to be classed as 'principal names' in the co-called census of 1659, were already to be found in that province at that time. A few of them indeed occur transiently in mediaeval Irish records. In addition to those listed above and those dealt with individually in the text the following are among the most numerous now found in the six counties of the political entity known as Northern Ireland. The Scottish names are indicated by the letter S, the English by E.

Auld S	Gregg E S	Poots E
Balmer S	Halliday E	Ramsay S
Bamford E	Harbinson E	Richardson E
Barnett E	Harkness S	Richmond E
Blackwood E	Hawthorn S	Robertson S
Briggs E	Higginson E	Robson S
Brownlee E	Horner E	Rutherford S
Calvert E	Hull E	Shanks E S
Cathcart S	Humphreys E	Simpson E S
Chesnutt E	Hutchinson S	Spratt E
Clyde S	Hutton E	Steele E
Copeland E	Hyndman E	Steen E S
Crockett E	Jardine S	Sterling S
Cupples E	Jenkins E	Strong E
Dickey S	Kelso S	Tate E
Eccles E	Kidd E	Telford E S
Edgar E	Kirkwood S	Templeton S
Emerson E	Knox S	Todd E S
Erskine S	Lockhart S	Totten E
Esler E	Lorimer S	Trimble E
Ewart E S	Malcolmson S	Turtle E
Foster E	Matchett E	Waddell E
Gardiner E S	Meeke E	Whiteside E
Gaston E S	Park S	Wilkinson E
Geddes S	Parkes E	Willis E S
Gracey S	Pinkerton S	

Appendix II

NOTES ON THE SIMPLIFICATION OF THE GAELIC FORMS OF IRISH SURNAMES

It has been pointed out that my previous books on the subject of names contained very little reference to the modern tendency to simplify the spelling of the Gaelic forms of Irish surnames. This simplification if not carried too far is commendable, particularly now that the Roman alphabet is superseding the Gaelic one. Thus *Ó hInnse* is accepted for Henchy, *Mac Mathúna* is widely preferred to the cumbrous *Mac Mathghamhna* and *Ó Sé*, if a little naked looking, is displacing *Ó Séaghdha*. But as yet this change has not been authoritatively standardized. Take the name O'Rahilly, for example. Two quite eminent writers give it different forms in modern guise—*Ó Rathile* and *Ó Rathaile*. Again, should *Ó Gallachair* be preferred to *Ó Gallchúir*? Similarly some retain final IGH, others make this Í, e.g. for Downey. *Ó Dúnaigh* or *Ó Dúnaí*, or again *Mac Ránaill* (Reynolds) is put forward to replace *Mac Raghnaill* but this is objected to on the grounds that Á does not accurately represent the sound of AGH. I give below what appear to be generally accepted modernizations of some well-known surnames. (Many, of course, of the names in the text are not susceptible of simplification.) It will be seen that the principal abbreviations are effected by the substitution of F for BHTH and the dropping, where possible, of aspirated consonants both internal and terminal. In many cases this unfortunately tends to obscure the derivation of a name: *Mac Thréinfhir*, for instance, more readily suggests 'strong man' than *Mac Thréinir*. Finally, there is another type of 'rule' which will not command general agreement. Most of us readily accept the modern ruling that the genitive of *post* should be *poist* and that of *coll, coill*, but there is no point in expecting a Mr. Quill to change his name to *Ó Coill* from the hitherto usual form of *Ó Cuill*, which may have been in use by his family for generations, since this results in no simplification at all. This comment applies to a number of cases—*Réamann*, for *Réamonn*, to mention just one more. The Afrikaners, who have fought a long battle on behalf of their language, have abolished the letters C and Z: Zuid Afrika has become Suid Afrika, but Mr. Van der Zyl is still Van der Zyl not Van der Syl.

Our reformers should remember that surnames are heirlooms—not mere words.

The following are examples of the simplification referred to:

Boylan	Ó Baíolláin	Larrissey	Ó Learasa
MacCarron	Mac Carrúna	Laverty	Ó Laibheartaigh
Coffey	Ó Cofaigh	Leahy	Ó Laocha
O'Connor	Ó Conchúir	O'Leary	Ó Laoire
Costelloe	Mac Coisdeala	Lilly	Mac Ailile
Creegan	Ó Críogáin	Mackey	Ó Maca
Crowley	Ó Crualaoi	MacMahon	Mac Mathúna
Darcy	Ó Dorchaí	Meehan	Ó Miacháin
O'Dea	Ó Deá	Molloy	Ó Maoluaidh
MacDonagh	Mac Donncha	Moore	Ó Móra
O'Donoghue	Ó Donnchú	Moriarty	Ó Muireartaigh
O'Dowd	Ó Dúda	Murphy	Ó Murchú
Downey	Ó Dúnaí	MacMorrow	Mac Muirí
Doyle	Ó Dúghaill	MacNabb	Mac an Aba
Duffy	Ó Dufaigh	MacNally	Mac an Fhailí
Duggan	Ó Dúgáin	Neenan	Ó Naíonáin
Egan	Mac Aogáin	MacNellis	Mac Niallais
Fallon	Ó Fallúin	Newell	Ó Tnúail
O'Friel	Ó Fríl	Noonan	Ó Nuanáin
Gallagher	Ó Gallchúir	MacQuillan	Mac Uílín
MacGarry } Garrihy }	Mag Fheara	Rafferty	Ó Raifeartaigh
		Roe	Ó Rua
Gaynor	Mag Fhionnúir	Rohan	Ó Ruacháin
MacGovern } MacGauran }	Mag Shamhráin	MacRory	Mac Ruairí
		Seery } Freeman }	Ó Saoraí
Griffey	Ó Gríofa		
MacGuinness	Mag Aonasa	O'Shea	Ó Sé
MacHale	Mac Héil	Sheehan	Ó Síocháin
Healy	{ Ó hÉalaithe { Ó hÉilí	O'Sheil } Shields }	Ó Siail
Henchy	Ó hInnse	Sugrue	Ó Siochrú
Hickey	Ó hÍcí	Tiernan	Mac Tiarnáin
Hussey	Ó hEosa	Terry, Turley	Mac Toirealaigh
Kiernan	Mac Thiarnáin	Tierney	Ó Tiarnaigh
Kinneally	Ó Cionnaola	Traynor	Mac Thréinir
Kirwan	Ó Ciarabháin	Walsh	Breathnach

MAP

The map on the following pages shows the location of the Gaelic septs and the principal Hiberno-Norman families in the period after the Anglo-Norman invasion and before the upheavals of the seventeenth century.

It was prepared by the author and drawn and lettered by Nora O'Shea, one time heraldic artist to the Office of Arms, Dublin Castle.

311